The Network Starter Kit

Kevin Stoltz

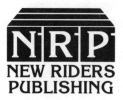

NRP
NEW RIDERS
PUBLISHING

New Riders Publishing, Indianapolis, Indiana

The Network Starter Kit

By Kevin Stoltz

Published by:
New Riders Publishing
201 West 103rd Street
Indianapolis, IN 46290 USA

Printed in the United States of America 1 2 3 4 5 6 7 8 9 0

```
Stoltz, Kevin, 1961-
    The network starter kit / Kevin Stoltz
       p.    cm.
     ISBN 1-56205-403-1
     1. Local area networks (Computer networks)  I. Title.
   TK5105.7.S83  1994
    004.6'8--dc20                                    94-34770
                                                        CIP
```

Warning and Disclaimer

This book is designed to provide information about networking. Every effort has been made to make this book as complete and as accurate as possible, but no warranty or fitness is implied.

The information is provided on an "as is" basis. The author and New Riders Publishing shall have neither liability nor responsibility to any person or entity with respect to any loss or damages arising from the information contained in this book or from the use of the disks or programs that may accompany it.

Publisher	LLOYD J. SHORT
Associate Publisher	TIM HUDDLESTON
Product Development Manager	ROB TIDROW
Marketing Manager	RAY ROBINSON
Director of Special Projects	CHERI ROBINSON
Managing Editor	MATTHEW MORRILL

About the Author

Kevin Stoltz is an independent consultant specializing in LANtastic networks and system integration for small businesses. He has been installing LANtastic networks for more than five years and is an Artisoft 5 Star dealer. He also is the leader of the Seattle area LANtastic User Group. He authored *Inside LANtastic 6* and *Inside LANtastic 5.0*, co-authored *The Modem Coach,* and contributed to *Ultimate Windows 3.1* and *Inside Lotus 1-2-3 for Windows 4.0*, all from New Riders Publishing.

Born and raised in Spokane, Washington, Kevin attended the University of Washington at Seattle where he earned a degree in aeronautical engineering. He worked for the Boeing Company for more than six years as an engineer and systems analyst. He and his wife started CompuPlus, which now operates a VAR specializing in networking and system integration for small businesses.

Kevin lives with his wife, son, and daughter in Mukilteo, Washington.

Dedication

To my wife Dana for keeping me focused and somewhat organized (not an easy task), and for the "chair" to keep me in my "hole" and out of the living room. And to my six year-old son Zak, for keeping life in perspective by reminding me that I wasn't spending very much time with him. And to my two year-old daughter Katie, for winning a much-needed vacation after this project, just for being "cute."

Trademark Acknowledgments

Simply LANtastic is a trademark of Artisoft, Inc. All rigts reserved. All terms mentioned in this book that are known to be trademarks or service marks have been appropriately capitalized. New Riders Publishing cannot attest to the accuracy of this information. Use of a term in this book should not be regarded as affecting the validity of any trademark or service mark.

Acknowledgments

Special thanks to the many people whose hard work, dedication, and sacrifices made this book possible:

Emmett Dulaney, for the wisdom and insight he brings to this project. His experience, suggestions, and valuable comments are a major contribution to the success of this book.

Rob Lawson, for managing the editorial flow and pre-production preparation of text. His attention to detail in addition to his valuable suggestions and advice are greatly appreciated.

Jim LeValley, for his recommendations, insight, and efforts to keep this book on schedule even when I wasn't. His suggestions helped get this book started and finished.

Lillian Yates, Laura Frey, and Mary Ann Larguier for their superb editing, recommendations, and attention to detail.

The entire production staff of New Riders Publishing whose hard work and long hours allow this book to be of the highest quality and content. Their efforts are most appreciated.

Artisoft, Inc. for producing powerful yet easy-to-use network products without which this book would not have been possible.

Product Director
EMMETT DULANEY

Team Leader/Production Editor
ROB LAWSON

Editors
LILLIAN YATES
LAURA FREY
MARY ANN LARGUIER

Senior Acquisitions Editor
JAMES LeVALLEY

Technical Editor
WILLIAM M. STEEN

Acquisitions Coordinator
STACEY BEHELER

Editorial Assistant
KAREN OPAL

Publisher's Assistant
MELISSA LYNCH

Cover Designer
JAY CORPUS

Book Designers
FRED BOWER
ROGER S. MORGAN

Production Imprint Manager
JULI COOK

Production Imprint Team Leader
KATY BODENMILLER

Graphics Image Specialists
TERESA FORRESTER
CLINT LAHNEN
TIM MONTGOMERY
DENNIS SHEEHAN
GREG SIMSIC
SUSAN VANDEWALLE

Production Analysts
DENNIS CLAY HAGER
MARY BETH WAKEFIELD

Production Team
DON BROWN, MONA BROWN,
AYRIKA BRYANT, AMANDA BYUS,
CHERYL CAMERON, ELAINE CRABTREE,
KIMBERLY K. HANNEL, DEBBIE KINCAID,
STEPHANIE McCOMB, MARC SHECTER,
SUSAN SHEPARD, DENNIS WESNER

Indexer
JEANNE CLARK

Contents at a Glance

Table of Contents

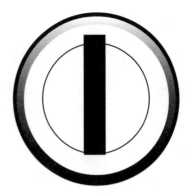

Introduction

As technology marches forward, the personal computer is used in more situations and for more purposes than ever thought imaginable. Computer use in business and in the home continues to grow, and any location with two or more computers usually can benefit by being networked.

A network allows previously isolated computers to communicate with each other and share resources that exist on other computers including programs, disk drives, and printers. By sharing a single resource such as a large disk drive or printer with every computer in the network, you don't have to purchase a printer or large hard disk for each computer. Besides being cost-effective, a network enables individuals to interact, sharing information and resources. Network applications enable more than one person to access a customer database, for example, or to perform invoicing or accounting functions concurrently.

The technology incorporated in networks today is advancing at an incredible rate. The cost of implementing a network is continually decreasing while network features are increasing. The question is no longer "Can I afford a network?" but rather "Can I afford to wait?"

Who Should Read This Book?

The Network Starter Kit is written for the individual with little or no knowledge about networks who needs to acquire a good working knowledge of networks in a short amount of time. This book is not intended for those who want detailed network theory. You will find *The Network Starter Kit* an extremely valuable source of information if you have any or all of the following needs:

- You don't know anything about networks and want to understand what a network is and how to use one.

- You need to plan and implement a network for use in your business or home office.

- You need to understand how your existing network operates and the general fundamentals that apply to all networks.

- You are a manager responsible for overseeing the implementation of a network in your business and need to understand what you are responsible for.

- You are training individuals or groups about networking and need a complete and easy-to-understand source of information able to provide the reader with a practical hands-on knowledge of networks.

What Makes This Book Different?

The Network Starter Kit is very different than other beginning network books. It is written the way most people learn, with an organized layout and plenty of examples and illustrations. You can learn *hands-on* how to use a network without having to buy anything else.

By building on the information contained in each chapter and emphasizing practical applications of networks, *The Network Starter Kit* leads you from knowing nothing about networks to possessing a good working knowledge of network fundamentals and use. *The Network Starter Kit* companion disk provides practical experience that expands your network knowledge one step beyond what other books can provide.

What Can You Expect To Learn?

Expect to learn a lot about network fundamentals as well as the actual implementation of a network. When you finish this book, you will have sufficient knowledge to plan, install, use, and manage a network.

The Network Starter Kit is a self-contained source of network information and practical hands-on experience. You begin by learning general networking fundamentals that apply to all networks. In the second part of the book, you get a chance to use your networking knowledge to install, use, and manage an actual network. Using the accompanying disk, you can install and become familiar with the use and operation of Artisoft's Simply LANtastic network without purchasing additional hardware. Or, with additional adapters and cable, you can install a complete functioning network between two computers that you can expand later to include more computers.

What's Included on the Accompanying Disks?

The Network Starter Kit companion disk includes the full version of Artisoft's Simply LANtastic network operating system for two computers. Also included in the back of the book is a coupon you can send to Artisoft to purchase Simply LANtastic network adapter cards, or you can use any other network adapters supplied with standard NDIS drivers.

The accompanying disk also includes a special *stub* driver that enables you to install and run Simply LANtastic on your computer even if you don't have a network adapter installed.

How This Book Is Organized

The Network Starter Kit is divided into two general parts. Part 1, "Fundamentals," provides the information required for you to have a good working knowledge of networks. Part 1 covers the general principles and concepts as they apply to all networks. Everything from networking history, through hardware and software components, through troubleshooting and management is covered in Part 1.

Part 2, "Implementing a Network," shows you how to implement Artisoft's Simply LANtastic network, which is included on the accompanying disk. Complete coverage of Simply LANtastic is discussed in Part 2 including detailed installation procedures, configuration, management, and even example sessions using Simply LANtastic with your application software.

Each chapter in this book covers specific topics progressing from general introductory concepts and ideas through a more detailed examination and discussion of network usage, administration, and management.

Part 1: Fundamentals

Chapter 1, "History of Networking," discusses the sequence of events that led to where networks are today, including the technological advances required for networks to evolve.

Chapter 2, "Network Nodes and Their Function," examines the capability and function of each computer in a network, including the different types of networks and how resources such as disk drives and printers are shared in a network.

Chapter 3, "Hardware Components," explains the many hardware components that are used in a network and the function of each.

Chapter 4, "Software Components," discusses the software used to create a functioning network, including the network operating system and the standards that govern the development of network software.

Chapter 5, "Peer-to-Peer Networks," looks at the features and capability of the most popular peer-to-peer networks.

Chapter 6, "Server-Based Networks," examines the features and capability of the most popular high-performance server-based networks available today.

Chapter 7, "Network Applications," discusses how to use the various types of application software on a network, including anything from single-user applications to applications written specifically for use on a network.

Chapter 8, "Printing on a Network," explains how network printing is different than printing from a stand-alone computer, and the many features and benefits obtained by printing on a network.

Chapter 9, "Managing Users and Resources," discusses how to manage user accounts and shared resources to make the most efficient use of your network while maintaining security.

Chapter 10, "Troubleshooting," discusses what can go wrong with your network, what to look for, and the necessary steps to resolve any problem you might have.

Part 2: Implementing a Network

Chapter 11, "Installing Simply LANtastic," explains how to install on your computer, in both a DOS and a Windows environment, the Simply LANtastic network operating system included on the accompanying disks.

Chapter 12, "Users, Printers, and Shared Drives," discusses how to set up shared resources such as disk drives and printers in Simply LANtastic, and how to connect to and use the shared resources once they have been set up.

Chapter 13, "Managing a Network," looks at several issues you might encounter when managing a Simply LANtastic network, including everything from disabling the network on a computer to configuring your network to sharing a CD-ROM drive.

Chapter 14, "Running DOS and Windows Sessions," examines several example sessions of how to use your Simply LANtastic network with your application software to improve the efficiency and productivity of your daily tasks.

The Appendix, "Planning a Network," discusses how to determine your network requirements, and the steps to plan and implement a network.

The Glossary defines the many terms discussed throughout the book.

Conventions Used in This Book

As you read through this book, you find that special formatting has been used throughout the text to help you get the most out of this book. To simplify the book's discussions when special notes or special formatting is used, several conventions have been established.

Where appropriate, special typefaces are used as well. *Italics* are used to define terms introduced for the first time in a chapter, as well as to emphasize words. This typeface is used for screen messages.

The Network Starter Kit features some special "sidebars," such as the following, which are set apart from the normal text by icons.

A note includes extra information that you should find useful, and complements the discussion at hand, instead of being a direct part of it. A note may describe special situations that can arise under certain circumstances.

New Riders Publishing

The staff of New Riders Publishing is committed to bringing you the very best in computer reference material. Each New Riders book is the result of months of work by authors and staff who research and refine the information contained within its covers.

As part of this commitment to you, the NRP reader, New Riders invites your input. Please let us know if you enjoy this book, if you have trouble with the information and examples presented, or if you have a suggestion for the next edition.

Please note, though: New Riders staff cannot serve as a technical resource for questions about software- or hardware-related problems. Please refer to the documentation that accompanies your hardware and software, or to the applications' Help systems.

If you have a question or comment about any New Riders book, there are several ways to contact New Riders Publishing. We will respond to as many readers as we can. Your name, address, or phone number will never become part of a mailing list or be used for any purpose other than to help us continue to bring you the best books possible. You can write us at the following address:

New Riders Publishing
Attn: Associate Publisher
201 W. 103rd Street
Indianapolis, IN 46290

If you prefer, you can fax New Riders Publishing at
(317) 581-4670.

You can send e-mail to New Riders from a variety of sources. NRP maintains several mailboxes organized by topic area. Mail in these mailboxes will be forwarded to the staff member who is best able to address your concerns. Substitute the appropriate mailbox name from the list below when addressing your e-mail. The mailboxes are as follows:

ADMIN	Comments and complaints for NRP's Publisher
APPS	Word, Excel, WordPerfect, and other office applications
ACQ	Book proposal inquiries by potential authors
CAD	AutoCAD, 3D Studio, AutoSketch, and CAD products
DATABASE	Access, dBASE, Paradox, and other database products
GRAPHICS	CorelDRAW!, Photoshop, and other graphics products
INTERNET	Internet
NETWORK	NetWare, LANtastic, and other network-related topics
OS	MS-DOS, OS/2, and all OS except UNIX and Windows
UNIX	Unix
WINDOWS	Microsoft Windows (all versions)
OTHER	Anything that doesn't fit the above categories

If you use an MHS e-mail system that routes through CompuServe, send your messages to the following address:

mailbox @ NEWRIDER

To send NRP mail from CompuServe, use the following address:

MHS: *mailbox* @ NEWRIDER

To send mail from the Internet, use the following address format:

mailbox@newrider.mhs.compuserve.com

NRP is an imprint of Macmillan Computer Publishing. To obtain a catalog or information, or to purchase any Macmillan Computer Publishing book, call (800) 428-5331.

Thank you for selecting *The Network Starter Kit!*

Part One: Fundamentals

In This Chapter. . .

In this chapter you learn about the history of networking and computing (as it relates to networking), and the progression of events and technology that led up to the creation of the *local area network* (LAN). The advancement of the PC and the requirements that led to the implementation of networks on PCs also are discussed.

Specifically, this chapter covers the following topics:

- The computing technology used with some of the early computers such as mainframe and minicomputers.
- The impact of the introduction of the PC on computing.
- The growth of the PC in both power and capability leading to the need to network PCs.
- Local area networks and wide area networks.

This chapter also introduces the following terms:

Bit	Binary
Download	Byte
Downsize	Main frame
Dumb terminal	Microcomputer
Host	Minicomputer
Local area network (LAN)	Modem
Network interface card (NIC)	On-line service
Network operating system (NOS)	Protocol
Time-sharing service	Resources
Wide area network (WAN)	Upload
American Standard Code for Information Interchange (ASCII)	RS232C

History of Networking

As computers find their way into our daily lives, they are used to solve more and more of our problems. A single computer can be extremely valuable because of its ability to process information independently from any outside influence. Stand-alone computers are used successfully for a variety of tasks including word processing, database management, accounting, financial analysis, graphic design, desktop publishing, *computer aided design* (CAD), and much more. However, consider the additional capabilities available if you could connect your computer to other computers and access the information contained within them; the door would open to an even greater wealth of information. Consider the benefits realized if you and a colleague could access a customer database and make changes to it at the same time. Or, suppose you have an accounting system for your business. You might spend a couple of hours a day invoicing customers, while someone else enters inventory received, while still another person enters payments from customers into the accounts receivable section of the accounting program. Wouldn't it be nice if instead of taking turns using the accounting computer, each person could have his or her own computers, enabling them to enter their accounting information whenever they want? And wouldn't it be nice if all the data entered from the different computers would update the same accounting data files so the others using the accounting program would have instant access to the current data? A network makes this, and much more, possible.

A *network* is two or more computers connected to allow the sharing of information and resources. The information to be shared may consist of files and data such as daily sales information, graphical data such as charts and clip-art images, and documents. Resources are the devices or data storage areas on a computer that are accessed by another computer using the network. Resources that one computer may share with another computer on a network typically include disk drives, directories, and printers. Programs like any other file on a computer may be shared and used by accessing the program by means of a shared resource.

To truly understand what a network is and how networks enhance our ability to use computers more efficiently, it is important to understand how networks have evolved into what are available today. It also is useful to understand other methods used to access computer systems that may not necessarily be considered networking but for all intents and purposes provide a similar end result. By considering other methods of accomplishing the same result you can determine if you are using the correct tool for the job. Although a network enables you to save a file to a 3 1/2-inch floppy disk on another computer, for example, if that is the only task for which you use your network, it makes more sense to purchase a 3 1/2-inch floppy drive for your computer rather than a network.

Early Computers

One of the early means of supplying information to a computer for processing was by using punch cards. First you sat at a keypunch machine and, by typing on a keyboard, created a series of rectangular cards with small rectangular holes in them; each card represented a line of program code or data that was later fed into the computer for processing. Next you took your stack of punch cards to the punch card reader, at which you placed the stack of cards in the hopper and pressed a button to begin reading. The information contained on the punch card was then read into a large mainframe computer system where in time it was processed and the results were printed out. The process of reading in information and processing it all at once is known as *batch processing*. With batch processing, as soon as the information is sent for processing, there is no further interaction between the user and the computer until after the results are printed.

The next major advancement in the way to submit data to the mainframe computer for processing was with the use of dumb terminals. Now, instead of having to sit down at a key punch machine and create punch cards, you sat down at a *dumb terminal* (which consists of a screen and keyboard that are directly connected to the mainframe computer) and type in the information necessary (see fig. 1.1).

Dumb Terminals get their name from the fact that no processing is actually performed at the terminal itself. It is simply used to send data to the host computer by means of the keyboard and to receive data from the host computer by means of the display.

A host is the computer to which dumb terminals are connected. Host computers can be mainframes or other smaller computers.

In the 1960s a new type of commercial network service known as time sharing began to flourish. *Time-sharing* allowed terminals to be placed at locations geographically isolated from the host computer, such as at a place of business or in specified computer centers, which could be used to access the computing resources available from a host computer. The dumb terminals were connected to the host computer by the means of leased telephone lines (see fig. 1.2). The host computer allocated and divided its time between the different terminals accessing it. Because a mainframe computer was big and expensive, often the host computer was a less powerful computer. When a batch job was submitted, the host computer sent the job to the mainframe computer to be processed. When the mainframe computer finished processing the job, this intermediate host computer stored the results and sent them back to the dumb terminal or the appropriate printer. Often, several of the smaller host computers were used to provide dumb terminals access to a single mainframe computer.

Figure 1.1

Dumb Terminals connected directly to a mainframe computer.

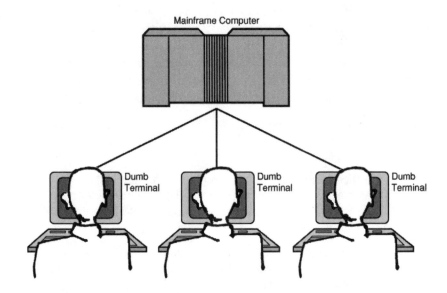

Two different types of networks were used at this stage to allow communication between the computers. The connection of the many dumb terminals to the host computers was considered one network. The connections between the host computers and the mainframe computer was another network. Even though the path between the terminals and the final mainframe computer was not direct, the two networks allowed the path to appear as though it was, resulting in the entire system being referred to as a single network.

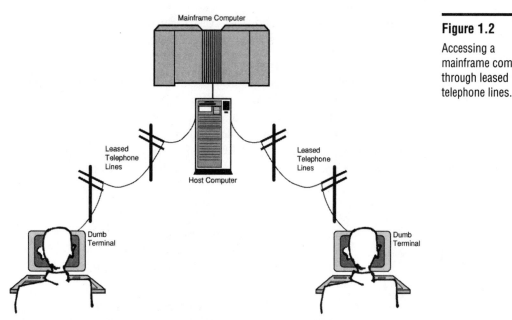

Mainframe Computer

Leased
Telephone
Lines

Leased
Telephone
Lines

Host Computer

Dumb
Terminal

Dumb
Terminal

Figure 1.2

Accessing a
mainframe computer
through leased
telephone lines.

During this same time period, many additional advances occurred
that made the access and use of the computing resources of a
mainframe and other host computers even easier. Instead of the
standard batch processing required previously, there was the
ability to process information in real time. *Real-time processing*
enabled the user to view the results of the processed information
as it was typed in. Real-time processing enabled the creation of the
airline reservation system in use today. Developed by IBM and
American Airlines, the SABRE system allowed dumb terminals to
be connected to a host mainframe computer that provided airline
flight and seating information. Reservations were made and
confirmed using the SABRE system, which consisted of nearly
2,000 terminals connected to the host computer using some 12,000
miles of leased telephone lines.

As more and more time-sharing services became available, users
of those services found themselves in an interesting predicament.
Each service typically had its own terminal and required a separate leased line for the connection. A separate terminal usually

was required because each host computer had its own method of communicating with the terminals; there was not a standard.

The *American Standard Code for Information Interchange* (ASCII) standard was adopted in 1964 by the American Standards Organization. The ASCII standard allows for 128 characters, which include the letters in the alphabet, the 10 numeric symbols (0–9), as well as several other symbols, to be represented in a binary format of 0s and 1s (see fig. 1.3). The binary format for the ASCII character set uses a 7-bit representation that allows for 128 possible combinations.

Binary is the most basic number system used by computers. Binary represents each number as either a 1 or a 0. In binary, each digit (0 or 1) is referred to as a bit. A byte is represented by 8 bits.

A single bit can represent two combinations, 0 or 1. Two bits together can represent four combinations—00, 01, 10, and 11. The more bits combined, the more combinations possible. Seven bits allows for 128 combinations while eight bits allows for 256 combinations.

Figure 1.3

An example of ASCII characters and their binary and decimal representation.

Example ASCII Characters

ASCII Character	Binary Representation	Decimal Representation
0	0110000	48
1	0110001	49
2	0110010	50
3	0110011	51
•		
•		
•		
A	1000001	65
B	1000010	66
C	1000011	67
D	1000100	68
•		
•		97
a	1100001	98
b	1100010	99
c	1100011	100

With ASCII established as the standard method used to transmit characters, another standard was needed to specify how the data would be transferred over the wire. RS-232C was developed to specify the voltages and electrical communication parameters used to connect devices.

The solution to the requirement of a leased line for each terminal was the modem and the dial-up connection. A modem connected to the terminal dialed the number for the host computer. A modem connected to the host computer answered and the terminal was connected to the host computer using standard telephone lines. When finished, the connection was terminated and the phone line was used for other purposes. Dial-up connections resulted in a substantial savings because a special leased line no longer was required for access to the host computer.

The RS232C standard was developed specifically to prescribe the method used to connect Data Terminal Equipment (the terminal at which the user sat) with Data Communications Equipment (the modem connected to the telephone lines).

Today RS232C is used for connecting all kinds of devices to computers including modems, a mouse, serial printers, and even other computers.

As technology advanced, the access to computer network services also advanced, resulting in more capability and less cost. Mini-computers, which were less powerful but also much less expensive than mainframe computers, were purchased and used by many companies for tasks such as accounting and inventory management. With the advent of ASCII and the RS-232C standards, a single dumb terminal often was used to access many different types of host computers and services. Additional standards were developed and adopted to specify the protocol (or rules) to be used for communication.

Introduction of the PC

In 1981, IBM introduced the IBM PC and set the stage for the future of personal computing. Although several personal computers (also called microcomputers) were introduced a few years before the IBM PC, it was the IBM PC that provided the initiative for what was to be a revolution in computing. Personal computers (PCs) provided the computing capability in a single unit to be used by an individual. Instead of having a dumb terminal connected to a host computer, you now had an independent computer sitting at your desk. Of course the PC was not as powerful as a mainframe or minicomputer, but this was not necessary as it only had to serve the needs of one user.

When IBM designed the PC, it was created with an open architecture, which meant that the PC was able to use components designed and manufactured by other companies. Due to the open architecture of the IBM PC and the fact that the IBM name was on a personal computer, the PC became an industry standard for microcomputers. Many manufacturers jumped on the bandwagon and began developing software and hardware products for the PC. With most of the specifications for the IBM PC available and in hand, other manufacturers, COMPAQ being the first and most notable, also began making IBM PC-compatible computers.

Technology continued to advance and the combination of competition and the technological advances caused prices to decrease and computing power to increase.

The flexibility, adaptability, and lower price of personal computers caused sales to explode. A huge industry was born ready to respond to the needs of its customers. Although initially intended for simple computing tasks such as mathematical calculations, simple accounting functions, basic database management, and word processing, the PC began to evolve into much more. With the advent of programs such as the VisiCalc and Lotus 1-2-3 spreadsheet programs, and the Wordstar word processing program, the PC became an invaluable asset to businesses.

Although the PC was capable of running programs and processing data independent of another computer, the need to access
other computer systems still existed. Software was developed that
enabled the PC to be used in place of a dumb terminal to connect
to a host computer through either a modem or direct connection.
However, the PC was not a dumb terminal, and thus was able to
reduce the cost incurred when connecting to a host computer
using time-sharing services.

The PC could be used to type in data that normally would be
typed in at a dumb terminal while being on-line with a time-
sharing service, thereby saving phone line and host computer
connect charges. After the data was entered in the PC and saved
to a file, the host computer could be connected to and the data
transferred (also called uploaded) from the PC to the host computer at a faster rate than if it was typed directly from a dumb
terminal. The PC also could be used to capture data that was sent
from the host computer to a file (also called downloading) that
then could be used on the PC or sent to another computer.

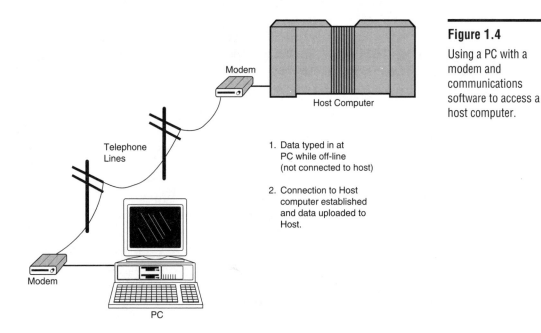

Modem

Host Computer

Telephone
Lines

1. Data typed in at
   PC while off-line
   (not connected to host)

2. Connection to Host
   computer established
   and data uploaded to
   Host.

Modem

PC

Figure 1.4

Using a PC with a
modem and
communications
software to access a
host computer.

Modern Day Communications

A modem and communications software allow a PC to connect to on-line services. On-line services differ from time sharing in that they are primarily a source of information, including news, weather, databases, and encyclopedias. Time-sharing services enable you to use a host computer to run a program and process data that you supply from an off-site terminal. On-line services also are used to exchange messages with others and to ask and answer questions about particular topics. On-line services usually have forums or conferences that are categorized by topics such as networking, aviation, or any other subject. Computer hardware and software manufacturers frequently have a forum on an on-line service such as CompuServe, America Online, or Prodigy. In addition to exchanging messages with questions and answers, on-line services also have files that can be downloaded. These are anything from sample programs to databases to clip art.

Communications software enables your PC to emulate a terminal and connect to a host computer using a modem and phone lines. Also referred to as *Terminal Emulation Software*, communications software provides additional features to enable you to upload and download files.

The host computer for an on-line service can be connected to (networked with) several other computers that provide additional services to subscribers of the on-line service. For example, you can access the SABRE airline reservation system from on-line services such as CompuServe and Prodigy. When you access the SABRE system from an on-line service, a special program called EAASY SABRE is run that provides access to the airline flight information on the SABRE host computer. The actual process occurring "behind the scenes" is very complicated. However, when using the on-line service, it appears as if you are simply accessing another feature. With features like EAASY SABRE included in on-line services, the distinction between an on-line service and a time-sharing service is not as clear.

Today, the term time-sharing rarely is used. Terms like "accessing," "tied into," or even "on-line" are used to describe when a person is accessing another host computer.

PC computers can be set up as a *bulletin board system* (BBS). A BBS is similar to an on-line service but is operated on a much smaller scale. With a modem and the appropriate BBS software, nearly any PC can be set up as a BBS. If you have a modem and communications software, which allows your PC to act as a terminal, you can connect to a computer that has been set up as a BBS. BBSs enable you to exchange messages with others as well as upload and download files. Many computer hardware and software manufacturers maintain a BBS so that you can ask questions about their product as well as download related files that can consist of utility programs and other data.

One of the largest networks that can be accessed using a PC is the Internet. Often referred to as the "Information Superhighway," the Internet is comprised of computers from colleges, universities, and corporations all over the world. The Internet currently connects over 5,000 networks and is used by five to ten million users worldwide, and it is growing at an incredible rate! By accessing computers connected to the Internet, you can obtain almost any information imaginable. While connected to the Internet, you can send and receive e-mail, transfer files between your computer and any host computer on the Internet, or even log in to a host computer as if you had a terminal that was directly connected to it.

The Need for Connectivity

With the advancement of technology came an evolution of the personal computer. Additional storage and processing capabilities were added to the PC, making the gap in processing power between the PC and the other mainframes and minicomputers smaller and smaller. In some cases, in fact, this has resulted in the

PC's power exceeding that of the host minicomputer or mainframe being used. While minicomputers and mainframes were expensive to purchase and maintain, the PC could be purchased inexpensively and maintenance costs were almost nonexistent.

Several PCs could be purchased and used for much less than a standard maintenance contract for a mainframe or minicomputer. The PC was still a stand-alone computer, however, and the technology to connect PCs to form a network had yet to be defined. Although PCs could access mainframe or minicomputers acting as dumb terminals using communications software, there was no way for PCs to communicate with each other.

Connecting PCs or microcomputers to form a network provides several benefits. The ability to access and use information from a common source is beneficial and in some cases a requirement for operations, such as accounting in which different people need access to the same data at the same time. Another immediate benefit of networking PCs is the ability to share printers and disk drives among PCs. For example, a single laser printer can be used by all computers in the network rather than purchasing a laser printer for each computer. Similarly, a large hard drive can be used by all computers in the network for storing data so that it may be accessed by others. Because most of the data is stored on the large hard drive, smaller, less expensive hard drives can be purchased for use in the other PCs in the network.

The Local Area Network

With the benefits of connecting PCs or microcomputers to share information among them identified, the *local area network* (LAN) was born. Long before the idea of PCs replacing mainframe or minicomputers was even considered plausible, the first PC LANs began to appear.

A *LAN* is a high-speed communications system that connects microcomputers or PCs that are in close proximity; usually in the same building. A LAN consists of the network hardware and software to connect previously isolated, or stand-alone, PCs to a network. A LAN provides the capability to share programs, information, and resources such as disk drives, directories, and printers among PCs.

Appearing as early as 1983, the LAN has continued to evolve into an integral part of PC connectivity. The LANs available today are reliable and include an abundance of powerful features, making the LAN an extremely powerful and flexible tool for sharing information among PCs.

The process of incorporating a PC or microcomputer into a LAN consists of installing a *network interface card* (NIC) in each computer. The NICs in each computer are connected with a special network cable. The final step to implementing a LAN is to load software, known as the *network operating system* (NOS), on each PC. The NOS works with the computer's operating system software to enable the application software (word processor, database, spreadsheet, accounting, and so on) running on the computer to communicate through the network with other computers.

A LAN differs significantly from a network in which a host computer is accessed and used by means of a dumb terminal or with a PC running communications software (see fig. 1.5). Because a PC in a LAN is a fully functional computer, the actual processing is performed on the individual PC. For example, suppose you need to revise a document that has been created and is stored on another PC. Although you could load the word processor program and data from another PC, the program actually would be running using the processor on your computer; not the processor on the other computer. You would read the data from the other computer and when finished with your changes, would write the data to the other computer. If you were accessing a host computer using a dumb terminal, the processing actually would be performed on the host computer because the dumb terminal only has the capability to send data from the keyboard and receive data to the screen.

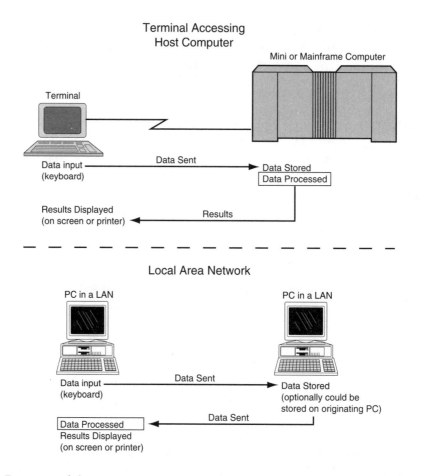

Figure 1.5

The processing that occurs with a terminal accessing a host computer compared to a PC in a LAN.

Because of the increasing power of the PCs and microcomputers available, as well as the sophisticated application programs that exist for these computers, many companies are changing their focus from the mainframe or minicomputers as their primary computing resource to the much smaller, but in many cases more powerful, microcomputer or PC. The process of converting (or porting) applications from mainframe or minicomputers to micro-computers on a LAN is known as *downsizing*.

The Wide Area Network

LANs can be connected to form a *wide area network* (WAN). LANs are used to connect PCs in close proximity; WANs, however, are not geographically limited in size. WANs usually use special hardware and phone lines provided by the telephone company to connect LANs. WANs also can use specialized hardware and software to include minicomputers and mainframe computers as elements on the network. The hardware used to create a WAN also can include satellite links, fiber optics, infrared devices, and laser devices.

The network of computers that compose the Internet are connected to form a WAN.

Summary

This chapter introduced you to the history of networking, helped give you a feel for how networking has evolved, and described the many paths networking has taken. The factors that contributed to the evolution of the networks used today were discussed. The LAN and its relation with other networks also was discussed.

With an understanding of the history of networking, you are now ready to learn more about the details of LANs.

In This Chapter. . .

In the previous chapter you learned about the history of networking and were introduced to the Local Area Network (LAN). With a basic understanding of the LAN, this chapter will take you to the next step that includes understanding the function and capability of each computer in a LAN. Specifically, you will learn the following:

- The difference between a server and a workstation.

- The difference between a nondedicated server and a dedicated server.

- The difference between a server-based network and a peer-to-peer network, including the advantages and disadvantages of each.

- How disk drives and printers are shared for use by others on the network.

- How shared disk drives and printers are used in a network.

The following terms are used in this chapter:

Client-server	Physical connections
Logical connections	Server-based LAN
Network Operating System (NOS)	
Peer-to-peer	
Server	
Workstation	
Dedicated server	
Node	
Nondedicated Server	

Network Nodes and Their Function

In the preceding chapter, you learned that a *Local Area Network* (LAN) consists of individual microcomputers (or PCs) connected together to allow information and resources such as disk drives and printers to be shared among computers.

Each computer in a LAN, or network node as they are often called, still retains its stand-alone properties, with the exception of any computer that has been configured specifically for other functions. The function, capability, and network features available to each node are determined by the network software, the network hardware, and the way each network node has been configured.

The *Network Operating System* (NOS) is the network software installed on each computer (node) that allows your computer to communicate with other computers in the network. The NOS determines the network features available to you and the capability of the network in general. The NOS also enables you to configure each network node so that it performs the functions you want. The NOS can enable you, for example, to configure one or more computers in your network to share its resources, such as disk drives and printers, with other computers. You can configure computers that are unable to share their own resources to access the resources that others share.

The first step to understanding how a LAN actually enables you to use the shared disk drives and printers connected to other computers is to understand the two different types of connections that exist in a network; physical and logical. A physical connection is an actual hardware connection such as a printer connected to your computer by means of a printer cable. A logical connection is a temporary connection which appears as a physical connection to your application software, but is created through the use of your network software. The NOS enables you to create and destroy logical connections at will without changing the physical layout of the hardware in your network.

Consider the following example in which the DOS substitute command (SUBST) is used to create a logical drive letter that points to another drive or directory. You can create a logical drive E, for example, that points to the C:\DOS directory on your computer by typing the following command at the DOS prompt:

```
SUBST E: C:\DOS
```

Anytime you perform an action that references drive E, C:\DOS is substituted for E:. Typing DIR E: produces the same result as typing DIR C:\DOS. The E: drive is a logical drive that doesn't really exist.

An easy way to understand a logical connection is to think of it as being a physical connection. For example, when a logical network connection is made from your computer to a printer connected to another computer, think of it as if you walked over to the other computer, unplugged the printer cable from the computer and then plugged it into your computer. The network provides the capability to use other devices connected to other computers without physically changing anything.

Suppose you need to use the laser printer which is physically connected to Dana's computer (see fig. 2.1). The computer (node) at which you are working needs to use the laser printer on Dana's computer (node). Dana's computer will service your computer's request to use the laser printer by making it available for you to use. The NOS enables you to specify which laser printer you want to use, and then establishes a temporary logical network connection between your computer and the laser printer. When you print from an application, the printed information is sent through the network to the printer specified, which in this example, is the laser printer connected to Dana's computer.

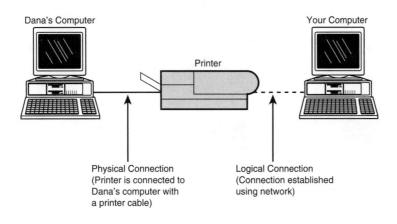

Figure 2.1

Physical and logical connections.

Servers and Workstations

The function of each network node is determined by how you configure the node when it is first installed in the network. At its most basic level, a network node may be configured as either a server or a workstation. The workstation is the computer at which you are sitting and performing your work, while a server is the computer you are accessing (see fig. 2.2).

Suppose Mike's computer has a database that contains the addresses and telephone numbers of all your customers, for example. With a network, you can sit at your computer and access the customer database on Mike's computer. Mike's computer in this example is the server because it is serving your request for information by sharing the information with you. Your computer is the workstation because it is accessing and using the shared information (the database) on Mike's computer.

Two different types of servers exist, nondedicated and dedicated. The quantity and type of servers in your network depend on the flexibility of the NOS you have selected and how you have chosen to configure the computers in your network.

Figure 2.2

The role of the server and the workstations.

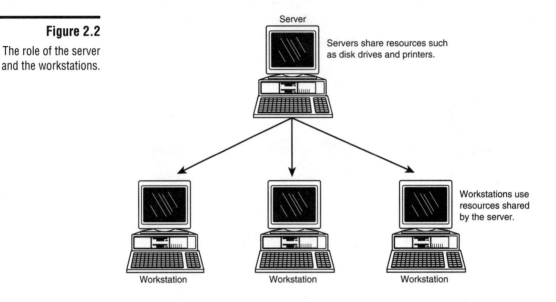

Workstation

A workstation is a computer that is able to use resources such as disk drives and printers that are located on other computers (servers). A workstation does not share its own resources with other computers and therefore other nodes may not access and use any resources on a workstation. With many networks, particularly nondedicated server style, a computer can function as both a server and a workstation.

The computer at which you are sitting and working is a workstation. As the name implies, even without a network, a workstation can be thought of as the station where you perform your work. When discussing a workstation in a network environment, the meaning is the same, with one addition; you have the ability to access and use the shared resources on other computers. The other computers you are able to access are the computers that have been configured as servers in your network.

Consider the example shown in figure 2.3. The workstations may access and use the shared resources on the server. In this example, the C: drive and the laser printer are the resources on the server that have been shared. The network allows both Workstation A and Workstation B to access and use the C: drive and laser printer on the server. The network also allows the workstations to use the shared resources on the server at the same time. Workstation A and Workstation B cannot access each other. Workstation B can use its own printer just as if there were no network. Workstation A may not use the printer connected to Workstation B.

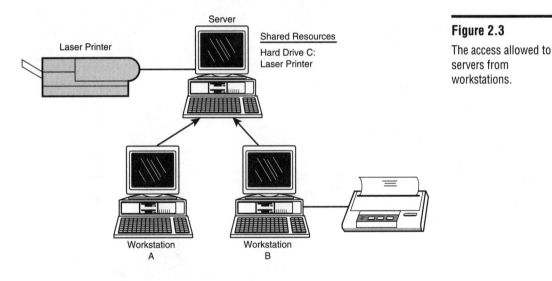

Figure 2.3

The access allowed to servers from workstations.

Nondedicated Server

A server is a computer that is capable of sharing its resources with other computers. The shared resources can include printers, disk drives, CD-ROM drives, directories on a hard disk, or even individual files.

A nondedicated server is a server that also can be used as a workstation. You can sit at a nondedicated server and use it as a workstation while at the same time it is sharing its resources with other computers. You may, for example, be editing a document and saving the changes to your C: drive while at the same time, another computer is accessing your C: drive to read and write data files.

Your NOS determines whether or not you may have nondedicated servers, their capability, and the quantity of nondedicated servers allowed.

Figure 2.4 is an example of a network with three nodes; two are configured as nondedicated servers and the other is configured as a workstation. The previous rules for servers and workstations still apply; workstations may access the shared resources on other servers but may not share their own resources. However, because a nondedicated server also may be used as a workstation, any nondedicated server may access and use the shared resources of another server.

Figure 2.4

A three-node network with two nondedicated servers and a workstation.

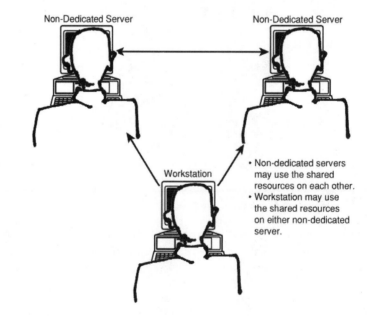

Dedicated Server

A *dedicated server* is a server that may not perform any tasks other than those required to share resources with network nodes. Unlike a nondedicated server, a dedicated server may not be used as a workstation. A dedicated server usually operates a version of the NOS, which optimizes the speed at which data moves between the server and the other network nodes. Because the dedicated server is used only for network-related tasks, any additional overhead that would be required if the server was to also act as a workstation is eliminated, resulting in increased performance. Users do not have any reason to have physical contact with a dedicated server, except to check or clear connections, and check the system status. As such, dedicated servers are often kept isolated and even in locked rooms to prevent someone from inadvertently turning the computer off or trying to use the computer as a workstation, which could result in the loss of valuable data.

Networks use dedicated servers in situations where the performance of the server must be at its best. Consider the case in which the same large customer database must be accessed by 20 computers in a network concurrently. The customer database to be shared is located on the server. Sharing a large database with 20 computers concurrently could tax the processing power of even the fastest PC. To maximize the efficiency of the server, it is configured as a dedicated server and runs the version of the NOS to allow it to be a dedicated server and optimize its efficiency, thereby maximizing its speed at processing network tasks.

You can dedicate servers to perform specific tasks. You use a file server specifically for sharing files with other nodes in the network. You use a print server for sharing the printers connected to it with the network. You use a fax server specifically for sharing a fax board with other computers in the network.

More specific uses for nondedicated servers are as nondedicated file servers, nondedicated print servers, or nondedicated fax servers.

Server-Based and Peer-to-Peer LANs

LANs generally are classified into one of two categories: server-based and peer-to-peer. A server-based LAN, also referred to as Client-Server, typically consists of a single dedicated server that shares its resources with the other nodes in the LAN (see fig. 2.5). The other nodes in the network are configured as workstations (or clients) and may use only the shared resources on the server. Because the server is dedicated, it may not be used as a workstation. The sole purpose of the dedicated server is to serve the needs of the network nodes accessing it.

Figure 2.5

A server-based network showing a single server that may be accessed by the workstations.

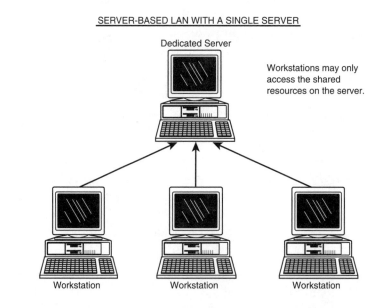

SERVER-BASED LAN WITH A SINGLE SERVER

Dedicated Server

Workstations may only access the shared resources on the server.

Workstation   Workstation   Workstation

In larger LANs, a server-based LAN may include more than a single dedicated server (see fig. 2.6). For example, each department in a company may have its own dedicated server. Engineering may have its own server, sales another, accounting another, and so on. The server in engineering may be used to store all the data and CAD drawings for the products manufactured by the company. The server for the sales department may contain product specifications used by the sales staff in addition to a customer database. Although each department may use its own server, any server could be accessible, if necessary, to any department unless security concerns make it prohibitive to do so. If security is an issue, user names and passwords could allow only those authorized to have access to a particular server. User names and passwords are useful when making available accounting and other sensitive information that should only be available to specific individuals.

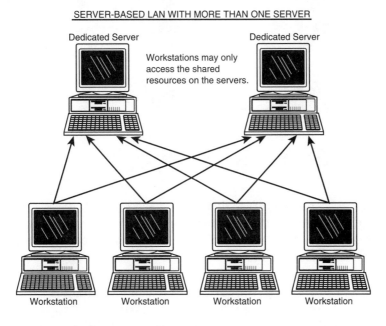

Figure 2.6

A server-based network with multiple servers.

A peer-to-peer LAN allows every computer in the network to be configured as a nondedicated server so any computer in the network can share its resources with any other computer in the network (see fig. 2.7). A peer-to-peer LAN offers much more flexibility than a server-based LAN because the the peer-to-peer LAN allows any computer in the network to share its resources with any other computer in the network. The flexibility that a peer-to-peer

LAN provides also can make it more confusing to manage than a server-based LAN. Instead of keeping track of the shared resources and users on a single or just a few servers, you have to keep track of the configuration of each nondedicated server in the network—which can be every computer in a peer-to-peer LAN.

Figure 2.7

A peer-to-peer LAN.

PEER-TO-PEER NETWORK

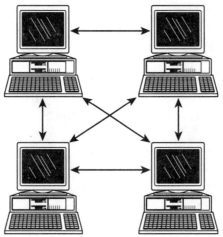

Every non-dedicated server may access the shared resources on every other non-dedicated server in the network.

Even though a peer-to-peer LAN allows you to set up every node in your network as a nondedicated server, most peer-to-peer LANs also give you the flexibility to set up nodes as workstations or as dedicated servers. Most dedicated servers run a special version of the NOS software, which optimizes the efficiency of the server and prevents it from being used as a workstation. You can treat a nondedicated server as a dedicated server if you want to by simply not using it as a workstation. Although the server may not run a special version of the NOS to optimize its efficiency as a server, the fact that you are not also using it as a workstation will improve the performance.

Comparing Server-Based and Peer-to-Peer LANs

Understanding the difference between a server-based network and a peer-to-peer network does not necessarily give you enough information to allow you to choose the network type that is right for your situation. However, with a few examples of how specific tasks would be accomplished in a server-based network as compared to a peer-to-peer network, you will have a strong foundation from which to choose the best network for your requirements.

Consider the most basic operation of transferring a file from one computer to another. Without a network you would first copy the file from the hard disk on your computer to a floppy disk. Then you would walk over to the computer to where you wanted the file transferred, put the disk into the disk drive, and then copy the file from the floppy disk to the hard disk on that computer.

Figure 2.8 helps illustrate the process to copy a file from one computer to another using both a server-based network and a peer-to-peer network. In a dedicated server network, copying a file from workstation A to workstation B would require two steps. While sitting at workstation A, you first copy the file from workstation A to the dedicated server C. Next, move to workstation B and copy the file from dedicated server C to workstation B. In a server-based network you cannot copy files directly between workstations; workstations only may access servers. In a peer-to-peer network, you can copy the file directly between nondedicated server A and nondedicated server B. Because a nondedicated server can be used as a server (to share resources) and as a workstation (to access the shared resources), you can copy the file from node A to node B while sitting at either node A or node B.

The previous example clearly shows that a peer-to-peer network is more flexible when it comes to accessing different nodes in the network. The increased flexibility, however, may come at the cost of other features such as more difficult administration, compromised security, and performance in some situations.

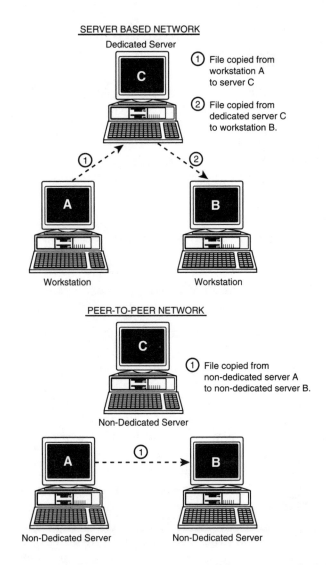

Although server performance is maximized by using a dedicated server, overall network performance is increased by distributing network tasks between several servers. Consider the example in which a customer database and an accounting database share a server (see fig. 2.9). Two workstations from the sales department access the customer database while two other computers from the accounting department access the accounting database. With a single server, both databases are located on the same server, which then has to support all four workstations. With two servers, the customer database is placed on server A and the accounting database on server B. The two sales workstations access the customer database on server A and the two accounting workstations access the accounting database on server B. Distributing the two databases between two servers causes the two servers to have roughly half the workload as a single server with both databases.

Distributing tasks between multiple servers as previously described can be accomplished with both a server-based network or a peer-to-peer network. In a peer-to-peer network it is a simple matter to put one database on one node and the other database on another node since all nodes will typically be configured as nondedicated servers. In a server-based network, however, if you don't already have two dedicated servers, performing this feat would require you to purchase an additional dedicated server. Again, the choice between a server-based network and a peer-to-peer network is one of flexibility, economics, and performance.

Table 2.1 summarizes the advantages and disadvantages of server-based and peer-to-peer networks. Keep in mind that each NOS is different, independent of whether it is considered server-based or peer-to-peer, and may include features normally found in the opposite type of network.

Table 2.1
Summary of the Advantages and Disadvantages of
Server-Based and Peer-to-Peer Networks

Server-Based Network

Advantages

Use of dedicated servers results in better server performance (faster).

Network administration is easier because there is a limited number of servers to keep track of.

continues

Table 2.1, Continued
*Summary of the Advantages and Disadvantages of
Server-Based and Peer-to-Peer Networks*

Server-Based Network

Disadvantages

Usually have to purchase an additional high-performance computer to be used as a dedicated server that cannot be used for anything else.

Cannot share resources on network nodes other than the resources shared by dedicated servers.

If server fails, network activities pretty much shut down.

Peer-to-Peer

Advantages

Complete flexibility to share resources on any node in the network.

More economical because each nondedicated server also may be used as a workstation.

Flexibility to distribute network applications among several servers for improved overall network performance with no increase in cost.

Disadvantages

Can be difficult to administer (manage) because of the large amount of flexibility.

Nondedicated servers are slower than dedicated servers.

Nondedicated servers use more RAM than a workstation.

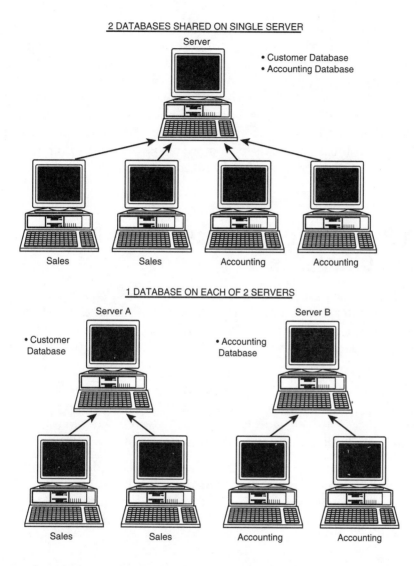

2 DATABASES SHARED ON SINGLE SERVER

Server

• Customer Database
• Accounting Database

Sales   Sales   Accounting   Accounting

1 DATABASE ON EACH OF 2 SERVERS

Server A   Server B

• Customer
Database

• Accounting
Database

Sales   Sales   Accounting   Accounting

Figure 2.9

Comparison of using a single server for two databases and using a separate server for each database.

Sharing and Accessing Network Resources

Before you can access the shared resources such as disk drives and printers on a server from your workstation, you must first configure the server to specify which resources to share. As soon as the server has been configured and the shared resources specified, you may access and use the shared resources, provided you have the proper authorization to do so. When you specify the resources to share and then, later, the shared resources you wish to use, for the most part you use DOS naming conventions. Therefore, it is beneficial to be comfortable with DOS before proceeding to discuss the methods used to share resources on a server and then access the server's shared resources from another network node.

A Review of DOS Devices, Drives, and Directories

The methods used to share and use shared resources in a LAN are a slight extension of what you already know about DOS. Therefore, the more comfortable you are with DOS, the easier it will be to understand the new features provided by your network.

Figure 2.10 shows a typical computer and its resources (drives and printers). Also shown is the directory tree structure for drive C. In this example, the computer has a floppy disk A, a floppy disk B, a hard disk C, and a CD-ROM drive E. Also connected to the computer is a laser printer on LPT1: and a dot matrix printer on LPT2:.

After your computer starts, there are certain default parameters established and used by DOS. The default is the value assumed by DOS unless you have specified otherwise. For example, after starting your computer your DOS prompt may appear as the following:

```
C:>
```

The C:> prompt indicates that your default drive is C. If you type **DIR** at this point, you would see a directory listing of the files on your C drive. Because you did not specify a drive letter after the DIR command, DOS assumes you want to see a directory listing of the C drive. If, on the other hand, you actually wanted to see a directory listing of the files on the CD-ROM drive (E), you would type **DIR E:**. To change your default drive from C to E, you would type **E:** and press Enter. Your default drive is now E and your DOS prompt appears as:

E:>

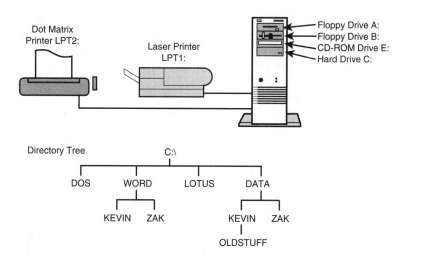

Dot Matrix Printer LPT2:

Laser Printer LPT1:

Floppy Drive A:
Floppy Drive B:
CD-ROM Drive E:
Hard Drive C:

Directory Tree   C:\

DOS   WORD   LOTUS   DATA

KEVIN   ZAK   KEVIN   ZAK

OLDSTUFF

Figure 2.10

A computer showing its resources and the directory tree of the C drive.

In addition to a default drive, you will also have a default directory. Your computer may have several directories and in each directory there may be several files. When you first start your computer, the default directory is usually the root directory, which is represented with the back slash character \.

Your DOS prompt will show the current default directory in addition to the default drive letter if your AUTOEXEC.BAT file contains the following statement:

PROMPT = PG

Assuming your current default drive/directory is the root directory on the C drive, your prompt would appear as:

C:\>

To make your current default directory the DATA directory, you would type the following at your DOS prompt:

```
C:\>CD DATA
```

The DOS command shown above to change the default directory to DATA assumes your current default directory is the root. If your default directory were somewhere other than the root directory, you would precede the directory name with the \ character:

```
C:\>CD DATA
```

Preceding a directory name with the \ character tells DOS to look for the DATA directory as the next level down from the root directory. Otherwise, without the \ character, DOS looks for the DATA directory beneath the current default directory.

The DOS PATH statement specifies where DOS should look for a program (files with a COM or EXE extension) or DOS batch files (files with a BAT extension) if not found in the current default drive/directory. The different search directories are separated with a semicolon (;). For example, if you wanted DOS to look for program files in the root, and DOS directories on drive C in addition to the current default drive/directory, you would include the following path statement in your AUTOEXEC.BAT file or you could type it at a DOS prompt:

```
PATH = C:\;C:\DOS
```

To start a software application, you specify the drive, directory, and the name of the program. If the application you want to run is located in one of the directories specified in your path statement, DOS will find the application and execute it.

Assuming you want to start the word processing program Microsoft Word (WORD.EXE), located in the WORD6 directory, you would normally type the following commands at your DOS prompt:

```
C:\>CD \WORD6
C:\WORD6>WORD
```

Typing CD \WORD6 changes the default directory to WORD6 as shown by the change in the prompt from C:\> to C:\WORD6>. Next, typing WORD executes the WORD.EXE program file, which starts Microsoft Word.

While running a program such as Word, you typically will read a file from your hard disk, make changes to the file, and then save the changes to your hard disk. When you read and write files from and to your hard disk, you specify the drive, directory and name of the file. Most application programs also have a default drive and directory that they use if you don't specify one, allowing you to simply type the file name without the drive and directory information.

When you install application software such as Word, you specify the port to which your printer is connected and the type of printer. For the computer shown in figure 2.10, you specify that a laser printer is connected to the port on your computer with the DOS device name LPT1:, and a dot matrix printer is connected to the port with the DOS device name LPT2:. When you print from an application program or even directly from DOS, to send the printed results to the laser printer you specify LPT1: and to send the results to the dot matrix printer you specify LPT2:.

With an understanding of DOS drives, directories, and devices, you are ready to expand that knowledge as it applies to sharing resources and accessing shared resources across the network.

Creating Shared Drives and Printers

Each server in your network is able to share its resources (such as disk drives, directories, and printers) with others in the network. Before a server is able to share its resources with others, you must first configure the server to specify which resources you want to share. You can share as many or as few resources as you want on a server. Most networks also enable you to specify the users that may have access to specific shared resources. For example, you may want to share a general data directory with everyone in your network. Whereas the data directory may be accessible to all, you may want to limit access to the entire hard disk drive on the server to a select few with special privileges.

When specifying a resource to share, you give the shared resource a name and then specify the actual DOS drive/directory or device name that the shared resource name points to on the server. The name you choose for the resource is how the resource will be known by other nodes in the network. For example, you might specify a network resource name of BIG-DRIVE, which refers to the C drive on the server.

Each server in your network is also given a name when the network is installed. The network name enables you to specify which server you want to access. The combination of server name and shared resource name enables you to specify exactly which shared resource you want to access. Because server names are different, you could have the same resource names on different servers.

Assume that you want to set up the computer shown in figure 2.10 as a server. You want to share the two printers, the C drive, the CD-ROM drive (E), and the DATA directory on drive C. Also assume that the server has the network name of KATIE. Figure 2.11 shows the shared resources for server KATIE. The following is a description of each shared resource on server KATIE:

- **LASER => LPT1:** The shared resource name LASER points to the laser printer that is connected to port LPT1:. When a network node accesses the LASER resource on server KATIE, it will actually be accessing the laser printer that is connected to LPT1: on server KATIE.

- **PRINTER => LPT2:** The shared resource name PRINTER points to the dot matrix printer connected to port LPT2:. When a network node accesses the PRINTER resource on server KATIE, it will actually be accessing the dot matrix printer that is connected to LPT2: on server KATIE.

- **CD-ROM => E:** The shared resource name CD-ROM points to the CD-ROM drive, which is accessed using drive letter E: on server KATIE. When a network node accesses the

CD-ROM resource on server KATIE, it will actually be accessing the E: drive on KATIE, which is the CD-ROM.

- **BIG-DRIVE => C:** The shared resource name BIG-DRIVE points to the root directory of hard disk C on server KATIE. When a network node accesses the BIG-DRIVE resource on server KATIE, it will actually be accessing the C drive on server KATIE.

- **USERDATA => C:\DATA** The shared resource name USERDATA points to the C:\DATA directory on server KATIE. When a network node accesses the USERDATA resource, it will actually be accessing the C:\DATA directory on server KATIE.

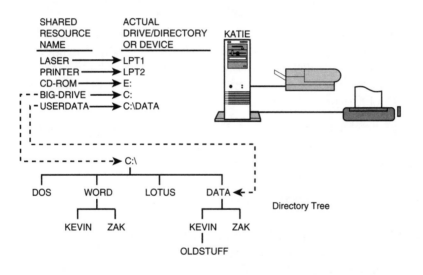

Figure 2.11

Creating shared resources on a server.

When a network node accesses a shared resource on a server, the only information available to the user accessing the shared resource is the shared resource name. The actual drive/directory or device on the server that the resource name points to is usually not visible to the user. Therefore, it is important when setting up shared resources on a server to use a shared resource name that is somewhat descriptive of the actual physical resource that is being accessed.

In figure 2.11 the directory tree for the C drive is also shown. Notice how the BIG-DRIVE shared resource name points to the root directory (\) on drive C. When a network node accesses the BIG-DRIVE resource, it will have access to the root directory and any directory below it which, in this case, is every directory on the hard disk. Similarly, when a network node accesses the USERDATA resource, it will have access to the C:\DATA directory and any directory below it, which includes C:\DATA\KEVIN, C:\DATA\KEVIN\OLDSTUFF, and C:\DATA\ZAK. A network node accessing the USERDATA resource will not have access to any directories above (or adjacent to) the C:\DATA directory.

After you have specified the resources to share on a server, most NOSs also enable you to specify user names and passwords of those who access the server as well as the type of access each user has. For example, some users may have access to all the shared resources on the server, whereas others may only have access to a specific resource such as USERDATA (which points to the C:\DATA directory).

Once the shared resources on the server have been established, other computers in the network may access and use the shared resources.

Sharing CD-ROM Drives

CD-ROM drives and other similar drives, such as Read/Write Optical drives, are often referred to as non-DOS drives because they require special device drivers to use with your computer. Many NOSs include provisions that enable you to share CD-ROM drives with other nodes in the network.

When you configure the shared resources on a server, to specify a CD-ROM drive as a shared resource, the NOS typically has an additional selection enabling you to specify that the drive is a CD-ROM drive. Once the CD-ROM drive resource is specified and configured on the server, other nodes can access and use the shared CD-ROM drive resource as though it were any other shared drive resource on the server.

You can read information from a CD-ROM drive but
cannot write to it.

Using Shared Drives and Printers

Having specified the shared resources on each server in the
network, the shared resources may be accessed and used by other
nodes in the network. A workstation wanting to access a shared
resource on a server may do so by establishing a logical connection to the shared resource on the server.

The first step to establishing a network connection is to log in to
the server that has the resource to which you want to connect.
When you log in to a server, you generally must specify a user
name and password. If the server enables you to have access to it,
you are logged in and may proceed to establish logical connections to the shared resources on the server. The requirements for
logging in to a server vary with the NOS and how the network is
configured. Some networks require that each user has a specific
user name and password, whereas others don't require any user
names or passwords to access a server. Chapter 9, "Managing
Users and Resources," contains detailed information about the
different types of user accounts and requirements.

After logging in to a server (if logging in is required), you are
ready to establish a logical connection between your workstation
and a shared resource on the server. In this example, assume that
you want to use the hard disk on the server and the laser printer
connected to the server (see fig. 2.12).

To establish a connection to a shared drive resource on another
computer, you first choose a drive letter that your workstation
uses to access the shared resource. The process of establishing a
logical connection to a shared resource using a drive letter (such
as K) or a device name (such as LPT1) is called *redirecting* or
mapping a drive (or device).

You choose to redirect (or map) drive letter K to point to the BIG-DRIVE resource on server KATIE. When you access the BIG-DRIVE resource on server KATIE, KATIE knows that you actually want to access hard disk C. Now when you access your K drive you are actually accessing the C drive on server KATIE.

Now assume you want to be able to use the laser printer connected to server KATIE from your computer. You redirect your printer port LPT1 to point to the shared resource LASER on server KATIE. When the LASER shared resource is accessed on server KATIE, KATIE knows that you want to connect to the laser printer on the server's printer port LPT1. With your printer port LPT1 redirected to point to the LASER resource on server KATIE, whenever you print something to LPT1 it is sent automatically to the laser printer connected to server KATIE.

Finally, assume you want to make one more network connection to the USERDATA shared resource on server KATIE. You decide to redirect drive L to point to the USERDATA resource on server KATIE which in turn points to the C:\DATA directory. Now when you access drive L you are actually accessing the C:\DATA directory on server KATIE.

Figure 2.12

Using the shared resources on a server from a workstation.

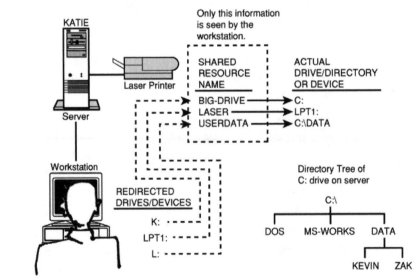

With your network connections established, you are able to use the shared resources on server KATIE. Using the information shown in figure 2.12, assume that you use the Microsoft Works program located on server KATIE. If Works were installed on your computer, you would type the following commands from the DOS prompt to start Works:

```
C:\>CD \MSWORKS
C:\MSWORKS>WORKS
```

The first statement changes your current directory to MSWORKS. Typing WORKS actually starts the program. With your K drive redirected to point to the BIG-DRIVE resource on server KATIE, typing the following commands at the DOS prompt would run Works from the server's hard disk:

```
C:\>K:
K:\>CD \MSWORKS
K:\MSWORKS>WORKS
```

The statements above show that in this example the only difference from the previous example is that you change your current drive to K before typing the other commands necessary to start Works. At the DOS prompt, typing **k:** changes your current default drive to K, which is redirected to the BIG-DRIVE resource (C:\) on server KATIE. Next you change to the MSWORKS directory and then type WORKS to start the program.

In a Local Area Network, the program is actually being run on your computer using your processor. When you start a program, the program files are transferred across the network to your computer where they are read and executed. A common mistake made by those not familiar with networks is to assume that because the program is stored on another computer, it is actually being executed on the other computer, which is not the case.

Now suppose you create a document in Works that you want to print on the laser printer. You already have redirected your LPT1 device to point to the LASER resource on server KATIE so when you print, your document automatically is sent to the laser printer connected to KATIE.

You've finished your document, and now you want to save it. Of course, you could save the document to your own C drive, but you can also save it to the drive on server KATIE. If you want to save the document with the name MYDOC in the DATA directory on server KATIE, specify the following when asked for the file name:

`K:\DATA\MYDOC`

This will save the file to the C drive on server KATIE in the DATA directory.

Using K specifies the BIG-DRIVE resource on server KATIE which points to the C drive on KATIE. \DATA is the directory, and MYDOC is the name of the file.

Now to look at one more variation on this example. You have already redirected your L drive to point to the USERDATA resource on server KATIE. Knowing that USERDATA points to the DATA directory on server KATIE's hard disk C, you could specify the following to save the file as the same name and in the same location as you did in the previous example:

`L:\MYDOC`

You don't have to specify the DATA directory because the L drive is redirected to that directory; specifying L without any directory will save to the DATA directory on server KATIE's drive C.

To better understand this concept, look at figure 2.13. Figure 2.13 shows the directory tree of the C drive on server KATIE and the redirected drives on the workstation. Once the network connections have been established, when you access drive K, you are accessing C:\ on server KATIE. When you access drive L, you are accessing C:\DATA on server KATIE. Using drive K, you can access any directory on server KATIE. Using drive L you can access the DATA directory and the two directories below DATA, KEVIN, and ZAK. The following shows what your prompt would look like when you are in the same directory using both the K drive and the L drive.

Actual Directory on Server KATIE	K Drive	L Drive
C:\DATA>	K:\DATA>	L:\>
C:\DATA\KEVIN>	K:\DATA\KEVIN>	L:\KEVIN>
C:\DATA\ZAK>	K:\DATA\ZAK>	L:\ZAK

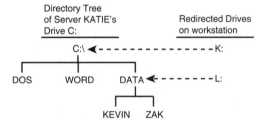

Figure 2.13

Summary of redirected K and L drives on workstation.

Notice that in the preceding table, if you were to list the directory of K:\DATA using the DOS DIR command and then list the directory of L:\, you would see the exact same files; this is because in both cases you are actually looking at the exact same directory, which is C:\DATA on server KATIE. Similarly, L:\ZAK and K:\DATA\ZAK are the exact same location, which is actually C:\DATA\ZAK on server KATIE.

Summary

This chapter discussed in detail the types of network nodes in a network and their function. You learned the difference between nodes configured as servers and workstations. You also learned the difference between nondedicated servers and dedicated servers and how each is used.

Server-based and peer-to-peer LANs were discussed and the advantages and disadvantages of each described. Specifying shared resources on a server and using the shared resources by a workstation were discussed in detail and several examples used to help illustrate the process.

Now that you have a good understanding of the function of the nodes in a network, the next chapter examines the hardware components required to implement a network.

In This Chapter...

This chapter discusses the hardware required to create a functioning network. Specifically, you'll learn about the following:

- Topologies or methods used to connect nodes in a LAN.

- LAN standards such as Ethernet, ARCnet, and Token Ring.

- Network adapters and how to pick the right one for your installation.

- The different types of network cable used in a LAN.

- Hardware devices that enhance network capability.

- The hardware required to incorporate your LAN into a *wide area network* (WAN).

This chapter also introduces the following terms:

Bus topology	VESA Local Bus (VLB)
Star topology	Wide area network (WAN)
Ring topology	Thicknet
Ethernet	PCI Local Bus
10BASE5, 10BASE2, and 10BASE-T	Unshielded twisted pair (UTP)
Thinnet	ARCnet
Extended Industry Standard	Concentrator and hub
Multistation Access Unit (MAU)	Token Ring
Industry Standard Architecture (ISA)	Micro Channel Architecture (MCA)
Carrier Sense Multiple Access with Collision Detection (CSMA/CD)	American National Standards Institute (ANSI)
Channel Service Unit/Digital Service Unit (CSU/DSU)	

Hardware Components

A *local area network* (LAN) combines network hardware and software, enabling your computer to share programs, files, disk drives, and printers with other computers on the network. The hardware components used to implement a network are available from many different manufacturers. Fortunately, the standards by which network hardware is manufactured are well defined, resulting in a high level of compatibility with different networks. Some companies' hardware components exceed the required specifications, resulting in greater reliability and better performance at a higher cost; other companies produce the product as inexpensively as possible.

This chapter discusses the many hardware implementations and components available to build your network.

Network Topologies

Network nodes (computers) need to be connected to communicate with each other. The way the nodes are connected is their *topology*. A network has two different topologies: a physical topology and a logical topology. The *physical topology* is the actual physical layout of the network—how the nodes are connected to each other. The *logical topology* is the method the network uses to communicate with the other nodes; the path network data takes between the different nodes in the network. The physical and logical topologies of a network can be the same or different.

The three standard network topologies are bus, star, and ring. Combinations of more than one topology also exist. For example, a tree topology is actually a combination of a bus topology and a star topology.

In a *bus topology*, each computer is connected to a common network cable segment (see fig. 3.1). The network segment is laid out like a linear bus or a long cable that stretches from one end of the network to the other and to which each node in the network is connected. The cable can be on the floor, in the walls, in the ceiling, or any combination of these so long as the cable is one continuous segment.

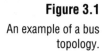

Figure 3.1

An example of a bus topology.

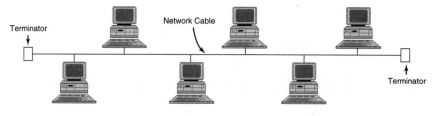

In a *star topology*, each computer is connected to a centrally located concentrator (or hub) (see fig. 3.2). The concentrator is a hardware device with several ports; you can plug a network cable connection into one of these ports.

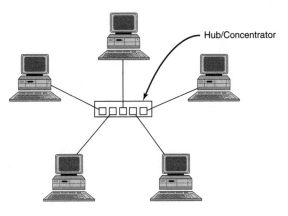

Hub/Concentrator

Figure 3.2
An example of a star
topology.

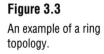

Hubs and concentrators are discussed in detail later in
this chapter.

In a *ring topology*, each computer is connected to the network in
the form of a ring (see fig. 3.3). Ring topologies almost always are
logical topologies with a physical star topology. Figure 3.4 shows
the way data flows in a logical ring topology that is connected in a
physical star topology. The physical topology shows each computer connected to a central device and resembles a star. The path
taken by the data from one computer to the other illustrates that
the logical topology is a ring.

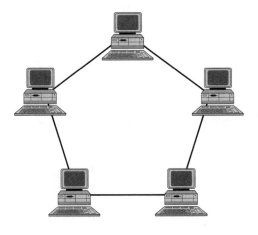

Figure 3.3
An example of a ring
topology.

Figure 3.4

An example of a physical star topology with a logical ring topology.

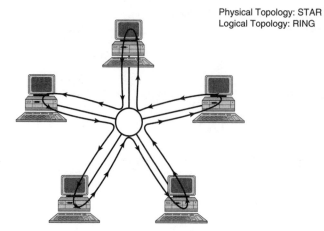

Physical Topology: STAR
Logical Topology: RING

A tree topology actually is a combination of a bus and a star topology. Many concentrators used in Ethernet physical star topology networks also have a connector on the back that connects the concentrator to a physical bus topology network (see fig. 3.5).

Figure 3.5

An example of a tree topology.

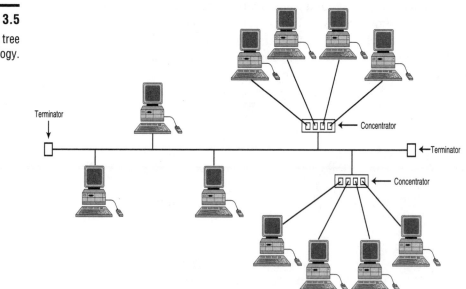

LAN Standards

Networks are comprised of many different components that must work together to create a functioning network. The components that comprise the hardware pieces of the network include network adapter cards, cables, connectors, concentrators, and even the computer itself.

Network components usually are manufactured by several different companies. Therefore some understanding and communication among the manufacturers regarding how each component works and interacts with the other components in the network is necessary.

Fortunately, standards have been developed that define the way to connect hardware components in a network, and the protocol (or rules) to use when communicating on the network. All the data flowing over the network cable must be sequenced and distinguishable so the many nodes can ensure that the correct data arrives at the intended location.

A *protocol* is a set of rules that define how communications are to take place in a network, including the format, timing, sequencing, and error checking and correction.

A *standard* is an adopted network specification or set of specifications that includes guidelines and rules pertaining to the type of components to use, how to connect the components, as well as the communications protocols to use.

The three popular standards in use today are Ethernet, ARCnet, and Token Ring. Ethernet and Token Ring are standards endorsed by the *Institute of Electrical and Electronic Engineers* (IEEE), whereas ARCnet is an industry standard and has recently become an *American National Standards Institute* (ANSI) standard.

Ethernet

Ethernet, also referred to as IEEE 802.3, is the most popular standard for LANs used today. The 802.3 standard uses a logical bus topology and either a bus or star physical topology. Ethernet transmits data across the network at a rate of 10 Mbps (megabits per second).

Ethernet uses a data transmission method known as *Carrier Sense Multiple Access with Collision Detection* (CSMA/CD). Before a node sends any data across an Ethernet network, it first listens to see if any information is being transferred by another node. If not, the node then transfers information across the network. All the other nodes listen, and the node the data is meant for receives the information. In the event that two nodes attempt to send data across the network at the same time, each node senses the collision and waits a random amount of time before resending.

The logical bus topology used by Ethernet enables each node to take its turn broadcasting information across the network. The failure of a single node does not cause the entire network to fail. Whereas CSMA/CD is a quick and efficient way to transmit data across the network, a heavily used network can reach a saturation point. As more nodes attempt to broadcast information across the network, the chance of collisions is greater and the efficiency of the network is reduced substantially. With a properly designed network, however, network saturation rarely is an issue.

Three types of Ethernet implementations exist—10BASE5, 10BASE2, and 10BASE-T—that define the type of network cable used, the length specifications, and the physical topology used to connect nodes in the network.

Thicknet (10BASE5)

10BASE5 also is called standard Ethernet, Thick Ethernet, or Thicknet, and was the first type of Ethernet to be developed and used. Thicknet has a physical bus topology implementation that consists of a segment of network cable with terminators at the ends (see fig. 3.6). The terminators include a resistor that dissipates the network signal instead of allowing it to be reflected back in the network cable. The *network interface card* (NIC) in each computer is the communications interface between the computer and the network cable, and is connected to an external transceiver by means of a drop cable. The transceiver is connected to the Thick Ethernet cable segment and acts to transmit and receive network data between the computer and the network.

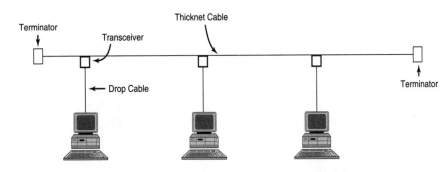

Figure 3.6

Thick Ethernet physical topology.

Thicknet is relatively difficult to work with compared to the other two implementations, 10BASE2 and 10BASE-T. Because it was the only available Ethernet for a period of time, however, Thicknet is implemented in several installations. Thicknet also requires a separate external transceiver for each computer in addition to the NIC. Thicknet therefore rarely is used for new Ethernet installations.

Thinnet (10BASE2)

10BASE2 often is referred to as Thinnet, Thin coax, Thin Ethernet, or Cheapernet. Thinnet is implemented using a physical bus topology that consists of a network cable segment with terminators at each end (see fig. 3.7). The NIC in each computer is directly connected to the Thinnet cable segment, bypassing the need for an external transceiver. The transceiver is incorporated onto the NIC.

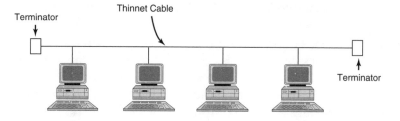

Thinnet is very popular in small businesses and for smaller installations because it is the least expensive method of implementing
an Ethernet network using a relatively small number of nodes.
Thinnet also is less susceptible to electrical interference than
twisted pair. A disadvantage of Thinnet is that a break in any part
of the network cable causes the entire network to stop functioning.
As a result, troubleshooting a cable problem with Thinnet can be
difficult.

Twisted Pair (10BASE-T)

10BASE-T also is referred to as *UTP* (unshielded twisted pair), or
twisted pair. Unlike Thick or Thin Ethernet, 10BASE-T is implemented using a physical star topology. Each node is connected to
a central hub or concentrator (see fig. 3.8). The NIC in each computer is connected to the concentrator (or hub) by means of a
network cable segment.

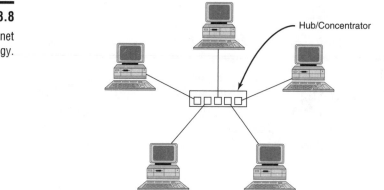

You might prefer 10BASE-T over 10BASE2 because of its flexible star topology. A break in a cable in a 10BASE-T network only disables the computer on the end of the break rather than the entire network, as opposed to 10BASE2. 10BASE-T is more expensive for small networks to implement than 10BASE2 because it requires an additional concentrator. The twisted-pair cable used in 10BASE-T is less expensive than the cable used for Thin Ethernet, however, so as more nodes are added, the additional expense of a concentrator becomes smaller compared to the additional expense incurred by using the more expensive Thinnet cable.

Token Ring

Token Ring, also called IEEE 802.5, was developed by IBM and a few other manufacturers. Operating at a speed of either 4 Mbps or 16 Mbps, Token Ring uses a logical ring topology and a physical star topology (see fig. 3.9). The NIC in each computer is connected to a cable that is plugged into a central hub called a *Multistation Access Unit* (MAU). You can connect the MAUs from different rings so that the previously separate rings exist as a single network.

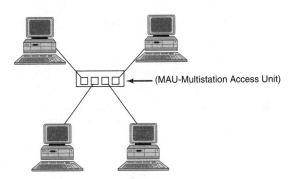

(MAU-Multistation Access Unit)

Figure 3.9

Token Ring physical topology.

Token Ring uses a token passing scheme that passes a token to each computer in the network (see fig. 3.10). A token can be thought of as a way to gain access to the network. The computer in possession of the token is allowed to transmit its information to another computer on the network. When finished, the token is given to the next computer in the ring. If the next computer has information to send, it accepts the token and proceeds to send the information; otherwise the token is passed to the next computer in the ring and the process continues.

Figure 3.10

A logical Token Ring topology.

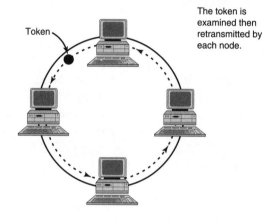

Token

The token is examined then retransmitted by each node.

The MAU automatically bypasses a network node that is not turned on. Because each node in a Token Ring network examines and then retransmits each token, however, a malfunctioning node can cause the entire network to stop working. Token Ring tends to be less efficient than CSMA/CD (used in Ethernet) in networks with light network activity because it requires additional overhead. As network activity increases, however, Token Ring becomes more efficient than CSMA/CD. This is because Token Ring avoids the collisions that occur in the CSMA/CD scheme that result in having to resend data.

ARCnet

Developed in the 1970s by Datapoint Corporation, *Attached Resource Computing Network* (ARCnet) is an industry accepted standard, although it doesn't bear an IEEE standard number. In October of 1992, ANSI recognized ARCnet as a formal standard as part of the ANSI 878.1 LAN standard. Supporting a data transfer rate of 2.5 Mbps, ARCnet uses a logical bus topology and a slight variation of the physical star topology (see fig. 3.11). Each node in the network is connected to either a passive hub or an active hub. A *passive hub* is not powered and serves to distribute the network signal over short distances. An *active hub* is powered and also amplifies the network signal to enable the network to cover longer distances. The NIC in each computer is connected to a cable that in turn is connected to either an active or passive hub.

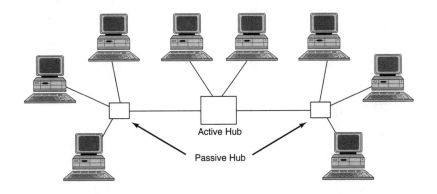

Active Hub

Passive Hub

Figure 3.11
ARCnet's physical topology.

Several variations of the ARCnet standard have evolved over the years including linear bus ARCnet, which uses a physical bus topology, and twisted-pair ARCnet, which uses UTP cabling. These variations improve on the already flexible nature of the ARCnet standard, enabling the nodes in the network to be configured in almost any physical topology.

ARCnet uses a token passing scheme to manage the flow of data between nodes in the network. When a node is in possession of the token, it can broadcast data across the network. All nodes except the intended recipient ignore the data. As the token is passed to each node, the node can send data. Because each node can send data only when it has the token, collisions that might occur with a scheme such as CSMA/CD used by Ethernet do not occur with ARCnet. Therefore, ARCnet is less susceptible to network saturation than Ethernet.

ARCnet once was the most popular standard for LANs, but, partly because of its relatively slow speed (2.5 Mbps compared to Ethernet's 10 Mbps), it rarely is used for new installations.

New Technologies

As networks expand in both physical area and in the number of nodes that comprise them, manufacturers must develop new network technologies that solve the problems produced by larger networks and increased network traffic. As users transfer more data across the network and the network extends over larger distances, the requirement for greater speed and longer network cables becomes apparent. Several new technologies exist that address the needs of today's networks, including Fast Ethernet, FDDI/CDDI, and ATM.

Fast Ethernet

Fast Ethernet, also called 100BASEX, is an extension of the Ethernet standard that operates at a speed of 100 Mbps; a ten-fold increase over standard Ethernet's 10 Mbps.

Another implementation of a Fast Ethernet technology is Hewlett-Packard's 100BASEVG technology that operates over existing UTP cabling at 100 Mbps.

FDDI and CDDI

Fiber Distributed Data Interface (FDDI) is a standard for transferring data over fiber-optic cable. The ANSI standard X3T9.5 for FDDI specifies a speed of 100 Mbps. Because fiber-optic cable is not susceptible to electrical interference, or as susceptible to network signal degradation as standard network cables are, FDDI accommodates much longer cables than other network standards. FDDI uses a logical ring topology with token passing.

In addition to fiber-optic cable, the ANSI FDDI standard also has provisions for 100 Mbps operation over UTP cabling—often referred to as *Copper Distributed Data Interface* (CDDI).

ATM

ATM, which stands for *Asynchronous Transfer Mode*, is a set of international standards for transferring data, voice, and video information over a network at very high speeds. Operating at speeds between 1.5 Mbps and 1.5 Gbps (gigabits per second; 1 Gbps = 1,000,000,000 bits per second), ATM incorporates parts of Ethernet, Token Ring, and FDDI standards to transfer data.

With the growth of multimedia (sound, data, and video) applications, ATM shows great promise for the future because of its ability to transfer sound, data, and video information quickly and efficiently.

Network Adapters

To communicate with the rest of the network, each computer must have a *network interface card* (NIC) installed. NICs also are often called network adapters, network adapter cards, or just network cards. The NIC is a card that usually plugs into a slot in your computer (see fig. 3.12). The network cable is connected to the NIC, which is then connected to the other nodes in the network.

Many NIC manufacturers adhere to each of the LAN standards discussed in the preceding section. Although most network adapters are installed inside your computer, some are installed externally. If you have a notebook computer without any expansion slots in which to plug an internal network adapter, for example, you can use an external network adapter that plugs into the parallel port on your computer (where you normally plug in your printer).

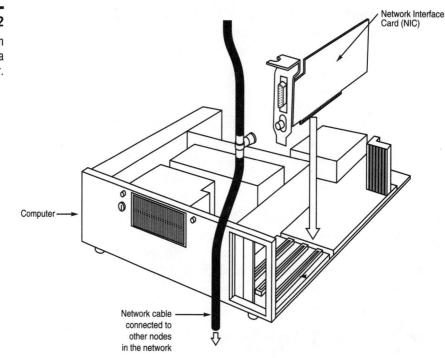

Figure 3.12

A NIC plugged into an expansion slot in a computer.

The type of network adapter you purchase determines the topology you use, so be sure to obtain the appropriate network adapter for the topology you want to use. If you buy twisted-pair Ethernet adapters, for example, you will use a physical star topology with a concentrator. If you buy Thinnet adapters, you will use a physical bus topology.

Hardware Requirements

The network adapter is the interface between the network and the computer. On one hand, the network adapter is connected to the network and must communicate with the other nodes in the network using the proper protocols. On the other hand, the network adapter must communicate properly with the computer in which it is installed and not conflict with the other computer devices such as the monitor, hard drive, mouse, floppy drives, and so on.

For any network adapter to operate as the interface between your computer and the network, it first must meet the following two criteria:

1. It must be the proper type for the network to which you are connecting: It must use the appropriate protocols to communicate with the rest of the network, and have the proper connector to attach to your network's cable.

2. It must have the proper connector to plug into the computer's expansion slot. Computers from different manufacturers have different types of expansion slots. If you have a notebook or laptop computer, chances are you do not have an expansion slot, in which case you need a network adapter that plugs into a port you do have, such as the parallel printer port.

Most computers have *Industry Standard Architecture* (ISA) expansion slots. ISA expansion slots are either 8 bit or 16 bit. Accordingly, network adapters for ISA expansion slots also are available as 8-bit or 16-bit adapters. 16-bit adapters can transfer twice as much information at a time between the computer and network adapter. Some of the ISA computers have expansion slots such as *VESA Local Bus* (VLB) or PCI Local Bus. These expansion slots enable data to be passed to the adapter plugged into the local bus slots (provided the adapter is a VLB or PCI adapter) at a much faster rate than the standard ISA slots.

Other types of expansion slots are *Micro Channel Architecture* (MCA), which are used in many of the IBM PS/2 computers, and *Enhanced Industry Standard Architecture* (EISA). Many notebook computers now have one or two *Personal Computer Memory Card International Association* (PCMCIA) expansion slots into which you can plug a special adapter approximately the size of a credit card.

After you identify the proper network adapter for your computer, you can install and configure it. Most of the new network adapters do not have any jumpers that you have to change. If any changes to the configuration are required, they are made using a software configuration program that comes with the network adapter. Other network adapters might have jumpers that enable you to change the configuration depending on their position. *Jumpers* are small devices that plug over two pins on an adapter card to electrically short the pins together, thereby changing a configuration setting on the adapter card.

Although many network adapters have several options that can be changed or specified during configuration, two settings have the biggest impact as to whether your network adapter operates in your computer: the hardware *interrupt request line* (IRQ), and the *input/output* (I/O) address.

Most devices in a computer, such as the floppy drive, hard drive, mouse, parallel port (printer), serial port (modem), and network adapter use an IRQ. The IRQ enables the device to interrupt the microprocessor from the task it currently is performing to service the request of the device interrupting it. IRQs are given numbers; usually each device has its own IRQ or a conflict arises between the two devices. If an IRQ conflict does occur, the devices can fail to operate properly resulting in the computer locking up.

The I/O address is a location in the memory of a computer that is used for input and output of data. Any device that uses an I/O address must have its own unique I/O address or data being sent to or received from a device might get mixed up with the data from another device, which most likely would result in your computer locking up or not operating correctly.

In most situations, the default values of the IRQ and I/O addresses work fine. If you have devices such as a scanner or CD-ROM drive, however, you may have to change the settings from their default values to avoid conflicts between your network adapter and the other device.

Ethernet Adapters

Today most networks are based on the Ethernet standard and therefore most likely use an Ethernet network adapter card. As discussed previously, the three primary Ethernet standards are 10BASE5 (Thick Ethernet), 10BASE2 (Thin Ethernet), and 10BASE-T (unsheilded twisted pair). Because each of these Ethernet standards uses a different type of cable to connect the nodes, the Ethernet adapter must have the appropriate connector for the type of Ethernet network you are installing.

Figure 3.13 shows four different Ethernet network adapter cards. The connectors shown on the right side of each card are where the card actually plugs into the computer's expansion slot. The connectors on the bottom of each card shown in the figure are where the network cable connects to the adapter.

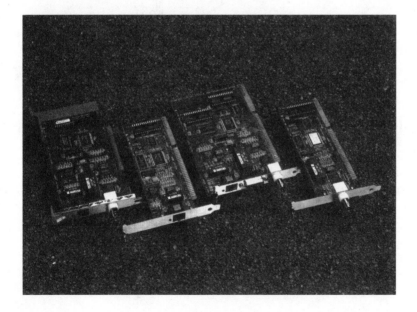

Figure 3.13

Four Ethernet network adapter cards.

Figure 3.14 shows the three different connectors associated with the three types of Ethernet: 10BASE5, 10BASE2, and 10BASE-T. Some Ethernet adapters have only one of these connectors; others have two or all three. An Ethernet adapter that has all three connectors supports the three types of Ethernet, although usually only one connector can be used at a time. Also, the price of such an adapter is usually greater than that of an adapter that only supports one or two types of Ethernet.

Figure 3.14

Figure 3.14

The three types of connectors found on different Ethernet adapters.

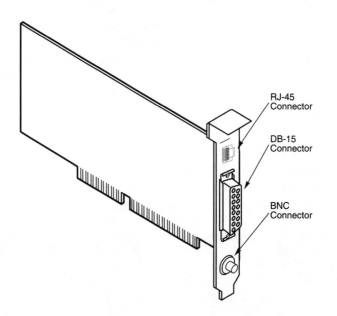

RJ-45
Connector

DB-15
Connector

BNC
Connector

10BASE5 (Thick Ethernet)

10BASE5, or Thick Ethernet, uses a DB-15 connector on the network adapter. The DB-15 connector is a female 15-pin D-style connector (refer to fig. 3.14). The Thick Ethernet cable connected to the rest of the network is connected to an external transceiver that is connected in turn to the DB-15 connector on the network adapter (see fig. 3.15).

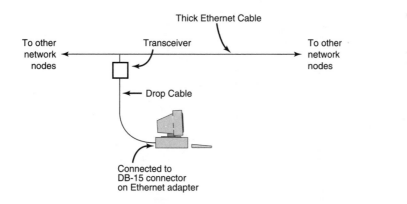

Figure 3.15

A network node connected to Thick Ethernet.

10BASE2 (Thin Ethernet)

The connector on the network adapter for 10BASE2 (also called Thin Ethernet or Thinnet) is a BNC connector that resembles a cable connector on a television. You attach a BNC connector using a half-twist motion, however, rather than by screwing it on (refer to fig. 3.14). The Thinnet cable is connected to the connector on the network adapter card with a BNC T connector (see fig. 3.16). The bottom part of the T is connected to the BNC connector on the network adapter card. The other two parts of the T are connected to the Thinnet cable running to the other nodes on the network. Although Thinnet uses a physical bus topology, the nodes appear to be daisy-chained together because cables extend from computer to computer. In reality, however, the network adapter taps into the network cable segment using the BNC T connector; if the connector is removed from the network adapter card, nothing happens to the network connection (except that the disconnected computer no longer can access the network).

Figure 3.16

A network node
connected to Thin
Ethernet.

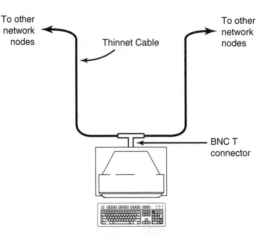

10BASE-T (Unshielded Twisted Pair)

Ethernet adapters supporting 10BASE-T use an RJ-45 connector
that is similar to the RJ-11 connector used for most telephone
installations, with the exception that the RJ-45 connector is larger
and has eight conductors rather than four (refer to fig. 3.14).
The UTP network cable has an RJ-45 plug on each end. One end
of the cable is plugged into the RJ-45 jack on the network card,
and the other end is plugged into the RJ-45 jack on the concentrator (see fig. 3.17). The other nodes in the network are connected to
the concentrator in a similar fashion.

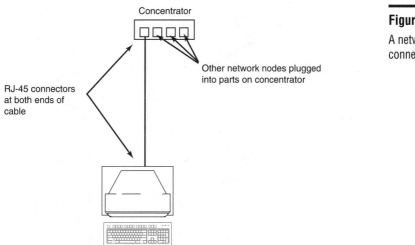

Concentrator

RJ-45 connectors
at both ends of
cable

Other network nodes plugged
into parts on concentrator

Figure 3.17
A network node
connected to UTP.

ARCnet Adapters

Once the standard of choice, ARCnet has been overshadowed by
the increased speed and manufacturers' support of the Ethernet
standard. Supporting data transfer speeds of 2.5 Mbps, ARCnet
network adapters can support a connection to a coax network
cable or a UTP network cable. The connector used on the back of
an ARCnet network adapter for the standard coax cable connection is the same BNC connector used for Thin Ethernet (see fig.
3.18). An alternative cabling scheme uses UTP cable with the same
RJ-11 connector used in telephone installations. ARCnet adapters
can have a BNC connector to support the coax cable or an RJ-11
to support UTP cabling. Adapters supporting both cabling
schemes can have both connectors.

Figure 3.18

Connectors used on
different types of
ARCnet adapters.

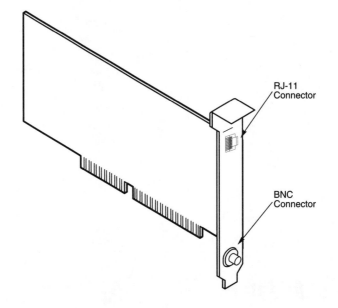

Figure 3.19 shows the way the ARCnet adapter in each node is
connected to the network. A physical bus topology, a star topology, or a combination of the two can be used with RG-62 coax
cable. A physical star topology is used with UTP cabling.

In the physical star topology using coax cable, the RG-62 coax
cable is connected on one end to the BNC connector on the
ARCnet adapter, and on the other end to the BNC connector on
the hub. The physical star topology with UTP cable uses a similar
connection scheme with UTP cable and RJ-11 connectors.

The combination physical bus and star topology using coax cable
enables up to eight nodes to be connected. The nodes are connected in the bus topology using BNC T connectors. The node at
the end of the cable segment has a terminator connected to one
side of the T connector. The opposite end of the cable segment is
connected to an active hub that in turn is connected to other nodes
or hubs.

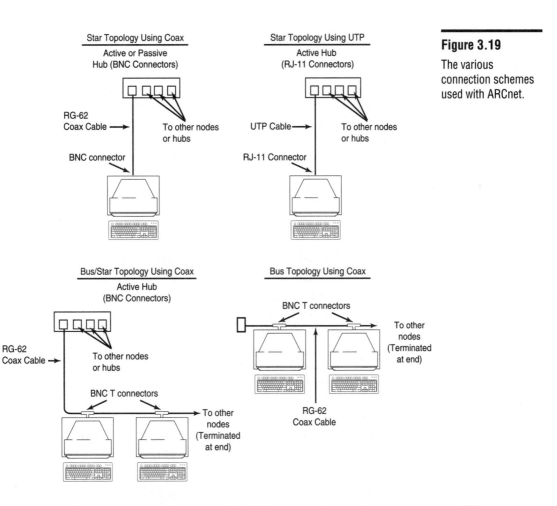

Figure 3.19

The various
connection schemes
used with ARCnet.

The network adapters used for ARCnet configured in a
physical bus topology are different from those configured
in a physical star topology, although the BNC connector
on the adapter is the same. When acquiring ARCnet
network adapters, be sure to purchase the correct
adapter for the type of physical topology you are using.

The physical bus topology uses the same connection scheme as
Thin Ethernet with a slightly different coax cable. Each node is
connected to the network cable using a BNC T connector. The
node on each end of the network cable has a terminator on one
side of the BNC T connector.

Proprietary Adapters

A *proprietary network adapter* is an adapter that does not adhere completely to established standards. Some proprietary adapters incorporate parts of the standards; for example, they use the correct connectors and cabling, but with a different protocol scheme for communicating among the network nodes. Other proprietary adapters do not adhere to any part of a standard.

Proprietary network adapters usually are manufactured for the exclusive use of a particular *network operating system* (NOS), or a special version of the NOS. They can benefit both buyers and manufacturers in the following ways:

- Producing a proprietary network adapter prevents the purchase of network adapters from other manufacturers. This allows the manufacturer of the proprietary adapter to set the price of the adapter and prevents the possibility of competition. Some manufacturers offer incentives to their customers for purchasing their proprietary network adapter rather than a competitor's standard network adapter. Instead of requiring the purchase of a separate copy of the NOS for each node in the network (as is usually the case), for example, a manufacturer might allow you to use the same copy of the software for the entire network if you purchase all your network adapters from them.

- In some situations, proprietary network adapters can be produced less expensively than standard network adapters. This was especially true when standard network adapters such as Ethernet were expensive. However, due to the continuing decrease in the price of Ethernet adapters, Ethernet is now relatively inexpensive to implement in a network. Therefore, the possible cost benefit of a proprietary network adapter today is rarely a justifiable incentive for its purchase.

- A proprietary network adapter can be developed so that its installation is simpler than that of a standard network adapter, for example, with special cable and connectors that are impossible to install incorrectly.

- A proprietary network adapter can offer superior performance in comparison with existing adapters that adhere to a standard. In some situations, a manufacturer produces a proprietary network adapter that eventually becomes a standard because of its widespread appeal for use in many network situations.

Before using a proprietary network adapter, carefully consider the advantages and disadvantages. Some factors to consider include cost, performance, options for upgrading or expanding the network in the future, support policies from the manufacturer, and overall flexibility.

Wireless Adapters

Recently a new type of network adapter has appeared that uses radio signals instead of network cable to transmit data across the network. Several manufacturers are producing wireless network adapters with slightly different implementation schemes. Some manufacturers produce a network adapter that is used in place of your standard network adapter. Others require you to have a standard network adapter in your node and then add a device that takes the network signal from your existing network adapter and converts it to a radio signal; the signal is then broadcast to other wireless nodes.

Wireless network adapters typically are used in situations in which it is inconvenient to run standard network cable. Such is the case with a node such as a notebook computer that frequently is moved to various locations, but still requires access to the network. Wireless network adapters tend to offer lower performance and higher cost than conventional network adapters, and therefore usually are used only in special situations in which conventional network adapters are not appropriate.

Network Cable

Each network standard defines the required type of cabling and the specifications to connect the network nodes. Because of high speeds and the large amount of data that is transmitted across a network, cable specifications and rules for use are very strict. Using network cable with the wrong specifications ultimately causes a failure in your network communications.

The standards specified for network cable length usually refer to cable segments. A network *cable segment* is a continuous section of cable that is not interrupted by a device such as a concentrator or repeater (these terms are discussed later). Connectors can be included in a network cable segment because they simply tap into the segment without interrupting or changing the network signal.

Network cable is available in premade lengths from a number of sources such as retail computer stores and network vendors. In addition, companies that specialize in data and telecommunications cables can configure custom length cables to your requirements. If you have a lot of cable to install, or special cable requirements, you can purchase bulk cable and install the connectors yourself. If you choose this latter method, it is critical that you obtain the correct tools, connectors, and instructions to properly install the connectors.

Ethernet

Three types of cable can be used in an Ethernet network: Thick Ethernet (10BASE5), Thin Ethernet (10BASE2), and UTP (10BASE-T). The network cables used for each type of Ethernet cannot be mixed, although devices exist that enable you to connect different types of Ethernet network segments (these are discussed later in this chapter).

Thick Ethernet

The cable used for Thick Ethernet is a special type of coax cable (see fig. 3.20). The center conductor is surrounded by a dielectric insulator that is surrounded by a foil shield. Around the foil shield is a braided conductor that is surrounded by another foil shield that is again covered by a braided conductor. The outermost part of the cable has a protective covering.

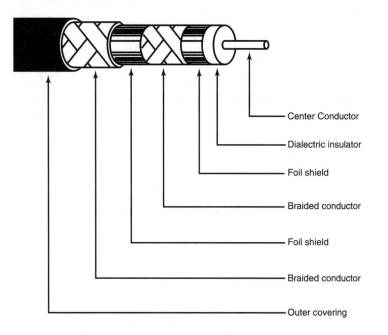

Figure 3.20
Thick Ethernet cable.

Center Conductor

Dialectric insulator

Foil shield

Braided conductor

Foil shield

Braided conductor

Outer covering

Thick Ethernet rarely is used for new installations and is discussed here only as a reference for the large number of existing sites that need to expand or adapt.

The rules for the installation and configuration of Thick Ethernet cable segments are as follows (see fig. 3.21):

- The maximum network segment length is 500 meters (1,641 ft.).

- Each network segment must have a 50-ohm terminator at each end.

- No more than five network segments can be connected in series, only three of which can be populated (have nodes connected to them).

- The maximum number of transceivers per segment is 100.

- The maximum number of nodes on a network is 1,024.

- Transceivers cannot be placed closer together than 2.5 meters (8 ft.).

- Drop cables cannot be longer than 50 meters (164 ft.).

- The maximum distance between any two stations is 3,000 meters (9,848 ft.).

The connectors used for Thick Ethernet cable are called N-series coax connectors.

Figure 3.21

Thick Ethernet cable requirements.

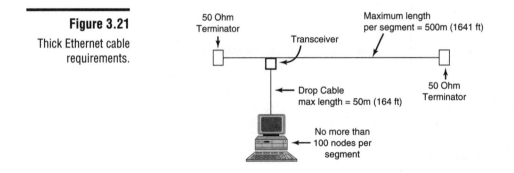

Thin Ethernet

Thin Ethernet cable, a type of RG-58 coax, consists of an inner conductor surrounded by a dielectric insulator, a foil shield, a braided conductor, and a protective outer covering (see fig. 3.22).

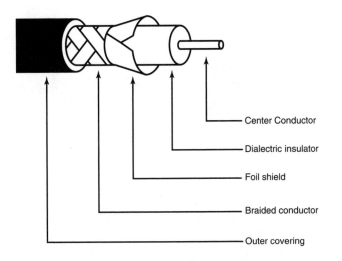

Figure 3.22
Thin Ethernet cable.

Center Conductor

Dialectric insulator

Foil shield

Braided conductor

Outer covering

The following rules apply to the installation and configuration of
Thin Ethernet cable (see fig. 3.23):

- The maximum segment length is 185 meters (607 ft.).

- Each network segment must have a 50-ohm terminator at
  each end.

- No more than five network segments can be connected in
  series, only three of which can be populated (have nodes
  connected to them).

- The maximum number of nodes per segment is 30.

- The minimum cable distance between network adapters is .5
  meters (1.6 ft).

- The maximum number of nodes on a network is 1,024.

- The maximum distance between any two nodes is 1,425
  meters (4,678 ft.).

BNC type connectors are used for Thin Ethernet.

Figure 3.23

Thin Ethernet cable
requirements.

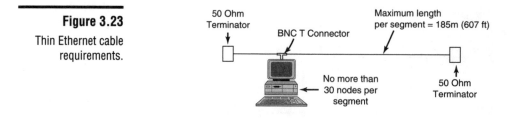

Figure 3.23

Thin Ethernet cable
requirements.

UTP Ethernet

UTP is a cable that consists of wires twisted together in pairs (see fig. 3.24). UTP Ethernet uses a total of four conductors (or two pairs) for transmitting and receiving the network signal. Because the standard RJ-45 connectors have eight connection points, the cable usually installed has eight conductors although the network actually uses only four of them.

Figure 3.24

UTP cable.

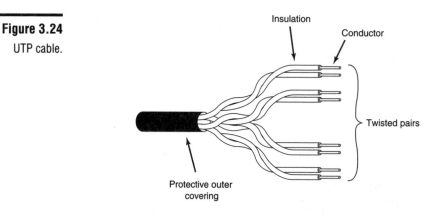

The following rules apply to the installation and configuration of UTP Ethernet cable (see fig. 3.25):

- The maximum cable length between a node and concentrator is 100 meters (328 ft.).

- Pins 1, 2, 3, and 6 on the RJ-45 connector are used and wired straight through. Pins 1 and 2 transmit; pins 3 and 6 receive.

- Up to 12 hubs can be attached to a central hub.

- Without using bridges, UTP Ethernet cable can accommodate a maximum of 1,024 workstations.

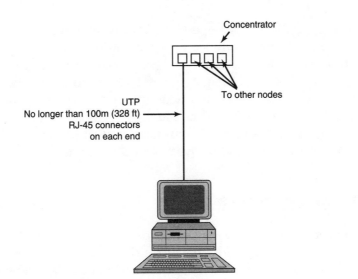

Figure 3.25
UTP cable
requirements.

Fiber-Optic Cable

Fiber-optic cable, often referred to as fiber, transmits data using a
series of light pulses transmitted down a fine glass fiber strand.
A single fiber cable typically consists of a fiber surrounded by a
buffer coating (see fig. 3.26). Kevlar surrounds the buffer coating
for added protection and strength. The outer protective cover is
composed of PVC or black polyurethane. Fiber cable often contains more than one fiber.

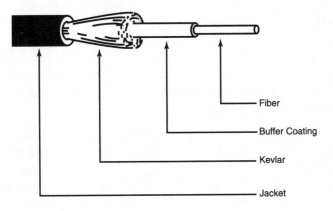

Figure 3.26
A fiber-optic cable.

Fiber is capable of high-speed data transmission and is not susceptible to outside interference as is conventional wire cable. Working
with fiber requires special care; its splices and connectors are more
costly and difficult to manage than those of conventional cabling
techniques. Although network adapters that connect directly to
fiber now are available, fiber usually is used to connect networks
that require high-speed communication over distances longer than
those covered by standard network cable segments.

Proprietary Cable

Proprietary, also called nonstandard, cable is cable used with
proprietary network adapters. Proprietary cabling schemes also
can be used with standard network adapters. A nonstandard
cabling scheme can use the standard cable specified for a selected
network configuration, but with different connectors. Following is
a list of several nonstandard cabling schemes:

- Nonstandard cable and connectors used with proprietary
  network adapter cards

- Standard cable and nonstandard connectors used with
  standard network adapter cards

- Nonstandard cable and connectors used with standard
  network adapter cards

Often, proprietary network adapters are designed to simplify
connecting the nodes in a network. An example of nonstandard
cable and connectors used with proprietary network adapter
cards is a proprietary network adapter that accepts a phono jack
similar to the jack used for headphones on a stereo or radio. The
cable connected to the plug might be a type of coax such as that
used for regular cable TV.

Nonstandard cabling schemes that are used with standard network adapters also exist, making connecting the nodes to the
network more convenient. An example of a nonstandard cabling
scheme used with standard network adapters is a cable system
used with Thin Ethernet adapters as shown in figure 3.27. This

system, developed by AMP Inc., consists of a tap assembly connected to the Thin Ethernet cable rather than the standard BNC T connector. The tap assembly typically is located in the wall at each location where a network node can be connected. The drop cable assembly consists of a tap plug that plugs into the tap assembly in the wall at one end of the cable, and a insulated BNC plug that connects to the BNC connector on the network adapter card on the other end.

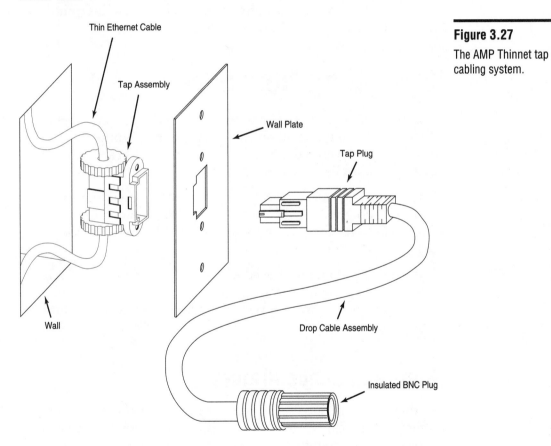

Thin Ethernet Cable

Tap Assembly

Wall Plate

Tap Plug

Wall

Drop Cable Assembly

Insulated BNC Plug

Figure 3.27

The AMP Thinnet tap cabling system.

An advantage of the AMP cabling system is that you can plug in and unplug network nodes without causing a disruption in the primary Thin Ethernet cable. A second advantage is that the drop cable assembly can be nearly any length. The AMP system therefore is much more convenient than a standard Thin Ethernet cable installation that most likely has two cables coming out of the wall and cannot be disconnected without bringing down the network. The drop cable assembly actually has in it the equivalent of two Thinnet cables. When calculating network cable lengths, multiply the length of the drop cable assembly by two.

Expanding Networks

The cable length requirements discussed in the previous section do not restrict most small networks. As your network grows, however, you eventually might need to extend its cable length or exceed the number of specified nodes.

Fortunately, several devices are available that extend the length of your network. In this section the discussion is limited to the devices used for Ethernet, although similar devices exist for some of the other network standards.

The devices and methods used to expand your network each have a specific purpose or function. Many devices, however, incorporate the features of another type of device to increase flexibility and value.

Hubs and Concentrators

As discussed previously, hubs, or concentrators (as they more commonly are called), are a central connection point for network nodes that are arranged using a physical star topology as in 10BASE-T Ethernet. Concentrators are devices that are physically separate from any node in the network, although some concentrators actually plug into an expansion port in a network node. The concentrator has several ports on the back side of the card to which the cable from the other network nodes are attached.

Multiple concentrators can be connected to enable the connection of additional nodes. Consider the example shown in figure 3.28, in which two four-port concentrators are connected. Here both concentrators use UTP cable (10BASE-T) and RJ-45 jacks for connection. One port on each concentrator is used to connect to the other concentrator. The cable used to connect the concentrators is the same cable used between the concentrator and the network nodes, except that the wires are crossed over between the two connectors on each end.

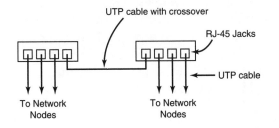

Figure 3.28

Connecting two concentrators using a cross-over UTP cable.

Using a cross-over UTP cable also enables you to connect two computers with 10BASE-T adapters without using a concentrator.

Many concentrators have a BNC connector on the back in addition to the normal RJ-45 jacks. The BNC connector enables you to chain together concentrators using Thin Ethernet coax cable (see fig. 3.29). With the BNC connector, you do not have to waste an RJ-45 port on each concentrator for connection to another concentrator; instead that port can connect an additional network node. In addition to the concentrators connected with the Thin Ethernet cable, you also can install network nodes with Thin Ethernet adapters on the same Thin Ethernet cable segment.

Figure 3.29

Connecting two
concentrators using
Thinnet cable.

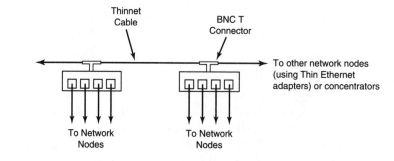

Repeaters

A *repeater* is a device that enables you to extend the length of your network by amplifying and retransmitting the network signal. For example, the maximum cable segment length for a Thin Ethernet cable is 607 feet. By putting a repeater on the end of the cable, you can connect another Thin Ethernet cable segment of up to 607 feet for a total of 1,214 feet (see fig. 3.30).

Figure 3.30

Extending the
maximum allowable
network cable length
with a repeater.

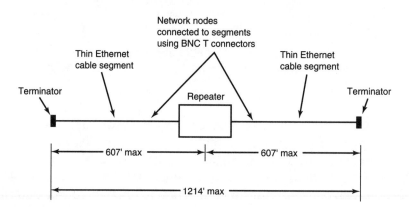

Multiport repeaters enable you to connect more than two network cable segments. For example, with a multiport repeater, you can connect multiple Thin Ethernet cable segments to form a combination of physical bus and star topologies (see fig. 3.31). It's important to keep in mind that although the multiport repeater enables you to create a physical star topology using multiple physical bus topologies, the primary purpose of a repeater is to extend the maximum allowable network cable length.

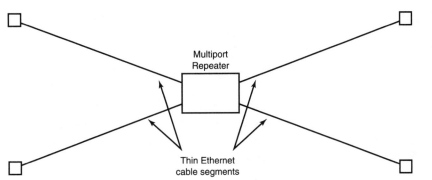

Figure 3.31

Using a multiport
repeater to extend
maximum allowable
network cable length
while creating a star
physical topology.

Bridges

A *bridge* is a device that connects two separate LANs to create
what appears to be a single LAN. Bridges look at the address
associated with each packet of information. Then, if the address is
that of a node on the other network segment, the bridge passes the
packet to the segment. If the bridge recognizes that the address is
that of a node on the current network segment, it does not pass
the packet to the other side. Consider the case of two separate
networks, one operating on Thin Ethernet, and the other using a
proprietary cabling scheme with proprietary network adapters
(see fig. 3.32). The function of the bridge is to transmit information
destined for a node on one network to the intended destination on
the other network.

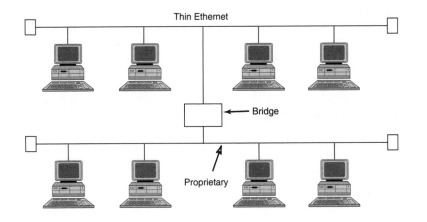

Figure 3.32

Using a bridge to
connect similar
networks.

For those familiar with the *Open System Interconnection* (OSI) model (discussed in Chapter 4, "Software Components"), a bridge operates at the media access layer (layer 2).

Bridges also are often used to reduce the amount of network traffic on a network segment. By splitting a single network segment into two segments and connecting the two using a bridge, the overall network traffic is reduced. To help illustrate this concept, consider the example shown in figure 3.33. Before a bridge is incorporated in the network, all the network traffic is on one segment. AB represents information sent from node A to node B, BC represents information send from node B to node C, and CD represents information sent from node C to node D. By incorporating a bridge and splitting the network cable segment into two segments, only two activities occur on each segment rather than three. The bridge keeps network activity isolated to each segment unless a node on one segment sends information to a node on another segment (in which case the bridge passes through the information).

A bridge also can be used to connect two Thin Ethernet network segments using wireless communications (see fig. 3.34). In this example, a bridge is connected to each network segment. The bridge includes a transmitter and receiver for sending the appropriate information between segments.

Bridges come in all sizes and shapes. In many cases, a bridge is a device similar to a computer, with connectors that attach separate networks. In other cases, a bridge actually is a computer with a network adapter from each network that is to be connected. Special software enables the passing of appropriate information across the network adapters from one network segment to the destination network segment.

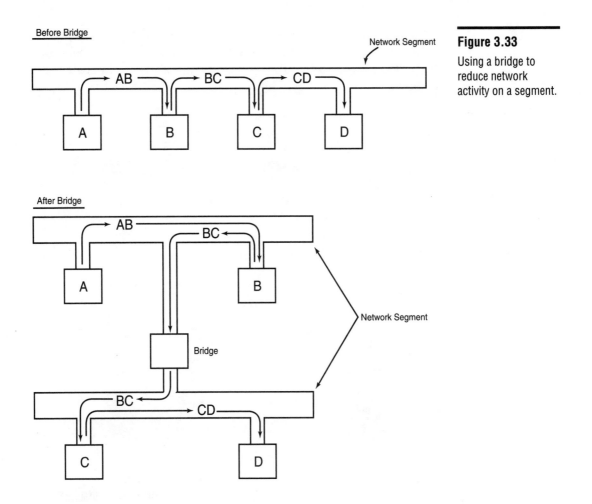

Figure 3.33
Using a bridge to reduce network activity on a segment.

Routers

Routers are similar to bridges except that they operate at a different level. Routers typically require that each network has the same NOS. With a common NOS, the router can perform sophisticated functions that a bridge cannot, such as connect networks based on completely different logical topologies, like Ethernet and Token Ring. Routers also are often intelligent enough to determine the most efficient path to send data across if more than one path exists. Along with the added sophistication and capability provided by routers, though, comes a penalty of increased cost and decreased performance (routers have higher overhead costs than bridges).

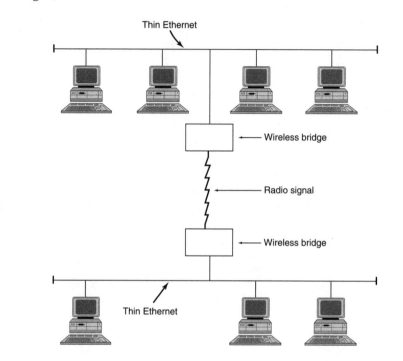

 For those familiar with the OSI model (discussed in Chapter 4, "Software Components") a router operates at the network layer (layer 3).

Gateways

A gateway enables nodes in your network to communicate with different types of networks or devices. You might, for example, have a LAN consisting of IBM-compatible computers, and another comprised of Macintosh computers. In this situation, a gateway enables your IBM computers to share files with the Macintoshes. This type of gateway also enables you to share printers between the two networks.

Some gateways enable you to connect to other types of devices, such as fax machines. A fax gateway, for example, enables all the nodes in your network to connect to a fax machine (or fax board).

Wide Area Networks

A *wide area network* (WAN) is a network created by connecting two or more LANs that are physically isolated from each other, such as networks in two different buildings. The most common method of connecting LANs to form a WAN is to use connection services available from the phone company.

The phone company provides diverse services to connect LANs, each supporting various communication speeds. A bridge or a router connected to a *Channel Service Unit/Digital Service Unit* (CSU/DSU) connects the LAN to the WAN (see fig. 3.35). A CSU/DSU is a sophisticated high-speed modem that connects the network with the telephone lines.

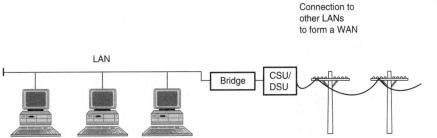

Figure 3.35

Connecting a LAN to a WAN.

Phone company services include dial-up connections, leased lines, and packet switching. A *dial-up connection* is a temporary connection to the WAN, established as needed. A *leased line* is a permanent connection to the LAN. *Packet switching* is a service that enables connections between several LANs. With packet switching, several LANs are connected to a service that can recognize for which LAN an information packet is destined, and then route the packet to the appropriate destination.

The data transfer speeds supported by the various services range from 19.2 Kbps to 45 Mbps. A service called T1 supports a data link of 1.544 Mbps. A T1 line also can be split into a total of 24 64 Kbps channels. Another popular service called 56 Kbps is significantly less expensive than a T1 line.

As modem technology advances, high-speed modems are used to connect multiple LANs using standard telephone lines. 14.4 Kbps modems now are available at extremely low prices and are sometimes used if the data transfer requirements are minimal. As 28.8 Kbps modems become more readily available, expect their usage to increase. Keep in mind, however, that a 28.8 Kbps modem, which is twice as fast as a 14.4 Kbps modem, is still only half as fast as a 56 Kbps line. (A 56 Kbps line is considered one of the low-performance services available from the phone company.)

Technologies are available that connect multiple LANs to form a WAN in a similar way that a CSU/DSU enables a bridge or router to connect a LAN to the phone company system. These devices include infrared, laser, and microwave.

Summary

In this chapter, you learned about the many hardware components and devices available to build a network. You also learned about the various network topologies, and established standards for their use. The different types of network adapters and the cable used to connect them were discussed. Finally, the devices available to expand your network beyond the size allowed by the various specification standards were discussed, as was using these devices to build a WAN.

In This Chapter. . .

This chapter discusses the software components that enable your computer to communicate with the other nodes in the network. Specifically, you learn about the following:

- What the network operating system (NOS) is and what it does.

- What low-level drivers are and what they do.

- The established communication standards and their purpose in developing network software.

- Memory usage concerns resulting from loading network software into the existing memory on your computer.

This chapter also introduces the following terms:

Internetwork Packet   Sequenced Packet
Exchange (IPX)   Exchange (SPX)

Network Basic Input/Output   Xerox Network
System (NetBIOS)   System (XNS)

Network BIOS

Redirector

Transmission Control Protocol/
Internet Protocol (TCP/IP)

Network Driver Interface
Specification (NDIS)

Network Adapter Driver

Open Systems
Interconnection
(OSI) Model

Software Components

The *network interface cards* (NICs), cables, and other devices that connect your computers to form a network are only some of the requirements of a functioning network. Network software also is required for the existing operating system and application programs on your computer to communicate with other computers on the network. Low-level drivers that communicate directly with the network adapters enable the network to operate. Additional software including the *network operating system* (NOS) enables the computer's operating system and application programs to communicate with other nodes in the network.

The Network Operating System

The NOS is the group of core software programs that enable your computer to communicate with other nodes in the network. Through it, you can access the shared resources on other servers in your network. The NOS also provides the features required for a node configured as a server to share its resources with other nodes in the network. Most NOSs include utility programs that establish network connections, manage user accounts and passwords, and manage shared resources on the servers.

Because each NOS is different, the commands required to start the network also are different. Starting the network involves launching several different network programs; therefore, the commands to start the network on each computer usually are included in a DOS batch file.

A *DOS batch file* is a text file that contains a list of commands. When you execute the DOS batch file by typing its name, the commands within the batch file are executed as if you had typed each command separately at the keyboard.

Figure 4.1 shows the different layers that comprise the network software. The software in each layer (except for the network driver) is considered part of the NOS.

Figure 4.1

The layers of network software.

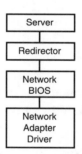

The *network adapter driver* software communicates directly with the NIC. The network *basic input/output system* (BIOS) includes the functions used by the NOS to send and receive network information. At the heart of the NOS is a program called the *redirector*. The redirector intercepts read and write requests and redirects them to the appropriate device, either a disk drive on the local computer or a disk drive on one of the network servers. Finally, if the computer is a server, the server program provides the capability for the node to share its resources with others.

When your computer is started, it performs some self-tests and then proceeds to load its operating system software, such as DOS, from the hard drive. After the operating system is loaded and running, the network software, which coexists with the operating system and provides the additional features required for network operation, is loaded.

Figure 4.2 is a DOS batch file used in a LANtastic network to start the network software on a computer. When the user employs this batch file, the computer is configured as a nondedicated server. The name of the DOS batch file is STARTNET.BAT. Because STARTNET.BAT has a BAT file extension, DOS knows to execute the commands contained within the file when STARTNET is typed at a DOS prompt. NR is the low-level driver software for the network adapter; AILANBIO is the network BIOS; and REDIR is the redirector program. The statement STATION1 on the REDIR line is the node's network name. SERVER is the server program.

```
STARTNET.BAT

NR
AILANBIO
REDIR STATION1
SERVER
```

Figure 4.2

Using a batch file to start the network.

To better understand the role of each of the network software programs, consider what happens when an application program attempts to read data from a disk drive without a network, as shown in figure 4.3. The application program issues a read command to the operating system, which is DOS in this example. DOS then issues the appropriate commands to the system BIOS. The BIOS is the software that interfaces directly with the computer's hardware, such as the disk drive. The BIOS reads the information from the disk drive and passes it to the operating system (DOS), which then passes it to the application program requesting it.

Figure 4.3

Read request processing without a network.

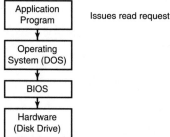

With a network, the task of reading data from a disk drive is more involved. If the application program issues a read request, the redirector program intercepts that request and determines whether the drive to be accessed is a local or network drive (see fig. 4.4). If the drive is local, the redirector passes the request to the operating system, which processes it as previously described. If the drive is a network drive, the redirector passes the request to the network BIOS, which sends it to the network through the network adapter. The server processes the network request and passes the information back across the network. The requesting node receives it and passes it to the application program.

Figure 4.4

Read request processed by the redirector.

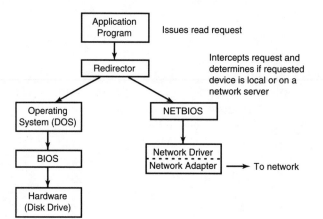

Each layer of the network software passes information to the next layer in a specific format expected by the next layer. Otherwise the communication within the network software breaks down and the network becomes inoperable.

Low-Level Drivers

A *low-level driver* is software that facilitates the communication between the NIC and the network BIOS by acting as the interface between the two. The low-level driver communicates directly with the NIC. The network BIOS expects to see data sent to it by the network adapter in a specific format. Otherwise it can't understand it. Similarly, the network BIOS sends data to the network driver in a specific format. The network adapter driver receives the information and converts it to a format that the NIC understands.

Although many NOSs include drivers for several network adapter cards, it is very difficult for the NOS to have a driver for every available NIC. Two common solutions to this dilemma exist. The first is that the NIC manufacturer make its adapter compatible with an adapter that is supported by the NOS. In most cases, an optional jumper or setting enables a NIC to emulate a common network adapter such as the Novell NE2000. If your NOS doesn't directly support your adapter, you can set the adapter to the NE2000 mode, for example, and then specify to the NOS that you are using a NE2000 adapter. Almost every available NOS supports Novell's NE2000 network adapter. Although emulating Novell's NE2000 network adapter enables the adapter to work with the NOS, any special features of the adapter usually are not available when emulating the NE2000.

The second method of ensuring that your NOS is compatible with your network adapter is to use an NDIS driver. The *network driver interface specification* (NDIS), developed by Microsoft, provides a common set of rules for network adapter manufacturers and NOS developers to use for communication between the network adapter and the NOS. Most network adapters now come with an NDIS driver. If the NOS you use supports NDIS, as do most, you can use any network adapter that has an NDIS driver.

Although NDIS provides compatiblity between any network adapter and NOS that supports it, the primary reason NDIS was developed was to support multiprotocol stacks—enabling you to run different network protocols concurrently using the same network adapter. Running multiprotocol stacks enables you to use the network adapter in your computer for your LAN while also using it to access a mainframe computer that uses a completely different protocol, such as *Transmission Control Protocol/Internet Protocol* (TCP/IP). Without support for multiprotocol stacks provided by NDIS, you would have to unload one stack and then load another stack to gain access to a system that uses a different protocol. This usually entails rebooting your computer.

A standard that serves the same purpose as Microsoft's NDIS is the *Open Datalink Interface* (ODI) specification developed by Novell. ODI supports multiprotocol stacks and naturally is the standard supported in Novell's NetWare NOSs.

Novell's *(Open Data-Link Interface Network SUPport)* ODINSUP was written to provide support for NDIS and coexistence between NDIS and ODI. This enables workstations to connect to virtually anything.

Communication Standards

Standards ensure a common means of communication between the products of various vendors. The previous chapter discussed the hardware components used to construct a network and the standards developed to ensure that the components from different manufacturers connect and communicate with each other. Because network software also is produced by multiple manufacturers, it is necessary that these companies follow standards that foster communication among different software products.

> The term protocol is used extensively in discussions of network standards. A *protocol* is simply a set of rules that specify how network communications occur. Network manufacturers adhere to these rules to ensure that their products are compatible with products produced by other manufacturers.

The OSI Model

The *International Standards Organization* (ISO) developed the *Open Systems Interconnection* (OSI) model as a guideline for developing standards for networking computing devices. Because of the complexity of connecting devices in a network and integrating them so they operate properly, the OSI model includes seven different layers ranging from the physical layer, which includes network cables, to the application layer, which is the interface to the software application being run (see fig. 4.5).

Layer 7	APPLICATION
Layer 6	PRESENTATION
Layer 5	SESSION
Layer 4	TRANSPORT
Layer 3	NETWORK
Layer 2	DATA LINK
Layer 1	PHYSICAL

Figure 4.5
The OSI model.

The OSI model establishes the guidelines by which software and devices from different manufacturers work together. Although manufacturers of network hardware and software are the primary users of the OSI model, a general understanding of the model might be extremely beneficial as you expand your network or connect networks to form a *wide area network* (WAN).

The seven layers of the OSI model are *physical, data link, network, transport, session, presentation,* and *application.* The first two layers (physical and data link) are the hardware that comprises the LAN, such as the Ethernet cables and network adapters. Layers 3, 4, and 5 (network, transport, and session) are the communications protocols, such as *Network Basic Input/Output System* (NetBIOS), TCP/IP, and Novell's *NetWare Core Protocol* (NCP). Layers 6 and 7 (presentation and application) are the NOS that provides network services and functions to the application software.

A detailed discussion of the purpose of each OSI model layer follows.

Physical Layer

The physical layer (layer 1) defines the interface with the physical media, including the network cable. The physical layer governs issues such as the strength of the network signal, the voltages used for the signal, and the distance of the cables. The physical layer also governs types and specifications of cables including the *Institute of Electrical and Electronic Engineers* (IEEE) 802.3 Ethernet cables (Thick Ethernet, Thin Ethernet, and UTP), the *American National Standards Institute* (ANSI) *Fiber Distributed Data Interface* (FDDI) standard for fiber cable, and many others (see fig. 4.6).

Figure 4.6

Cable standards covered by the OSI physical layer.

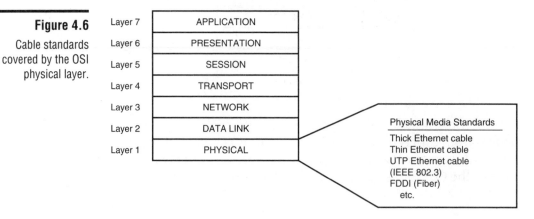

Data Link Layer

The data link layer, layer 2, defines the protocol that detects and corrects errors which occur when transmitting data through the network cable. The data link layer is responsible for the stream of network data that is divided into packets or frames of information. When a packet of information is received incorrectly, the data link layer causes the packet to be sent again. The data link layer is divided into two sublayers: the *Media Access Control* (MAC), and the *Logical Link Control* (LLC). Bridges, described in Chapter 3, operate at the MAC sublayer.

Standards based on the data link layer include the *IEEE 802.2 Logical Link* standard, *Point-to-Point* (PPP), IEEE standards for *Carrier Sense Multiple Access with Collision Detection* (CSMA/CD) and Token Ring, and the ANSI FDDI Token Ring standard (see fig. 4.7). The PPP protocol is used in WANs for communications across links, such as T1 lines.

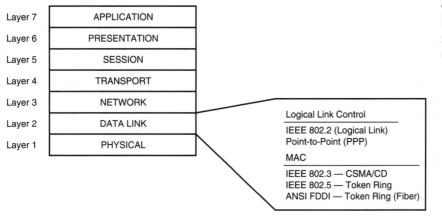

Layer 7	APPLICATION
Layer 6	PRESENTATION
Layer 5	SESSION
Layer 4	TRANSPORT
Layer 3	NETWORK
Layer 2	DATA LINK
Layer 1	PHYSICAL

Logical Link Control
IEEE 802.2 (Logical Link)
Point-to-Point (PPP)

MAC
IEEE 802.3 — CSMA/CD
IEEE 802.5 — Token Ring
ANSI FDDI — Token Ring (Fiber)

Figure 4.7
Standards for the data link layer.

Network Layer

Layer 3, the network layer, defines how data is routed from one network node to the next.

Standards that pertain to the network layer include Novell's *Internetwork Packet Exchange* protocol (IPX), *Internet Protocol* (IP), and Apple's *Datagram Delivery Protocol* (DDP) (see fig. 4.8). IP is part of the TCP/IP protocol standard developed by the Department of Defense and is used with the Internet (often referred to as the "Information Superhighway"). DDP was developed for computers manufactured by Apple, such as the Macintosh.

Routers, discussed in Chapter 3, operate at the network layer.

Figure 4.8

Standards for the network layer.

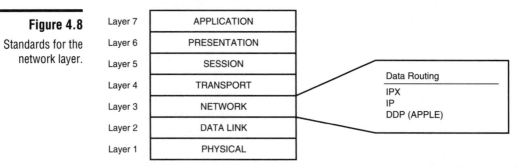

Transport Layer

Layer 4, the transport layer, provides and maintains the communication link. The transport layer is responsible for responding appropriately if the link fails or cannot be established.

Standards that pertain to the transport layer include the *International Standards Organization* (ISO), *Transport Protocol* (TP), and Novell's *Sequenced Packet Exchange* (SPX) protocol (see fig. 4.9). Other standards that perform important functions at the transport layer include the Department of Defense's *Transmission Control Protocol* (TCP), which is part of TCP/IP, and Novell's NCP.

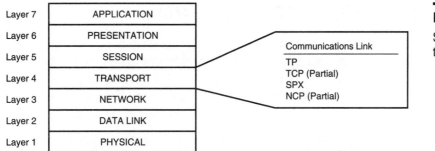

Figure 4.9
Standards for the transport layer.

Session Layer

Layer 5, the session layer, controls the network connections between nodes. The session layer is responsible for creating, maintaining, and terminating network sessions.

The TCP performs important functions at the session layer, as does Novell's NCP.

Presentation Layer

Layer 6, the presentation layer, is responsible for the format of the data. The presentation layer translates data between specific formats to ensure that the data is received in a format that is meaningful to the device on which it is presented.

Application Layer

Layer 7, the application layer, is the highest defined layer in the OSI model. The application layer is responsible for providing user applications and network management functions, and for providing the operating system with network services such as file transfer.

Network Protocol Standards

An operational network requires that each node on the network communicates with any node configured as a server. The network adapters must be able to send and receive network signals among the nodes in the network. In addition, information sent among the nodes must be in a format that can be understood by each node.

Several protocols serve as rules for network communication. These communication protocols tend to operate between the network adapter driver and the NOS software. Popular network communication protocols include NetBIOS (or NetBEUI), TCP/IP, IPX and SPX, and *Xerox Network System* (XNS).

NetBIOS and NetBEUI

NetBIOS operates in a fashion similar to that of the standard BIOS in every computer. Whereas the standard BIOS is the communication interface between the computer's hardware devices and the operating system, the NetBIOS is the communication interface between the network adapter and the NOS. NetBIOS was developed originally by IBM.

The standard NetBIOS implementation spans layer 3 (the network layer) and layer 5 (the session layer) of the OSI model. Many NetBIOS–compatible networks emulate the layer 5 implementation of NetBIOS, but use a different transport (layer 4) and network (layer 3) layer protocol, such as TCP/IP, IPX, or XNS.

NetBIOS Extended User Interface (NetBEUI) is Microsoft's implementation of NetBIOS.

TCP/IP

The Department of Defense developed TCP/IP to connect a wide variety of dissimilar host computers around the world. Today TCP/IP is the protocol of choice for connecting dissimilar systems, including mainframe and minicomputers running the UNIX operating system. Many NOSs now support the TCP/IP protocol for connecting PC LANs to other types of computers, both mini-computers and mainframes. TCP/IP also is the protocol that connects the thousands of computers that form the Internet.

TCP/IP was developed prior to the existence of the OSI model, although the four layers used in TCP/IP have similar counterparts in the OSI model (see fig. 4.10). The TCP/IP process layer, which includes applications such as Telnet and *file transfer protocol* (FTP), is similar to the OSI application and presentation layers. The *host-to-host* layer (or TCP) is equivalent to the OSI session and transport layers. The *Internet layer* (IP) is similar to the OSI network layer. Finally, the network access layer is similar to the OSI data link and physical layers.

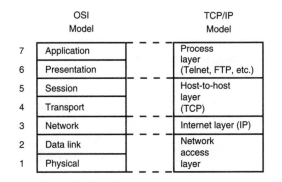

Figure 4.10

A comparison of the TCP/IP model with the OSI model.

IPX and SPX

IPX is Novell's protocol for specifying the rules for exchanging packets across a network. IPX is a network layer (layer 3) protocol. Novell has several other protocols that span other layers, including NCP.

SPX is Novell's protocol for enabling two workstations to communicate across a network. SPX ensures that data is transferred in sequence and arrives at its intended destination. SPX is a transport layer (layer 4) protocol.

XNS

XNS is Xerox's network communications protocol upon which Novell's IPX and SPX network protocols are based. XNS is the long-standing protocol of choice for NOSs developed by 3Com Corporation. XNS spans the network through the session layers (layers 3 through 5).

Memory Usage Concerns

Every computer operating in a network must have network software installed and running. The network software is loaded into memory, where it remains ready to perform network-related tasks while there is power to the computer. When the computer is turned off, the contents of the memory are cleared. Therefore, when the computer is turned on again, the network software must be loaded into memory again.

When you start your computer, it loads DOS, the network software, and possibly some other drivers or programs such as a mouse driver or a CD-ROM driver. Most DOS application programs are able to use only the first 640 KB of memory (also called conventional memory). Most of the software, including DOS and the network software, also is loaded into conventional memory. Therefore, you might not be able to run your application software if your application program requires a relatively large amount of conventional memory. (Even if you have 4 MB (4096 KB) of memory installed on your computer, most applications use only the first 640 KB.)

Conventional memory is the memory from 0 KB to 640 KB (see fig. 4.11). Most DOS applications use this memory. Software drivers and *terminate-and-stay-resident programs* (TSRs) also are loaded into conventional memory.

The memory area between 640 KB and 1024 KB (1 MB) is reserved for display adapters and other hardware devices, including some network adapter cards. This memory is called *upper memory*.

Memory above 1024 KB (1 MB) is called *extended memory* (XMS). Most DOS applications cannot use this memory area. Microsoft Windows and disk-caching programs such as SMARTDRIVE use extended memory.

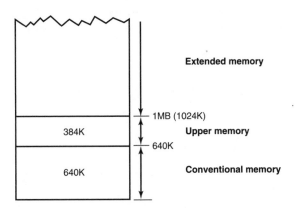

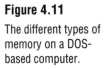

Figure 4.11

The different types of memory on a DOS-based computer.

If you have an 80286 computer with at least 384 KB of available extended memory, MS-DOS 5.0 and above enable you to load most of DOS into an unused portion of the upper memory area.

If you have an 80386 computer or higher, and at least 384 KB of extended memory, MS-DOS 5.0 and above enable you to load drivers including network software into any unused portion of the upper memory area.

With the ability to load DOS and other drivers into upper memory, you can free additional conventional memory for your application programs.

Summary

In this chapter, you learned about the software components of a network and their functions. You examined the NOS, as well as the many levels of software that comprise it. The communication standards for an operational network were discussed as well as the OSI model from which most of the standards are derived. Finally, you learned about some memory usage concerns, and the options to maximize available memory for application software.

In This Chapter. . .

Today's peer-to-peer networks offer sophisticated features and flexibility. Chapter 2, "Network Nodes and Their Function" introduced the concepts of peer-to-peer and server-based networks, and compared the advantages and disadvantages of each. This chapter takes the peer-to-peer network concept one step further by looking at some of the specific features and capabilities of the following five most popular peer-to-peer networks:

- Artisoft LANtastic
- Artisoft Simply LANtastic
- Novell Personal NetWare
- Microsoft Windows for Workgroups
- Performance Technology POWERLan

Peer-to-Peer Networks

Peer-to-peer networks offer many sophisticated features and the flexibility required by even the most demanding installations. Chapter 2 discussed the peer-to-peer network concept in detail. This chapter expands on the information discussed in Chapter 2, taking a closer look at particular peer-to-peer networks and the implementation of specific features in each.

The general function of all peer-to-peer networks is the same: to share devices such as printers, and share information contained on disk drives between nodes in the network. Each *network operating system* (NOS) provides the basic peer-to-peer network features in different ways. Some are easier to install than others; however, others are easier to use. Some provide more options for configuring nodes as servers and workstations, yet others are faster.

When you evaluate a peer-to-peer network, several factors determine which peer-to-peer network suits your needs. Not all networks incorporate every network feature. Carefully consider the following points before choosing a network:

- **Features.** The features available in each network can vary substantially. Only you can determine if the network you are evaluating has the features that suit your needs. Seek advice from others, but remember the advice you receive reflects their own personal experience. Try to obtain advice from those with firsthand knowledge of the networks you are investigating.

- **Ease of Installation.** If you are installing the network hardware and software, an important consideration is the ease of installation. What questions will have to be answered to successfully install the network? How do you determine the answers? What if you change your mind later? How comfortable are you with the whole concept of installing and configuring a network? Make sure the network is easy to install or you have the experience and knowledge necessary to successfully perform the installation. Even the best network with all the features to suit every possible need is useless if you can't install it correctly.

If someone else is installing your network, it's very important that the person(s) performing the installation understands your requirements for installation and has the necessary knowledge and experience to perform a successful installation.

- **Configuration and Management Options.** Immediately after the network is installed, you can set up specific user accounts and shared resources on each server. You should consider carefully the options available for setting up and managing shared resources and user accounts. You want to know about user-account and shared-resource access restrictions. In addition, you want to be able to change restrictions as your requirements change. You also want to be able to add, modify, or remove specific shared resources on a particular server at any time.

- **Ease of Use.** Once the network is installed, the ease with which you can use it ultimately determines if it meets your requirements. Often the original network setup and configuration determines how easy it is to use.

> Most networks enable you to include network commands in DOS batch files so that users don't have to know a lot to successfully use the network.

It's important that the included network utility programs that establish network connections are intuitive and easy to use. If you operate in a Windows environment, there should be network utilities in Windows to establish network connections. Similarly, if you operate primarily in a DOS environment, network utility programs should be available to run from DOS.

An important fact to keep in mind is: If it isn't easy to use, most people won't use it!

- **Cost.** Cost is always a concern. There is a point at which the cost to implement a network exceeds the benefits of having a network. When figuring the cost of your network, in addition to the cost of the network hardware and software, include the cost of installation. If you are installing the network yourself, put a value on your time. If it takes you eight hours to install what would take a professional two hours to install, having a professional install your network might actually cost you less.

After you determine how much a network costs, determine how much it will save you. You immediately save the cost of buying a larger hard disk or a laser printer for each computer. Also, try to assign a value to the increased productivity you obtain by having a network. If the savings never outweigh the cost incurred, maybe you are installing a network for the wrong reason.

- **Flexibility.** As your needs change or as you replace computers and components, the network must be flexible enough to adapt to these changes. Some of the questions you might ask yourself to determine how flexible your network really is are as follows:

  You previously configured a node as a workstation and now need to configure it as a nondedicated server so you can access its resources. Will you be able to change the configuration?

  How easy is it to share a newly added printer in the network?

  Can a CD-ROM drive be accessed across the network?

- **Expandability.** Every business wants to grow. As you grow, it's important to know if and how your network will grow with you. As new computers are added to the network, you need to know what equipment is required and any limitations or restrictions for adding new equipment. How many nodes can the network support? What if you want to connect two separate networks? How many dedicated servers can exist?

- **Interoperability.** If you need to access nodes on different networks, find out what kind of support is available for your network. To access a mini- or mainframe computer running the UNIX operating system, your network probably needs to support the *Transmission Control Protocol/Internet Protocol* (TCP/IP). To access servers on other types of networks, your NOS needs to have the appropriate support.

- **Conforms to Standards.** In general, a network that conforms to the established standards, such as Ethernet, is likely to be expanded or changed later at a low cost. If, for example, you purchase a network that has proprietary network adapters, and you later decide to change NOSs, you have to buy new network adapters. If, on the other hand, your network uses standard Ethernet adapters and you change to a different NOS, you can use your existing Ethernet adapters.

- **Security.** When you implement a network, security almost always becomes a concern. Prior to the implementation of a network, each computer is independent and the only way a person can access its data is to walk over and use it. However, as part of a network, users on other nodes can access the data and files on other computers. When choosing a network, it's important to understand what security options are available for restricting access of specific users or restricting access to selected shared resources.

- **Fault Tolerance.** It's important to consider what happens if a node or a component in the network fails. Does the entire network become disabled? What features are available to help reduce the risk of losing valuable information in the event of a hardware failure? The answers to these questions will take you a long way toward understanding the effect of a failure on your network and on the network's shared data.

- **Maintenance.** What type of periodic maintenance is required if any? Do any hardware components need to be maintained? What about software maintenance?

- **Stability.** Product stability is an important issue. In other words, what is the likelihood of a failure occurring due to a bug or a glitch in the design? You also want to consider how stable the companies that manufacture the network hardware and software are.

- **Technical Support.** Check on the technical support policies of the company that manufacturers the network hardware and software before choosing a network. If you encounter problems, you want to know what technical support is available, when it's available, and how much it costs. Each network company has a different policy for technical support.

- **Guarantee.** If, after installing your network, you discover it doesn't work for your situation, you'll want to know what kind of a guarantee you have on your purchase. Many reputable companies offer a no questions asked, money-back guarantee on your purchase of network hardware and software within a specified amount of time.

It's important to keep in mind that if you purchase standard network hardware such as Ethernet adapters, and later decide to change your NOS, you do not have to replace your existing network hardware.

The following sections describe the primary features of the most popular peer-to-peer networks.

LANtastic

Artisoft's LANtastic is the leading peer-to-peer network offering a tremendous number of features and capabilities. LANtastic has received numerous industry awards for its sophisticated features, flexibility, and ease of use.

Artisoft manufactures a complete line of network products including network adapters that can be used with LANtastic. Artisoft's Ethernet adapters are software-configurable and offer compatibility with Novell network adapters. Artisoft also manufactures a proprietary 2 Mbps adapter for use with LANtastic.

The standard software-only version of the LANtastic NOS includes support for both DOS and Windows environments. LANtastic is licensed per node, meaning you have to purchase a licensed copy for each computer in your network, and is available in 1-, 5-, 10-, 25-, 50-, and 100-user packages. If you purchase a five-user package, for example, and later need to add a computer to your five-node network, you can purchase a single-user version for the new computer; you do not have to buy the 10-user version and reinstall LANtastic on each computer.

LANtastic is available in a software-only configuration (previously described), a LANtastic network add-on kit, and a starter kit. The LANtastic network add-on kit includes an Artisoft Ethernet network adapter and a single-node license of the LANtastic NOS. Artisoft pioneered the network starter kit concept by including everything necessary to set up a two-node LANtastic network in one package, including a two-node version of the LANtastic software, two network adapters, and cable.

Artisoft also manufactures several other products that enhance and expand your LANtastic network, including 8- and 12-port 10Base-T concentrators, LANtastic for the Macintosh, LANtastic for TCP/IP, and more. LANtastic for the Macintosh allows your LANtastic network to communicate with a Macintosh network using a computer configured as a gateway. LANtastic for TCP/IP allows your LANtastic network to communicate with computers running the TCP/IP protocol.

CorStream Server is a separate, high-performance, dedicated-server product available for LANtastic networks requiring the best performance possible from a dedicated server. CorStream Server is based on a 32-bit operating system offering robust security and fault tolerance features.

LANtastic Z is a separate product that provides a two-node LANtastic network between two computers using parallel ports, serial ports, or a connection using modems. Using these methods to connect two computers is much slower than installing a network adapter in each computer.

You can use Central Station for remote dial-in access to the network, as a print server (a printer can be connected to it instead of connecting it to a server), or even to connect a node such as a notebook computer to the network using the node's parallel port.

Features

LANtastic includes utilities for network connections and management in both DOS and Windows. You also can establish connections to network drives and printers using the NET command line at the DOS prompt or in a batch file, or by using the DOS NET or Windows NET programs.

LANtastic allows the sharing of printers, drives, directories, and even individual files. You can share CD-ROM drives with nodes on the network. You also can share other types of non-DOS drives with LANtastic including write once, read many (WORM) drives, and rewritable optical drives.

You can configure nodes in a LANtastic network as workstations, nondedicated servers, dedicated servers, or any combination thereof. LANtastic includes a program called ALONE that configures a LANtastic node as a dedicated server, providing better performance than a nondedicated server.

LANtastic operates on older XT and 286-class computers with at least 640 KB of RAM (more if running Windows). LANtastic does not restrict the network functionality of older computers that operate as workstations or nondedicated servers.

Mail

LANtastic Mail provides e-mail features across the network in both Windows and DOS. Also included is Artisoft Exchange, which consists of a sophisticated mail and scheduling program that runs with Windows.

Exchange Mail is an object-oriented program that enables you to create, read, and manage mail by manipulating objects to perform tasks (see fig. 5.1). The program contains an object that represents your "in" basket, another that represents the mail you have sent, and so on. Exchange Mail includes a fax gateway so that you can send messages and information to fax machines. The LANtastic Mail gateway enables you to send mail to those in your network who are not running Exchange Mail. The pager gateway enables you to page individuals or send short messages to alpha pagers, which are pagers that display messages. Gateways allowing communication with MCI Mail and MHS-compatible systems are available separately.

The Artisoft Exchange Scheduler works with Exchange Mail to schedule personal and group appointments (see fig. 5.2). When you change a group appointment, Exchange Scheduler sends an Exchange Mail message notifying users of the change.

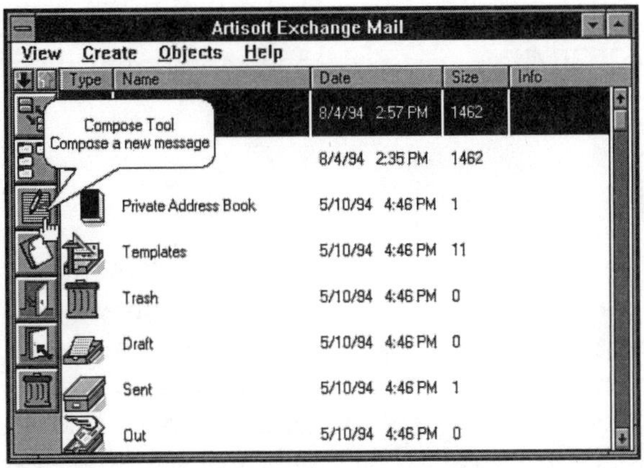

Figure 5.1
Artisoft Exchange
Mail.

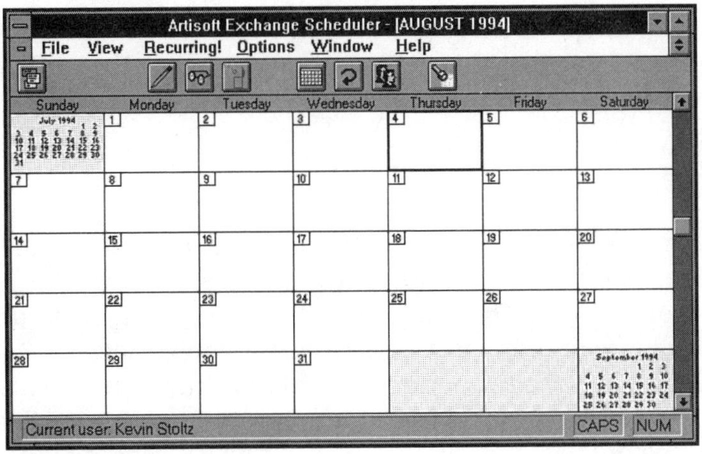

Figure 5.2
Artisoft Exchange
Scheduler.

Standards Support

LANtastic supports many network adapters from other manufacturers, such as ARCnet and Ethernet. LANtastic also has *Network Driver Interface Specification* (NDIS) support to ensure compatibility with nearly all currently manufactured network adapters.

LANtastic supports connections with other types of networks, including Novell, Microsoft, and IBM, using the *NetWare Core Protocol* (NCP) and *Server Message Block* (SMB) protocols.

LANtastic for TCP/IP enables LANtastic nodes to access systems running the TCP/IP protocol, such as mainframe and minicomputers running the UNIX operating system.

Security

LANtastic has sophisticated, yet easy to implement, security for restricting user access to shared resources. Thirty levels of security are implemented using *access control lists* (ACLs). ACLs specify the users or groups of users that are allowed to access specific resources as well as the type of access they have. LANtastic supports the use of individual and wild-card accounts to access servers, and supports up to 500 users per server.

LANtastic supports the use of account servers that enable you to set up your user accounts on a single server. The other servers can retrieve user account information from the account server.

Printing

LANtastic includes a *remote printer server program* (RPS) that enables a node, whether configured as a server or a workstation, to despool print jobs from a server. RPS also enables more than one printer to despool print jobs from the same printer queue, which provides the maximum amount of printing possible. LANtastic also supports *immediate despooling*—allowing printing to start before the application program finishes sending the print job to the network print spooler.

Other Features

The Linkbook feature, which is similar to the Windows clipboard but operates across the network, provides Windows *Dynamic Data Exchange* (DDE) support.

LANtastic includes an autoreconnect feature that automatically reestablishes a network connection in the event that a server is rebooted. LANtastic also enables network connections to be specified but not actually established until the redirected drive or printer is accessed. Thus, the computer to be accessed can be turned off except when it is in use.

LANtastic supports the use of *global resources*—resources set up on one server that actually define a shared resource on another server. When you establish a connection to a global resource, LANtastic finds the destination to which the global resource points and automatically establishes the connection between that computer and your computer.

The LANtastic server program is modular, enabling you to load only the features you need. As you specify server features, the server's approximate memory usage is automatically calculated and displayed. Because better performance usually comes at a cost of less available memory for application programs, the ability to view the servers memory usage allows the balancing of server performance with memory usage.

Installation

The LANtastic installation program automatically searches your drive for Windows. If it finds Windows, LANtastic runs the Windows version of the installation program; otherwise it runs the DOS version of the installation program. The installation program walks you through a series of steps asking specific questions about how you want to configure your network node. Each question is displayed on a separate screen and includes a complete description. Some of the information LANtastic enables you to specify during installation follows:

- The network name of your computer.

- The drive and directory in which you want to install the LANtastic software.

- If you want to share your disk drives and printers with other computers. This is how you specify whether you want your computer configured as a nondedicated server or a workstation.

- The type of network adapter card installed in your computer.

- If you want to install and use the Artisoft Exchange Mail and Scheduler programs, and if so, the post office location for Mail.

- Whether you want your LANtastic node to connect to a Novell file server, Windows for Workgroups, Windows NT Server, or Microsoft LAN Manager networks.

- Connections to disk drives and printers on other computers.

After specifying the options you want installed on your LANtastic node, the LANtastic installation program automatically installs LANtastic and updates your computer's system files (AUTOEXEC.BAT and CONFIG.SYS). If Windows is installed on your computer, the Windows configuration files also are updated. The LANtastic program group is created showing the available LANtastic utility programs (see fig. 5.3). After completing the installation process, when you turn on your computer, the network automatically starts with the configuration options specified during installation.

Figure 5.3

The LANtastic program group in Windows.

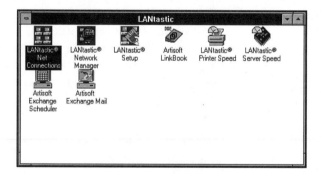

Although LANtastic provides extensive support for user accounts and security, the installation program automatically creates a wild-card account, which enables anyone to access any server without setting up specific user accounts. In addition, the LANtastic installation program sets up default shared resources on each server. For example, the C-DRIVE resource name can be set up to point to the physical C drive on the server. The default wild-card account * and default shared resources for the server set up during installation enable you to start using LANtastic immediately after it's installed.

Configuration and Management

The DOS or Windows LANtastic Network Manager program sets up and manages user accounts (see fig. 5.4). You also can set up wild-card accounts that provide groups of users access to a server without setting up an account for each user. After setting up user accounts on a server, copy those accounts to another server to avoid having to set up separate accounts on each server.

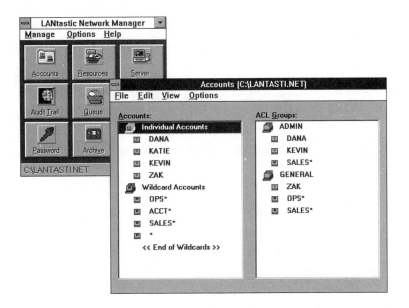

Figure 5.4

The Accounts dialog box in the LANtastic Network Manager program in Windows.

You can specify parameters for each account including the account name, description, and password; ACL groups to which the account belongs; expiration date of the account; number of concurrent logins allowed for this account; time of day the account users can log in; and account privileges.

You can set up ACL groups and specify the users that belong to them. ACL groups or user accounts can access a specific shared resource on a server.

Specifying the time of day that a user account is allowed to log in to a network server prevents access to the network during unauthorized times.

Several privileges provide an account special access to various features of LANtastic (see fig. 5.5). The privileges are described as follows:

- Super ACL prevents enforcement of the ACL for this account, thereby giving the account access to all resources without restrictions.

- Super Queue enables the user to view and control all jobs in the print queue.

- Super Mail enables the user to control all items in the mail queue.

- User Audit enables the user to issue NET AUDIT commands to create audit entries in a server's audit log.

- System Manager enables the user to perform system manager functions, such as remotely shutting down servers and logging out users.

- Operator Notify provides the user with special system messages that require operator intervention, such as a depletion of printer paper.

- Remote Despooler enables an account to access the server and despool print jobs using the remote printer server program.

- Network Manager enables the user to view the status information and performance statistics of a server.

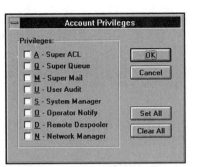

Figure 5.5

The Account
Privileges dialog box
in the Windows
LANtastic Network
Manager program.

Shared resources are defined on each server using the DOS or
Windows LANtastic Network Manager program (see fig. 5.6).
Shared resources can be printers, disk drives, specific directories on
the drives, or even individual files. Support for CD-ROM drives,
WORM drives, and other non-DOS drives also exists. Several
resource names can refer to a single printer, enabling you to use
different printer setup strings. You can, for example, set up one
printer resource to print in portrait mode, and another to print in
landscape mode.

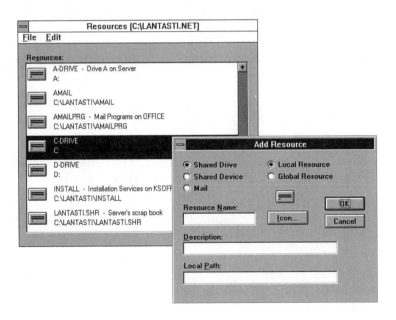

Figure 5.6

Adding a shared
resource in Windows.

Each shared resource has an ACL that determines which user accounts or ACL groups are allowed access to the resource, and the type of access they have (see fig. 5.7). The following list describes the 12 possible ACL rights for each User/Group Name accessing a particular shared-drive resource:

- **Read Access.** Able to open files for reading.

- **Write Access.** Able to write to files.

- **Create File.** Able to create files. The user or group must have Write Access to be able to save information to the file.

- **Make Directory.** Able to create a new directory.

- **File Lookup.** Able to display directory listings.

- **Delete File.** Able to delete files.

- **Remove Directory.** Able to delete directories.

- **Rename File.** Able to change the name of a file.

- **Execute Program.** Able to run programs.

- **Change File Attribute.** Able to change the attributes of a file, such as Read-Only or Hidden.

- **Indirect File.** Able to create and use indirect files within the shared directory.

- **Physical Access.** Able to connect to DOS devices directly without going through server's spooler.

The shared resource in the example is a large hard disk with the name THE-GIG. The ACL for this resource contains a list of User/Group Names and the associated Access Rights for each.

LANtastic enables you to create ACL groups that contain a list of individual or wild-card accounts, thereby the ACL group name can be specified in the ACL for a shared resource. As new accounts are added, you can place them in an ACL group that is already defined for the shared resource. By placing a new account in an established ACL group, the new account automatically has ACL rights defined for each shared resource.

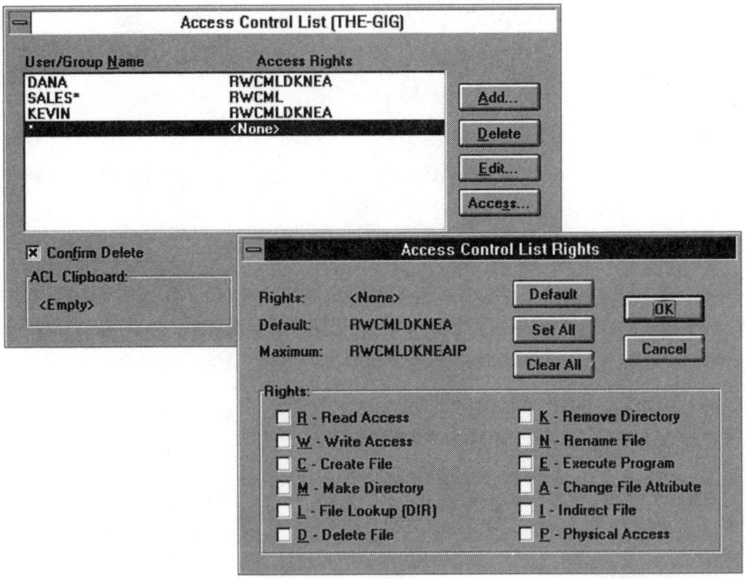

Figure 5.7

The Access Control List Rights dialog box for a specific User/ Group Name for a shared-drive resource in Windows.

LANtastic provides extensive printer configuration and management features (see fig. 5.8). Each shared-printer resource can have several different parameters specifying the available network features. The following is a description of the possible parameters for each shared-printer resource:

- **Description.** A description of the shared-printer resource that is displayed when network connections to the printer are established.

- **Output Device.** The name of the DOS device to which the printer is physically connected, such as LPT1 or COM1.

- **Notification.** Sends a message to a user with the Operator Notify privilege when an event that needs user intervention occurs, such as when the printer paper jams or the printer runs out of paper.

- **Notification T/O.** The time that must elapse before the Notification message is sent.

- **Banner Page.** Before each print job, sends a banner page to the printer indicating user name, network node name, time and date, and other information about the print job.

- **Form Feeds.** Sends a form feed to the printer after each print job causing the last part of the print job to be ejected from the printer.

- **Immed Despool.** Causes the print job to begin printing immediately, even before the application program finishes sending the job to the print queue.

- **Despool Timeout.** If immediate despooling is enabled, this is the amount of time the currently despooling print job can remain idle before it is closed and another job is sent to the printer.

- **Lines Per Page.** The number of lines of standard text to be printed on each page.

- **Tab Width.** The number of spaces the spooler inserts in the print job each time a tab character is encountered. This feature is useful if your application program sends tabs but your printer doesn't support them.

- **Paper Width.** The width of the printed banner page.

- **Chars/Second.** The minimum number of characters per second the spooler attempts to send to the printer. This setting is extremely valuable when used to speed up network printing, which is normally slowed down by applications such as Windows.

- **Setup Delay.** The number of seconds the spooler waits between sending the setup string to the printer and sending the data to be printed.

- **Cleanup Delay.** The number of seconds the spooler waits after sending the cleanup file. The cleanup file is sent to the printer after a print job and often includes commands, for example, to reset the printer.

- **Edit Setup String.** This option enables you to specify a setup string to be sent to the printer before sending a print job, or a cleanup file or string that is sent to the printer after sending a print job. Setup strings usually perform actions such as resetting the printer, setting the printer to landscape mode, and so on.

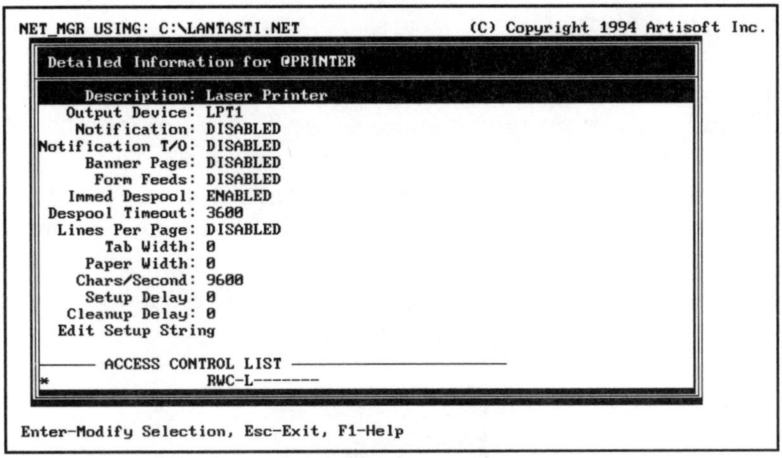

```
NET_MGR USING: C:\LANTASTI.NET              (C) Copyright 1994 Artisoft Inc.
┌─────────────────────────────────────────────────────────────────────────┐
│ Detailed Information for @PRINTER                                         │
│    Description: Laser Printer                                             │
│   Output Device: LPT1                                                     │
│    Notification: DISABLED                                                 │
│  Notification T/O: DISABLED                                               │
│     Banner Page: DISABLED                                                 │
│      Form Feeds: DISABLED                                                 │
│   Immed Despool: ENABLED                                                  │
│  Despool Timeout: 3600                                                    │
│  Lines Per Page: DISABLED                                                 │
│       Tab Width: 0                                                        │
│     Paper Width: 0                                                        │
│    Chars/Second: 9600                                                     │
│     Setup Delay: 0                                                        │
│   Cleanup Delay: 0                                                        │
│  Edit Setup String                                                        │
│                                                                           │
│        ── ACCESS CONTROL LIST ──────────────                              │
│ *              RWC-L────────                                              │
└─────────────────────────────────────────────────────────────────────────┘
  Enter-Modify Selection, Esc-Exit, F1-Help
```

Figure 5.8

The LANtastic Network Manager printer information screen in DOS.

The LANtastic server program is modular, so that you can load only the options you want to use. The Server Startup Parameters options enable you to choose from several general LANtastic features to use for your server (see fig. 5.9). As you specify different operating parameters for your server, the Approximate Memory Usage window changes to display the effect your selection has on the memory usage of the server.

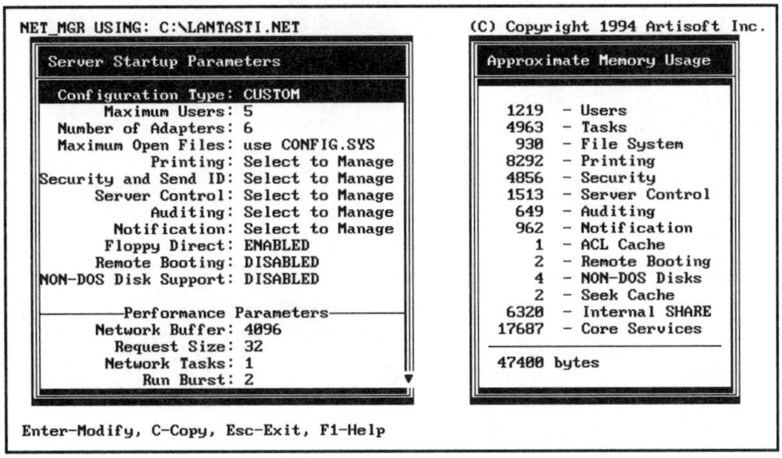

```
NET_MGR USING: C:\LANTASTI.NET              (C) Copyright 1994 Artisoft Inc.
┌──────────────────────────────────┐  ┌─────────────────────────────────┐
│ Server Startup Parameters        │  │ Approximate Memory Usage        │
│┌─────────────────────────────────┤  ├─────────────────────────────────┤
││Configuration Type: CUSTOM       │  │                                 │
││    Maximum Users: 5             │  │  1219  - Users                  │
││ Number of Adapters: 6           │  │  4963  - Tasks                  │
││Maximum Open Files: use CONFIG.SYS│ │   930  - File System            │
││        Printing: Select to Manage│ │  8292  - Printing               │
││Security and Send ID: Select to Manage│ 4856  - Security             │
││ Server Control: Select to Manage │  │  1513  - Server Control         │
││        Auditing: Select to Manage│  │   649  - Auditing               │
││    Notification: Select to Manage│  │   962  - Notification           │
││   Floppy Direct: ENABLED         │  │     1  - ACL Cache              │
││  Remote Booting: DISABLED        │  │     2  - Remote Booting         │
││NON-DOS Disk Support: DISABLED    │  │     4  - NON-DOS Disks          │
││                                  │  │     2  - Seek Cache             │
││   ──Performance Parameters──     │  │  6320  - Internal SHARE         │
││  Network Buffer: 4096            │  │ 17687  - Core Services          │
││    Request Size: 32              │  │                                 │
││   Network Tasks: 1               │  │ 47400 bytes                     │
││       Run Burst: 2            ▼  │  │                                 │
│└─────────────────────────────────┘  └─────────────────────────────────┘
  Enter-Modify, C-Copy, Esc-Exit, F1-Help
```

Figure 5.9

The Server Startup Parameters screen and the Approximate Memory Usage window in the DOS LANtastic Network Manager program.

Using LANtastic

One of LANtastic's strongest features is its ease of use. The DOS and Windows Net programs make network connections a breeze. The Windows LANtastic Net program enables you to perform all your network activities in Windows (see fig. 5.10). You start the DOS LANtastic Net program by typing NET at the DOS prompt. DOS LANtastic Net performs the same functions as its Windows counterpart. The following is a description of the Windows LANtastic Net program menu selections:

Figure 5.10

The LANtastic Net menu in Windows.

- **Drives**. Establishes network connections to shared-drive resources on other computers.

- **Printers**. Establishes network connections to shared-printer resources on other computers.

- **Mail**. Enables you to send and receive LANtastic mail or Exchange Mail (if you are using Windows and have installed Artisoft Exchange). If you have the Artisoft Sounding board, you can send and receive voice mail.

- **Chat**. Enables you to have a real-time chat session with another user by using your keyboards to type messages to each other. The information typed by one user immediately appears in a window on the other user's display. If you have the Artisoft sounding board, you even can have a voice chat session.

- **Jobs**. Enables you to view and manage print jobs in a server's queue.

- **Computers**. Enables you to log in or log out of another computer on the network. To view the jobs in the print queue, for example, you must be logged in to the computer with the queue you want to view.

A quick way to terminate all the drive and printer redirections for a particular server is to log out of the server; all drive and printer redirections are terminated when you log out.

- **Account**. Enables you to view the information for your account on any server in the network. You also can disable your account or change your password using this selection.

- **Manage**. Enables you to perform management functions on other servers including shutting down a server, logging a user off a server, and viewing performance statistics for a server. You even can take control of a server so that what you type on your keyboard is sent to the keyboard of the computer you are controlling, and your display shows what is on the screen of the computer you are controlling.

The computer you are controlling must be running a DOS text application. You cannot control a computer running Windows or another graphics-based application.

Establishing a drive connection to a shared resource on another computer using the Windows LANtastic Net program is very easy. Select **D**rives, and the Drive Connections dialog box appears. Select the resource to which you want to connect from the A**v**ailable for Connection list, and drag and drop it on the drive letter slot you want to use in the My C**o**nnections list (see fig. 5.11). If the computer with the resource you want to use doesn't appear in the A**v**ailable for Connection list, select the Comp**u**ters button to connect to any server you want. Establishing network printer connections by selecting <u>P</u>rinters from the LANtastic Net menu is equally as easy.

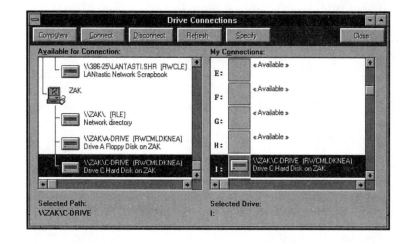

Artisoft Exchange Mail and Scheduler is the latest addition to LANtastic and is included with LANtastic at no extra charge. Like the other features of LANtastic, Exchange is an extremely powerful and flexible program but also is easy to use. Exchange Mail and Scheduler are actually two programs although Exchange Scheduler relies heavily on Exchange Mail to perform it's group scheduling features. To send an Exchange Mail message, select the <u>M</u>ail option from the LANtastic NET program menu. Exchange Mail starts. Select the compose tool, and you are prompted to select the users to whom you want to address your message. Type your message and select the Send tool, and your message is sent (see fig. 5.12).

Specifications and Requirements

LANtastic operates on any PC or compatible computer with at least 640 KB of RAM. To use LANtastic with Windows, an 80286-based computer or higher with at least 2 MB of RAM is required (4 MB is recommended).

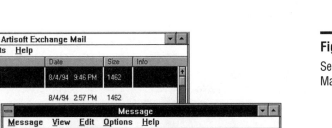

Figure 5.12
Sending an Exchange
Mail message.

A computer configured as a workstation requires between 15 KB and 30 KB of RAM depending on the configuration. A computer configured as a nondedicated server requires between 43 KB and 70 KB of RAM depending on the configuration.

LANtastic supports up to 500 users per server and requires DOS 3.1 or DOS 3.3 and higher.

Cost and Technical Support

LANtastic is available in many different software and hardware configurations.

Each computer requires a licensed copy of LANtastic and a network adapter. The LANtastic NOS and network adapters are available separately; however, Artisoft discounts the price substantially if you purchase a LANtastic starter kit or an add-on kit. The starter kit includes everything necessary to network two computers including LANtastic for two nodes, two Ethernet network adapter cards, and a 25-foot Thinnet cable and terminators. The

LANtastic add-on kit, enables you to add a node to your LANtastic network. The add-on kit includes a single-node version of LANtastic, an Ethernet network adapter, and a 25-foot Thinnet cable. Artisoft offers a 30-day, money-back guarantee on all their products and a five-year limited warranty on all hardware.

Technical support is available Monday-Friday, 7:00 a.m.–5:00 p.m. Mountain Time. Although most companies today charge for technical support, Artisoft continues their tradition of offering free technical support for all their products.

Simply LANtastic

LANtastic was designed from the start to be a powerful, yet easy to use, peer-to-peer network operating system offering features unmatched by competitors. Realizing the importance of ease of use, especially for small businesses, Artisoft introduced Simply LANtastic, which offers fewer features but is even easier to use than the award-winning LANtastic.

Simply LANtastic is a scaled-down version of the LANtastic NOS designed to implement the most widely used features of LANtastic. Intended for the small business and home office, Simply LANtastic does not include some of the security and extensive management features of LANtastic. Simply LANtastic is designed to be a powerful NOS that is easy to set up and use.

The network software included with this book is a two-node version of Simply LANtastic. Detailed information regarding the installation, use, and management of a Simply LANtastic network is discussed in Part Two.

The standard package of the Simply LANtastic NOS includes support for both DOS and Windows environments. Simply LANtastic is licensed per node, meaning you must purchase a licensed copy for each computer in your network.

The Simply LANtastic NOS is available separately or bundled with two proprietary network adapters and a cable in a starter kit. Add-on kits that include a single-node version of Simply LANtastic and a proprietary Simply LANtastic network adapter card and cable also are available.

Simply LANtastic uses 8-bit Ethernet proprietary network adapters with a special coax cable that has phone plugs on the end like those used to plug an earphone into a radio. The cabling system cannot be installed incorrectly; it is truly a "plug and play" situation. The Simply LANtastic NOS also supports many other network adapters including Artisoft's own Ethernet adapters and any other network adapter provided with NDIS drivers.

Features

Simply LANtastic includes utilities that enable you to share and use shared resources in both DOS and Windows environments. In addition, you can connect to shared resources using DOS NET command-line commands included in batch files to further simplify use of this program.

You can configure nodes in a Simply LANtastic network as workstations, nondedicated servers, or a combination of the two. Simply LANtastic nodes also can access and use the shared resources on regular LANtastic servers. Simply LANtastic supports up to 30 users per server.

Simply LANtastic does not require or support specific user accounts. The computer accessing the resource—not the user—determines restrictions to shared resources.

You can specify shared resources such as disk drives, directories, and printers in either DOS or Windows. Simply LANtastic also supports the use of a CD-ROM drive across the network.

Access restrictions for shared resources can be specified as Full access, Read-Only access, or No access. You also can specify which computers have access to a specific shared resource by placing the name of the computer in the access list for the shared resource. You can use wild cards in the access list to specify a group of computers with similar names.

Simply LANtastic includes e-mail for sending messages and attachments (including files) across the network using both the Windows and DOS interfaces. Mail created in the Windows interface is interchangeable with mail created using the DOS interface.

Simply LANtastic can operate on older XT and 286-class computers with at least 512 KB of RAM (more if running Windows).

Simply LANtastic includes an autoreconnect feature that automatically reestablishes a network connection in the event that a server is rebooted. Simply LANtastic also enables network connections to be specified but not actually established until the redirected drive or printer is accessed. Thus, the computer to be accessed can be turned off except when it is in use.

Installation

The Simply LANtastic installation program automatically searches your drive for Windows. If it finds Windows, it runs the Windows version of the installation program; otherwise it runs the DOS version of the installation program. The installation program walks you through a series of steps by asking you specific questions about how you want to configure your network node. Each question is displayed on a separate screen and includes a complete description (see fig. 5.13). Some of the information you specify during installation follows.

- The network name of your computer.

- The drive and directory in which you want to install the LANtastic software.

- If you want to share your disk drives and printers with other computers. This is how you specify if you want your computer configured as a nondedicated server or a workstation.

- The type of network adapter card installed in your computer.

- Connections to the disk drives and printers on other computers you want established when you turn on your computer.

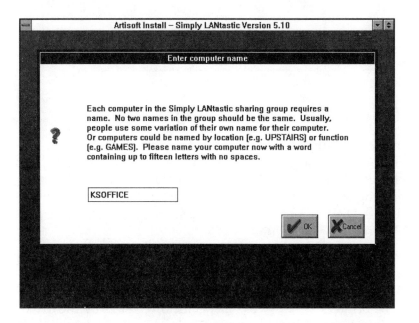

Figure 5.13
A Simply LANtastic installation screen in Windows.

After specifying the options you want installed on your Simply LANtastic node, the Simply LANtastic installation program automatically installs Simply LANtastic and configures it to your specifications. The system files on your computer (AUTOEXEC.BAT and CONFIG.SYS) are updated so when you turn on your computer, the network automatically starts with the specified configuration options. If you have Windows, the Windows configuration files are updated so you can run Windows with Simply LANtastic. After installation on a computer with Windows, the Simply LANtastic program group is created (see fig. 5.14).

The Simply LANtastic installation program automatically sets up default shared resources on each server. For example, the C-DRIVE resource name is set up to point to the physical C drive on the server. Therefore, after you install Simply LANtastic, you can use it immediately; further configuration isn't necessary.

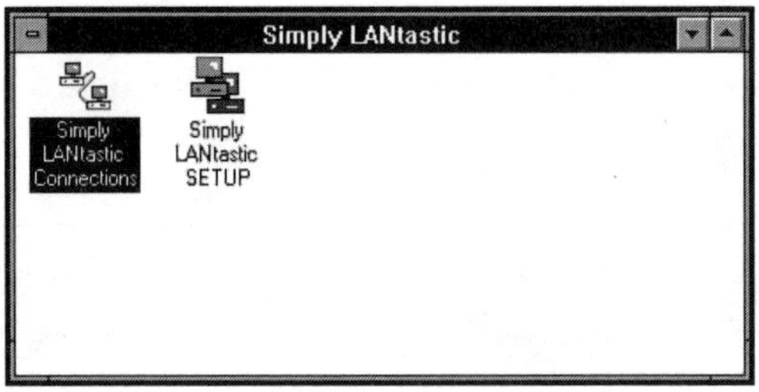

Figure 5.14

The Simply LANtastic
program group in
Windows.

Configuration and Management

The configuration and management of a Simply LANtastic network are easy and pleasant tasks. The installation program automatically defines basic shared resources for drives and printers.
The program creates a shared resource for the A floppy drive
called A-DRIVE, for example, and a shared resource named
@PRINTER for the printer.

You can define or change shared resources on each server using
the Share Drives and Printers option in the DOS or Windows
LANtastic Connections program (see fig. 5.15). Shared resources
can be printers, disk drives, or specific directories on the drives.
Simply LANtastic also supports sharing CD-ROM drives across
the network. You can use several resource names to refer to a
single printer, allowing the use of different printer setup strings.
You can, for example, set up one printer resource to print in
portrait mode and another to print in landscape mode.

Each shared resource has an Access List that determines which
computers are allowed access to the resource and the type of
access they have (see fig. 5.16). The shared resource in the figure is
a hard disk with the shared resource name C-DRIVE. The Access
List for this resource contains a list of Computer Names and the
associated Access for each.

The Access right options are Full Access, Read-Only, and No
Access. You can switch between the selections by clicking on the
Access button. In addition, you can use wild cards in the Computer Name list. In figure 15.16, SALES* refers to any computer
whose name begins with SALES, such as SALES1 or SALES-BOB.

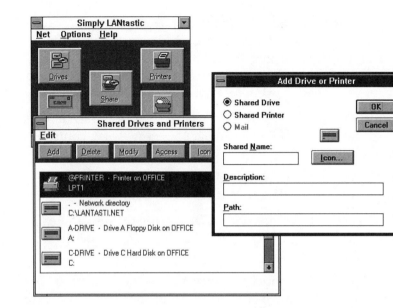

Figure 5.15

Adding a shared resource using the Simply LANtastic Connections program in Windows.

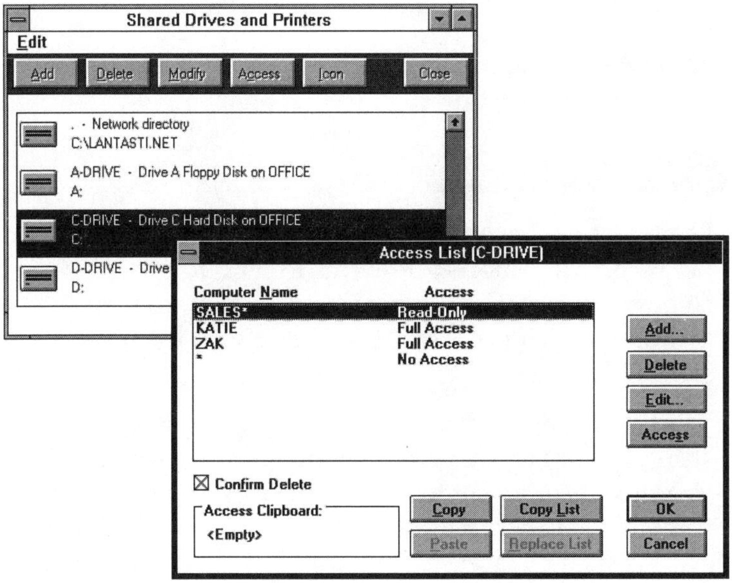

Figure 5.16

The Access List dialog box for a shared-drive resource in Windows.

Simply LANtastic provides extensive printer configuration and management features (see fig. 5.17). Each shared-printer resource has several different parameters specifying available network features. The following is a description of the parameters you can specify for each shared-printer resource:

- **Description.** A description of the shared-printer resource that is displayed when you establish printer network connections.

- **Port.** The name of the DOS device to which the printer is physically connected, such as LPT1 or COM1.

- **Send Form Feed.** Sends a form feed to the printer after each print job causing the last part of the print job to be ejected from the printer.

- **Tab Width.** The number of spaces the spooler inserts in the print job, each time it encounters a tab character. This feature is useful when the application program sends tabs to a printer that doesn't support them.

- **Paper Width.** The number of characters to be printed on a line when printing text files.

- **Lines per Page.** The number of lines printed on each page if printing standard text.

- **Characters per Second.** The minimum number of characters per second the spooler attempts to send to the printer. This setting is extremely valuable for speeding up network printing, which is normally slowed down by applications such as Windows.

- **Setup.** Clicking on this button enables you to specify a setup string to send to the printer before sending a print job, or a cleanup file or string to send to the printer after sending a print job. Setup strings sent to a printer usually perform actions such as resetting the printer, setting the printer to landscape mode, and so on.

Using Simply LANtastic

Simply LANtastic is very easy to use; it enables you to establish network connections with little effort. You can establish network connections using the DOS or Windows Simply LANtastic Connections programs, or by typing a NET command at the DOS prompt. Start the DOS Simply LANtastic Connections program by typing **NET** at the DOS prompt. It performs the same functions as the Windows Simply LANtastic Connections program. Following is a description of the selections on the Windows Simply LANtastic Connections program menu (see fig. 5.18):

- **Share.** Enables you to set up and configure shared resources for the server as described in the previous section.

- **Drives.** Establishes network connections to shared-drive resources on other computers.

- **Printers.** Establishes network connections to shared-printer resources on other computers.

- **Mail.** Enables you to send and receive Simply LANtastic Mail.

- **Jobs.** Enables you to view and manage print jobs in a server's queue.

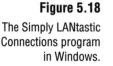

Figure 5.18

The Simply LANtastic
Connections program
in Windows.

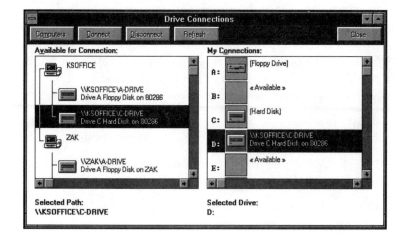

Establishing a drive connection to a shared resource on another computer using the Windows Simply LANtastic Connections program is very easy. Select **D**rives, and the Drive Connections dialog box appears. Select the resource to which you want to connect from the A**v**ailable for Connection list, and drag and drop it on the chosen drive letter slot in the My C**o**nnections list (see fig. 5.19). If the computer that has the resource you want to use doesn't appear in the A**v**ailable for Connection list, select the Co**m**puters button to connect to any server you want. Establish network printer connections in a similar manner by selecting **P**rinters from the Simply LANtastic Connections program menu.

Figure 5.19

Establishing network
drive connections
using the Simply
LANtastic
Connections program
in Windows.

Sending and receiving Simply LANtastic Mail is as simple as selecting **M**ail from the Simply LANtastic Connections program menu. The My Mail dialog box displays mail sent to you in the Incoming Mail list and mail you sent to others in the Outgoing Mail list (see fig. 5.20). To read mail, select the item you want to read and then select the **R**ead button. To send mail, select the **T**ext button if you want to type your message, or press the **F**ile button if you want to send a file.

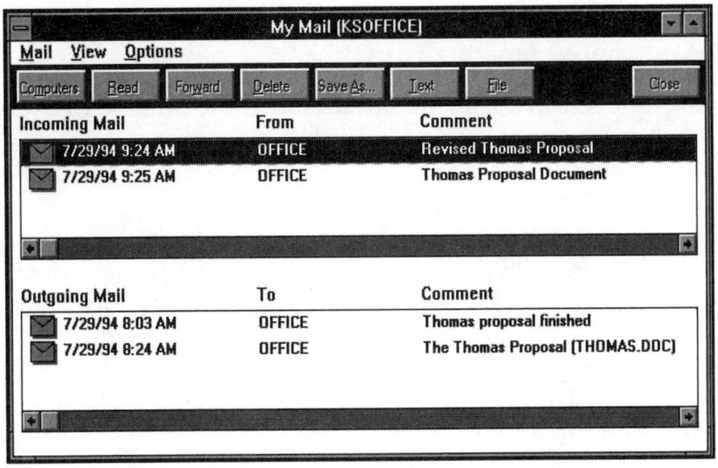

Figure 5.20

Sending and receiving mail using Simply LANtastic in Windows.

Specifications and Requirements

Simply LANtastic operates on any PC or compatible computer with at least 512 KB of RAM. To use LANtastic with Windows, an 80286-based computer or higher with at least 2 MB of RAM is required (4 MB is recommended).

A computer configured as a workstation requires 15 KB of RAM. A computer configured as a nondedicated server requires 43 KB of RAM.

Simply LANtastic supports up to 30 users per server. You can connect a maximum of 20 computers if you're using Simply LANtastic adapters.

Simply LANtastic requires DOS 3.1 or DOS 3.3 and higher.

Available Configurations and Technical Support

Artisoft has done an admirable job of bringing powerful yet easy to use network products to the workplace at an affordable price.

The Simply LANtastic NOS software is licensed per node, meaning each computer must have a separate licensed copy of the software. The Simply LANtastic software included in this book is a two-node version that is worth several times the cost of this book if purchased separately.

The Simply LANtastic Starter Kit includes the Simply LANtastic NOS for two nodes, two Simply LANtastic network adapters, and a 25-foot cable.

Included with this book is a coupon you can use to order two Simply LANtastic network adapters from Artisoft for $120. With the Simply LANtastic software included with this book and the network adapters, you can set up a complete two-station Simply LANtastic network for less than $150!

Simply LANtastic Add-On Kits are used to add another node to your Simply LANtastic network. Simply LANtastic Add-On Kits include a Simply LANtastic network adapter, a single-node version of the Simply LANtastic software, and a 25-foot cable.

Artisoft offers a 30-day, money-back guarantee on all their products and a five-year limited warranty on all hardware.

Technical support is available Monday-Friday, 7:00 a.m.–5:00 p.m. Mountain Time. Unlike many networking companies that offer free technical support for only a short time and then begin charging, Artisoft offers free lifetime technical support for all their products.

Personal NetWare

Personal NetWare is networking giant Novell's answer to a peer-to-peer network. Replacing Novell's NetWare Lite peer-to-peer NOS, Personal NetWare includes several features that make it interoperable with Novell's entire NetWare product line.

Personal NetWare is licensed per node, meaning you must purchase a licensed copy for each computer in your network. Personal NetWare is available in a single-node version and a five-node version.

Novell DOS 7 includes Personal NetWare, enabling you to implement a peer-to-peer network simply by adding a network adapter card to each computer running Novell DOS 7.

Features

Personal NetWare operates under DOS and Windows and includes both DOS and Windows utility programs for establishing network connections and managing network users and shared resources. You can configure nodes in a Personal NetWare network as either workstations or nondedicated servers.

Personal NetWare offers a feature called Single-Network View that combines all the user accounts and shared resources on each server in a single database that is duplicated on every server.

With Single-Network View, a user logs in to the network once to automatically connect to every server on the network. Management is simplified because user accounts need to be set up only once. Because user accounts are duplicated on every server, if a server is turned off, the user account information is still available on the remaining nodes. User account restrictions enable you to control the time of day of logins, set password and password expiration dates, and disable user accounts.

You can view all shared resources available on the network with Single-Network View after you log in. Accessing and using shared resources also is simplified because all available shared resources are visible from a single screen; you don't have to access each server manually to see the shared resources on that server. Full, Read-Only, Write-Only, and No rights control access to resources.

Network nodes running Personal NetWare can log in to and access directly NetWare servers running NetWare 2.*x*, 3.*x*, or 4.*x*. The Personal NetWare client software enables you to start with an inexpensive Personal NetWare network, and, when the time is right, add or convert an existing station to a NetWare 2.*x*, 3.*x*, or 4.*x* server. You do not have to make any changes to the other nodes in the network running Personal NetWare. Each Personal NetWare node then can access the NetWare 2.*x*, 3.*x*, or 4.*x* server in addition to the Personal NetWare nondedicated servers.

You can conserve server memory by disabling unnecessary services such as print sharing, file sharing, security, and diagnostics.

Novell's *NetWare Management System* (NMS) supports server management in Personal NetWare. NMS provides a graphical view of the network and monitors the network for any problems. Personal NetWare also supports *Simple Network Management Protocol* (SNMP), used in several management utilities from other manufacturers.

Personal NetWare includes *Client Virtual Loadable Modules* (VLMs) that enable the addition of future network services without replacing software. In addition, you can load VLMs in the standard, expanded, or extended memory of a computer to free additional memory for DOS applications. VLMs automatically detect and use the different types of memory on each computer, thereby saving conventional memory for DOS applications.

An autoreconnect feature automatically reestablishes a network connection if a server is turned off or rebooted.

Specifications and Requirements

Each Personal NetWare server supports up to 50 workstations and as many as 50 server connections.

Personal NetWare uses approximately 92 KB of RAM when configured as a workstation and 145 KB of RAM when configured as a nondedicated server.

Personal NetWare can operate on older XT and 286 class computers with at least 640 KB of RAM.

DR DOS 6.0 or higher, or MS-DOS 3.0 or higher, is required.

Technical Support

Novell offers 24-hours-a-day, 7-days-a-week technical support. Free, unlimited technical support is offered for the first 30 days after purchase.

Comparison

Advantages:

Strong support of NetWare 2.*x*, 3.*x*, and 4.*x* makes Personal NetWare a peer-to-peer network that can grow as your network grows.

The usage and capabilities of VLMs make a strong argument in favor of Personal NetWare, especially their capability to free precious conventional memory by being loaded into expanded and extended memory.

Personal NetWare is bundled with Novell DOS 7, making it a giveaway if you plan to upgrade to Novell DOS 7.

Disadvantages:

Personal NetWare is a first-generation product; it needs some polishing from Novell to be on par with some of the other NOSs discussed in this chapter.

The Windows interface is weak compared to the other peer-to-peer networks.

Neither electronic mail nor scheduling is included in the standard package as it is with the other peer-to-peer networks.

Windows for Workgroups

Microsoft Windows for Workgroups is a Windows-based peer-to-peer network. All network connections and management are performed in Windows. You can think of Windows for Workgroups as Microsoft Windows with a few added features that enable connected computers to use shared resources. In fact, if you are familiar with Windows, the migration to Windows for Workgroups is extremely easy.

Windows for Workgroups is an enhancement to standard Windows, providing 32-bit operation for faster file access and network operation. Because of the performance improvements over standard Windows, many manufacturers include Windows for Workgroups (without the network features enabled) with their stand-alone systems in place of standard Windows.

Later, you can purchase network adapters and cable to create a functioning Windows for Workgroups network.

Computers connected in a Windows for Workgroups network are organized into workgroups. A workgroup is given a name and usually consists of a group of computers in the same department or with a similar function that typically need to share information and resources. That's not to say a computer in one workgroup can't share resources with a computer in another workgroup. Workgroups are simply a way to organize the computers in the network, and do not impose restrictions on the accessibility of a computer to shared resources. You might have a workgroup called ACCOUNTING, for example, that is comprised of all the computers in the accounting department. Another workgroup called MARKETING includes all the computers in the marketing department. Although the computers in accounting rarely need to communicate with the computers in marketing, if a user in accounting wants to use a laser printer in marketing, he or she can connect to the laser printer the same way he makes a connection to a shared resource in the same workgroup.

Microsoft Windows for Workgroups is licensed per node, meaning you must purchase a licensed copy for each computer in your network, and is available in three different configurations: the full Microsoft Windows for Workgroups package, the Microsoft Workgroup Add-on for Windows, and the Microsoft Workgroup Add-on for MS-DOS. The full Microsoft Windows for Workgroups package includes the software for a single node on the network. The Microsoft Workgroup Add-on for Windows enables users to upgrade if they are currently running Windows or a earlier version of Windows for Workgroups. The Microsoft Workgroup Add-on for MS-DOS enables computers running DOS to be configured as a server or client. In this manner, the computers can share resources with, or use shared resources on, other computers running Windows for Workgroups or the Workgroup Add-on for MS-DOS.

Features

You can configure nodes running Windows for Workgroups as either workstations or nondedicated servers.

Windows for Workgroups includes multiprotocol support and can access servers using other NOSs including Novell NetWare, Microsoft Windows NT Server, Microsoft LAN Manager, and Novell NetWare 2.x, 3.x, and 4.x.

Windows for Workgroups comes bundled with several useful programs and utilities. Microsoft Mail is included for sending, receiving, and managing electronic mail, and Microsoft Schedule provides individual and group scheduling functions. The WinMeter utility enables users to monitor their PC's utilization by local applications. as well as network requests. The Net Watcher utility enables users to see who is connected to their PC and what shared resources are being accessed. The Chat utility enables two users to carry on a chat session by typing information on their keyboards. The information from one participant is immediately displayed in a window on the other's computer.

Network DDE is supported by the Clipbook Viewer. You can save and store in the Clipbook Viewer, which other users may access and use, items normally contained in the Windows Clipboard. In the Clipbook Viewer, you can cut and paste DDE links across the network the same way the Windows Clipboard is used on a local computer.

Windows for Workgroups has NDIS support to ensure compatibility with nearly all currently manufactured network adapters as well as to provide access to other network transport protocols including TCP/IP, XNS (Xerox Network System), and others.

Individual user accounts are set up on each computer. When Windows for Workgroups is first started, you are required to enter a user name and password to gain access to the computer, which in turn enables you to access all the shared resources on the network. Multiple user names and passwords can exist on the same computer.

Shared resources allow three types of access: Read-Only, Full, and Depends on Password. The Depends on Password option enables you to specify a Read-Only password or a Full Access password. The first time a user connects to a shared resource that requires a password, the password for that user is added to the user's password list. Therefore, subsequent connections by this user to the shared resource won't require the password.

Installation

Installing Windows for Workgroups is an easy task and is almost identical to a standard Windows installation with a few additional steps for network support.

To start the Windows for Workgroups installation program, place the setup disk in drive A and at the DOS prompt type **A:SETUP**, and the installation program starts.

As with Windows, you can choose between the Custom and the Express setup. Unless you want to specify the programs and Windows features to install, select the Express setup. Some of the information Windows for Workgroups permits you to specify during installation is as follows:

- The installation drive and directory where Windows for Workgroups is to be installed. The default is C:\WINDOWS.

- Your name.

- The network name for your computer.

- The name of the workgroup to which you want your computer to belong.

- The type of network adapter installed in your computer as well as any necessary configuration settings such as the IRQ (Interupt ReQuest) value and the base *input/output* (I/O) address.

- Any additional protocols or networks you want access to, including Novell NetWare and Microsoft LAN Manager.

When you install Windows for Workgroups, if your computer is powerful enough to operate as a server (at least an 80386SX computer with 3 MB RAM), it automatically is configured as a peer (nondedicated server/workstation). Otherwise, it's configured as a client only and is not able to share its resources with other computers.

If your computer is configured as a peer, the installation program does not set up any shared resources; you need to specify them later.

When you finish the installation process, you are prompted to reboot your computer before starting Windows for Workgroups. The installation program automatically changes your system files CONFIG.SYS and AUTOEXEC.BAT to include the necessary commands to run Windows for Workgroups.

To start Windows for Workgroups after installation, type WIN at the DOS prompt. Notice how Windows for Workgroups Program Manager looks like the standard Windows Program Manager screen you are accustomed to (see fig. 5.21).

Figure 5.21

The Windows for
Workgroups Program
Manager.

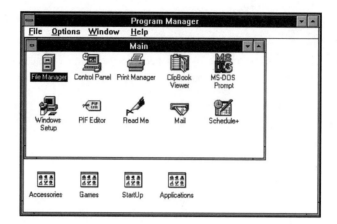

Configuration and Management

After you install Windows for Workgroups, you need to specify
any drives, directories, and printers you want to share with
others. The installation program does not assume you want to
share any resources. However, specifying shared drive, directory,
and printer resources is not difficult.

You specify shared drives and directories using the Windows for
Workgroups File Manager program. File Manager in Windows for
Workgroups has been enhanced over the standard Windows
version to include network features that enable you to share
drives and directories and easily establish network connections to
shared drive and directory resources on other computers.

To specify a shared drive or directory, select the drive or directory
you want to share from the list. Then select the Share icon, which
appears as a hand holding a folder. The Share Directory dialog
box appears, enabling you to specify the information for the
shared resource (see fig. 5.22).

The **S**hare Name field contains the name of the shared resource as
it appears to other computers in the network. The **P**ath is the
actual drive or directory you are to share. The Access Type for the
shared resource may be **R**ead-Only, **F**ull, or **D**epends on Password. (If you want to specify a password for Read-Only or Full
access, select **D**epends on Password.)

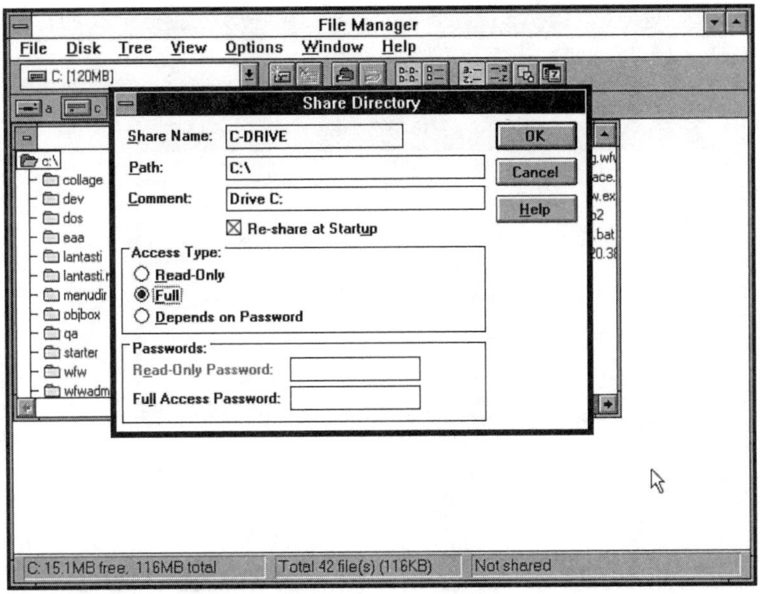

Figure 5.22

Sharing a drive or
directory resource in
Windows for
Workgroups.

Selecting the Re-share at Startup option causes the resource
specified to be shared automatically each time you start Windows
for Workgroups. If you don't select this option, the resource
specified is shared for only the current session.

After you specify the shared-drive resources, for any shared
resources the file folder icons appear as hands holding a file folder
(see fig. 5.23).

Specifying a shared-printer resource is similar to specifying a
shared-drive resource, except the shared-printer resource is
specified in the Print Manager program. The Windows for
Workgroups Print Manager—enhanced over the standard Windows version—provides features for sharing and using shared-
printer resources.

To specify a shared-printer resource, after selecting the printer to
be shared, select the icon that appears as a hand holding a printer.
The Share Printer dialog box appears. Type the shared resource
name for the printer in the Share as text box (see fig. 5.24). After a
printer becomes shared, an icon that looks like a hand holding a
printer appears next to the printer name in the Print Manager list.

Figure 5.23

The Windows for
Workgroups File
Manager program
showing the shared
resources.

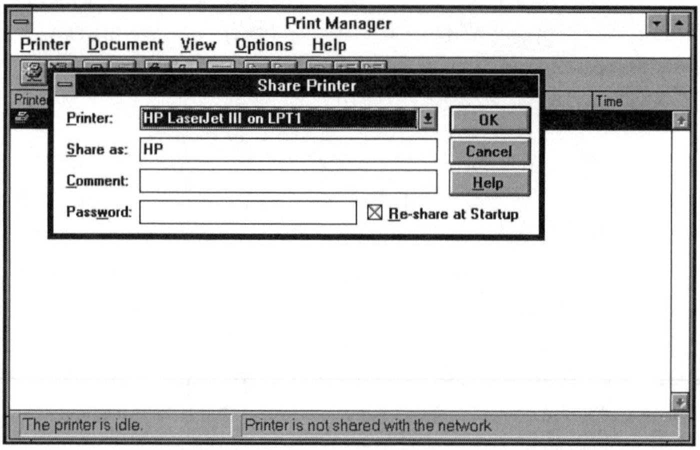

Figure 5.23

The Windows for Workgroups File Manager program showing the shared resources.

Figure 5.24

Specifying a shared-
printer resource in
Windows for
Workgroups Print
Manger.

Figure 5.24

Specifying a shared-printer resource in Windows for Workgroups Print Manger.

Using Windows for Workgroups

Establishing connections to network drives and printers is a simple task in Windows for Workgroups. Use the File Manager program to establish network drive connections and the Print Manager program for network printer connections.

To connect to a network drive in File Manager, select the icon that appears as a drive, and the Connect Network Drive dialog box appears (see fig. 5.25). The various workgroups and the computers in the workgroup appear in the **S**how Shared Directories on list. Selecting a specific computer from the list causes the shared drive or directory resources for that computer to appear in the Shared Directories on list. Select from the **D**rive selection field the drive you want to redirect to the shared resource. If you want to establish this connection each time you start Windows for Workgroups, select the Reconnect at Startup option. Otherwise, the connection exists for this session only.

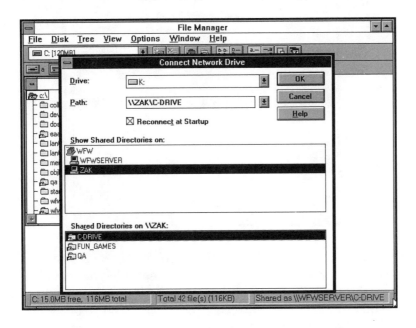

Figure 5.25

Establishing a network drive connection in Windows for Workgroups using File Manager.

After you establish network drive connections, the redirected drives appear as icons next to the icons representing the physical drive on your computer.

To establish network printer connections using Print Manager, select the icon that appears as a printer connected to a network cable. The Connect Network Printer dialog box appears (see fig. 5.26). The various workgroups and the computers in the workgroup appear in the **S**how Shared Printers on list. Selecting a specific computer from the list causes the shared-printer resources for the selected computer to appear in the Sha**r**ed Printers on list. Select from the **D**evice Name selection field the device you want to redirect to the shared resource. If you want to establish this connection each time you start Windows for Workgroups, select the Reconnec**t** at Startup option. Otherwise the connection is established for this session only.

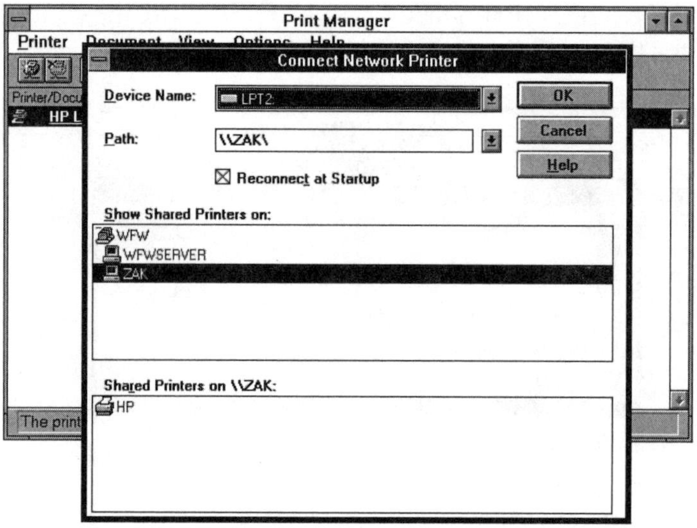

Figure 5.26

Establishing a network printer connection in Windows for Workgroups Print Manager.

Microsoft Mail and Schedule are sophisticated, yet easy to use, programs that enable you to send and receive electronic mail as well as perform individual and group scheduling functions. With Mail you can incorporate objects (files, charts, and so on) into your mail messages using *Object Linking and Embedding* (OLE) technology. OLE enables you to place objects in your message which the recipient may select to start an application to view a spreadsheet file, for example. Sending a message in Mail is as easy as selecting the Compose icon, specifying to whom you're sending the message, typing the message, and selecting the **S**end button (see fig. 5.27).

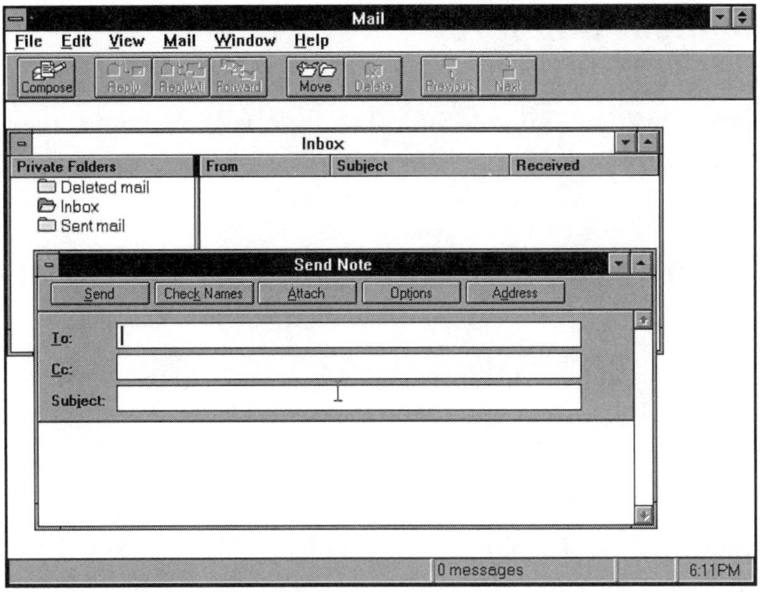

Figure 5.27
Sending a message in
Windows for
Workgroups Mail.

Schedule enables you to easily schedule your own time as well as
schedule meetings to which others are invited. Schedule simplifies
scheduling group meetings because it can identify times at which
meeting participants are available.

Specifications and Requirements

Full-peer operations (those able to share resources) require a
computer with an 80386SX or higher processor and a minimum of
3 MB of memory. (A computer with 2 MB of memory can operate
as a client only.)

Using the Workgroup Add-on for MS-DOS, an XT or 286 can
access shared resources and share resources in the DOS environment. The redirector program uses either 11 KB or 88 KB of
conventional memory depending on its features (11 KB for basic
access to shared files and printers, and 88 KB for features including Mail access). The server program requires an additional 22 KB
of conventional memory.

DOS 3.3 or higher is required.

Technical Support

Technical support is available Monday-Friday, 9:00 a.m.–9:00 p.m. Eastern Time. Unlimited technical support is available for the first 90 days. After that, Microsoft charges you for support.

Comparison

Advantages:

Microsoft Windows for Workgroups is an easy to use network offering for the Windows user an especially smooth transition to a networking environment.

Disadvantages:

Windows for Workgroups requires at least a 386-based PC or better with a minimum of 3 MB of RAM for a node to operate as a server, and 2 MB of RAM for a node to operate as a workstation (client). The standard package does not support XT or 286 computers.

POWERLan

Performance Technology's POWERLan is an extremely capable peer-to-peer network offering features and capabilities on the same caliber as the leading peer-to-peer network LANtastic. Included with POWERLan are utilities that enable network connections and management in both DOS and Windows.

POWERLan is available in several software configurations including a two-user starter pack, a single-user add-on, and a five-user pack. Also available is a five-user pack that includes the POWERserve dedicated server product and a five-user mail program called DaVinci eMAIL. Ten- and 20-user add-on packs, as well as unlimited user packs supporting up to 255 computers, are available.

POWERserve is a 32-bit dedicated server product that maximizes the performance of a node configured as a dedicated server in a POWERLan network. You can purchase POWERserve as an add-on to POWERLan.

POWERbridge is a separately available product that enables you to connect multiple LANs independent of their topologies. POWERbridge can extend the 255-computer limitation of a POWERLan network.

POWERfusion, another separately available product, provides access to UNIX-based computers.

Features

You can configure nodes in a POWERLan network as workstations, nondedicated servers, dedicated servers, or any combination thereof.

Use the DOS or Windows interface to set up and manage user accounts. You can configure each user account with password protection. You can set an expiration date for an account and the time of day that an account is allowed to log in to the network. You also can create group accounts to be used, for example, by all the users in one department within a company.

Another powerful feature of POWERLan is its user database. The user database exists on every server and is duplicated automatically. Each time an account is added, modified, or deleted, the user database on each POWERLan server is updated with the changes. The user database enables a user to log in to the network once rather than log in to each server that has a resource to access.

Shared resources are defined on each server using either the DOS or Windows interface. Shared resources can be disk drives, specific directories on each drive, and printers. Support for sharing CD-ROM drives also is included. Shared resources also can be password protected, requiring a password to gain access to the shared resource.

POWERLan also has very strong support for shared-printer resources. In addition to specifying individual network printers to which to send a print job, you can group printers into pools (also called classes) and send print jobs to a printer class. Suppose you have three laser printers in your office. You can group those three printers into a class. If you select the class to print to, when you print from an application program, the printed output is sent to any available printer in that class.

Additional printing features supported include immediate despooling that allows printing to begin before the application program finishes sending the print job to the printer. You also can share printers that are connected to workstations with the rest of the network.

Connecting to network drives and printers is accomplished by selecting a plug from an available drive letter or printer port and plugging it into a shared resource represented as an electrical outlet.

You can minimize the POWERLan Print Manager in Windows to an icon that displays the number of print jobs in the queue and the status of your print job while you're working in another application.

The users, groups, and shared resources on a server can be managed from any computer on the network. Cloning users eases the setup requirements for new users. When a user is cloned, the properties and privileges of the new user account are duplicated from the user account from which they were cloned.

POWERLan provides a connection to Microsoft networks using the SMB protocol. Connectivity to Novell NetWare also is provided, enabling users to connect to NetWare servers and POWERLan servers using the same interface. The interface displays both NetWare and POWERLan resources. POWERLan also supports NDIS and *Open Datalink Interface* (ODI). This flexibility ensures support for most network adapter cards, including Ethernet, ARCnet, and Token Ring.

Also available with POWERLan is DaVinci eMAIL, a powerful electronic mail package for sending mail and attachments to other users.

Specifications and Requirements

POWERLan operates on any IBM-compatible PC. For POWERLan to run as a dedicated server using POWERserve, a 386-based PC or better with at least 640 KB of RAM (more if running Windows) is required.

POWERLan uses approximately 15 KB of RAM when configured as a workstation and 35 KB of RAM when configured as a nondedicated server.

Up to 255 users are supported per server. DOS 3.3 and higher is required.

Technical Support

Technical support is available Monday-Friday, 10:00 a.m.–6:00 p.m. Eastern Time.

Comparison

POWERLan is an extremely powerful peer-to-peer network offering an extensive feature set. Of the networks discussed in this chapter, only peer-to-peer leader LANtastic offers the same broad range of features and flexibility.

Summary

In this chapter, you learned about the factors to consider when choosing a peer-to-peer network as well as the general features of five of the most popular peer-to-peer networks. The features of

Artisoft LANtastic, Artisoft Simply LANtastic, Novell Personal NetWare, Microsoft Windows for Workgroups, and Performance Technology POWERLan were discussed.

LANtastic is the leading peer-to-peer network by which all other networks are judged. Simply LANtastic is very easy to set up and use, but doesn't offer the broad range of features that LANtastic does. Novell's Personal NetWare offers good support for connecting to NetWare servers but has a weak Windows interface and, as a first-generation product, lacks many of the features of LANtastic and will require time to acquire some of the polishing touches associated with a mature NOS. Microsoft's Windows for Workgroups offers an excellent Windows interface and is easy to use, but requires a 386-based computer with 3 MB of RAM for peer-to-peer operation and doesn't include support for computers running DOS in the standard package. The features available in Windows for Workgroups are only a small subset of those available in LANtastic. Performance Technology's POWERLan is the only peer-to-peer network offering a feature set of the same caliber as LANtastic.

In This Chapter. . .

This chapter discusses the general features of server-based networks and points to consider when evaluating a server-based network. Chapter 2, "Network Nodes and Their Function," introduced the concepts of peer-to-peer and server-based networks and compared the benefits and possible disadvantages of each. This chapter takes the server-based network concept one step further by looking at some of the specific features and capabilities of the following six most popular server-based networks:

- Novell NetWare 2.2
- Novell NetWare 3.*x*
- Novell NetWare 4.*x*
- Microsoft Windows NT Server
- Microsoft LAN Manager
- IBM OS/2 LAN Server

This chapter also introduces the following terms:

Enterprise network

RAID

Disk mirroring

Disk duplexing

Server-Based Networks

As discussed in Chapter 2, "Network Nodes and Their Function," server-based networks usually incorporate one or more dedicated servers, which may be accessed by workstations (clients). A *server-based network* is often referred to as client-server, indicating that the server shares its resources with others while the client uses the shared resources on the dedicated server.

Whereas peer-to-peer networks offer more flexibility with resource sharing by enabling every computer in the network to access every other computer, the same flexibility can turn into an administrative nightmare if your network has a large number of nodes. Many peer-to-peer networks now include features that make them appealing to larger network installations with many nodes. And it also is true that server-based networks are becoming easier to use and include features found in peer-to-peer networks. Nevertheless, peer-to-peer and server-based networks appeal to substantially different markets.

A server-based network typically is comprised of powerful dedicated servers with large hard disk drives often supporting several hundred nodes. Unlike the *network operating system* (NOS) found in most peer-to-peer networks that sit on top of DOS, the server-based NOS usually takes advantage of the powerful features of 32-bit microprocessors such as the 80386 and 80486. The dedicated server's NOS either replaces the existing operating system, such as DOS, with the 32-bit NOS or is based on a 32-bit operating system, such as IBM's OS/2 or Microsoft Windows NT. The client software is installed on each workstation and resides with the operating system's software, allowing the node to access and use each server's shared resources.

Because server-based networks frequently are connected to a *wide area network* (WAN), in general they tend to overshadow their peer-to-peer counterparts by their widespread support of different networks, operating systems, and network protocols. For example, even the oldest server-based NOS discussed in this chapter has support for Macintosh, UNIX, and OS/2 environments.

Supporting a large number of network nodes adds several more requirements to the NOS. Security is a major requirement—the security of the data from unauthorized access and protection against accidental loss of valuable information. Several fault-tolerant data-protection schemes protect against the accidental loss of valuable information on hard disks. A data duplication scheme known as *Redundant Array of Inexpensive Disks* (RAID) uses multiple disk drives and different methods to duplicate the information from one drive to another so in the event of a drive failure, another drive with the same information may be used.

To protect against the loss of data, most server-based networks incorporate RAID or another similar method of writing information to multiple drives concurrently. One form of RAID (RAID 1)—often referred to as *disk mirroring*—causes all data to be written to two different drives, so the data on the two drives are identical. Disk duplexing actually duplicates the entire disk-drive hardware channel, which includes both the disk drive and the drive controller. Disk duplexing additionally protects against data loss caused by faulty disk drive controllers.

Another feature found in some of the more powerful server-based networks—including Novell NetWare—is the ability to use multiple disk drives to store and transparently access data files that are larger than the storage capacity of a single drive.

The following sections describe some of the factors you should consider to determine which NOS suits your needs and the primary features available in the most popular server-based networks.

Evaluating Server-Based NOSs

Many of the same factors used to evaluate peer-to-peer networks will assist you in determining the best server-based network for your needs. Server-based networks appeal to different markets and serve different needs than peer-to-peer networks, therefore you'll find additional factors to consider than those used when evaluating peer-to-peer networks. In addition, you may find that you are thinking about the same factors in a different way when evaluating server-based networks. Carefully consider the following points before choosing a server-based network for your situation:

- **Features.** The features available in a server-based NOS may seem a little overwhelming at first. Before evaluating the features available with each NOS, you need to determine your needs; what features do you require? Then look at the features available with the NOS you are evaluating. From the list of features available, identify those that provide solutions to your requirements. Also, identify the requirements on your list that the NOS you are evaluating cannot meet.

- **Consultants and System Integrators.** In the process of planning for and evaluating server-based networks, at some point you need to decide whether you feel comfortable evaluating your needs and implementing a solution yourself, or prefer to seek help from another source. If your network will be relatively small, then you may feel comfortable doing everything yourself. If, however, your network is very large, it may be wise to seek the services of a professional.

Consultants can help you plan and implement your network. A *system integrator* is a person or group of persons with the skills and experience necessary to successfully implement your network by taking the hardware and software pieces available from several manufacturers and making them all work together. A consultant helps you plan your network and a system integrator turns your plans into reality. Often a consultant's and systems integrator's functions overlap and, in many cases, the consultant is the same individual or company as the system integrator.

If you require the services of a professional, expect to pay for those services from the start. Whereas you may find a knowledgeable person to answer your questions on the sales floor of a computer store, chances are that person does not have the knowledge or experience to provide the assistance you require. It's okay to ask questions of the salesperson, but eventually you need to seek the advice of a professional.

Before putting your important network project in the hands of a consultant or system integrator, be sure to establish the qualifications of the person you will be hiring. Factors to consider are experience, compatibity with others in your company, and references.

Do not make the mistake of assuming a salesperson is a consultant. Unfortunately, salespeople sometimes appear to have a great deal of knowledge when in reality their experience is limited. A professional consultant, on the other hand, will take the time to listen to your requirements, ask you several questions, and evaluate your requirements thoroughly before suggesting solutions.

- **Installation.** If you will be installing the network hardware and software, an important consideration is the ease of installation. How difficult will the installation be? What questions will have to be answered to successfully install the network? How do you determine the answers? What if you change your mind later? And, how comfortable are you with the whole concept of installing everything yourself?

  If a professional will be installing your network, then the ease of installation doesn't necessarily concern you. It's still very important, though, that the person(s) you hire has the proper experience and qualifications to successfully perform the installation.

- **Configuration Options.** Immediately after the network is installed, you will most likely want to set up specific user accounts and shared resources on your server. If someone other than yourself is installing your network, you probably want them to do the initial setup while you observe so you can add, modify, or remove users and shared resources at a later date. Carefully consider the options available for setting up shared resources and user accounts. You want to know the access restrictions that may be imposed on user accounts and shared resources. In addition, you want to be able to change any restrictions that have been specified as your requirements change.

- **Management and Maintenance Options.** As your network grows, management and maintenance options become increasingly important. You want to be able to change specific parameters for user accounts such as the time of day a specific account is allowed to access the network or perhaps how often a password must be changed. You want to know what features are available to help save you time specifying which users may access a particular shared resource and the type of access the account may have.

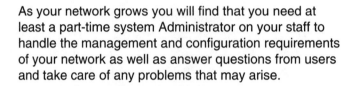

As your network grows you will find that you need at least a part-time system Administrator on your staff to handle the management and configuration requirements of your network as well as answer questions from users and take care of any problems that may arise.

You also want to find out what kind of maintenance is required and the features available to aid in performing routine maintenance. For example, are there steps you must perform to check the validity of the data on the server's hard disk? Or, will the network slow down as users access more and more data from the server? Will someone have to organize the data on the server or will the NOS automatically take care of that?

- **Ease of Use.** Even in a complex network, ease of use is critical. You need to make sure the network you choose is easy for your users to understand and use. At the very least, you want to make sure you can configure the network in such a way that you can tell each user what they need to do to use the network. For example, you may have chosen to redirect drive K to point to a resource on the server used for storing all your data files when each computer is booted. In this situation you may tell each user, "Whenever you open or save a file make sure you use drive K. That way all your data is stored in a common location so others may access it and we can back it up."

- **Cost.** Cost is always a concern. At some point, the cost to implement a network exceeds the benefits obtained by having one. When figuring the cost of your network, in addition to the cost of the network hardware and software, include the cost of planning, installation, and the ongoing support required. If you will perform these tasks yourself, put a value on your time; if it takes you eight hours to install what it would take a professional two hours to install, unless you place a low value on your time, having a professional install your network might cost you less.

After you determine how much a network will cost, determine how much it will save you. By not having to buy a larger hard disk in each computer or having to purchase a laser printer for each computer you have an immediate cost savings. Also, try to assign a value associated with the increased productivity obtained by having a network. If the savings obtained by having a network never outweigh the cost incurred, maybe you are installing a network for the wrong reason.

- **Flexibility.** As your needs change or as you replace computers and components in your network, the network must be flexible enough to adapt to the changes. A server-based network isn't as flexible in its ability to share resources on all computers in a network as peer-to-peer networks are so you need to carefully consider issues related to flexibility. Some of the questions you may ask yourself to determine how flexible your network really is are as follows:

  As your needs change, how flexible is the network to meet your new requirements?

  If you previously configured a node as a workstation and now want to use it as a dedicated server, how easy will the conversion be? Can you have more than one dedicated server in your network?

  How easy is it to share a newly added printer in the network? Does it have to be connected to the server or are there features that enable you to access it if it's connected to a workstation?

  Can users access a CD-ROM drive across the network?

- **Expandability.** As you anticipate growth in your business, it's important to know if and how your network will grow with you. As new computers are added to the network, you need to know what equipment is required and any limitations or restrictions for adding new equipment. How many nodes will the network support? What if you want to connect two separate networks? How many dedicated servers can exist?

- **Interoperability.** If you need to access nodes on different networks, find out what kind of support is available for your network. To access a mainframe or minicomputer running the UNIX operating system, your network probably needs to support the *Transmission Control Protocol/Internet Protocol* (TCP/IP). To access servers on other types of networks, your NOS needs to have the appropriate support.

- **Security.** When evaluating peer-to-peer networks, you have to determine whether security is a required feature. Because server-based networks typically have many nodes and users, network security features always are part of the NOS, although each server-based NOS incorporates security differently. All server-based networks have security features built in, including password protection of user accounts and restrictions on the access of shared resources.

  When evaluating a NOS, it's important to understand what security features are available for restricting access of specific users or restricting access to selected shared resources.

- **Fault Tolerance.** The bigger your network is, the more important fault tolerance becomes. When planning your network, you need to consider the following questions:

  What happens if a node or a component in the network fails? Does the entire network become disabled?

  What features are available to help reduce the risk of losing valuable information in the event of a hardware failure?

Are there features such as disk mirroring or duplexing that reduce the chance of losing data in the event of a disk failure?

What kind of backup procedures are available and how are they implemented?

The answers to these questions will take you a long way toward understanding the effect of a failure on your network and the data shared by the network nodes.

- **Stability.** Unfortunately, even powerful expensive server-based NOSs are released before all the bugs are worked out. You should carefully consider how long the product has been on the market and whether there have been any maintenance releases to this version indicating that problems discovered have been corrected.

Most software, including NOSs, use version numbers to distinguish between the different software releases. Major releases that include significant changes in the features and operation usually are indicated by a number such as 4.0 or 5.0. Minor releases that add relatively simple features or capabilities are indicated by a number such as 4.1 or 5.1. Minor releases often include fixes to problems (bug fixes) in addition to new features. Maintenance releases or bug fixes correct problems discovered in the software and are indicated by a number such as 4.01, 5.11, or 6.1A.

- **Technical Support.** Check on the technical support policies of the company before choosing a network. If you encounter problems, you want to know what technical support is available, when it's available, and how much it costs. Each network company has a different policy for technical support.

Many companies now charge you for technical support of their product. As ridiculous as it may sound, they usually charge even if the problem you are having is a result of a bug in their software.

- **Guarantee.** If, after installing your network, you discover it doesn't work for your situation, you'll want to know what kind of a guarantee you have on your purchase. Some companies offer a no-questions-asked money-back guarantee on your purchase of network hardware and software within a specified amount of time.

Novell NetWare

Novell is the world leader in NOSs and commands over 60 percent of the market. First introduced in 1983, NetWare has progressed through several names and versions. Advanced NetWare 1.0 and Advanced NetWare 1.2, both introduced in 1985, represented the first NOSs to take full advantage of the 80286 microprocessor's protected mode capability. Advanced NetWare 2.0 was introduced in 1986. In 1987, *System Fault Tolerance* (SFT) NetWare, which provided features to improve the system reliability including disk mirroring, disk duplexing, and *Transaction Tracking System* (TTS), was introduced. NetWare 2.15, which added support for the Apple Macintosh when purchased with NetWare for Macintosh, was introduced in 1988. In 1989, NetWare 386 3.0 was introduced: a full 32-bit version of NetWare taking full advantage of the capabilities of the 80386 microprocessor. In 1990, NetWare 386 3.1 was introduced, adding more features as well as improved performance and system reliability.

In 1991, Novell consolidated all the previous versions of NetWare for the 80286 into NetWare 2.2. Also introduced was NetWare 3.11. In 1993, NetWare 4.0 was introduced to provide the latest technology available in client-server networks and included features for large enterprise networks.

An enterprise network is similar to a WAN. An *enterprise network* is a network that connects all the computers in a company regardless of their location or type.

General Features

The two versions of NetWare available today include NetWare 3.*x* and NetWare 4.*x*. NetWare 2.2 is a discontinued product but is discussed in this chapter due to the large number of networks still using it and its continued availability in some outlets.

The *x* shown in version numbers can represent any number. For example, 4.*x* could represent 4.01, 4.2, etc. The discussion in this chapter focuses on the features of the major release and not necessarily on the minor changes or bug fixes.

The various versions of NetWare have in common several innovative and powerful features. NetWare contains the following features that primarily improve system performance:

- **Multitasking.** The NetWare NOSs are all *multitasking,* meaning they can perform more than one task at a time. Multitasking allows the network requests from more than one user to be processed simultaneously, resulting in better performance than a NOS based on DOS for example.

- **Disk caching.** NetWare has built-in *disk caching,* which allows data from the hard disk to be read into an area of RAM known as the cache before the data is requested by the network. When data is first accessed from the hard disk, in addition to being passed across the network to the requesting workstation, the data also is read into the cache. The next time the data is requested, there is a good chance the information will be in the cache, resulting in much faster access than if the information had to be read from the hard disk again.

NetWare also implements a read-ahead cache that anticipates the information that will be required from the hard disk next and reads that information into the cache.

Finally, NetWare incorporates background writes to the hard disk. When an application writes data to the network drive, it actually is held in the cache until the server has time to write the data from the cache to the hard disk. By waiting until the server isn't too busy to write the data, performance is increased.

- **Elevator seeking.** *Elevator seeking* is a method used by NetWare to improve disk drive performance. By caching incoming read requests from the network, NetWare is able to sort the requests based on the current location of the read-write head of the hard disk. The information closest to the current location of the hard disk's read-write head is read first and the information farthest from the read-write head is read last. This reduces the amount of movement required by the read-write head and increases the effective data throughput of the hard disk.

- **Overlapped seeks.** *Overlapped seeks* is another technique used by NetWare to increase the throughput of a hard disk. If a computer has multiple disk drives with separate drive controllers, NetWare is able to read from both disk drives at once, which increases disk drive performance and efficiency.

- **Indexed File Allocation Tables (FATs).** NetWare uses a *file allocation table* (FAT) to determine the location of data on a hard disk. If a file stored on the hard disk is larger than 2 MB, NetWare indexes the FAT, thereby speeding the rate at which data may be located on the hard disk.

The reliability of your network system and the integrity of the data stored on your network server need to be sound. The various versions of NetWare include the following features to ensure system reliability and data integrity:

- **Read-after-write verification.** All data that is written to a NetWare server's hard disk immediately is read from the hard disk and compared with the contents of memory. This ensures that the data stored on the hard disk is indeed the same data that was written to it.

- **Hot Fix.** *Hot Fix* is a technology NetWare uses in conjunction with Read-after-write verification and other technologies to identify bad spots on the hard disk. When NetWare identifies a bad spot on the hard disk, NetWare marks it as bad, thereby preventing that spot from being used.

- **Duplication of directories and FATs.** NetWare maintains two copies of the directory on the hard disk. With two copies of the directory, NetWare is able to recover the directory of files in the event the original directory becomes corrupted.

  In addition to duplicate directories, the FAT also is duplicated to maintain the integrity of all the data on the hard disk in the event of a problem such as a corrupted FAT.

- **System Fault Tolerance (SFT).** NetWare's SFT features provide disk mirroring, disk duplexing, and TTS. TTS is a method NetWare uses to prevent files from becoming corrupted because invalid data is written to them. If an invalid transaction is written to the hard disk due to a system failure, the TTS is able to back out the invalid transaction, restoring the hard disk to the state it was in before the invalid transaction was written.

Security is an important feature in any network that contains sensitive data that should be available only to selected individuals. NetWare includes several features that enforce the security requirements of data on the server including user accounts, passwords, and user profiles. Each user logs into a server with a user name and password. User profiles list the resources a particular user has access to as well as the type of access the user has for each shared resource.

Additional security features enable the system Administrator to specify the date and time a user may log in to a particular server, as well as the location from which a user may log in. Security features can detect intruders and lock them out of the system as well as notifying the system Administrator of an attempted access by an intruder.

NetWare supports a variety of server and client operating systems including DOS, Microsoft Windows, OS/2, Macintosh, and UNIX. In addition, a number of communications protocols, which include Novell's IPX/SPX, Apple's AppleTalk, TCP/IP, and *Open Systems Interconnection* (OSI) transport protocols, are supported.

Each variation of NetWare supports Novell's *Open Data-Link Interface* (ODI) specification, which supports the use of multiple protocols through a single network adapter. The combination of ODI network adapter drivers supplied by Novell with those supplied by the various network adapter manufacturers allows nearly any network adapter to be used with NetWare.

Basic Usage

NetWare contains several utilities as well as DOS command-line commands that enable you to perform network connections and manage the network. Login scripts also are used to establish network system default parameters and network connections. You can think of a login script as NetWare's equivalent to a DOS batch file; the login script contains a series of commands that NetWare processes to perform the specified actions.

NetWare uses two basic types of login scripts: system login scripts and user login scripts. The *system login script* is executed each time a user logs in to the network and contains instructions such as the default drive mappings, default search mappings, and greeting messages. The *user login script* also is executed each time a user logs in to the network and contains commands specific to each user, such as additional drive mappings.

Drive Mappings is a NetWare term that refers to redirected drives. The term Map refers to the process of redirecting drives. The term *Search Mappings* refers to the order in which the mapped (redirected) drives are searched for programs or commands if the programs or commands are not found in the current default drive or directory. A Search Mapping in NetWare is similar to the Path statement in DOS.

The SYSCON Utility

The *System Configuration* (SYSCON) utility is used to manage the system configuration of a NetWare server (see fig. 6.1). SYSCON enables you to set up NetWare's accounting function, view file server information, set up user accounts and groups, and perform other administrative functions.

Figure 6.1
NetWare's SYSCON main menu.

The Accounting option enables you to charge users for the use of the file server based on the types of actions performed and the length of time they are connected to the server.

The Change Current Server option enables you to access a different server and perform management functions on it.

The File Server Information option enables you to view information about the operating system for the selected NetWare server.

The Group Information option enables you to place accounts in groups that have specific privileges assigned to them. When a user account is created, it automatically becomes a member of the EVERYONE group. Therefore any global rights specified for the EVERYONE group also apply to the new user account. When groups are created several parameters may be specified including the name of the group, the members of the group, and the privileges or rights of the group.

The system Administrator uses the Supervisor Options menu to perform several configuration tasks on the server such as specifying system defaults, managing server configuration files, managing system login scripts, and specifying default user account parameters and login time restrictions (see fig. 6.2). Selecting the Default Account Balance/Restrictions option displays the Default Account Balance/Restrictions window, enabling you to specify several default parameters that will apply to user accounts as they are created (see fig. 6.3).

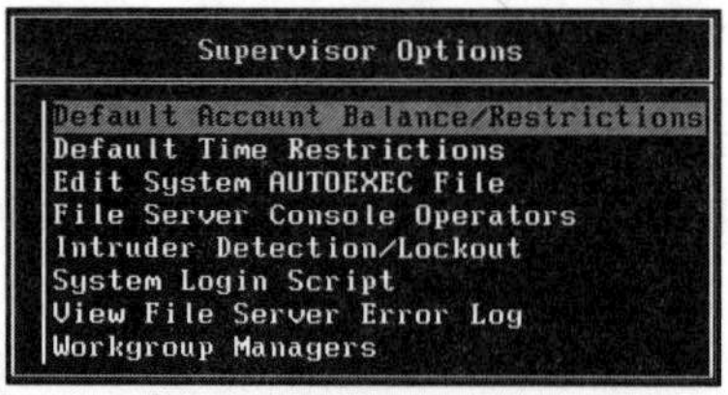

Figure 6.2

The SYSCON Supervisor Options menu.

```
             Supervisor Options

Default Account Balance/Restrictions
Default Time Restrictions
Edit System AUTOEXEC File
File Server Console Operators
Intruder Detection/Lockout
System Login Script
View File Server Error Log
Workgroup Managers
```

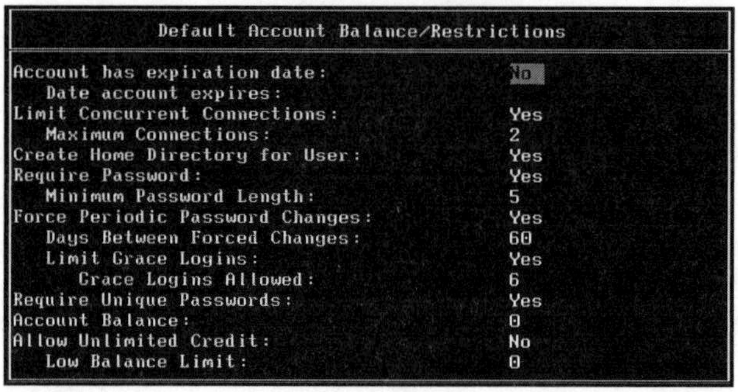

Figure 6.3

The SYSCON Default Account Balance/ Restrictions window.

```
        Default Account Balance/Restrictions

Account has expiration date:                     No
   Date account expires:
Limit Concurrent Connections:                    Yes
   Maximum Connections:                          2
Create Home Directory for User:                  Yes
Require Password:                                Yes
   Minimum Password Length:                      5
Force Periodic Password Changes:                 Yes
   Days Between Forced Changes:                   60
   Limit Grace Logins:                           Yes
      Grace Logins Allowed:                       6
Require Unique Passwords:                         Yes
Account Balance:                                 0
Allow Unlimited Credit:                          No
   Low Balance Limit:                            0
```

The User Information option enables you to set up and modify individual user accounts. Selecting this option displays two windows: the User Names window, which shows the user accounts already set up, and the User Information window, which enables you to specify specific configuration parameters for a user account (see fig. 6.4). A new user account is created by pressing the Ins key and responding with the appropriate information when prompted.

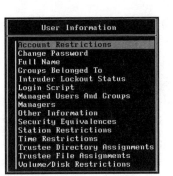

Figure 6.4

The SYSCON User
Information window.

The following is a description of the options in the User Information window:

- **Account Restrictions.** This selection enables you to specify the password and connection parameters for a specific account.

- **Change Password.** This selection is used to change the password for a specific account.

- **Full Name.** This selection is used to specify a description for the account such as the user's first and last name.

- **Groups Belonged To.** This selection enables you to specify the account groups of which this account is a member.

- **Intruder Lockout Status.** This selection enables you to view whether a user has been locked out by the intruder lockout feature.

- **Login Script.** This selection allows a login script to be added or managed for a specific user account. Login scripts also may be copied from other user accounts.

- **Managed Users and Groups.** This selection identifies the user accounts and groups over which the current user account has control. The selected user may grant or revoke specific access rights for the accounts listed.

- **Managers.** This selection lists the manager or managers of a selected user account.

- **Other Information.** This selection shows when the selected user last logged in to the network as well as the maximum server disk usage allowed for the selected user. Also listed is the user's ID.

- **Security Equivalences.** This selection is used to assign the security rights of one user to another user.

- **Station Restrictions.** This selection enables you to specify the workstations that a specified user may use to log in to the network.

- **Time Restrictions.** This selection enables you to specify the times that a specific user may access the network using 1/2 hour increments.

- **Trustee Directory Assignments.** This selection enables you to view the directories a user has rights to and to specify additional directories that a user may access.

- **Trustee File Assignments.** This selection enables you to view the files a user has rights to and to specify additional files that a user may access.

- **Volume/Disk Restrictions.** This selection enables you to limit the amount of space on a selected Volume/Disk that a user may access.

The Session Manager Utility

The Session Manager is a menu-driven utility that enables you to map drives, view and specify search mappings, and send messages to individuals and groups (see fig. 6.5).

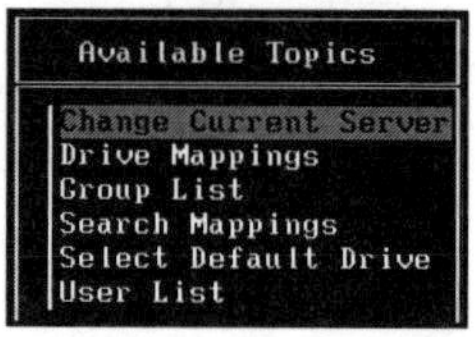

Figure 6.5

The NetWare Session Manager main menu.

Following is a description of the selections available from the Session Manager main menu:

- **Change Current Server.** This selection enables you to connect to another server.

- **Drive Mappings.** This selection enables you to add and delete drive mappings. To add a drive mapping, press the Ins key, specify the drive letter to use, then type the path of the resource you want to connect to or press Ins again and select the resource you want to connect to using the displayed menu options.

- **Group List.** This selection displays a list of all the groups. To send a message to all the members in the group that are currently logged in to the network press the Ins key.

- **Search Mappings.** This selection displays the search mappings, which is the order the mapped drives will be searched for a command or program if the command or program is not found in the current drive or directory (see fig. 6.6). You can add or delete search mappings using this selection.

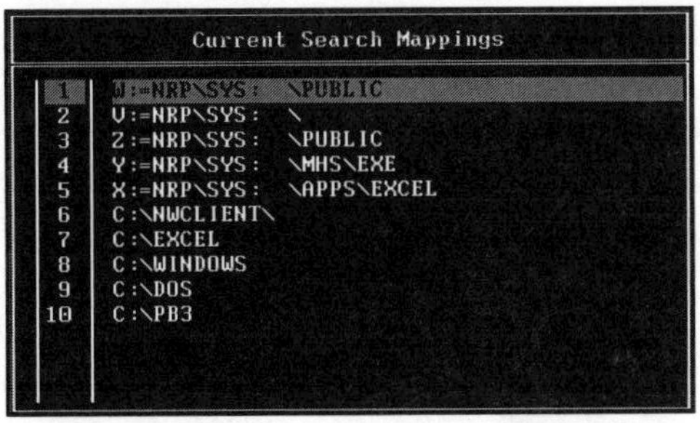

Figure 6.6

The Current Search Mappings window in Session Manager.

- **Select Default Drive.** This selection displays all your mapped drives and enables you to select the default drive that will be active when you exit the Session Manager (see fig. 6.7).

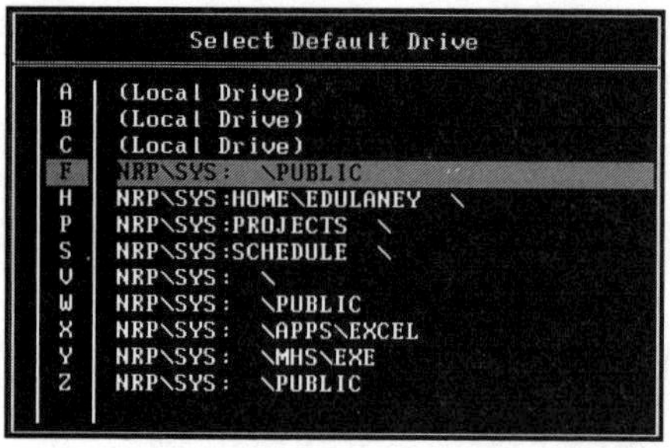

Figure 6.7

The Select Default
Drive window in
Session Manager.

```
              Select Default Drive
   A   (Local Drive)
   B   (Local Drive)
   C   (Local Drive)
   F   NRP\SYS:  \PUBLIC
   H   NRP\SYS:HOME\EDULANEY    \
   P   NRP\SYS:PROJECTS    \
   S   NRP\SYS:SCHEDULE    \
   U   NRP\SYS:    \
   W   NRP\SYS:    \PUBLIC
   X   NRP\SYS:    \APPS\EXCEL
   Y   NRP\SYS:    \MHS\EXE
   Z   NRP\SYS:    \PUBLIC
```

- **User List.** This selection displays a list of all the users logged in to the network. You can view information about a selected user, or send a message to the user by pressing the Ins key.

NetWare 2.2

Novell NetWare 2.2 sustains the largest installed base of Novell's NOSs. NetWare 2.2 was developed when the 80286 was used for file servers and is the only version of NetWare that supports using an 80286-based computer as a server.

Novell no longer sells NetWare 2.2 although it is still available in many outlets. NetWare 2.2 is a very mature and stable product offering a broad range of powerful features for the small- to medium-sized business. NetWare 2.2 is the only NetWare version that can have a server configured as either a dedicated server or a nondedicated server. This makes NetWare 2.2 especially appealing to small businesses on a budget that don't want to sacrifice an existing computer or purchase a new one for use as a dedicated server.

As a 16-bit NOS, NetWare 2.2 lacks the power and speed of the newer 32-bit NetWare 3.x and NetWare 4.x NOSs, although the performance offered by NetWare 2.2 usually is sufficient for smaller networks.

Features

As mentioned previously, NetWare 2.2 is the only version of NetWare that enables you to configure servers as either dedicated or nondedicated. Configuring a NetWare 2.2 server as nondedicated allows the server to be used as a workstation in addition to serving network requests.

NetWare 2.2 supports the most popular desktop operating systems including DOS, Microsoft Windows, and OS/2. Support also is available to allow Macintosh computers to access a NetWare 2.2 server. Additionally, UnixWare clients may access a NetWare 2.2 server. A NetWare 2.2 client may access a computer running UnixWare using terminal emulation software provided with UnixWare.

Value Added Processes (VAPs), programs that run on the server to increase the functionality of the server, are supported. A common VAP is the print server VAP, which allows the NetWare 2.2 file server also to share printers.

NetWare 2.2 supports SFT Level I and SFT Level II. SFT Level I provides the following features:

- Duplicate directory and FATs.

- Verification of directories when the computer is started.

- Read-after-write verification and Hot Fix technology to allow on-the-fly hard disk defect identification and correction.

- *Uninterruptable Power Supply* (UPS) support providing users with notification of an imminent server shutdown due to a power outage.

On NetWare 2.2 dedicated servers, SFT Level II provides disk mirroring, disk duplexing, and TTS to ensure the protection of valuable data.

The NetWare 2.2 server utilizes the *Internetwork Packet Exchange* (IPX) Protocol; support for TCP/IP and *Network File System* (NFS) connections are not available on the server. Individual workstations, however, can utilize the 2.2 client software, which includes support for TCP/IP and NetBIOS. This means that users can access TCP/IP through their workstations on a 2.2 network, but not through the server.

NetWare Print Server software is included, enabling users to share printers physically connected to the server and printers connected to workstations. Up to 16 printers may be shared. The print server may be loaded as a VAP on the server or as an executable file on a workstation.

Specifications and Requirements

NetWare 2.2 supports a maximum of 100 users although Novell strongly recommends upgrading to NetWare 3.*x* if the number of users exceeds ten.

The maximum amount of RAM supported is 12 MB. The largest storage capacity supported is 2 GB with a maximum individual file size of 255 MB.

The maximum number of concurrent open files per server is 1,000 with a maximum of 32,000 directory entries per volume. Thirty-two volumes per server are allowed.

A NetWare 2.2 server requires an 80286-based or higher computer with a minimum of 2.5 MB of RAM.

A NetWare 2.2 workstation may be a PC running DOS, Windows, OS/2, or an Apple Macintosh computer.

In the summer of 1994, Novell discontinued selling NetWare 2.2. Prior to that, it was available in a five-user and ten-user version.

NetWare 3.*x*

Novell NetWare 3.*x* is a 32-bit multitasking dedicated server NOS. NetWare 3.*x* features extensive file and printer sharing, extensive security features, and support for most operating systems including UNIX and OS/2.

NetWare 3.*x* is targeted at businesses of all sizes with various needs because it is flexible enough to integrate PC-type servers, minicomputers, and DOS, Windows, UNIX, and Macintosh workstations into a single network.

NetWare 3.*x* currently is Novell's best-selling NOS. NetWare 2.2 no longer is offered because it is relatively old technology. Although NetWare 4.*x* is Novell's latest network offering, it has not been widely accepted because it is not yet viewed as a stable product.

Features

NetWare 3.*x* supports a modular design allowing *NetWare Loadable Modules* (NLMs) to be loaded on and removed from a server without bringing down (rebooting) the server. NLMs are programs similar to VLMs used in NetWare 2.2 and provide added functionality to the NetWare server. All server-based applications and utilities are NLMs and may be loaded or un-loaded at any time without bringing down the server. Other available NLMs for NetWare 3.*x* include TCP/IP transport proto-cols, *Application Programming Interfaces* (APIs), and a source-routing NLM providing special routing capabilities for NetWare packets.

In addition to multitasking, NetWare 3.*x* also is multithreaded, meaning each task may have separate processes within it that execute concurrently.

NetWare 3.*x* includes client support for workstations running DOS and Windows. Client support for OS/2 is included with the OS/2 operating system. Client support for workstations running UNIX and *Network File System* (NFS) also is available. NetWare 3.*x* supports up to five Macintosh clients at no additional cost.

An internal router enables a NetWare 3.*x* server to connect up to 16 different networks that appear as a single network. The networks connected may use a different physical media or topology.

NetWare 3.*x* supports multiple name spaces allowing clients running different operating systems to use the file naming conventions to which they are accustomed.

Access to network resources is controlled through user accounts, passwords, trustee rights, file rights, and directory rights. Additional security features include intruder detection and lockout, as well as time-of-day login restrictions.

NetWare 3.*x* supports SFT Level I and SFT Level II. SFT Level I provides the following features:

- Duplicate directory and file allocation tables.

- Verification of directories when the computer is started.

- Read-after-write verification and Hot Fix technology to allow on-the-fly hard disk defect identification and correction.

- *Uninterruptable Power Supply* (UPS) support providing users with notification of an imminent server shutdown due to a power outage.

SFT Level II provides disk mirroring, disk duplexing, and TTS to ensure the protection of valuable data.

Hard disk backup and restore services are provided by NBACKUP and SBACKUP, which are included with NetWare 3.*x*. NBACKUP is a DOS client-based backup allowing a NetWare 3.*x* server to be backed up from a client workstation. SBACKUP is an NLM that the network supervisor may use to perform hard disk backups at the server.

The *Remote Management Facility* (RMF) enables you to perform management tasks on a server from your own workstation. RMF may be operated over the network or across the telephone line and enables you to configure servers, load and unload network services, and execute any console command without bringing down the server.

NetWare Print Server software is included, enabling users to share printers physically connected to the server and printers connected to workstations. Up to 16 printers may be shared and multiple print servers may be run on a single network. Printers physically connected to the server are managed using the print server software, whereas printers physically connected to workstations are managed by *terminate-and-stay-resident* (TSR) software that runs on the workstation.

NetWare 3.*x* includes two messaging products: NetWare Basic MHS and FirstMail. NetWare Basic *Message Handling Service* (MHS) enables users to send messages to others on the same NetWare server. An upgrade is available that allows messages to be sent to other NetWare servers and across asynchronous and internetwork links. FirstMail is an easy-to-use, menu-driven mail utility allowing e-mail to be created, sent, read, and managed. FirstMail exists in both DOS and Macintosh versions and also has features that attach files to mail, maintain addresses, and organize mail in folders.

NetWare 3.*x* interoperates with NetWare 2.2 and NetWare 4.*x* and also supports network access to shared CD-ROM drives.

Specifications and Requirements

NetWare 3.*x* supports up to 250 users. The maximum amount of RAM supported is 6 GB (1 GB = 1024 MB). The largest storage capacity supported is 32 TB (1 TB = 1024 GB) with a maximum individual file size of 4 GB.

The maximum number of concurrent open files per server is 100,000 with a maximum of 2,097,152 directory entries per volume. Sixty-four volumes per server are allowed, with up to 32 logical drives per volume.

A NetWare 3.*x* server requires an 80386-based computer or higher with a minimum of 6 MB of RAM.

A NetWare 3.*x* workstation (client) can be a PC running DOS, Microsoft Windows, or OS/2 with the client software provided. Additional software is available to include clients consisting of Macintosh computers or any UNIX NFS workstation including Sun Microsystems, HP Apollo, IBM RS6000, SCO UNIX, NeXT, and many other UNIX NFS workstations in your network.

NetWare 3.*x* is available in 5, 10, 25, 50, 100, and 250 user licenses.

NetWare 4.*x*

NetWare 4.*x* is Novell's latest and most technologically advanced dedicated server NOS offering all the features of NetWare 3.*x* in addition to extensive new features. NetWare 4.*x* can integrate separate multiserver computing environments into a single network.

NetWare 4.*x* is a powerful 32-bit multitasking NOS that is targeted at companies with multiserver networking needs including the requirement to integrate separate networks into a single network regardless of location, distance, language, and size.

Although it offers extremely powerful features and capability, NetWare 4.*x* has been met with some resistance from network users who considered the early versions of the product to be unstable.

Features

NetWare 4.*x* includes all the features of NetWare 3.*x* and adds new enterprise network features which allow the smooth integration of multiple networks into a single network.

In addition to multitasking, NetWare 4.*x* also is multithreaded, meaning each task also may have separate processes within it that execute concurrently.

NetWare Directory Services (NDS) is the technology that turns a separate multiserver network into a single enterprise system. NDS is discussed in the following section, "NetWare Directory Services."

NetWare 4.*x* provides new administration tools to allow the administration of any network node whether it is a DOS, Windows, Macintosh, or OS/2 computer. In addition to new administration tools, all the tools available as separate utilities in previous versions of NetWare are integrated into a single intuitive interface.

NetWare 4.*x* includes multiple language capability including English, Spanish, French, German, and Italian.

NetWare 4.*x* supports a similar modular design as NetWare 3.*x*, allowing NLMs to be loaded on and removed from a server without bringing down (rebooting) the server. Most NLMs developed for NetWare 3.*x* also work with NetWare 4.*x*.

NetWare 4.*x* also interoperates with NetWare 2.2 and NetWare 3.*x* and includes support for sharing CD-ROM drives and other optical disk formats.

NetWare 4.*x* provides print services through the NetWare Print Server application. Up to 255 printers may be shared and multiple print servers may run concurrently. A single utility allows the configuration of DOS, NFS, and Macintosh printers. Printers and queues are defined in NetWare Directory Services. The NetWare Administrator utility is used to manage printers and provides a graphical view of NDS resources, easing the administration of network print services.

NetWare 4.*x* supports *Simple Network Management Protocol* (SNMP), which provides network information to any SNMP management console.

NetWare 4.*x* provides improved performance over WAN links. See the section "WAN Performance Improvements," later in this chapter for more information.

NetWare 4.*x* provides new data storage management features including data compression. See the section "Data Compression and Storage" later in this chapter for more information.

NetWare Directory Services (NDS)

A database distributed over multiple servers that allows access to all network resources regardless of their geographic location, NDS replaces the bindery database in previous NetWare versions, which only handled a single server.

NDS enables users to log in once to gain access to all the network resources they are authorized to use regardless of the number of servers and their geographic location. Instead of logging in to a single server as was done in previous versions of NetWare, a single login gains access to every server in the network the user is authorized to use.

Using NDS, the entire network can be viewed as a single integrated network, and the user doesn't have to be concerned that resources exist on different servers in different locations.

NDS uses an object-oriented structure in which you define entities such as users, groups, volumes (shared drive resources), and printers as objects. Each object has properties associated with them. For example, a user may have properties which include the user's name, address, and telephone number. Each property has an associated value. NDS enables users to locate objects by searching for an object's values.

NDS is organized in a directory tree structure in which each object is part of the directory tree. To ensure database reliability and efficiency, the NDS database is distributed over several servers.

WAN Performance Improvements

NetWare 4.*x* provides features for improved performance over WAN links including burst mode technology, "largest packet" negotiating, and SAP Restrict.

Burst mode, sometimes called *packet burst*, is a technique that allows multiple packets of information to be sent over the network without waiting for verification from the receiving node that a packet was received. Because a WAN link operates at a much slower rate than a LAN, waiting for verification that a packet was received from a node located on the other side of a WAN can take a relatively long period of time. Sending additional packets before the receipt verification is received allows more data to be sent through the WAN link, resulting in significantly improved performance.

NetWare 4.*x* includes a *largest packet* negotiating capability that allows the two nodes involved in a data transmission to determine the largest size packet that both nodes can support. Sending a larger size packet results in less packets sent over the network resulting in improved throughput.

Finally, NetWare 4.*x*'s *Service Advertising Protocol* (SAP) Restrict controls and reduces the distribution of service information transmitted between servers in the network, which reduces the network traffic flowing over the WAN link, thereby increasing efficiency.

Data Compression and Storage

NetWare 4.*x* supports automatic data compression, which results in less drive space being used for storage of data. You can select which files, directories, or volumes are to be compressed and, because compression occurs as a background task, it has no effect on server performance. When a file that is compressed is accessed, it is automatically decompressed as it's being accessed.

Another feature of NetWare 4.*x* allows files that are not used often to be automatically transferred to less expensive storage media such as optical drives or tape drives. Any files transferred remain part of the directory as if they were never moved. When accessed by a user or application, the files are automatically copied back over to the primary storage device, which is usually a hard disk.

The *High Capacity Storage System* (HCSS) enables you to integrate rewritable optical disk drives into the network.

Specifications and Requirements

NetWare 4.*x* supports up to 1,000 users. The largest storage capacity supported is 32 TB (1 TB = 1,024 GB) with a maximum individual file size of 4 GB.

The maximum number of concurrent open files per server is 100,000 with a maximum of 2,097,152 directory entries per volume. Sixty-four volumes per server are allowed with up to 1,024 logical drives per volume.

A NetWare 4.*x* server requires an 80386-based computer or higher with a minimum of 8 MB of RAM. More memory may be required depending on the number of users, the NLMs used, and the size of the network hard disks.

A NetWare 4.*x* workstation may be a PC running DOS, Microsoft Windows, Microsoft Windows NT, or OS/2; or a Macintosh

computer (five-user client included) with the included client
software. NetWare 4.*x* client software is also available separately
for any UNIX NFS workstation including Sun Microsystems, HP
Apollo, IBM RS6000, SCO UNIX, NeXT, and many other UNIX
NFS workstations.

NetWare 4.*x* is available in 5, 10, 25, 50, 100, 250, 500, and 1,000
user licenses.

Windows NT Server

Microsoft Windows NT Server incorporates a 32-bit NOS into the
Windows NT environment. By itself, Windows NT offers a peer-
to-peer network solution. Windows NT Server provides a server-
based (client-server) network solution.

Windows NT Server offers several impressive features and an
exceptional user interface. Unfortunately, it requires a minimum
of 16 MB of RAM and therefore is more expensive to implement
than most other dedicated server NOSs.

Features

Windows NT Server supports Intel- (80386-25 and higher) and
RISC-based systems. Symmetric multitasking is supported, which
may use up to four microprocessors concurrently to process
information, resulting in much faster processing capability than a
single microprocessor.

In addition to multitasking, Windows NT Server is also
multithreaded, meaning each task may also have separate processes within the task that are executing concurrently.

Windows NT Server also supports centralized management and
control of individual user accounts and global groups. Users may
use a single network login to access and use available shared
resources. Centralized management allows user accounts to be

managed from a single computer. Management functions may be delegated to specific individuals and the allowed level of management features specified.

Preemptive multitasking enables you to run multiple applications concurrently and allows the network operations to take precedence over other less critical processes resulting in better network performance.

Windows NT Server includes extensive Macintosh services. A Macintosh computer can access a Windows NT Server as if it were accessing an AppleShare server. Files are automatically translated to the appropriate format for sharing across the two platforms. PC and Macintosh users can share the same printers; Macintosh users can even print Postscript jobs to a non-postscript PC printer. Macintosh accounts are managed just like any other account.

Windows NT Server supports integration with several other networks (with additional software) including Windows-based networks, Novell NetWare, Banyan VINES, LAN Manager for OS/2, UNIX, VMS, and SNA networks.

Network adapter cards are automatically detected during installation and may be configured at that time.

Windows NT Server supports *Simple Network Management Protocol* (SNMP) to allow the integration of Windows NT Server with existing management tools.

Fault tolerance features include disk mirroring and disk striping with parity (RAID 5), which uses several disks to store data by writing to and reading from multiple disks at a time. A failure of a single drive does not bring down the server. The data that existed on the failed drive is reconstructed by the server based on the information on the other drives.

Windows NT offers several easy-to-use utilities for network configuration and management. File Manager provides easy management of files and directories. Print Manager allows the installation and sharing of network printers in addition to the management of print jobs. The Control Panel customizes the server, including setting up network services and communication protocols. User Manager sets up, modifies, and manages user and group accounts. Disk Administrator sets up and manages drive resources including fault tolerance features. Event Viewer enables you to view the system, application, and security events enabling you to troubleshoot problems and monitor unauthorized user activity.

Windows NT Server also provides remote dial-in network access to resources and applications for computers running Windows NT, Microsoft LAN Manager, and Windows for Workgroups. Administrative functions may also be performed from a remote location.

Protocols that Windows NT Server supports include NetBEUI, TCP/IP, IPX/SPX, and NDIS.

Specifications and Requirements

Windows NT Server requires an 80386DX-25-based computer or better with a minimum of 16 MB of RAM, and 90 MB of available hard disk space or a Windows NT-compatible RISC based computer with 16 MB of RAM, and 110 MB of available hard disk space.

Clients to a server running Windows NT Server may include systems running Windows NT, Windows for Workgroups, and Macintosh computers. Other clients supported with additional software are computers running Windows, DOS, and OS/2.

Windows NT Server is available for use on a single server with unlimited users, or in a 20-server license pack.

Microsoft LAN Manager

Microsoft LAN Manager is Microsoft's predecessor to Windows NT Server. LAN Manager uses 32-bit operation but sits on top of Microsoft's OS/2, which is a 16-bit multitasking operating system.

LAN Manager is actually an application that runs on OS/2, meaning OS/2 must be installed and then LAN Manager; LAN Manager does not replace the operating system.

As the technology incorporated in LAN Manager is relatively old, performance doesn't measure up to some of the other NOSs discussed such as NetWare 4.*x*.

Features

LAN Manager supports centralized management and control of user accounts and shared resources. Access control lists specify the individual or group accounts that have access to a specific shared resource and the permissions each account has.

Diskless workstations (computers without any disk drives) can boot from a LAN Manager server and run DOS, Windows, and OS/2 over the network.

Several fault tolerance features are included. The Hot Fix services automatically detect and transfer data from a flawed area of the hard disk to an area free of defects. Disk mirroring and duplexing prevent data loss in the event of a hard disk failure. UPS-support notifies users in the event of an imminent server shutdown due to a power outage. Tape-backup software provides efficient backup of critical data to tape.

LAN Manager supports the *High Performance File System* (HPFS), which allows for faster access to data than the standard DOS-based system by including features such as larger data storage block sizes, disk caching, contiguous file allocation, and efficient file indexing.

SNMP and NetView allow LAN Manager servers to be accessed and managed by third-party management systems.

LAN Manager Print Station allows printing to printers connected to any Windows- or DOS-based client; printers don't have to be connected to the server for other nodes to use them.

Dial-up remote access enables remote users to use network resources, access e-mail, and administer servers off-site.

Users may use a single network login to access and use available shared resources on multiple servers. Servers are organized into groups called *domains* that may be accessed and managed as if they were a single server.

LAN Manager clients may include PCs running DOS, Windows, Windows for Workgroups, and OS/2. Apple Macintosh client support is available separately. Protocol support also is available to connect clients to Novell NetWare servers.

LAN Manager includes support for the NetBEUI protocol as well as support for TCP/IP and NDIS.

Specifications and Requirements

LAN Manager requires an 80386-based computer or better with a minimum of 9 MB of RAM.

Clients running DOS can be any PC with at least 512K of RAM. Clients running Windows must have a minimum of 1 MB of RAM and an 80286 microprocessor (Windows 3.1 and later). Clients running Microsoft OS/2 require an 80286 microprocessor with at least 4.5 MB of RAM. Clients running Windows for Workgroups must have an 80286 microprocessor or better with a minimum of 2 MB of RAM.

LAN Manager is sold retail as a server package with additional client packs available from Microsoft or downloadable from its BBS. The client packs allow for unlimited client access to a LAN Manager server.

IBM OS/2 LAN Server

IBM OS/2 LAN Server has its roots in Microsoft LAN Manager because IBM purchased the technology from Microsoft. IBM has improved the technology significantly and OS/2 LAN Server rivals the best in terms of performance and features. OS/2 LAN Server uses 32-bit operation and works in conjunction with IBM's OS/2 2.*x* multitasking operating system.

OS/2 LAN Server is available in an entry-level version and an advanced version. The entry-level version is a low-cost solution and allows the use of a nondedicated server. The advanced version of OS/2 LAN Server provides high performance and additional fault tolerance and administrative features.

Features

OS/2 LAN Server features a single system image that allows the resources available across the network to appear as a single, integrated system. Servers are organized into groups called domains that may be accessed and managed as if they were a single server. A single login is required to access all the network resources in a domain.

Peer-to-peer operation is available to nodes running OS/2, allowing those nodes to share and use each others' shared resources including programs, files, and printers. Client (or requestor) support is available to workstations running DOS, Windows, and OS/2 2.0 and higher. OS/2 LAN Server for Macintosh allows DOS, Windows, OS/2, and Macintosh users to connect to the same network. Coexistence with NetWare servers allows DOS and OS/2 clients to connect to NetWare servers.

Diskless workstations (computers without any disk drives) can boot from OS/2 LAN Server and run DOS, Windows, and OS/2 over the network.

IBM NetView allows NetView management utilities to manage a OS/2 LAN Server network.

User Profile Management (UPM) is provided to allow management of user and group accounts and passwords using a graphical interface. A similar interface is available for LAN Server for Macintosh.

Several fault tolerance features are included in OS/2 LAN Server Advanced. OS/2 LAN Server Advanced automatically detects and transfers data from a flawed area of the hard disk to a good area. Disk mirroring and duplexing are supported to prevent data loss in the event of a hard disk failure. UPS support notifies users in the event of a imminent server shutdown due to a power outage.

OS/2 LAN Server Advanced supports the use of multiprocessors in selected IBM hardware. Multiprocessor support allows different tasks and programs to be executed using different processors simultaneously, resulting in exceptional performance improvements.

OS/2 LAN Server supports HPFS, which allows for faster access to data than the standard DOS-based system by including features such as larger data storage block sizes, disk caching, contiguous file allocation, and efficient file indexing.

OS/2 LAN Server is available in many different languages for worldwide use.

OS/2 LAN Server supports the NetBIOS protocol in addition to TCP/IP. NDIS support also is included.

Specifications and Requirements

OS/2 LAN Server supports up to 1,000 users on a single server.

OS/2 LAN Server requires IBM OS/2 2.0 or higher to be installed on the computer prior to installing OS/2 LAN Server.

OS/2 LAN Server requires an 80386-based computer or better with a minimum of 2.5 MB of RAM for the entry-level version and a minimum of 9 MB of RAM for the advanced version.

OS/2 LAN Server Entry edition is available as is the OS/2 LAN Server Advanced edition. The client requestors, which allow client access to the servers, are sold separately.

Summary

This chapter discussed the features of server-based networks. The primary features that distinguish a server-based network from a peer-to-peer network were discussed as well as what to consider when evaluating a server-based network. The chapter also identified the features and specifications of the six most popular server-based networks.

In This Chapter...

In this chapter, you learn about using application programs with your network. The chapter covers application programs written specifically for use on a network, as well as how to use your existing single-user application programs with your network. You will become familiar with several examples of problems that might occur and the procedures to solve them. Specifically, this chapter covers the following topics:

- How to use your existing application software with your network.

- How to run a single-user application program from a server.

- How data is shared on a network.

- Tips for changing the configuration of an application program so you can use it in a network environment.

- Using network applications.

- Installing network applications on a server.

- Installing installation programs on a server.

- Using Microsoft Windows in a network environment.

This chapter also introduces the following terms:

Batch file	Default drive
Single-user application	Multiuser application
Attributes	Record locking

Network Applications

A network enables previously isolated computers to communicate with other computers connected to the network. Application programs and data that were installed previously and isolated on individual computers now are available for other network nodes to access and use. The question now becomes one of whether your existing applications will run on the network, or will you have to purchase different copies. The answer depends on the way the software was written, how it sees or does not see the network, and what you intend to do with it.

All kinds of different software applications exist. Some applications are written specifically for use with a network and others are not. Just because you have a stand-alone version of XYZ Spreadsheet, once you put in a network, you don't necessarily have to run to the store to buy a network copy. A lot of issues come into play, such as how many people will now use the spreadsheet, where it will be installed, and so on. If there are currently four users with XYZ installed on their machines, and when you finish there will still be only four users, then a viable solution is to leave those four machines exactly as they are, in terms of the spreadsheet, and place only the spreadsheet data on the network. Every user is running a single application and only the data is being shared.

The same application program might have a single-user version and a multiuser version for use on a network. A common misconception is that once you install a network, you must change all your application software to the network version. Upgrading an application program to the network version can be expensive, and many programs don't have a network version available. Fortunately, in most cases, a single-user version of an application program operates fine with a network.

One component you definitely want to examine before determining whether you need to change your software to match your hardware is licensing. Very carefully read the fine print and see how different vendors handle networking in terms of their product. Some allow you to place a stand-alone package on a network so long as only one user at a time uses it. Others ask that you purchase a copy for every user who can access the software. Needless to say, the former is preferred over the latter.

Software application programs tend to fall into three categories: single-user or stand-alone, network aware or network supporting, and network version.

The *single-user* (or stand-alone) version of a software application is sold for use on a single computer system. Almost every application program is available in a single-user version. The software you purchase for your computer prior to installing a network is undoubtedly a single-user version.

Application software that is *network aware* (or network supporting) was written with networks in mind. You purchase a separate copy of the software to install on each computer. The software may or may not support the simultaneous use of the data files by more than one user.

The network version of a software application program is installed on a server. Multiple users can access and run the software from the server. If it makes sense to share the same data files between multiple users concurrently, the network version of the software usually supports concurrent multiuser access to the same data files. Record locking prevents two users from saving changes to an individual record at the exact same time. In the event this occurs—in software that does not contain this feature—one user's changes would override the other's.

The following sections discuss in detail how to use the different types of software in a network environment, and contain some tips on how to install and configure software applications on your network.

Using Single-User Applications on a Network

Whether or not an application is network-aware, it most likely enables you to run an application with a network without any difficulty. In fact, with the proper precautions, you can run a single-user application from the shared drive on a server across the network on your computer. Again, remember to check your licensing agreement carefully before continuing.

Using Your Existing Applications

The stand-alone applications that you install on your computer before you install your network normally operate fine after you install the network. This is because their operation is still limited locally.

You can determine whether an application is local or shared (on the server) based on where the executable program that starts the application resides. If XYZ.EXE is on the local drive, then it is a local application—even though all the spreadsheet files it uses may be on the server. If XYZ.EXE is on the server, then it is a shared application—even if every file but that one is on the local PC.

Unless you change your computer's configuration when you install the network, any previously installed software is still available and can be accessed in the same way.

Using Applications Installed on a Server

You often can run single-user applications at your computer from a server on the network. To do so, install the application program on a server in the network. The network enables you to redirect a drive letter on your computer to point to the drive or directory on the server that contains the program you want to run. Using the redirected drive, you access the program on the server and run it on your computer.

When you purchase a program, the license agreement stipulates how you are allowed to use it. The license agreements for many (but not all) programs permit you to install the software in any fashion you choose so long as no more than one person operates each licensed copy of the software at a time.

Check your program's license agreement for any restrictions associated with installation on a network server.

To better understand how to run an application from a server on your computer, consider the example shown in figure 7.1. In this example, the objective is to run Microsoft Word from the server on a local workstation. In the two-node network shown in figure 7.1, the node with the network name KATIE is configured as a non-dedicated server, and the node with the network name ZAK is configured as a workstation. Each computer has a hard disk drive C, and the directory tree for drive C on each computer is shown.

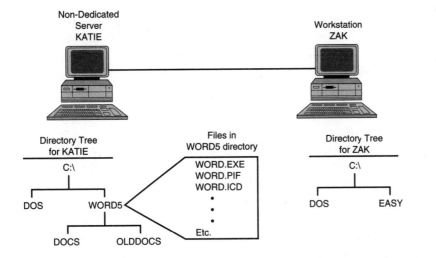

Figure 7.1

Running a single-user application from a server.

If you are sitting at KATIE, with the DOS prompt on your screen, start Word the same way you do without a network by typing the following commands:

```
C:\>CD \WORD5
C:\WORD5>WORD
```

If the AUTOEXEC.BAT file located in the root directory on your hard disk contains the command PROMPT=PG, the DOS prompt displays the name of the current directory in addition to the current drive letter as part of the prompt, as shown in the preceding example.

Now assume that you have redirected the K drive on ZAK to point to the C drive on KATIE. To run Word from the C drive on KATIE while sitting at ZAK, type the following commands at the DOS prompt:

```
C:\>K:
K:\>CD \WORD5
K:\WORD5>WORD
```

The first command (K:) changes the default drive to K, which is redirected to point to the C drive on server KATIE. The CD \WORD5 command makes WORD5 the current directory. Type **WORD** to start the program.

> In most situations, the performance of an application running from your local drive is better than the performance of an application running from a redirected network drive. Therefore, if maximum performance is critical, install your application on your local drive unless you have limited available drive space.

Now that you have successfully run a single-user application from a server, you need to be aware of a few important subjects:

- **Default data drive.** Many programs enable you to specify a default drive and directory in which to save your data. In the example above, if you specify the WORD5\DOCS directory on drive C of server KATIE, the full path is C:\WORD5\DOCS. If you sit at workstation ZAK, Word looks for the default directory (\WORD5\DOCS) on drive C of ZAK and doesn't find it (because from ZAK the \WORD5\DOCS directory is located on the redirected drive K).

- **Batch files.** You can start many application programs by typing the name of a DOS batch file. The DOS *batch file* might include several commands that are required to start the application. If the commands reference a drive letter such as C, and you access the application using a redirected drive such as K, the batch file cannot locate the required files on the C drive.

- **Configuration files.** When installed, some programs record locations for other files that the program uses in a *configuration file*. A good example of this is a word processor such as Microsoft Word. Although Word starts and appears to operate correctly when run across the network, if you try to run the spell check routine, an error appears indicating that

Word cannot find the spell files. The reason for the error is that the Word configuration specifies the location of the spell check files as drive C and not drive K. Therefore, to access the spell check files, you must change the Word configuration for the location of the spell check files from the C drive to the K drive.

You can change the location of the configuration information of some programs simply by changing the information screen within the program. Other programs, however, might require that you reinstall them to change the location of the configuration files.

Installing Single-User Applications on a Server

One method you can use to prevent the possible problem of invalid default drive specifications in your configuration is to install the program from a workstation onto the server.

Without a network, you specify your C drive as the location of the installation when you install a single-user program. With a network you can redirect a drive letter such as Z and specify the redirected drive as the location for the installation. Because the network creates a logical Z drive, you can choose Z when the installation program asks you to specify to which drive you want to install the program (and its associated files).

If you install a program on a nondedicated server, you also can redirect a drive on the nondedicated server to point to a shared drive resource on the same nondedicated server. The method to do this is the same as if you were redirecting a drive on a workstation.

To run the program you just installed from any workstation (or nondedicated server), redirect the same drive letter used for the installation to point to the shared resource on the server that contains the program. Run the program using the appropriate redirected drive letter.

To make it easier to understand accessing and running programs from a server using a redirected drive, remember to think of the redirected drive as another physical drive on your computer.

Moving Single-User Applications to a Server

You might have a single-user application installed on your computer that you want to move to a server and run off the server's drive.

Moving a program from a local drive to a redirected drive is the same as moving a program between two drives on your computer. Most application programs and their associated support files are installed in a specific directory. To move the application to a server, copy the directory and its contents from your computer to the server.

When moving an application from your computer to a server so users across the network can access the application, do not forget to consider the possible problems previously mentioned regarding the default data drive, batch files, and configuration files attempting to use invalid drives or directories.

Consider an example in which you want to move the WP directory and its contents, including any subdirectories, from the workstation ZAK to the server Katie (see fig. 7.2). The first step is to redirect a drive letter (K in this example) on ZAK to point to the physical C drive on Katie. With drive K on ZAK redirected to point to the C drive on server KATIE, you now have a means of copying the information from the WP directory (and its subdirectories) to the new location on KATIE.

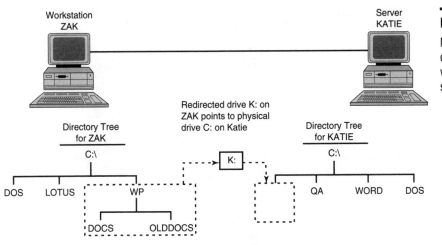

Figure 7.2

Moving the WP directory from workstation ZAK to server KATIE.

You can use several methods to perform the operation. Using DOS, the following command issued at the DOS prompt while you are sitting at ZAK copies the WP directory and its contents to the C drive on server KATIE:

```
XCOPY C:\WP\*.* K:\WP\*.* /S/E
```

The preceding XCOPY command copies all the files (*.*) in the WP directory on the C drive to the WP directory on the K drive (which is redirected to point to the physical C drive on KATIE). The /S switch causes any subdirectories under WP also to be copied (DOCS and OLDDOCS) and the /E causes the subdirectories to be copied even if they are empty.

After copying the WP directory from ZAK to KATIE, you probably want to delete from ZAK the directory and its files to prevent having the exact same information in two different locations.

If you have Microsoft Windows, you can use the Windows File Manager Program to move the WP directory from the C drive on workstation ZAK to the C drive on server KATIE (see fig. 7.3). From the File Manager main menu, select **F**ile and then select **M**ove. In the Move dialog box, specify C:\WP in the **F**rom field and K:\ in the **T**o field. Select OK and the WP directory is moved from the C drive (on ZAK) to the K drive, which is the physical C drive on server KATIE. File Manager also automatically deletes the WP directory on ZAK after moving it to KATIE.

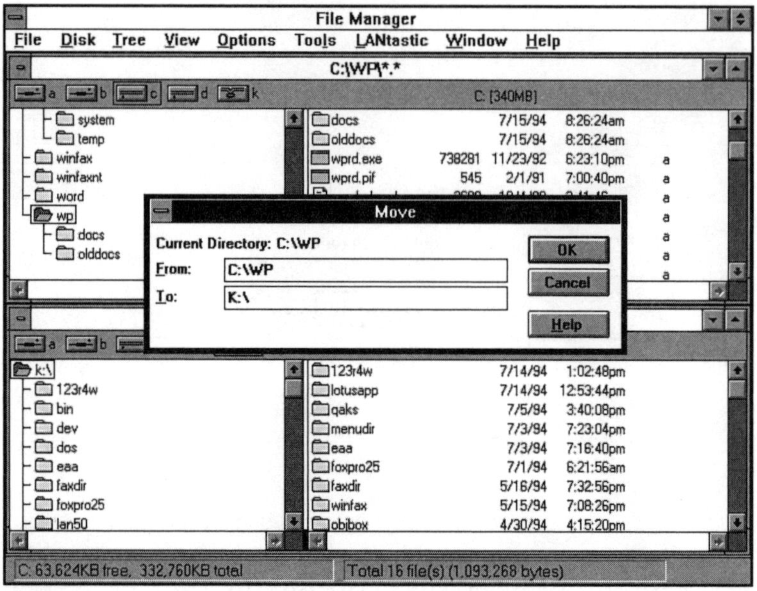

Figure 7.3

Moving the WP
directory from
workstation ZAK to
server KATIE using
Windows File
Manager.

Multiuser Access of a Single-User Application

In some situations, more than one person can use a single-user application installed on a server at the same time. Before attempting this, make sure the following statements are true:

1. Your license agreement for the software you are sharing enables you to install it on a server for multiuser access. Legally, you probably are required to purchase the same number of licensed copies of the software as users who concurrently access the shared copy.

2. Data files with the same name are not used by anyone using the shared application or by the application itself. The network prevents more than one copy of a file with the same name from being used with a single-user application program. If either a user or the application itself attempts to use a file with the same name, the computer displays an error message or the application crashes resulting in the loss of data.

If the previous statements are true, use the following procedures to enable more than one user to access and use an application program at the same time.

> In a peer-to-peer network, if your computer is configured as a nondedicated server, other nodes can access an application at the same time you access it by performing the following procedures.

Normally, when more than one person tries to access any file, whether a program file or a data file, the network allows access to the first person, but denies any others access until the first person closes the file. Access is denied to others to prevent data currently being accessed or modified by one person from unintentionally being overwritten by another. Most program files always are read and never written to. Therefore, you can specify to the *network operating system* (NOS) or your computer's operating system that those files are read-only, allowing more than one person (or node) to read concurrently the information contained in the files.

Each NOS might have a different procedure for making a file read-only. Many NOSs enable you to use the DOS ATTRIB command. To make all the files in your current directory read-only, for example, type the following command at the DOS prompt:

```
ATTRIB +R *.*
```

The +R sets the files to read-only. The same statement with a -R removes the read-only setting from the files so that you also can write to them. The *.* specifies all files. You can specify just the executable program files (EXE) by replacing *.* with *.EXE.

Most NOSs offer rights and attributes beyond those confined to the PC operating system. With these, it is possible to limit a user to reading an entire subdirectory without being able to create additional subdirectories beneath, or to writing files without being able to alter them.

A classic example of this is the NetWare method of handling e-mail. Every time a new user is added to the network, a subdirectory off the root\mail directory is created for them. This subdirectory is given a mixture of numbers and letters to confuse those who find it and prevent them from easily identifying it with the owner. The new user is indeed the owner of the file, but everyone else is given the permission to create files in it.

Normal users (not an administrator), when making a DIR listing, do not see these subdirectories present—as far as they are concerned, they do not even exist. When they send a letter to Kristin, for example, their file goes into the Mail\4F00005G subdirectory. They have the permissions necessary for their mail program to place the file there. Once there, they cannot list it with DIR, nor read, write to, change, alter, or delete it. Kristin, on the other hand, can see the file is there, because she has all permissions to that one subdirectory, and she can read, write, alter, delete, or do anything else she wants to it. If she replies, the cycle repeats with her now able to send, but unable to do anything else to, the other person's subdirectory.

You cannot delete or write over a DOS file marked as read-only. Before deleting or writing over a file, such as when you reinstall a program, remove the read-only setting from any files specified as read-only with the command "attrib -r {filename}".

Sharing Data on a Network

One of the primary reasons for implementing a network is to share data. The capability of different computers to access and use programs and data from a common location creates many flexible and powerful options.

In many situations a company implements a network without considering obtaining the network version of the software. Often the ability to share printers and store data files in a common location more than justifies the purchase and installation of a network.

Figure 7.4 is an example of such a situation. A company that uses *computer-aided design* (CAD) workstations to produce drawings for the products they manufacture can benefit greatly by implementing a network rather than having several stand-alone computers. CAD workstations typically are powerful computer systems with large monitors and hard disks. In this situation, the company installs the CAD program on each workstation. The drawings are stored in a common location on the server and can be accessed by everyone. Because the component drawings used in most situations occupy a significant amount of disk space, storing them on the server eliminates the requirement for extremely large hard disks on the workstations. In addition, instead of purchasing an expensive plotter and laser printer for each computer, the company can access and use a single plotter and laser printer connected to the server to use across the network.

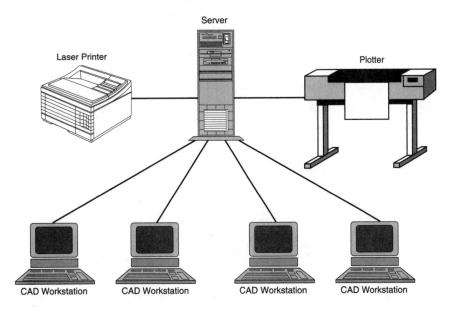

Figure 7.4

A sample network configuration for CAD workstations.

File and Record Locking

File and *record locking* are methods to prevent more than one user from accessing the same file or the same part of a file (record) at the same time. To prevent data files from being overwritten or the contents of the data from becoming corrupt, networks and application programs must support some form of file or record locking.

In the case of file locking, when someone accesses or modifies a file, the network allows access only to the person currently using the file; all others are locked out and cannot access or modify the file until the person using the file finishes his or her work and exits the program.

You can use different levels of file locking depending on your network and application. When you're using a single-user application, an attempt to use a file being used by another person usually results in a DOS error message such as `Sharing Violation` or `Access Denied`. Applications that are network aware often display their own error message such as `File already in use` or `Not able to access file at this time`. You can use file locking when updating a document in your word processor program, or records in a database.

If, while you're working on the document, another user tries to open the file to make changes, access is denied to them until you finish. Then they can open the document (with your latest changes) and modify the contents.

Many network applications enable more than one person to access and use the same data file concurrently. These are called *multiuser applications*. To allow multiuser access to the same data file, multiuser applications employ record locking. Record locking enables several users to access the same file but prevents more than a single person from using a specific record in the file.

Figure 7.5 illustrates record locking as it is used in a database program. Databases are tables of information that are divided into rows (called *records*) and columns (called *fields*). The example shown is a database that consists of customer names and telephone numbers. In the table are three fields: one for the customer's first name (FNAME), one for the customer's last name (LNAME), and one for the customer's telephone number (NUM-BER). Each record contains the information for a different customer. The name of the file that contains all this information is CUSTOMER.

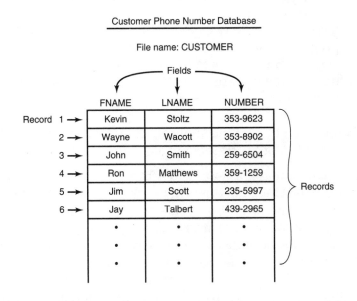

Figure 7.5

A database table to illustrate record locking.

Although almost all programs that store large amounts of information store it in a table format as shown in figure 7.5, often the data is presented to the user in a different format, as in a form. A form is used to display and edit a single record at a time. If your database has several fields, a form greatly simplifies entering and modifying the information by eliminating the other records from the screen.

In an application that supports record locking, such as that shown in figure 7.5, any number of users can open the CUSTOMER file. Only one person at a time, however, can change the contents of any particular record; all others are either completely locked out of the record or only can view it.

The level of sophistication of record locking can vary for each application. Some applications prevent any kind of access if a record currently is being used by someone else. Other applications enable you to view a record that another user is modifying. Still others update your display while other users are making changes.

Using Network Applications

Network applications enable more than one person to access and use the program concurrently and can enable more than one person to access the same data file concurrently with the use of record locking. Usually a network application is installed and accessed from a server. A network-supporting application that includes record locking also can be referred to as a network application even though the application resides on individual nodes with the data file residing in a common location.

The popular database program Q&A by Symantec is a perfect example of a product that offers network support with record locking in both the single-user version and the network version (see fig. 7.6). In the first scenario a separate licensed copy of Q&A is installed on the hard disk on each workstation (shown in the upper part of fig. 7.6). The workstations can access and use the same database file on the server. Q&A supports record locking in this configuration. When browsing through different records (or forms), if another person currently is editing the record you are viewing, the computer displays a message near the bottom of the screen indicating that you can view the record but cannot change it (see fig. 7.7). After the other user modifies the record, the changes appear on your display when you reenter the screen. You then can make your changes to the record.

In the second scenario, the network version of Q&A is installed on the server along with the Q&A database file (see the lower part of fig. 7.6). Each workstation runs the Q&A program by accessing it from the server. The workstations also access the database from the server. The operation and features of Q&A are identical whether running single-user copies on each workstation and accessing the data from the server, or accessing both the Q&A

program and data from the server. The only difference is that performance tends to be better with Q&A installed on each workstation because the program files don't have to travel across the network to each workstation when running the program.

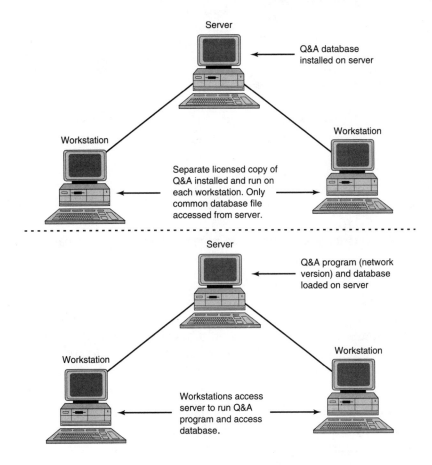

Server

Q&A database installed on server

Workstation

Workstation

Separate licensed copy of Q&A installed and run on each workstation. Only common database file accessed from server.

Server

Q&A program (network version) and database loaded on server

Workstation

Workstation

Workstations access server to run Q&A program and access database.

Figure 7.6

Comparing the use of the single-user version of Q&A with the network version.

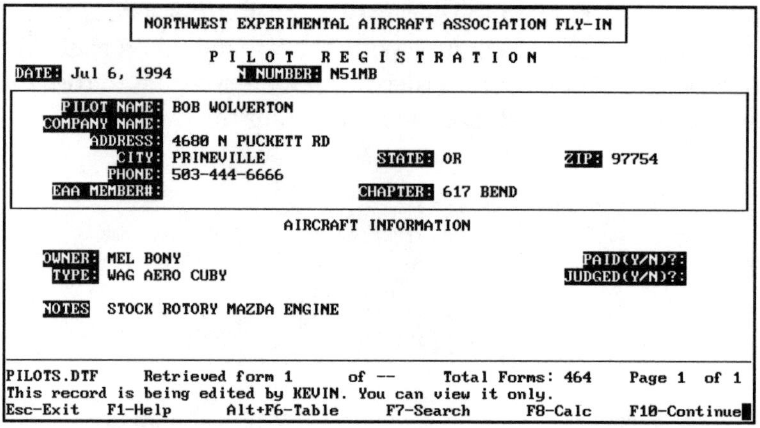

Figure 7.7

A Q&A database form
indicating on the next
to last line that
another user is
modifying the
current form.

```
┌─────────────────────────────────────────────────────────────────────┐
│        NORTHWEST EXPERIMENTAL AIRCRAFT ASSOCIATION FLY-IN             │
│                 P I L O T   R E G I S T R A T I O N                   │
│ DATE:  Jul 6, 1994      N NUMBER:  N51MB                              │
│  ┌──────────────────────────────────────────────────────────────┐   │
│  │ PILOT NAME:  BOB WOLVERTON                                     │   │
│  │COMPANY NAME:                                                   │   │
│  │     ADDRESS:  4680 N PUCKETT RD                                │   │
│  │        CITY:  PRINEVILLE          STATE:  OR      ZIP:  97754   │   │
│  │       PHONE:  503-444-6666                                     │   │
│  │ EAA MEMBER#:                       CHAPTER:  617 BEND          │   │
│  └──────────────────────────────────────────────────────────────┘   │
│                        AIRCRAFT INFORMATION                           │
│   OWNER:  MEL BONY                            PAID(Y/N)?:             │
│    TYPE:  WAG AERO CUBY                      JUDGED(Y/N)?:            │
│                                                                       │
│   NOTES   STOCK ROTORY MAZDA ENGINE                                  │
│                                                                       │
│                                                                       │
│ PILOTS.DTF      Retrieved form 1      of --     Total Forms: 464    Page 1  of 1 │
│ This record is being edited by KEVIN. You can view it only.          │
│ Esc-Exit   F1-Help     Alt+F6-Table     F7-Search      F8-Calc     F10-Continue │
└─────────────────────────────────────────────────────────────────────┘
```

When you request information from a server, it has to read that information from its hard drive and transmit it down the wire. Assuming that you have an identical machine for the server as for your workstation, there is always a better response time when the application is local as opposed to remote. The hard disk read time is going to be the same, and your savings will be the length of time it takes to send the signal down the wire.

The flip side to installing all applications on local machines however, comes when a new version of the software is released. If the application is on the server, you only have to reinstall or update one time. If it is on 500 workstations, you have to go to 500 different physical locations with your set of floppies and do the dirty work.

Many other applications take advantage of the multiuser features provided by a network, including file and record locking. Database and accounting applications that keep track of customers, invoicing, sales, and other items that multiple users need to access at the same time are natural candidates for networks. Any type of situation in which you need to share or exchange information is a candidate for a network application.

Installing Network Applications on a Server

Installing a network application on a server is very similar to installing an application on a stand-alone computer. Normally you install network applications from a workstation to a server. Prior to beginning the installation process, you need to redirect a drive on the workstation at which you are sitting to point to the shared resource on the server to be used for the installation.

When choosing a redirected drive letter to use for installation, remember that you most likely will be required to use the same drive letter later when accessing and running the application, so plan accordingly.

Each network application you install has different requirements for, and a slightly different method of, installation.

Up to this point it has been assumed that when you redirect a drive letter to point to a resource on a server, you access the entire drive on the server. In the previous examples you redirected a drive on your computer to point to a physical drive on the server. In many situations, however, you do not want to give an individual access to the entire hard disk on the server, but only to the directory that contains the necessary application or data. In this case, redirect a drive on your computer to point to a resource on the server that is a directory instead of pointing to the entire drive. You install the application to the chosen redirected drive. After the installation is complete and you are ready to run the program, redirect the same drive to the shared resource on the server that was used for installation. Because you access the same location using the same drive letter, any configuration files with the drive and directory information defined can access the appropriate files, and the application runs fine.

To help illustrate the process of installing an application to a shared resource on a server that points to a directory instead of an entire drive, consider the example shown in figure 7.8. Assume you have a network application that contains every law in existence. You want to install the application on your server for everyone's access. You also use your server to store all your accounting and payroll information, to which only a small group of individuals have access. You want everyone to be able to access the new application without compromising the security of your accounting and payroll information. Redirect the V drive on your computer to point to the VIEWS resource on the server. Now install the application on the V drive.

Figure 7.8

Installing an application to a drive redirected to a directory resource.

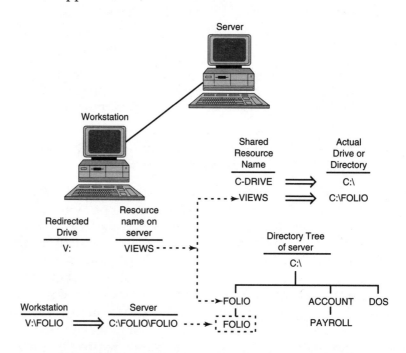

Most installation programs try to create their own directory in which to place the program file. Because V already points to C:\FOLIO on the server, if you install the program files in the V:\FOLIO directory as the installation program likely recommends, the program files actually are installed in the C:\FOLIO\FOLIO directory on the server. There is nothing wrong with accepting the suggestion of the installation program, but it is important to understand where the program files actually are installed.

Because the V drive actually is redirected to the VIEWS resource on the server that points to the FOLIO directory on the server's C drive, any files installed on V actually are installed to the FOLIO directory or subdirectories below it on the server's C drive. You can access neither the root directory on the server (C:\) nor any other directories at the same level as FOLIO using the V drive, leaving secure all information other than that contained in the server's FOLIO directory.

Suppose you already installed the application to the server's hard disk, but you redirected drive V to point to the C-DRIVE resource instead of the VIEWS resource. Now that the application is installed, try to redirect V to point to the VIEWS resource. The application doesn't run properly, however, unless you redirect V to the C-DRIVE resource. The application doesn't run properly with V redirected to the VIEWS resource probably because it is looking for configuration files in the V:\FOLIO directory, which doesn't exist.

When you redirect your V drive to the C-DRIVE resource, V:\FOLIO actually is the C:\FOLIO directory on the server. When you redirect your V drive to the VIEWS resource, however, V:\FOLIO actually is the C:\FOLIO\FOLIO directory on the server.

The trick to making your application work properly is to create a subdirectory named FOLIO under the existing directory named FOLIO on the server and copy all the files from the server's C:\FOLIO directory to the server's C:\FOLIO\FOLIO directory. Now when you redirect your V drive to point to the VIEWS resource on the server, there is a directory V:\FOLIO that contains the appropriate files, and the application works correctly.

Installing the Installation Program on the Server

You can install the installation program for many applications from the floppy disks that accompany the application to a server's hard disk. Once you install the installation program and related files to the server's hard disk, you no longer need to use the floppy disks for subsequent installations. You can perform subsequent installations on other nodes by redirecting a drive to point to the shared resource on the server, and perform the installation by accessing the install program from the server.

One benefit of this type of installation is that you only have to feed in once the many floppy disks; all other installations access the required files from the server. Also, the installation process is speeded up considerably due to the speed at which the installation program can access the installation data from the server compared to that of floppy disks.

Microsoft Windows and Networks

Microsoft Windows is a graphical interface that enables you to perform various tasks. You can run different programs in Windows that you can size, move, and organize. Many available application programs that run with Microsoft Windows provide an easy-to-use and flexible environment in which to perform your tasks.

Microsoft Windows has extensive network support and you can run it on a stand-alone PC or from a server's hard disk. You can install the Microsoft Windows installation program and associated files on a server to enable Windows to be installed on several nodes by accessing the installation program and files from a network server.

To install the Windows installation program and related files onto a server's hard disk, first redirect a drive to point to the shared resource on the server where you want to place the Windows installation files. Then run the Windows administration setup by typing the following command at the DOS prompt:

SETUP /A

The installation program asks you a few questions, including where you want Windows to copy the installation files. Specify the redirected drive and directory on the server. All the files are copied to the location specified; you are prompted to change disks as required.

After you have performed this administrative setup, installing Windows on each node is greatly simplified. First, redirect a drive to point to the resource (subdirectory) where the installation program is located on the server. Next, run the installation program.

You can perform a complete Windows installation to the hard disk of each network node or install Windows to run across the network. The standard Windows installation installs the complete Windows program to your hard disk and supports network activity (such as managing files on other computers using File Manager). The network installation installs only a few configuration files on your hard disk; the remainder of the Windows program files are accessed from the server. The network installation saves disk space on your hard disk but results in slower Windows operation because you have to access the primary Windows files over the network. To run the standard Windows installation program, redirect a drive to point to the shared resource containing the Windows installation program and type the following at the DOS prompt:

SETUP

To perform the network installation, follow the steps above but type the following command at the DOS prompt:

SETUP /N

Windows, and many applications that run under it, make use of SWAP files or TEMP files. If you check your defined variables (with the SET command) you will see a listing for TEMP=. This file should always point to a local drive.

TEMP and SWAP data is usually large and you do not want that additional traffic across the network wire. Placing it locally saves you time and enables other operations to have quicker response times.

Additionally, if you place these files on the server, say for example F:\TEMP, what happens when Karen logs on and her TEMP variable is set the same? Our information collides within that directory, corrupts the data, and (hopefully) both Windows sessions crash. The "hopefully" is added because if they do not crash, the data will become more and more corrupted.

The only reason TEMP files should be on the server is if you are utilizing diskless workstations. In that scenario, pay careful attention to redirect each workstation's TEMP files to a totally separate subdirectory.

Many applications that run under Windows also enable you to install their installation program either on a server or on the network node.

Windows incorporates several unique features including *dynamic data exchange* (DDE). DDE enables you to create real-time links among information contained in multiple data files. Windows enables you to run simultaneously different programs in different windows. Therefore, if certain data is linked to the information in another window using DDE, the information in the second window is automatically updated as you change the information in the first. Some networks support network DDE that enables you to create real-time links among the data in Windows programs running on separate computers.

Summary

This chapter discussed using network applications and single-user applications in a network environment. You learned how to use your existing applications with a network and even how to run existing single-user applications from a server. Using file and record locking to enhance network applications was discussed. Some time-saving techniques available with a network, such as installing software from a server instead of from floppy disks, were discussed.

In This Chapter. . .

Sharing printers in a network offers many benefits, but with the benefits comes a new way of thinking about printing. This chapter discusses the various features and options available when printing in a network environment, as well as using your local printer in a network environment. Specifically, this chapter discusses the following:

- Considerations when using a network printer

- How network printing differs from stand-alone printing

- Understanding the network print spooler and queue

- How application software and printers work together

- How shared printers are used on dedicated server networks

- What a print server is and devices that can be used to connect printers in a network

This chapter also introduces the following terms:

Print server

Print spooler

Print queue

Printing on a Network

A common feature of all *local area networks* (LANs) is the capability of every node in the network to access a common printer. Although printer sharing isn't necessarily the most powerful feature of a network, it's rarely a feature that goes unused.

The capability of multiple network nodes to share a single printer results in an immediate cost savings. By sharing a printer in a network, you eliminate the need to purchase a printer for each computer.

Prior to installing a network, a typical small office might have three computers, each with its own printer (see fig. 8.1). One computer is used primarily for accounting and has a high-speed, dot-matrix printer for invoices and other accounting reports. Another computer is used to maintain a marketing database. The information produced from the marketing database is used internally; therefore this computer is stuck with the ancient dot-matrix printer. A third computer is used for general correspondence and has a laser printer.

Figure 8.1

A common small
office layout prior to
implementing a
network.

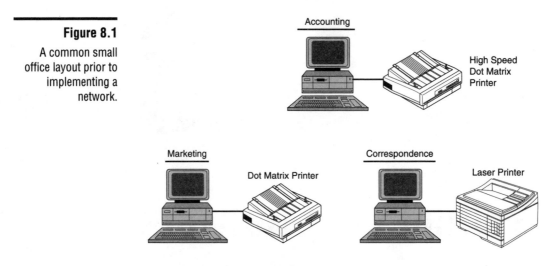

After the small office shown in figure 8.1 implements a peer-to-peer network, the same printers are still connected to the same computers. The big difference, however, is that any node in the network can print to any printer (see fig. 8.2). Marketing now creates mass mailings to send to everyone in the marketing database. Accounting now sends long accounting reports to the even faster laser printer. The correspondence computer now accesses a dot-matrix printer to print shipping labels.

Figure 8.2

The printing
capabilities of the
small office after
installing a peer-to-
peer network.

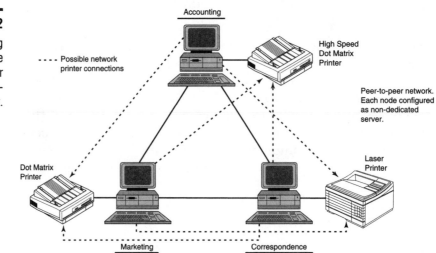

Understanding Network Printing

Network printing has many advantages over printing to a stand-alone printer. With the advantages come a few disadvantages, and some differences to which you may not be accustomed.

As discussed in Chapter 2, "Network Nodes and Their Function," you connect to a network drive by redirecting one of your printer device ports (usually LPT1, LPT2, or LPT3) to point to a shared-printer resource on a server. After you have redirected the selected printer device, any information sent to the selected device is routed by the network to the appropriate printer.

The Network Print Spooler

When you print from your computer or an application program to a network printer, the redirector sends the print job over the network to a temporary holding location on the server's hard disk called the *print queue*. A software routine in the NOS called the *print spooler* manages the queue and sends the job from the print queue to the printer (referred to as spooling to the printer).

In reality, the file you want to print is "copied" to a subdirectory on the print server, formatted for the appropriate printer. Other jobs that users are trying to print at the same time also are written to this subdirectory, and the subdirectory becomes the spooler. From here, the files are sent to the printer, in proper order, and deleted upon completion. When the print server also is on the file server, it becomes critical to leave enough free space on the hard disk for the spooling, because it still must copy the file to the appropriate directory.

LAN Server from IBM offers a great deal of flexibility in defining where the spooler is placed and the amount of disk space it is allowed. This is the exception rather than the rule, however you always should make certain you have sufficient disk space. The disk size is dependent upon the number of users you have, the number of print jobs they request, and the sizes of those print jobs.

Keep in mind that at some point, the printer will run out of paper without anyone noticing. When this happens, you want to be able to continue to spool print requests without running out of disk space.

The network print spooler manages the printing to each network printer. Without a network print spooler and the corresponding print queue, if more than one node prints simultaneously to the same printer, the two print jobs would try to print at the same time. This would result in a garbled mess coming from the printer.

To better understand the important role of the network print spooler and the print queue, consider the example in which three different network nodes are sending information to the same printer concurrently (see fig. 8.3). The print spooler accepts information from each workstation (A, B, and C) and stores the information for each print job in the print queue in a separate file . As soon as the first workstation finishes sending the print job, the spooler closes the file in the print queue and begins spooling the file to the printer. When finished with the first print job, the spooler looks for the next file in the queue ready to be printed and spools that print job to the printer. This print spooling process continues until the print queue is empty.

Figure 8.3

The function of the network print spooler.

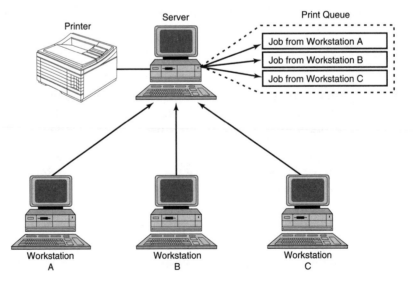

Print drivers format the file output according to the printer that you have configured. *Queue drivers* manage the queue—they take spooled files and send them to the printer. The usual sequence of operation follows:

1. Program
2. Print driver
3. Spooler
4. Queue driver
5. Print driver
6. Printer

When printing to a network, as opposed to printing to a local stand-alone printer, there is a delay from the time the application program starts sending data to the printer until the printer actually starts printing. The delay is caused by the print spooler waiting until the application finishes sending the entire print job before the spooler begins sending the information to the printer.

The delay in the beginning of actual printing may be annoying to some; however, it's important to understand two benefits associated with spooled network printing. First, because the network print spooler can accept information from the application program much faster than the printer can, the time you wait between when the application first starts sending information to be printed and when it finishes is much shorter. As a result of waiting less time for the application program to perform its printing routine, you can continue with your work much sooner. Also, because the print spooler is able to send print jobs to the printer as fast as the printer can accept the data, the overall throughput to the network printer is maximized, resulting in more efficient use of the network printer.

Older stand-alone applications sometimes spooled their print jobs before sending them to the local printer. They accomplished this by formatting the print job and writing it to the local hard disk, then slowly feeding this information to the printer. This was great in a non-networked environment because it is always much quicker to write to your local disk than to the printer. By slowly feeding it from the hard disk, the processor could divide processing between the print job and the user, and you could be busy working on something else, while the printing took place in the background.

In a network environment, however, programs that are not "network aware" format and write the print job to the local hard disk, then slowly feed it to the network. The network receives the information at a much slower rate than it should, and spools it in the subdirectory of the print server. It waits until all the data has been sent and written to this subdirectory, then slowly sends it out to the printer. The whole process takes more than twice as long as it should, AND there is the possibility that the network spooler will timeout while waiting on information from the local hard disk. If that happens, the print job comes out incomplete, or with other print jobs in the middle of it. (See the section, "Printer Timeout" later in this chapter for more information.)

Check the documentation on the individual applications if you have this problem. Many of them enable you to override their local spooling and send the output directly to the printer. Because the network spooler acts like the printer, this is exactly what you want.

Printing Features of the NOS

Although the network print spooler is at the heart of network printing, each *network operating system* (NOS) has additional features to control and enhance network printing. Some features are common to all NOSs, and some are unique to each individual NOS.

Printer Timeout

While receiving data from an application program, the network print spooler waits for an end-of-file character to be sent before it closes the print job and begins spooling the file to the printer. Some applications do not send the end-of-file character and, as a result, printing may not begin until the user exits the application. One solution to this anomaly is to press Ctrl+Alt+* after the application is finished sending the print job. This keystroke combination sends an end-of-file character to the print spooler. Many NOSs implement a printer timeout value as another solution. The *printer timeout value* usually is specified in seconds and is defined as the number of seconds the spooler waits after the last information is sent from the application before it automatically closes the print job. Printer timeout values of five or ten seconds usually are sufficient.

Some applications, especially those that print complicated graphics like desktop publishing programs, tend to process data, send a chunk of data to the printer, then process more data, send it to the printer, and so on. This process creates pauses between the streams of data being sent. Setting a printer timeout value too small in this situation causes the spooler to close the print job during one of the pauses and begin spooling it to the printer. When the next chunk of data is sent from the application, the spooler opens a new print file in the queue and begins accepting data in it. If the spooler has been receiving data from another node to be printed at the same time, there is a good chance the two print jobs will become mixed.

Figure 8.4 helps illustrate the previously described condition. Initially, both workstation A and workstation B are sending data to be printed. Because a pause greater than the timeout value is seen in the print data sent from workstation A, the spooler sees the information from workstation A as two separate print jobs, A-JOB-1 and A-JOB-2. As a result, the order of the print jobs in the queue is A-JOB-1, B-JOB-1, and A-JOB-2. In other words, the print job from workstation B is mixed between the print jobs from workstation A. To make matters even worse, if workstation A is sending graphics data to be printed, special printer codes are sent to the printer as the first part of the print job so that the printer understands that the data being sent is graphics data. The print job from workstation B is standard text data; therefore, the first part of the print job from workstation B sends special codes to the printer. The codes initialize the printer to receive text data. Now for the interesting part. When the second part of the print job from workstation A is sent to the printer, the printer interprets it as text data. In reality, however, the data in this case is graphics data. The result is pages and pages of garbage being printed, which leads to another important network printing feature—printer queue control.

Figure 8.4

The flow of print jobs from two different computers.

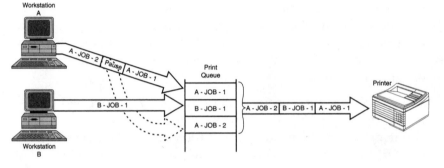

Printer Queue Control

Most NOSs incorporate features that enable you to view and manipulate print jobs in the queue. Each NOS incorporates a slightly different set of features, but in general most enable you to view information about each print job in the queue, such as its source, its size, and the date. In addition, you can usually stop a print job from spooling to the printer or delete the print job from the queue. In situations like those described in the preceding section, stopping a print job from spooling to the printer and deleting it from the queue can save many pages of wasted paper.

Immediate Despooling

Some NOSs incorporate a feature known as *immediate despooling* that allows spooling to the printer to begin before the application is finished sending the data to the spooler. With immediate despooling enabled, when the application begins to print, the data begins to print on the printer. Printing with immediate despooling enabled resembles printing without a network. Printer data still is managed by the spooler and passes through the print queue, so remember to set printer timeout values correctly.

Other Features

Several other features may be incorporated in the NOS to enhance network printing or give you more control over the network printing process.

Many NOSs enable you to specify *printer initialization strings*—special control codes sent to the printer before it receives a print job. You can use printer initialization strings to reset the printer to its default configuration or even to select a specific internal printer font to use for printing.

Often you can specify that a banner page be sent to the printer before each print job. *Banner pages*, which are separate pages printed before each document, usually include information such as which computer sent the print job, the name of the user, and the time and date. Banner pages make it easy to identify which print job is yours.

In the event of a problem with a printer such as a paper jam or a lack of paper, some NOSs provide features to notify specified users. Printer-notification features are especially valuable when printers are located at some distance from the users.

Another feature provided by some NOSs enables you to specify the number of characters per second the spooler should send to the printer. The spooler won't send more characters per second than the printer is able to receive. Sometimes the server must perform non-printing tasks that take priority over printing tasks, however, hence slowing the printing process. Increasing the characters-per-second value, however, can eliminate this problem.

Figure 8.5 is an example of a printer resource configuration screen for a single printer on a LANtastic network showing the variables within LANtastic that can be set for each individual printer resource.

```
NET_MGR USING: C:\LANTASTI.NET                    (C) Copyright 1994 Artisoft Inc.
┌─────────────────────────────────────────────────────────────────────┐
│   Detailed Information for @PRINTER                                   │
│  ─────────────────────────────────────────────────────────────────  │
│          Description: Laser Printer                                   │
│        Output Device: LPT1                                            │
│         Notification: DISABLED                                        │
│     Notification T/O: DISABLED                                        │
│          Banner Page: DISABLED                                        │
│           Form Feeds: DISABLED                                        │
│        Immed Despool: ENABLED                                         │
│      Despool Timeout: 3600                                            │
│       Lines Per Page: DISABLED                                        │
│            Tab Width: 0                                               │
│          Paper Width: 0                                               │
│         Chars/Second: 9600                                            │
│          Setup Delay: 0                                               │
│        Cleanup Delay: 0                                               │
│      Edit Setup String                                                │
│                                                                       │
│      ───── ACCESS CONTROL LIST ─────────────────────────             │
│     *                RWC-L--------                                    │
└─────────────────────────────────────────────────────────────────────┘
 Enter-Modify Selection, Esc-Exit, F1-Help
```

Notice in the figure that fields are offered for several key values:

- Banner Page—whether or not there will be one

- Form Feeds—almost always should be disabled because most applications automatically add this to the end of the document

- Timeout—in number of seconds

- Lines per page—another field usually defined by each individual application

Application Programs

When configuring an application program, you typically specify the type of printer (or printers) you have and the device name (port) to which the printer is connected (such as LPT1, LPT2, or LPT3). After specifying the printer configuration information, when you print something from your application program, the application knows what format in which to send the data, and to what device to send it.

The data format sent to the printer contains specific codes understood by the printer. The network doesn't need to know and doesn't care about the format of the data sent to the printer; the network spooler simply passes the data from the application to the printer.

The device to which the application sends its data is an important piece of information for the network because if the device (LPT1, for example) has been redirected, the network must intercept the print data and route it to the appropriate network printer.

Some applications take shortcuts to speed printing to local printers. Instead of passing the printer data to DOS, where it also can be redirected to a network printer, the application may use another method, which bypasses DOS and the network. For instance, even though you may have redirected a printer device, such as LPT1, to point to a network printer resource, printing may still be sent to the local printer, which is physically connected to LPT1. Most applications that bypass DOS for printing also have options to enable you to use the standard DOS printing routines, resulting in proper network printing. If your application does not route printer data through DOS or have an option to override this setting, you may be able to specify a printer device name other than LPT1, such as LPT2 or LPT3. Sometimes a printer device name such as LPT1.PRN or LPT2.PRN also works in this situation.

Many users have an application program configured for one type of printer but actually print to a different printer. Suppose, for example, you have a computer physically connected to an Epson LQ-570 dot-matrix printer (see fig 8.6). Your word processor application is configured for the Epson LQ-570 dot-matrix printer connected to LPT1. When you print a document from your word processing application, everything prints fine.

In this example the Epson LQ-570 dot-matrix printer defines the format the application uses for its print data and LPT1 defines where the data is sent.

Figure 8.6

An application program using physical and redirected printer connections.

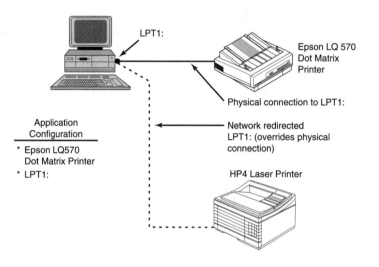

Now that you are networked, you decide to redirect your LPT1: device to point to the network HP 4 laser printer, and when you print from your word processing application the print job is sent to the HP 4 laser printer.

When you redirect a device (LPT1 in this example) to point to a network resource, the redirected device overrides any existing physical connection.

You notice that although the print job was sent to the laser printer, the printed page has strange characters and isn't formatted properly. Although the network often gets the blame when something like this happens, the problem is that the application is configured for the wrong printer. The network is just taking the information supplied by the application and sending it where you told it to go—to the HP 4 laser printer. The application program is sending the data in the format that the Epson LQ-570 understands, but the HP 4 doesn't; thus, the strange characters and incorrect format on the page. Change the printer configuration specified in the application from an Epson LQ-570 dot-matrix printer to an HP 4 laser printer to correct this problem. Remember that if you want to print locally, change the printer configuration setting back to LQ-570.

Printing on a Local Printer

A printer physically connected to your workstation does not have to be shared on the network. If your local printer is not shared with the network, you can print to it and expect the same operation as if the network didn't exist. Because you do have a network, however, you may redirect the device, such as LPT1, to which your printer is physically connected, to point to a shared-printer resource on the network. Using redirection, anything you print to the redirected device is sent to the network printer rather than your local printer. When finished using the redirected device, you can cancel the redirection and resume printing to your local printer.

Shared Network Printing (Dedicated Server)

If you have a server-based network, recall that workstations (or clients) generally can access and use the shared resources on the server, but the workstations cannot share their own resources. As a result, workstations cannot access the resources on other workstations—only on the server. Therefore, in a server-based network, the shared network printers usually are physically connected to a server.

Figure 8.7 illustrates which printers are available in a server-based network. This example shows a dedicated server and three workstations. Also, laser and dot-matrix printers are physically connected to the server. Notice that one of the workstations (workstation C) has a dot-matrix printer physically connected to it. The printers that are connected to the server can be shared with other nodes on the network. The dot-matrix printer connected to workstation C, however, can be used only as a local printer by workstation C, but cannot be shared with any other nodes on the network.

Figure 8.7

Shared network printers in a server-based network.

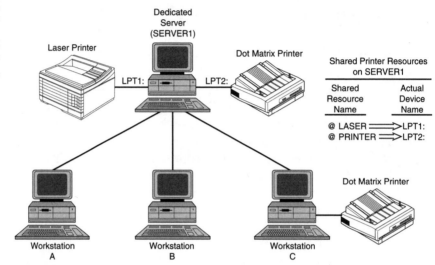

Suppose you are at workstation A. When you print to LPT1, you want to print to the server's laser printer, and when you print to LPT2, you want to print to the server's dot-matrix printer. To establish the network connection, redirect your LPT1 device to point to the @LASER resource on SERVER1 (refer to fig. 8.7) and redirect your LPT2 resource to point to the @PRINTER resource on SERVER1. If you have a LANtastic network, the following commands typed at the DOS prompt or included in a DOS batch file perform the desired redirections:

```
NET USE LPT1: \\SERVER1\@LASER
NET USE LPT2: \\SERVER2\@PRINTER
```

Figure 8.8 shows the LANtastic Windows interface that enables you to establish the same connections. You redirect a printer device by selecting the icon representing the shared-printer resource to connect to, and then dragging and dropping it on the device name (LPT1 or LPT2 in this example) used for the connection.

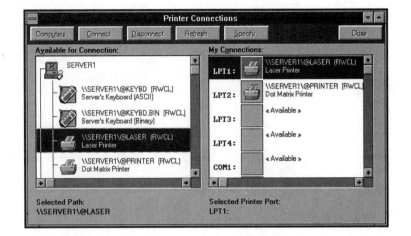

Figure 8.8

Establishing shared-printer connections using the LANtastic Windows interface.

Local and Shared-Network Printing (Nondedicated Server)

In a peer-to-peer network, any node configured as a server (either nondedicated or dedicated) can share printers with other nodes in the network. You may have a printer physically connected to the nondedicated server at which you are sitting that you want to use. In general, with a peer-to-peer network you can use the printer either as a local printer or as a network printer, but not both. The reason is that you don't want the network print spooler to send data to the printer while you are trying to print locally, nor do you want to send data to the printer when it is printing a network print job from another node.

Different NOSs react differently if a printer destination is used both locally and as a shared resource. In some cases, if you use the printer locally first, it is disabled for network access, and if it is used as a network printer first, it is disabled for local access. A general rule of thumb is if you are sharing a printer in a network, always establish a network connection to the printer before using it; do not attempt to use the printer locally.

Figure 8.9 is an example of printers shared in a peer-to-peer network. The example consists of three nondedicated servers in a peer-to-peer network with names DANA, ZAK, and KATIE. A dot-matrix printer is connected to server DANA, and a laser printer is connected to server KATIE. Both DANA and KATIE have printer resource names assigned to their respective printers. Any node in the network can access any shared printer.

Figure 8.9

Printers shared in a peer-to-peer network.

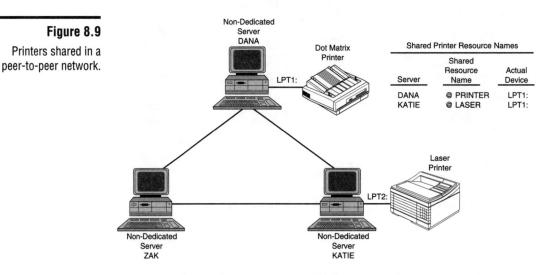

Suppose you want to configure each node so that when printing to LPT1, the data is sent to the laser printer connected to server KATIE, and when printing to LPT2, the data is sent to the dot-matrix printer connected to server DANA. In a LANtastic network, typing the following commands at the DOS prompt or including them in a DOS batch file on each node establishes these connections:

```
NET USE LPT1: \\KATIE\@LASER
NET USE LPT2: \\DANA\@PRINTER
```

Even though the laser printer is physically connected to server KATIE, you must include both of the preceding statements. Remember that when you redirect a device that has a physical connection, such as LPT1 on KATIE, the redirected device overrides the physical device (this is exactly what you want—to access a local printer through the network).

Server DANA's network printing parameters can be slightly confusing. With the two preceding redirections in effect, when DANA prints to LPT1, the print job is sent to the laser printer on server KATIE. When DANA prints to LPT2, the print job is sent to the dot-matrix printer on DANA. Don't let the fact that the dot-matrix printer on DANA is physically connected to LPT1 confuse the issue. When the shared-printer resource @PRINTER on DANA was defined, the physical device name was specified. From this point on, the network makes sure the data is sent to the correct location; all you have to do is tell the network the shared-printer resource name to which to print the data.

Print Servers

A *print server* is a server used primarily for network printing. When discussing network printing, the server to which the shared-network printer is physically connected is often referred to as the print server.

A *nondedicated print server*, manages network printing tasks but also can perform other functions, including serving as a workstation.

A *dedicated print server* is used only for printing. Many network installations with several heavily used printers incorporate the use of a dedicated print server. Because the speed at which a printer can accept data is relatively small compared to the rate the network spooler can spool data to the printer, dedicated print servers can be relatively low-performance computers. The only important requirement is that the print server has enough available disk space to hold the print jobs that may pile up in the queue waiting to be printed.

Print Server Devices

Often, you may want a printer located some distance from a computer. In a situation like this, special hardware is available that connects your printer to a device that connects directly to your network cable. Because these devices do not have a storage location for the print queue, typically the hard disk on one of the servers in the network is used. In addition, the shared-printer resource is configured on the same server that contains the print queue. When data is printed to the appropriate shared-printer resource, the server sends it to the device to which the printer is connected.

Remote Print Servers

Some NOSs support remote print servers. A *remote print server* can be a workstation that has special software that enables it to be used as a print server. With a remote print server, you can share printers that are physically connected to workstations with other nodes in the network. For example, using remote print-server software, the server-based network shown in figure 8.7 can share the dot-matrix printer connected to workstation C.

Printing with NetWare

NetWare uses three main utilities to handle the printing process—PRINTCON, CAPTURE, and PCONSOLE. PRINTCON is the first of the three, and is used to define printer setup configuration files.

CAPTURE is the redirection command used at each workstation to reroute print requests from the local ports to the network. The rerouting can be executed automatically when a user logs in (by adding it to their login script) or it can be executed from the command line. Figure 8.10 shows a sample capture of the network printers during a login sequence.

```
F:\>login edulaney
Enter your password:
Device LPT1: re-routed to queue TOSHIBA on server NRP.
Device LPT2: re-routed to queue LASER on server NRP.
Device LPT3: re-routed to queue LETTER on server NRP.
Device LPT3: re-routed to queue GRAPHICS on server NRP.
Good morning, EDULANEY.
```

Figure 8.10

Capturing network printers during a login.

To see if the printers have been redirected, at any time, a user can issue the command:

CAPTURE /SH

This command shows whether the printers are still active. To cancel connections once they are active, the command ENDCAP ends capturing, one port at a time, and returns the print destinations to local ports. ENDCAP /ALL returns all the ports to local configuration. Figure 8.11 illustrates this process.

```
C:\>endcap
Device LPT1: set to local mode.

C:\>capture /sh

LPT1:  Capturing Is Not Currently Active.

LPT2:  Capturing data to server NRP queue LASER.
       User will not be notified after the files are printed.
       Capture Defaults:Enabled       Automatic Endcap:Enabled
       Banner :(None)                 Form Feed       :No
       Copies :1                      Tabs            :No conversion
       Form   :0                      Timeout Count :10 seconds

LPT3:  Capturing data to server NRP queue GRAPHICS.
       User will not be notified after the files are printed.
       Capture Defaults:Enabled       Automatic Endcap:Enabled
       Banner :(None)                 Form Feed       :No
       Copies :1                      Tabs            :No conversion
       Form   :0                      Timeout Count :10 seconds

C:\>endcap all
LPT1:, LPT2:, and LPT3: set to local mode.

C:\>
```

Figure 8.11

Showing the active network print connections and canceling them.

Other parameters that can be used with capture enable you to specify what appears on the banner page (if there is one), the number of copies to print, and the length of timeout.

The last utility in the printing trilogy is PCONSOLE. PCONSOLE enables you to govern print jobs once they have been submitted. An individual user has complete control over his or her own print jobs, and an administrator has control over all print jobs. As shown in figure 8.12, the main menu enables you to change the current file server, check print queue information, and see print server information.

Figure 8.12

The main menu in PCONSOLE.

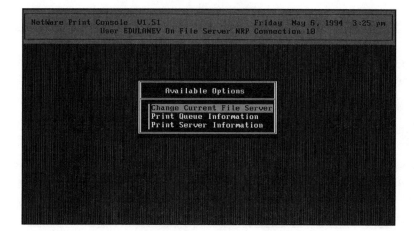

Most useful of all options is the ability to check current print job status. Selecting Print Queue Information from the main menu brings up a list of all queues that are recognized by the server. Using the arrow keys, you can move to any queue and press Enter. This brings up a list of available options, as shown in figure 8.13.

Selecting the first option, Current Print Job Entries, shows all jobs that are active on that printer, and the user who has them (see fig. 8.14). With appropriate permission (if it is your print job, or you are the administrator) you can delete a job before it finishes printing, add a job to the queue, or rearrange the order in which the listed jobs are sent to the printer.

Figure 8.13

Selecting a print queue to examine.

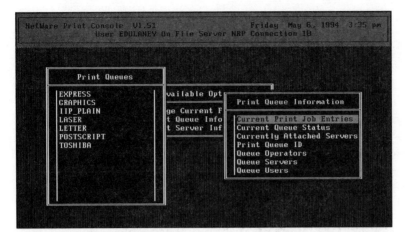

Figure 8.14

Current print jobs.

Summary

The capability of sharing printers is a widely used LAN feature. The network spooler used in conjunction with the print queue manages most of the network printing. Most NOSs also have several other features to enhance the printing features in a network.

Local printing capabilities in a network as well as the usage of network printers on nondedicated servers, dedicated servers, and other devices also were discussed.

In This Chapter. . .

This chapter discusses managing users and shared resources in your network. Included in the discussion are the issues of restricting user account access to satisfy security concerns and specifying access control lists for shared resources. In addition, this chapter examines disk and file management and how to organize your directory and file structure to maintain security while easing access to the shared resources. Specifically, the following topics are discussed:

- Using and managing individual accounts, wild card accounts, and group accounts.

- Restricting access to shared resources with *access control lists* (ACLs).

- Considering security and management issues for peer-to-peer and server-based networks.

- Managing and maintaining your disk and file structure on your server.

- Monitoring your server performance and implementing options when performance needs to be improved.

This chapter also introduces the following terms:

access control list (ACL)

group account

wild card account

disk caching

individual account

Managing Users and Resources

The capability of your network to meet your requirements is partially dependent on how well the users, resources, and overall network configuration are managed. The first step in achieving an efficient and effective network is to know the resources that will be shared, who will be allowed access to the shared resources, and what type of access each person will have.

The shared resources available to users depend on a number of factors, including the type of network (server-based or peer-to-peer), the location of the applications and directories that are to be shared, and the security and network performance requirements.

You can configure your network to allow as much or as little access to shared resources as you like, depending on how you choose to set up and manage your shared resources and user accounts.

Managing a network can be a pleasant or a stressful experience—it all depends on your attitude and how much thought you put into creating and maintaining a successful network. By knowing what to expect before experiencing the unexpected, you will always be one step ahead.

Managing User Accounts

Most networks allow the use of user accounts for accessing the network and the shared resources on the network. Maintaining a level of security is the single most important reason user accounts are created. Each computer configured as a server in your network is able to share its resources with other nodes in the network. Therefore, the type of data on each server and the level of security that must be maintained determine which resources are shared and which users may access the shared resources.

For small networks, security may not be much of an issue and specific user accounts with restrictions may not be necessary. For larger networks, however, security is a real concern and user accounts with restrictions in place are a requirement.

The security features incorporated in a *network operating system* (NOS) usually determine what types of user accounts are available. A NOS used primarily for small networks may not incorporate specific user accounts but rather may incorporate password restrictions on the access of shared resources. A NOS used for large networks not only has individual accounts but also supports the use of wild card and group accounts to enable users to be grouped into specific categories that determine the type of access they may have.

If you have more than a single server, such as in a peer-to-peer network or in larger server-based networks, many NOSs provide features to enable you to configure your accounts once and then either (manually or automatically) copy the accounts to other servers in the network or specify a common account server for the accounts.

The types of security features available for user accounts vary with each NOS. Some NOSs, including Artisoft LANtastic and Novell NetWare, have features that enable you to specify times and days a user is allowed to log in to and use a server. This feature ensures that network usage only occurs during certain times and often is used to prevent unauthorized network access during off hours.

Another user account security feature supported by Novell NetWare is the capability to detect and lock out intruders that have entered the wrong password for an account. When configuring NetWare you can specify the failed login parameters to identify intruders and the resultant account lockout to perform. An attempt by an intruder to log in using a specific account causes the account to be locked, preventing further logins until a time specified during the network configuration process.

Depending on the potential size, capability, and security requirements of a network, a NOS may support the use of individual accounts, wild card accounts, and group accounts.

Individual Accounts

An *individual account* is an account set up for use by a single person to log in to a network and use the shared resources or access the management utilities. To log in (or gain access) to a server, you are usually required to specify the name of the server you want to access, your user name, and your password. The server then checks its list of accounts and allows access if the information you entered is correct.

Each NOS supports different features for individual accounts. Figure 9.1, for example, shows the Account Information screen for an individual account for a server in a LANtastic network.

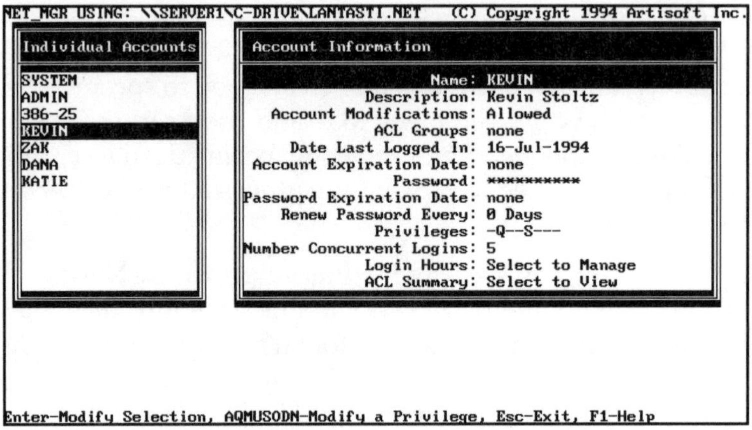

Figure 9.1

The Account
Information screen for
an individual account
in LANtastic.

```
NET_MGR USING: \\SERVER1\C-DRIVE\LANTASTI.NET     (C) Copyright 1994 Artisoft Inc.
┌─Individual Accounts─┐  ┌─Account Information──────────────────────────────┐
│SYSTEM               │  │                   Name: KEVIN                     │
│ADMIN                │  │            Description: Kevin Stoltz              │
│386-25               │  │   Account Modifications: Allowed                 │
│KEVIN                │  │             ACL Groups: none                     │
│ZAK                  │  │     Date Last Logged In: 16-Jul-1994             │
│DANA                 │  │ Account Expiration Date: none                    │
│KATIE                │  │               Password: **********               │
│                     │  │Password Expiration Date: none                    │
│                     │  │    Renew Password Every: 0 Days                  │
│                     │  │             Privileges: -Q--S---                 │
│                     │  │ Number Concurrent Logins: 5                      │
│                     │  │             Login Hours: Select to Manage        │
│                     │  │            ACL Summary: Select to View           │
└─────────────────────┘  └──────────────────────────────────────────────────┘

Enter-Modify Selection, AQMUSODN-Modify a Privilege, Esc-Exit, F1-Help
```

LANtastic provides many features for individual accounts. In addition to the common account name, password, and description information, the information allowed for an individual account includes options to enable the user to make changes (Account Modifications) to the account and the names of groups (ACL Groups) to which the account belongs. A password expiration date or the period in days that a new password must be set also can be specified. The account may have certain privileges associated with it that determine, among other things, the type of management functions available to the account (such as setting up new accounts or changing passwords for existing accounts). The time of day that the account may log in to the network also can be determined, as well as the number of people that may be logged in to the server concurrently using the same account name.

Additional features for individual accounts supported by some networks, such as Novell NetWare, include the capability to specify an account balance for charging users to access the network, and to limit the amount of disk space a user can use.

Many networks also support the use of a Guest account. A Guest account enables users without specific accounts to log in and use the network. A person logged in through the Guest account usually has limited capability, such as access to a single shared directory resource and printer.

It is the responsibility of each user to help maintain the security of the network by following established guidelines regarding the use and maintainance of passwords for individual accounts. To keep unauthorized individuals from gaining access to the network, consider the following guidelines:

- Always memorize the password for your account; don't write down your password.

- Choose a password that would be difficult for someone to guess but at the same time is easy for you to remember. Names are not good choices for your password because they are easy for someone to guess. You can create a suitable password by combining words and numbers such as the month you were born followed by the address of your house.

- Change your password frequently so there's no chance that someone can figure out your password by watching you type it over and over.

Most NOSs also have features that the system Administrator can implement to force users to change their passwords at specified intervals.

Wild Card Accounts

A *wild card account* is an account that enables several users to log in to a server using similar account names. Each wild card account has a single password that is used by each person who logs in using the account. Wild card accounts enable you to set up accounts for groups of people or departments with similar security privileges. A wild card account with the name SALES-*, for example, would allow users to log in to the server using names such as SALES-MIKE or SALES-KYLE.

Some NOSs use wild card accounts to eliminate the requirement to log in to a server. If you have a wild card account named * with no password, for example, you don't have to log in to a server before using shared resources on the server; you are automatically logged in when you try to use the shared resource.

Wild card accounts often have the same features as individual accounts, except that wild card accounts are usually used for groups of people.

Group Accounts

The term *group account* may be used by different NOSs to mean different things. Some NOSs refer to an individual account that allows more than one person at a time to use it as a group account. Other NOSs refer to a wild card account as a group account.

The more common definition of a group account is an account that contains a list of members composed of individual accounts or wild card accounts or both. Group accounts, or ACL Groups as they are sometimes called, are usually used to group together accounts that have certain access privileges to a shared resource.

Figure 9.2 shows a group account named ADMIN that has four accounts as members: the individual accounts KEVIN, DANA, and JOHN and the wild card account ACCTG-*. As you will see later, when specifying accounts that may have access to a particular resource, you can assign any type of account name. If, for example, you have a shared resource on your server named C-DRIVE that is the entire C drive on the server, you wouldn't want everyone to have access to the drive. Suppose you want the accounts KEVIN, DANA, JOHN, and ACCTG-* to have access to the C-DRIVE resource. You could specify each account separately as having access, or you could specify just the ADMIN account, of which KEVIN, DANA, JOHN, and ACCTG-* are members.

Some networks automatically assign each individual account to a particular group. Novell NetWare, for example, creates a group account called EVERYONE of which each new individual account is a member. Therefore, each individual account automatically has the access rights specified in the EVERYONE group.

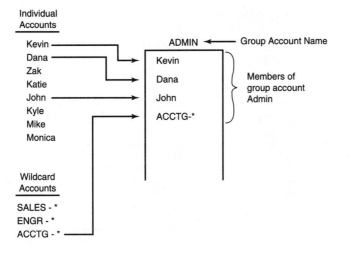

Figure 9.2

The accounts that are members of the ADMIN group account.

Login Scripts

A *login script* is a script or DOS batch file that executes a list of network commands to log a user into a certain server or group of servers and establish predetermined network connections.

Suppose that when you turn on your workstation, there are specific network connections you want to establish each time. You could create a login script (which amounts to a list of network commands executed in a batch file) to establish the connections for you. Figure 9.3 shows the shared resources that exist for two servers in a network: SERVER1 and SERVER2. Each time you turn on your computer, you want to redirect your K drive to point to the WORD shared resource on SERVER1, redirect your LPT1 device to point to the LASER shared printer resource on SERVER1, redirect your L drive to point to the LOTUS shared resource on SERVER2, and redirect your LPT2 device to point to the shared printer resource PRINTER on SERVER2. To establish the network connections automatically, you would create a login script or batch file that contained network commands such as the following:

```
NET LOGIN \\SERVER1
NET USE K: \\SERVER1\WORD
NET USE LPT1: \\SERVER1\LASER
```

```
NET LOGIN \\SERVER2
NET USE L: \\SERVER2\LOTUS
NET USE LPT2: \\SERVER2\PRINTER
```

Figure 9.3

Determining the
redirected drive and
devices to include in a
login script.

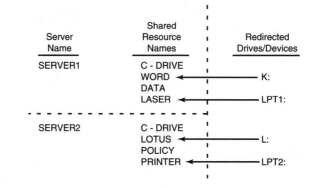

The command on the first line logs you in to SERVER1. The command on the second line redirects your K drive to point to the shared resource WORD on SERVER1. The command on the third line redirects your LPT1 device to point to the shared printer resource LASER on SERVER1. The command on the fourth line logs you in to SERVER2. The command on the fifth line redirects your L drive to point to the shared resource LOTUS on SERVER2. The last command redirects your LPT2 device to point to the shared printer resource PRINTER on SERVER2.

Login scripts perform several other functions in addition to logging in users to the network and establishing network connections. Login scripts can display greeting messages, run maintenance routines, check for mail, and execute specific functions depending on the value of a variable passed to the login script. Consider the following login script that displays information to the user, logs in the user to a server and establishes network drive connections, checks for mail, and backs up the user's data if it hasn't already been backed up for the current day:

```
@ECHO OFF
TYPE DAYINFO.TXT
ECHO *********************
ECHO * PLEASE LOG IN NOW *
ECHO *********************
```

```
NET LOGIN \\SERVER1 ?"Username: " ^"Password: "
NET USE K: \\SERVER1\%USER%
NET POSTBOX
IF NOT EXIST K:\BACKUP\%DATE% GOTO DONE
ECHO ****************************************************
ECHO * PLEASE WAIT WHILE A DAILY BACKUP IS PERFORMED... *
ECHO ****************************************************
CALL DBACKUP
:DONE
```

The TYPE DAYINFO.TXT statement displays the contents of the
DAYINFO.TXT file to the screen, which contains general system
information the user should know. Next the ECHO statements are
displayed to the screen prompting you to log in. The NET LOGIN
statement prompts you for your user name and password then
logs you in to SERVER1. Your K drive is redirected to point to the
shared resource name that is the same as your user name (indicated by the %USER% variable). The NET POSTBOX command
checks for mail addressed to you and notifies you if any exists.
Finally, the K:\BACKUP directory is checked to see if a file with a
name corresponding to the current date exists. If the file doesn't
exist, the daily backup routine is executed (CALL DBACKUP),
which performs a daily backup of the data on the redirected K
drive and creates the file with a name corresponding to today's
date in the K:\BACKUP directory. Otherwise the backup routine
is skipped by jumping to the DONE label.

Managing Shared Resources

Shared resources are created on the server to allow network nodes
to access drives, directories, and devices on the server. The type of
information stored on the server usually determines which resources you choose to share with others. Although you might
decide to allow some users access to specific directories on the
server, other users (such as the system Administrator) need to
have access to the entire drive.

The *system Administrator* or *system manager* is the person responsible for managing and maintaining the network. Responsibilities usually include the following tasks: adding and deleting users; specifying and managing shared resources on each server, including determining which users may access the shared resources; and file management functions, including designating the location of shared directories and applications on the server.

When you create a shared resource, many NOSs also enable you to specify the users who can access certain resources as well as the type of access each user can have. Other NOSs may offer password-protection features for individual shared resources to restrict access to the shared resource.

The type of network (peer-to-peer or server-based) and the mix of workstations, dedicated servers, and nondedicated servers also play a role in determining which resources you want to share and with whom.

Prior to implementing a network, you control access to your computer by not allowing others to sit at it. Once you implement a network, however, you need to consider and anticipate problems that might arise. If your computer is a workstation in a server-based network, you don't need to worry about security on your computer; no one else on the network is able to access it. You do, however, need to be concerned about the security of the data on the server. If your computer is configured as a nondedicated server in a peer-to-peer network, then you need to consider the security of your data and determine what to share and with whom.

The most important consideration when evaluating security requirements on a network is to realize that in a network several users are accessing and changing the information on a single computer (the server). An inappropriate action by a single user, such as deleting the wrong files, can adversely affect everyone. Therefore, you must take into account the detrimental effect the action of a single person can have on the rest of the users in the network, and structure the security and access rights and privileges accordingly.

Access Control Lists

An *access control list* (ACL) is a list of accounts that are allowed access to a particular shared resource. Each account in an ACL usually has a specified type of access to the shared resource, such as full access or read-only access.

Figure 9.4 is an example of an ACL for the C-DRIVE shared resource on a server. The account ZAK has full access to the C-DRIVE resource, whereas ADMIN has read-only access. If group accounts are allowed in the NOS, an account such as ADMIN could be a group of individual accounts or wild card accounts or both.

```
C - DRIVE ACL

Account          Access Rights
ZAK              FULL ACCESS
ADMIN            READ-ONLY
```

Figure 9.4

The ACL for the C-DRIVE shared resource.

Figure 9.5 shows how an ACL is actually specified in the LANtastic Windows interface. The Access Control List dialog box for the C-DRIVE resource lists three entries in the User/Group **N**ame field. Many types of access rights can be specified for each account in the list, including Read access (R), Write access (W), create file (C), create directory (M), and so on. In the example shown in figure 9.5, the account ZAK has full access rights and the account ADMIN (which could be an individual or a group account) has read-only access. All other accounts, as indicated by the asterisk (*), have no access.

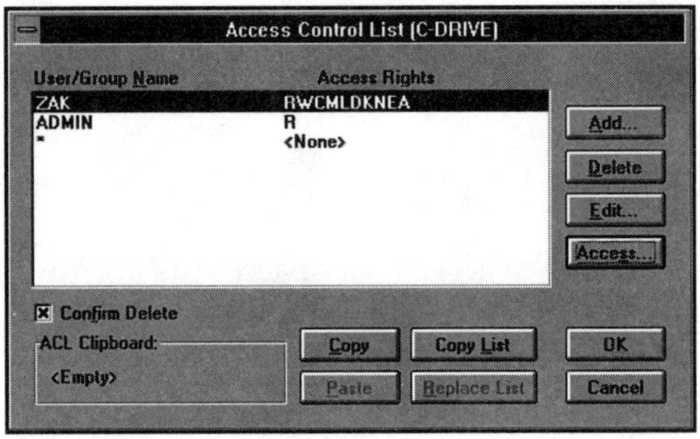

Figure 9.5

The Access Control
List dialog box for the
C-DRIVE resource in a
LANtastic network.

Access Control List (C-DRIVE)

User/Group Name	Access Rights
ZAK	RWCMLDKNEA
ADMIN	R
*	<None>

Add...
Delete
Edit...
Access...

X Confirm Delete

ACL Clipboard:
<Empty>

Copy   Copy List   OK
Paste   Replace List   Cancel

You can simplify management of your network by using group accounts in conjunction with ACLs for a shared resource. Suppose you have a shared resource on your server named DATA, which is used to store general files that all the users in your network use (see fig. 9.6). You have created a group account named GENERAL, whose members are every individual account in your network. Instead of listing each individual account in the DATA ACL, you can list the GENERAL group account. You might have several shared resources with the GENERAL group account in the ACL. If you use the GENERAL group account, when you add new individual accounts you can include the new account as a member of the GENERAL group account. Because the GENERAL group account is specified in the ACL of the shared resources, the new account automatically has access to the shared resources. If you weren't using group accounts, each time you added a new individual account you would have to modify the ACL for each shared resource to which the new account would have access.

If you do not have strict security requirements, most networks that support the flexibility of ACLs and group accounts also allow default configurations that give all users full access to every resource.

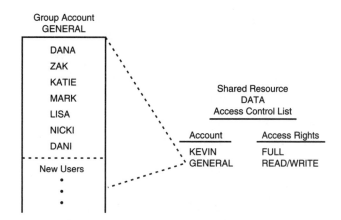

Figure 9.6

Using group accounts to simplify shared resource management.

Dedicated Servers

Server-based networks and sometimes peer-to-peer networks use dedicated servers. A dedicated server is usually placed in a secure location with limited access to prevent accidental damage or unauthorized use. Because a dedicated server cannot be used as a workstation, access to the contents of the dedicated server is usually by means of the network. Occasionally a few administrative functions are performed at the server by the system Administrator.

Although most users need to access only specific resources, such as the resources allowing them to run Word or Lotus 1-2-3, the system Administrator needs access to the entire drive (see fig. 9.7). In this situation, you probably want to create shared resources with specific access rights for different accounts. Only the system Administrator would have access to the C-DRIVE resource, which points to the C drive on the server. All users would have access to the WORD6 and the 123 resources, which point to the WORD directory containing Microsoft Word and to the LOTUS directory containing Lotus 1-2-3. Only key personnel would have access to the ACCOUNT resource, which points to the ACCTG directory containing the accounting information.

Figure 9.7

Identifying access rights for various shared resources on a server.

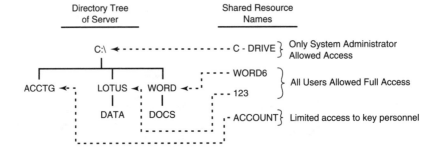

Recall that when you redirect a drive to point to a shared resource, you have access to the server's directory specified by that resource and to any subdirectories under it. A person accessing the 123 shared resource, for example, would have access to the LOTUS directory on the server as well as to the DATA directory beneath it. The system Administrator, by accessing the C-DRIVE resource, would have access to the root directory on the server's C drive in addition to the directories below it, which include ACCTG, LOTUS, LOTUS\DATA, WORD, and WORD\DOCS.

Besides having your dedicated server in a secure area, you need to consider other factors that could compromise the security of the information on the server or the reliability of the server itself. What happens, for example, if you lose power to the server due to an electrical outage? If someone is in the middle of updating a file when power fails, the effect on the data could be disastrous. It's bad enough to lose important data on a stand-alone computer, but if the directory on the server becomes corrupted everyone is affected. You can use an *uninterruptable power supply* (UPS) in situations such as this. The UPS provides power to the computer immediately after the primary power source fails and continues to supply power to the server for a specified amount of time thereafter. Many NOSs also have features that enable the UPS to send a signal to the NOS in the event of a power outage. The NOS then notifies the users of an imminent server shutdown allowing enough time for the users to save what they are doing and exit the program.

If your dedicated server shuts down and reboots for any reason, you also need to consider the sequence of events that occurs when the server is started again. Will it automatically start and resume dedicated server operation or are there a series of steps that must be performed to start the server? If steps are required, who knows what they are? Are they documented somewhere so the server can be started even if the system Administrator isn't available? If the server is locked in a secure area, who has the keys? There is nothing more frustrating to a user than to know that a few keystrokes typed at the server will get the network going again when there is nobody in the area with keys to the room the server is in.

Nondedicated Servers

Nondedicated servers usually are used in peer-to-peer networks and eliminate the requirement to purchase an additional computer for use as a dedicated server. Nondedicated servers function both as servers (to share resources with others in the network) and as workstations. Because a nondedicated server also functions as a workstation, it is not usually located in a secure location.

The management of shared resources discussed in the preceding section on dedicated servers also applies to nondedicated servers. The fact that nondedicated servers also are used as workstations introduces additional resource-management issues.

Care needs to be taken to ensure that access to a shared resource on a nondedicated server by another network node is not interrupted because the person sitting at the node inadvertently turns off the system.

An important point to keep in mind is that while you can specify shared resources and access rights to the shared resources for specific users, the person sitting at the computer has full access to the entire drive by accessing C. For this reason, you wouldn't want to move your accounting software to a computer other than one that is used by a person allowed to access the accounting data. The accounting program usually requires a password to gain access, although the password does not prevent an unauthorized individual from accidentally deleting important files.

Maintaining Disk and File Management

Managing the contents and organization of the drives and directories on a server is an important task in any network, regardless of the type. The proper organization of the drives and directories on your server can contribute to establishing a network that is easier to use, provides better security, and operates faster.

When you organize your drives and directories and the files within them, you are able to specify fewer resources to access for performing daily tasks. If you have an organized directory structure, you can back up your data more efficiently and with less time and effort.

In addition to organizing the shared drive and directory resources on the server, you need to consider the fault tolerance features available in the NOS to prevent the accidental loss of data. As a minimum, you need to have a plan in place to routinely back up the data on your server. Many of the server-based networks have fault tolerance features that when implemented can prevent the loss of data on the server. Features such as disk mirroring and duplexing protect against data loss due to failures of the system by duplicating the same information on two different hard disks; if one fails, the other can be used.

You also might find it valuable to have a system in place to record the usage and rate at which hard disk space is depleted on your server. By recording this information, you can anticipate future problems, such as running out of disk drive storage, and take the appropriate action to prevent them. Some NOSs actually let the system Administrator specify how much disk space a user is allowed when the user account is created.

Another important decision you need to make is what information you want to store on the server and what information you want to store on the local computer's hard disk. In most situations, a combination of storage on the server and the local computer's hard disk works best. Several factors determine the location of programs and data in each situation, however. If you have plenty of disk space on each computer's hard disk, in general, follow these guidelines:

- Data that will be accessed by others in the network should be stored on a server.

- Single-user applications should be stored on each computer's local hard disk.

- Multiuser applications should be stored on a server.

Of course there are exceptions to the above guidelines. Limited hard disk storage space on the local computer requires that more is stored on the server's hard disk. In this situation, it is advisable to store the single-user applications and data that is not to be shared with others in a private user directory on the server. You also can store all your data on the server for backup purposes—it's easier to back up information that exists in a single location (the server) than to routinely back up each workstation.

File and Directory Structure

The organization of the files and directories on your server can greatly simplify the maintenance of shared resources. Properly organized, you can access shared resources with fewer potential problems and easier use.

Consider the following example: Your file server has two application programs installed that are accessed by all users, an accounting program accessed by a few key individuals, and a data directory used to store the files created by the application programs (see fig. 9.8). The important fact to notice in this example is that for a user to be connected to the application directories (LOTUS and WORD) on the server in addition to the DATA directory, three drive redirections are necessary. On the workstation, drive D is redirected to point to the DATA shared resource on the server, drive W is redirected to point to the WORD6 shared resource on the server, and drive L is redirected to point to the 123 shared resource on the server.

Figure 9.8

Typical shared
resources on a server
and the workstation
redirections used to
access them.

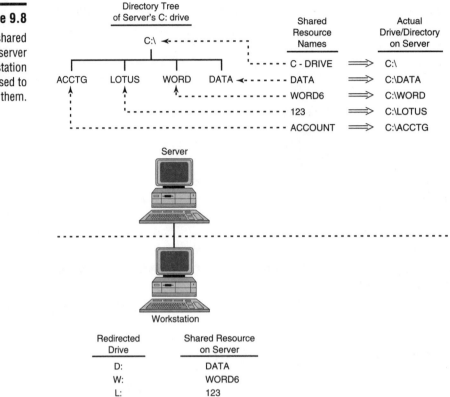

Now consider the alternative directory structure for the server's C
drive shown in figure 9.9. The only change is that the USERAPPS
directory has been added and the LOTUS, WORD, and DATA
directories have been moved to reside under the USERAPPS
directory instead of beneath the root directory as before. This
relatively basic change allows what was previously three separate
drive redirections to be replaced with one. The workstation now
redirects drive D, which points to the APPS shared resource on
the server. Instead of having to access the D, W, and L drives to
access the LOTUS, WORD, and DATA directories, the user can
access a single redirected drive D.

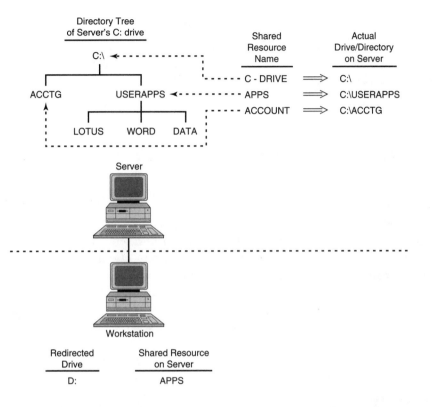

Figure 9.9

Shared resources on a server and the workstation redirections used to access them after changing the server's directory structure.

Table 9.1 illustrates the drive and directory used on the workstation to access the desired directories on the server with the original directory structure that requires three workstation drive redirections. Table 9.2 illustrates the revised directory structure that requires only one workstation drive redirection.

Table 9.1
Original Directory Structure of Server's Drive C

Workstation Drive/Directory	Actual Drive/Directory on Server
D:\	C:\DATA
W:\	C:\WORD
L:\	C:\LOTUS

Table 9.2
Revised Directory Structure of Server's Drive C

Workstation Drive/Directory	Actual Drive/Directory on Server
D:\DATA	C:\USERAPPS\DATA
D:\WORD	C:\USERAPPS\WORD
D:\LOTUS	C:\USERAPPS\LOTUS

You realize another benefit in organizing your server's directories as described in the preceding example. When you install new applications, you can install the application from a workstation and accept the default directory suggested by the installation program, such as LOTUS. Instead of the application appearing in the root directory of the workstation's redirected drive (which is actually a directory on the server), each application appears in its own directory as if it were installed on a local drive on the workstation.

Backups

By maintaining a backup of the programs and data on your server, you ensure against a potential disaster in the event that your server's hard disk fails or the data on the drive otherwise become corrupted.

A network provides many options for maintaining a backup of your programs and data. NOSs that support disk mirroring or disk duplexing automatically maintain a duplicate backup of your data, but they also require additional drives to do so.

In many cases, the method of choice for backing up servers in the network is the use of a tape backup. A tape backup enables you to copy any drive or directory to a small data tape cartridge. The tape cartridge can easily be removed from the tape backup drive and kept off the premises. In this way, a backup is maintained in the event of a fire or some other disaster that would destroy your computer.

Tape backup programs allow you to specify the drive or directory to back up. Normally, you would install the tape backup drive in a workstation. To back up a drive or directory on the server, you redirect a workstation drive to point to the shared resource on the server you want to back up. You then run the tape backup program, specify the redirected drive or directories on the drive to back up, and the process begins.

> If other nodes are accessing the files you are trying to back up, you receive a sharing violation error, which indicates that you are not allowed to access a file for backup because someone else is already accessing the file. To maintain a good backup, perform the backup when there is no chance of another user accessing the files, such as in the late evening or early morning.

Most tape backup programs include utilities that enable you to configure them to back up selected drives or directories automatically at predetermined times.

Suppose you wanted to back up the directory on your server that contains your accounting data (see fig. 9.10). The directory on the server you want to back up is C:\ACCTG\ACCTDATA. The shared resource on the server you use to access your accounting program and data is ACCOUNT, which points to the C:\ACCTG directory on the server's C drive. From the workstation, you redirect your K drive to point to the ACCOUNT shared resource on the server. You then run the tape backup program and specify the K:\ACCTDATA directory to back up your accounting data.

> The redirected K drive on your workstation points to the C:\ACCTG directory on the server's hard disk. Consequently, you need to specify the K:\ACCTDATA directory on the workstation to back up the C:\ACCTG\ACCTDATA directory on the server.

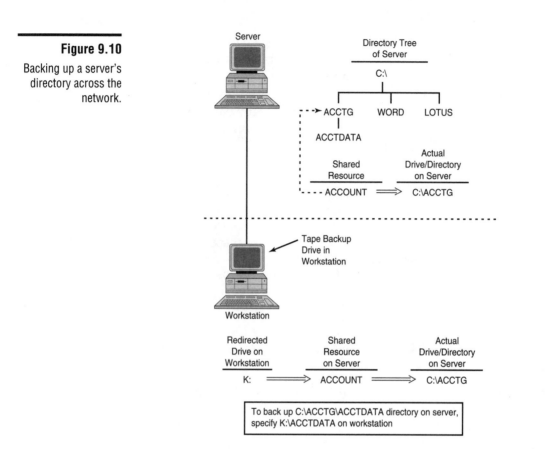

Figure 9.10

Backing up a server's directory across the network.

Although backing up a server is a relatively straightforward task, the following are several options for backing up individual workstations:

- If you have a peer-to-peer network, you can back up any nondedicated server the same way you backed up the server described previously.

- You can install a tape drive in each workstation or connect a portable tape backup drive to the workstation.

- You can copy to the server the information to be backed up and then back up the selected directory on the server using the tape backup drive.

- Some tape backup drives include software that runs on each workstation to enable a tape backup drive on another computer to back up the workstation's hard disk.

The workstation backup method you choose depends on several factors including cost, performance requirements, and available hard disk storage space. Installing a tape drive in each computer, for example, can be expensive. Using a portable tape backup drive is cost effective, but it can be difficult to locate the drive and awkward to plug it in to the back of the computer to perform the backup. Copying to the server the data to be backed up and then backing up the data requires two steps instead of one, and also requires sufficient disk space on the server's hard disk for the temporary storage of the backup data. Often the tape backup software installed on a workstation is loaded into memory as a *terminate-and-stay-resident program* (TSR), which uses valuable conventional memory and can cause problems with other application software.

A technique often implemented to back up important data on a network takes advantage of the power of the network to perform the backup function. The information on the server that needs to be backed up is actually copied to another node in the network. Often a batch file is created to perform the backup function from one network node to another. Suppose, for example, you want to back up the same accounting data directory that you did in the preceding example (see fig. 9.10). After redirecting drive K to point to the ACCOUNT resource on the server, you would issue the following command to back up all the information in the server's C:\ACCTG\ACCTDATA (K:\ACCTDATA) directory to the C:\ACCTBACK directory on your workstation:

```
XCOPY K:\ACCTDATA\*.* C:\ACCTBACK\*.*
```

To save hard disk storage space when backing up the data from one hard disk to another, you can use a compression program such as PKZIP that can take all the files specified for backup and compress them into a single file that requires less storage space on the hard disk.

continues

Most compression programs can run at the DOS command line and therefore can be included in the batch file in place of the XCOPY command in the previous example.

Monitoring Server Performance

As time goes on, the usage and demands made on the network and the network server(s) increase. The responsibilities that come with managing a network include monitoring the performance of the server and making any necessary adjustments to the network.

Several tools are available to help you to monitor a server's performance. Some NOSs include utilities that monitor the usage of the server so you can identify trends that may indicate a need to change the server's configuration.

Most NOSs enable you to change the operating parameters of the NOS to improve network performance. Before changing the configuration of the NOS, it's a good idea to establish measurements you can use to determine the effect on network performance of any changes made. If possible, develop a series of routines that simulate actual network tasks that would be performed in your situation. If, for example, you primarily run an accounting program and copy files over the network, set up a batch file that starts the accounting program, run a macro to perform some routine functions, and then exit the accounting program and copy a group of files across the network. Record the time it takes to perform the tasks so you can later compare it with the time recorded after changing the network parameters.

The following sections describe actions you can take to improve the performance of your network. The effect that each action has on network performance varies with each situation and is a function of many factors. These factors include the NOS, disk-drive speed and size, server power (386, 486) and speed, RAM, system configuration, network adapters, number of nodes on the network, usage of dedicated and nondedicated servers, and so on.

Drive Defragmentation

As data are saved, edited, and deleted from the server's hard disk, the information stored on the drive becomes fragmented. The more the drive is used, the worse the fragmentation becomes. The frequent drive access of network servers tends to exaggerate the rate at which drive fragmentation occurs. Eventually, the files on the server's hard disk become so badly fragmented that the performance of the drive is adversely affected. The result is poor network performance. Several utility programs are available (for DOS formatted hard disks) that you can run to defragment the drive in your computer. DOS 6.0 (and later) also includes a defragmentation program for defragmenting DOS formatted hard disks. Running a drive defragmentation program reads the existing data from the hard disk and writes it back to the drive in a consecutive format. When you access a file after defragmenting the hard disk, the drive is able to locate the file and read the contents consecutively instead of jumping all over the disk for the various pieces of information. The result is much better network performance.

To run a defragmentation program on a DOS formatted drive on a server, you must temporarily disable the server program.

NOSs other than DOS that use hard disk formats, such as Novell NetWare and OS/2's optional *High Performance File System* (HPFS), might not have defragmentation utilities readily available. The file structures used by these file systems, however, often are less susceptible to fragmentation problems than are DOS file structures.

Disk Caching

One of the best performance boosters for a network server is the implementation of a disk-caching program. Disk-caching programs use the server's RAM to temporarily hold information being transferred to and from the server's hard disk. With a disk-caching program, each time the hard disk is read, the information also is read into the *cache* (an area in the server's RAM). The next time information is needed from the hard disk, the disk-caching program first checks to see if it is located in the cache; if it is, the program reads it from there instead of from the hard disk. Reading information from RAM (the cache) is much faster than reading from the hard disk. Because a disk-caching program contains algorithms to maximize the efficiency of transferring the data, general system performance is greatly enhanced.

Disk caching should always be implemented on a network server. If it hasn't been used, implementing a disk cache improves system performance dramatically. In addition, the more RAM that can be devoted to the cache, the better the system performance.

Application Distribution

As you monitor the performance of the servers in your peer-to-peer network, you may discover an imbalance in the work load performed by each server. You might, for example, have a large database application to update customer information that is accessed from several nodes. In addition, the same computer might contain your accounting program, which has a high usage rate. Perhaps another server in your network is used primarily for word processing and storing documents from the word processor. In this situation, the performance of your network would probably benefit by distributing the two most widely used applications (database and accounting) between the two servers. By moving the database application to the other server, the two applications requiring the heaviest work load are divided between two servers instead of one. The result is improved network performance.

In a server-based network with more than one server, monitoring server work load and distributing applications between servers also is an effective way to improve network performance.

Additional and Dedicated Servers

As your network grows, a time will come when your existing server cannot provide the level of performance required. If you have a server-based network, the solution is to implement an additional dedicated server. If you have a peer-to-peer network, the solution is to transform one of your nondedicated servers into a dedicated server or to purchase an additional server to be used for dedicated or nondedicated use.

Summary

This chapter discussed managing users and shared resources, and the actions you can take to manage the network efficiently. The chapter also described the types of user accounts available and the usage of each. Techniques to restrict access to shared resources were examined. In addition, the chapter illustrated how you can improve the ease of managing and the usage of shared resources by changing the server's directory structure. Finally, the chapter discussed the importance of monitoring the server's performance and the actions you can take to improve server and network performance.

In This Chapter...

This chapter discusses what can go wrong when installing and using your network and the process to follow in identifying and resolving problems you might encounter. Specifically, the following topics are covered:

- Documenting your system configuration and keeping a problem log of any problems you encounter.

- Understanding the troubleshooting process of identifying and diagnosing problems, and then implementing solutions.

- Troubleshooting and isolating problems in network cable and connectors.

- Identifying problems with network adapter cards.

- Isolating and correcting conflicts between network adapter cards and other hardware devices installed in your system.

- Identifying software configuration problems.

Troubleshooting

A network consists of many technologically advanced components and software all working together. Every hardware and software component must work properly or you may encounter problems during installation or in the normal course of using your network.

This chapter helps you develop the basic network troubleshooting skills necessary to resolve network problems you may encounter. You also learn about specific network problems that may occur.

Documenting Problems

The key to identifying and solving problems is knowing where to look and what to look for. The true cause of a problem often is buried in what appears to be a completely unrelated symptom. By keeping detailed records of your system configuration and any problems encountered, you are able to resolve problems more quickly.

To ease your management tasks and the time you spend resolving problems, you should keep a record of the configuration of each computer in your network and a problem log to use for tracking problems. It's best to keep your records in a large three-ring binder if possible.

The binder that contains the configuration of your network computers should have a separate section for each computer and also a section for general network configuration. You should keep the following information for each computer:

- The general configuration of each computer:

     The brand and type of computer, such as a 486DX-33 clone.

     The amount of memory installed (1 MB RAM, 4 MB RAM, and so on).

     The size of the hard drive (120 MB, 255 MB, 440 MB, and so forth).

     Any other types of drives installed, such as a CD-ROM drive or any floppy drives.

     The type of monitor and video card installed, such as a 1024×768 color VGA monitor and a Diamond Speedstar Pro VESA Local Bus video card with 1 MB RAM.

     The quantity, type, and name of the communication ports installed such as COM1, COM2, LPT1, LPT2, and so on.

     Any peripheral components or devices such as a mouse, a CD-ROM drive, a modem, or a scanner. You also should keep track of the configuration of each device, such as the address or *input/output* (I/O) port used by any peripheral device.

     The network adapter installed and its configuration, including the I/O port and address if any.

- The network configuration of each computer, which contains the following information:

The version of the network software installed.

The function of the node on the network (dedicated server, nondedicated server, or workstation).

If configured as a server, the shared resources and user accounts allowed to use the server.

Any other general network configuration information that could change depending on which computer you're working on.

- The version of DOS installed.

- The configuration of the CONFIG.SYS and AUTOEXEC.BAT system files.

- The software application programs installed and their versions.

- The CMOS configuration of each computer, which includes the hard drive type and its specifications.

The CMOS configuration is a hardware configuration record maintained in the permanent memory of your computer. The CMOS configuration information usually contains the amount of memory, the type of monitor, the number and type of floppy drives installed, the time and date, and the number and type of hard drives installed, as well as their specifications.

Your computer uses the information contained in the CMOS configuration record to communicate with the peripheral components installed. If the CMOS configuration information is not correct, your computer probably won't work properly.

You can view or change your computer's configuration record by running a setup utility that comes with your computer. Sometimes this utility is on a separate disk, but often the setup utility is part of the *Basic Input/Output System* (BIOS) and may be started by pressing a special key, such as Esc or Del, just before your computer boots.

The general network configuration section of your binder should contain information about your network as a whole, including the type of network installed (Ethernet for example), the type of cabling used (thin coax, unshielded twisted pair, and so on), and a drawing of the physical layout of the cables, equipment, and nodes in your network. In addition you should keep track of the version of the *network operating system* (NOS) being used and any other information such as the type and location of any concentrators, repeaters, bridges, and so on, in your network.

The problem log you maintain should be organized similar to your system configuration binder, with a section for each computer in your network as well as a general network section. Each problem encountered should be recorded in the problem log on a separate page that contains the following information:

- A description of the problem.
- On which computer the problem occurred.
- The date the problem occurred.
- Who discovered the problem.
- The cause of the problem.
- The steps taken to solve the problem.

Each time a change is made to the configuration of your computer, whether it be a hardware or software change, be sure to document what has changed, for what purpose, the date of the change, and who made the change. By documenting changes, you can more easily isolate a problem caused by a configuration change. Also, you can isolate problems much easier knowing each computer's configuration.

Keeping an up-to-date problem log not only helps identify and correct problems, but also helps build a problem history that you can use to quickly determine the cause of a new problem.

The Troubleshooting Process

Problems you encounter with your network may occur during installation or may appear later during the normal network operation. The process used to troubleshoot and resolve problems depends on several factors, including when the problem occurs and if the problem is intermittent in nature.

A problem encountered while installing your network hardware or software is usually more difficult to isolate than a problem encountered after your network has been successfully operating for a period of time. The reason installation problems are relatively difficult to resolve is because the network has not been operational yet and there are so many possible causes of problems.

The most difficult problems to solve are those that are intermittent in nature and therefore difficult to duplicate. If you experience an intermittent problem, you have to rely on your experience and suspicion of the cause to come up with a possible solution. Because it's difficult to duplicate an intermittent problem, you have to implement a solution and wait to see if it fixes the problem. The first solution you try may not work; however, each solution you implement that doesn't solve the problem helps you eliminate another cause and brings you closer to a solution.

The troubleshooting process consists of three basic steps: identifying problems, diagnosing problems, and implementing solutions. Resolving a problem as quickly as possible requires that you follow the three basic troubleshooting steps in order. For example, suppose you are not able to access the server in your network from your workstation. Upon further investigation, you identify the problem as being that none of the workstations in your network are able to communicate with the server. After more investigation you diagnose the problem to be a fault in the network cable. After identifying and diagnosing the problem, the solution you implement is to replace the faulty cable.

Throughout your troubleshooting experience, you will find yourself asking the same three questions over and over again:

- Has it ever worked?

- Has it worked recently?

- What has changed?

Answering these three questions helps you eliminate the variables and find the cause of the problem much sooner.

Identifying Problems

To successfully diagnose a problem, you need to be able to identify the type of problem you have encountered. This requires that you isolate and duplicate the problem.

To isolate a problem you must be able to perform a repeatable sequence of steps that duplicate the problem. A problem that you cannot repeat is said to be intermittent; therefore identifying it as a problem is difficult. If you can duplicate the problem then you can determine the cause and find the solution.

Two questions you need to answer to identify a problem include: When does the problem occur? and What else is affected?

- **When does the problem occur?** You need to be able to identify when you encounter the problem. If the problem occurs during the installation of your network there are many potential causes that you need to diagnose. If the problem appears all of a sudden when your network otherwise appeared to be working fine, you'll have an easier time diagnosing the problem. If the problem is intermittent, a solution will be a little more difficult to find.

- **What else is affected?** To later diagnose the problem you need to know how widespread the problem actually is. The symptom may have appeared on a single workstation; however, after further investigation, you may discover the problem occurs on all workstations.

Diagnosing Problems

After you have identified the problem, you are ready to diagnose its cause. By knowing the cause of the problem, you can take the appropriate actions to solve the problem.

Diagnosing a problem requires that you evaluate everything you know about the problem and rule out the improbable causes. The information obtained when identifying the problem, such as when it occurs and what else is affected, is very valuable when diagnosing the cause.

A common and effective technique used to rule out the variables that aren't causing the problem is to start with the most basic configuration possible. The most basic configuration you can use depends on the problem you are having, but in general you want to temporarily change your configuration files, such as AUTOEXEC.BAT and CONFIG.SYS, to load only the software necessary for the network, and eliminate programs and software drivers such as the mouse driver, expanded memory drivers, disk cache programs, and other software that remains resident in your computer's memory. If the problem doesn't occur with the basic configuration, you know the problem most likely is related to the configuration and you can make changes one step at a time until you return to the configuration that had the problem. Somewhere along the way you will encounter the problem and then can conclude the cause. If, after changing to a basic configuration, the problem still occurs, either you have a hardware problem or the software configuration of the hardware is not correct.

The single most important question to answer when diagnosing a problem is, What has changed? If your network has been operating fine and nothing has changed, then a hardware component most likely has failed. However, if something has changed, the problem could be related to the recent change. A change could be anything from installing additional or different hardware or software to using a program that you didn't use before. It's possible that the problem has always been there but didn't appear until you ran a particular program.

After ruling out what couldn't have caused the problem, you will be left with only a few possible causes. With only a few causes you can implement a solution.

Implementing Solutions

After diagnosing the cause of the problem you are ready to implement solutions.

After you implement a solution, it's important to repeat the steps used when identifying the problem to try to duplicate the problem. If you can't duplicate the problem, it has been fixed. If the problem doesn't go away, implement another solution until the problem does disappear. If the problem you are trying to solve is intermittent, you have to implement a potential solution and then wait to see if the problem appears again.

When implementing solutions, change one thing at a time if possible. If the first solution doesn't solve the problem, reverse the change you just made and try another solution. For example, if you replaced a network adapter card in hopes of solving a problem and the problem didn't go away, put the old network adapter card back in the computer before you try another solution. This way you are changing one thing at a time and are able to confirm an exact diagnosis when the solution is found.

Because of the complexity of networks, computers, and software, you may find that a single solution sometimes solves what appeared to be multiple problems. In other situations, you discover that you may have to implement more than one solution for what appears to be a single problem.

There will be a point at which you decide the individual solutions you are trying aren't solving the problem and the time that is being expended is becoming excessive. In this situation you may find it beneficial to begin replacing more than one software or hardware component at a time. For example, you might replace the network adapters and cable at the same time, or you might choose to install a different computer in place of the node you are having trouble with to see if the problem is isolated to the node or the location in the network.

Specific Network-Related Problems

Understanding the troubleshooting process of identifying the problem, diagnosing the problem, and implementing a solution prepares you to tackle specific network-related problems you may encounter.

The following sections describe several different categories of problems you may encounter with your network. The beginning of each section lists the warning signs that may indicate a problem related to the topics discussed in that section. The following list describes the type of problems addressed by each section:

- **Network Cable**. Problems with the network cable and the connectors.

- **Hardware**. Problems with network adapters and concentrators.

- **Software Configuration.** Problems related to configuring network software, system files, and application software.

- **Hardware and Software Conflicts.** Problems encountered as the result of hardware devices and software in your computer conflicting with the network hardware and software.

When diagnosing problems with your network, suspect problems in the order they are listed above. For example, suspect a problem with the network cable before you suspect a problem with the hardware, and suspect a problem with the hardware before you suspect a problem with the software configuration. If, however, a network problem appeared as soon as you made a software change to your computer, then you could assume that the problem isn't related to the network cable or hardware and jump immediately to the software configuration section.

Network Cable

Warning signs:

- No communication between any nodes on the network (Thin Ethernet).

- Single node can't communicate with other network nodes.

One of the first symptoms of a possible problem with your network cable or connectors is the inability of your network nodes to communicate with each other.

If you suspect a problem with your network cable or connectors, perform the following steps to isolate the cause of the problem:

1. Verify that the cable and connectors used in your installation are the proper specification. Because of high network data transmission speeds, cable and connectors that are close to the required specifications do not work. Also, make sure that the maximum allowed network cable segment length for your installation hasn't been exceeded.

2. Check that the physical connections are secure and that the connectors (including terminators if required) are connected properly. Each connection point must be sound. If you discover a bad or loose connector, replace it. Make sure the physical cable layout is installed correctly.

For example, in a Thin Ethernet network, a BNC T connector must be connected to each adapter and a 50-ohm terminator must be connected to each end of the network cable segment (see fig. 10.1). Although the end of a cable can connect physically to the connector on the network adapter, the network does not operate properly with the cable in that configuration.

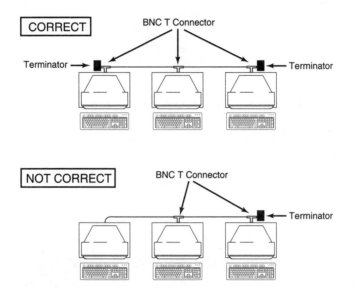

Figure 10.1

An example of correct and incorrect cabling for Thin Ethernet.

3. Using a multi-meter, check the cable for continuity. In a Thin Ethernet network, remove the terminator from one of the ends and check the resistance between the center pin and the outside ground on the terminator (see fig. 10.2). You should measure 50 ohms. Then check the resistance of the rest of the cable segment by measuring the resistance between the center conductor of the BNC T connector from which you removed the terminator and the outside ground on the connector.

Figure 10.2

Checking for
continuity in a Thin
Ethernet network.

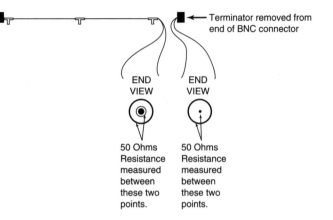

Figure 10.2

Checking for
continuity in a Thin
Ethernet network.

In a UTP (10BASE-T) network cable check for continuity between the ends of the cable. Pins 1, 2, 3, and 6 are used and wired straight through in normal installations (see fig. 10.3). If you are connecting two computers without using a concentrator, then a cross-wired scheme is used.

Figure 10.3

The wiring for a
10BASE-T network
cable.

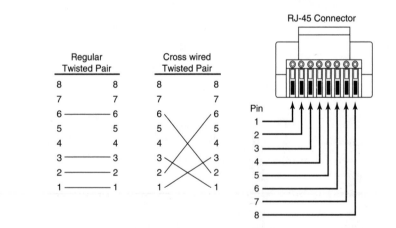

4. Identify the defective cable by configuring the cable to connect only two nodes, and add one node (or cable) at a time until the defective cable is found.

Hardware

Warning signs:

- No communication among any nodes on the network (UTP or 10BASE-T Ethernet).

- Single node can't communicate with other network nodes.

- Errors are displayed when network software is being loaded.

If you suspect a problem with a network adapter and have ruled out defective or improper cabling as a cause, the easiest way to verify your suspicion is to swap the network adapter with another. If after swapping out the network adapter the problem is still present, your network adapter may be configured incorrectly. Verify that the *interrupt request line* (IRQ) and I/O port settings used by your network adapter are not used by another device in your system. Also, check to make sure that the IRQ and I/O port settings specified by the network adapter driver software match the settings on your network adapter.

Many network adapters and NOSs include utilities to test the capability of a node to send and receive network signals across the network. Using one of these utility programs is a quick way to identify a problem with a network adapter or the network cable.

It is possible for a single connection point on a network concentrator to fail or for the entire concentrator to fail.

If you have a node that can't communicate with other nodes in your 10BASE-T network and you have ruled out defective or improper cabling as a cause, try plugging the cable from the node that can't communicate with the other nodes into a different port on the concentrator. If that doesn't work, use a cross-wired cable (refer to fig. 10.3) to connect two nodes at a time, and check for proper communications between the two nodes.

Software Configuration

Warning signs:

- Single node can't communicate with other network nodes.

- Network features seem limited or network node crashes frequently.

- Errors are displayed when network software is being loaded.

After eliminating the possibility of a failure in the network hardware or cabling, if you suspect a software configuration problem, the first step is to determine which configuration files are most likely to cause the problems you are encountering.

Generally there are three categories of configuration files: network software configuration files, system configuration files, and application configuration files.

The network software configuration files include the batch files used to load the network software into the memory in your computer. When the network software is loaded, each command executed must specify the correct switches for the NOS to operate correctly with the network adapter and the computer's operating system. Commands similar to those shown below might be part of a batch file to start the network on a node:

```
AEX IRQ=10 IOBASE=320
AILANBIO
REDIR OFFICE
```

The first command is the network adapter driver, which specifies an IRQ value of 10 and an IOBASE value of 320. If the network adapter isn't set for the exact save values, the network adapter and the network software won't be able to communicate, resulting in the network being unable to communicate with other network nodes. The third command invokes the network redirector program and specifies the name OFFICE, which is used as the network name of the node. If another node has the same network name, the network software won't install properly and the node won't be able to communicate with other nodes in the network.

For the network software to load properly, the commands in the network batch file must be executed in the proper order.

The system configuration files are used by the operating system, such as DOS, to specify environment settings and load software drivers required by the operating system and applications to communicate with the various hardware devices in the system. The files CONFIG.SYS and AUTOEXEC.BAT are the system files used by DOS. If you want your network to start when the computer is turned on, you need to make sure the appropriate commands are included in the system files. If there doesn't seem to be any sign of a network operating on your system, check to make sure the network software is being loaded when your system boots. If your node is configured as a server and network nodes accessing it frequently lock up when accessing the server, check to make sure the CONFIG.SYS file on the server and the workstation contain a sufficient number of file handles for the files that are opened by the workstation. The statement FILES=50 included in your CONFIG.SYS file usually is sufficient if your node is configured as a workstation; however, if your node is configured as a server, you may need to specify a value of 75 or more. Each file opened on a server by a workstation requires a file handle. With several workstations accessing applications that may open dozens of files, the FILES= specification required could be quite large for a server. DOS supports a maximum of 255 open files although many NOSs allow much larger values to be specified in the NOS configuration.

If your NOS uses the DOS share command for file and record locking, and nodes experience frequent lockups when accessing an application on a server, you may need to increase the number of locks and the filename space used by the SHARE command. The DOS SHARE command usually is specified in the AUTOEXEC.BAT file. If the SHARE command is specified without any parameters, the default value for locks is 20 and the default value for files is 2048, which is too small for a network server. A more common value is 250 locks and filename space of 4096 which you specify by including the following command in the AUTOEXEC.BAT file:

```
SHARE  /L:250  /F:4096
```

If your workstation is unable to redirect a drive letter past E, then you may need to include the LASTDRIVE statement in your CONFIG.SYS file. To allow redirecting drive letters from A to Z, include the following statement in your CONFIG.SYS file:

```
LASTDRIVE=Z
```

If your network appears to operate correctly but your application program cannot access files or use printers over the network, you might need to change the application program's configuration.

If you are unable to print from your application program, verify that a network connection to a shared printer resource has been established and that the redirected device name used (such as LPT2:) is the same device referenced by your application. Also, make sure the application does not bypass the operating system (DOS) and print directly to the device—doing so bypasses the network and results in the print job not being sent to the network printer.

If you are unable to access files across the network from your application program, verify that you have established a connection to the shared drive resource your application uses. The redirected drive letter and directory on the redirected drive must be the same as the drive or directory the application is trying to access.

Hardware and Software Conflicts

Warning signs:

- Single node can't communicate with other network nodes.
- Single node network connections fail or network operates inconsistently or intermittently.
- Network node crashes frequently.

If you have determined that the network cable and hardware are okay and the software configuration also appears to be correct, you may have a hardware or software conflict between your network and another device in your system.

The first step to perform if you suspect that you have a conflict is to change your system configuration files to the most basic software configuration possible. Temporarily remove all the software drivers and programs possible from your CONFIG.SYS and AUTOEXEC.BAT files. Following is an example of a CONFIG.SYS file:

```
DEVICE=C:\DOS\HIMEM.SYS
DEVICE=C:\DOS\EMM386.EXE NOEMS
FILES=75
BUFFERS=32
DEVICE=C:\DEV\MTMCDE.SYS
```

In this file you would temporarily remove each line that starts with DEVICE= because those statements are not necessary for your network to operate. The first two statements enable you to load software such as your network drivers into upper memory, and the last statement is a software driver for a CD-ROM drive. The following is an example of an AUTOEXEC.BAT file:

```
PROMPT $P$G
PATH C:\;C:\DOS
C:\DOS\SMARTDRV.EXE
C:\MOUSE\MOUSE
C:\TAPE\AUTOTAPE
CD\NETWORK
CALL NETWORK
CD\
```

In the preceding AUTOEXEC.BAT file, you would temporarily remove the three lines that start with C:\, which are not required for the network to operate. C:\DOS\SMARTDRV.EXE is the statement that loads the DOS disk cache program Smart Drive. C:\MOUSE\MOUSE loads the mouse driver into memory. C:\TAPE\AUTOTAPE is a program that automatically starts a tape backup on a specific day and time. The CALL NETWORK statement executes the batch file that loads your network software. If there were unnecessary commands in the NETWORK batch file, you would want to temporarily remove those commands also.

After removing the unnecessary commands from the various system files, reboot your computer and see if the network operates correctly. If the network operates correctly, replace one command at a time, reboot, and check for proper network operation until you are able to determine which command is conflicting with your network.

After removing the unnecessary commands, if your network still doesn't operate correctly, turn off your computer and temporarily remove the unnecessary interface cards from your computer, such as a sound card, CD-ROM interface, scanner interface, and so on. Reboot your computer and check for proper network operation. If the problem is a hardware or software conflict the network should now operate correctly. Reinstall one interface card at a time until you have determined the source of the problem.

When you have determined the source of the conflict, change the appropriate default setting on the device or software that is interfering and restart your computer to verify the changes have resolved the problem. Restore the other devices and software to their original settings.

Often you encounter a situation in which you can identify a conflict between a software driver or program and your network but you cannot make any configuration changes to the interfering program to resolve the problem. In situations like this, try changing the order in which the programs are loaded in your system files. For example, in the sample AUTOEXEC.BAT file discussed previously, for the automatic tape backup program to operate correctly with the network, you might have to change the order of the commands so AUTOTAPE is loaded after the network instead of before it. Similar changes often are required for devices such as CD-ROM drivers; in fact, in many situations you have to place one of the CD-ROM drivers after the redirector program, but before the server program in your network startup batch file for proper network operation.

Summary

This chapter discussed the troubleshooting procedures to follow in the event you experience problems with your network. Basic troubleshooting techniques were discussed in detail followed by specific situations you might encounter with your network. Problems encountered with network cabling and hardware were covered. In addition, problems that might be encountered due to software configuration or hardware or software conflicts between the network and other devices in the system were discussed.

Part Two:
Implementing a Network

In This Chapter. . .

The accompanying disks include a two-node version of Artisoft's Simply LANtastic. This chapter describes the installation of Simply LANtastic on your computers. Specifically, Chapter 11 covers the following topics:

- The Simply LANtastic software included on the accompanying disk.

- Installation and configuration of the Simply LANtastic *network interface card* (NIC).

- Installation of Simply LANtastic on a computer running DOS.

- Installation of Simply LANtastic on a computer running Microsoft Windows.

- Installation of the stub driver that enables you to use Simply LANtastic if you don't have a network adapter installed in your computer.

Installing
Simply LANtastic

Now that you have been exposed to *local area networks* (LANs) in some detail, you're ready to get your feet wet with some real networking.

The accompanying disks include the Simply LANtastic *network operating system* (NOS). In addition, the back of the book has a coupon you can send to Artisoft to purchase a Simply LANtastic network adapter for the computers in your network.

This chapter discusses how to install the Simply LANtastic network adapter and the Simply LANtastic NOS on your computer. If you don't have network adapters for your computers, you still can install and practice using Simply LANtastic on a single computer with the supplied stub driver.

Viewing the Disk Contents

Included on the accompanying disk is a complete two-node version of Artisoft's Simply LANtastic 5.1 NOS. The included two-node version of Simply LANtastic enables you to install and use Simply LANtastic on two computers.

If you don't already have NICs for the two computers on which you're installing Simply LANtastic, you can find information in the back of the book on how to purchase Simply LANtastic network adapters from Artisoft.

Also included on the accompanying disk is a stub driver that enables you to run Simply LANtastic on your computer without a network adapter installed in your computer. You use the stub driver in place of the network adapter driver. By using the stub driver, you can practice using the features of Simply LANtastic without having a network adapter installed in your computer.

Installing the Simply LANtastic Adapter

To set up your Simply LANtastic network, you must first install the Simply LANtastic NICs in each computer.

In addition to the Simply LANtastic network adapter, Simply LANtastic supports the Artisoft AE series and the NodeRunner series Ethernet adapters. Simply LANtastic also supports any network adapter supplied with an NDIS adapter driver.

The procedure for installing network adapters other than the Simply LANtastic adapter is similar to the following procedure.

To install the Simply LANtastic adapter, perform the following steps:

1. Turn off your computer, and remove any cables or equipment (such as the monitor) so you have room to work. Leave the power cord plugged in.

2. Find the screws that hold the cover on your computer. They usually are located in the back of the case, but some may be in the front or on the side (see fig. 11.1). If your computer is in a desktop case, there will most likely be five screws to remove. If your computer is in a tower case, you will most likely have to remove six screws.

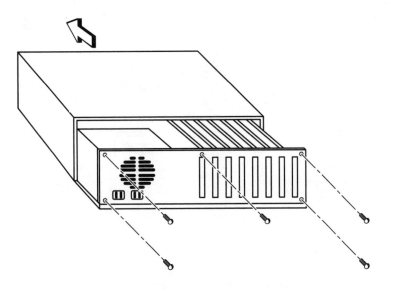

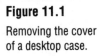
Figure 11.1

Removing the cover of a desktop case.

3. Remove the cover by sliding it forward (desktop case) or lifting it (tower case). Set the cover aside.

To remove the cover on some desktop cases, you might have to lift straight up or even slide the cover backward.

4. Locate an available 16-bit expansion slot in your computer. Remove the expansion slot cover by removing the screw holding the cover in place and pulling up on the cover (see fig. 11.2).

Figure 11.2

Accessing a 16-bit expansion slot.

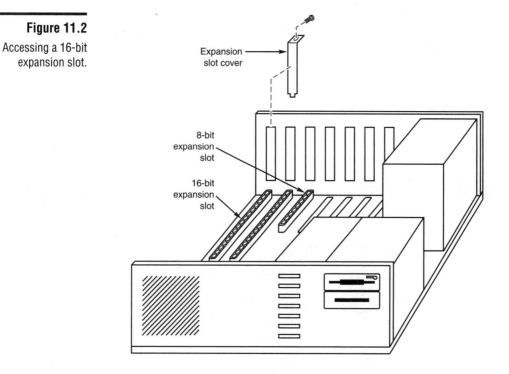

If you do not have an available 16-bit expansion slot in your computer, you can use an 8-bit expansion slot instead. If you use an 8-bit expansion slot, however, you need to reconfigure your Simply LANtastic adapter using the NRSETUP utility discussed later in this chapter.

5. Drain off any static electricity by touching the power supply (the big silver box inside the computer).

6. Remove the network adapter from its static protective bag, and position the bottom of the network adapter over the expansion slot. Press the network adapter firmly into the expansion slot (see fig. 11.3). Verify that the golden tabs on the bottom of the card are plugged into the expansion slot (not sitting on top of it).

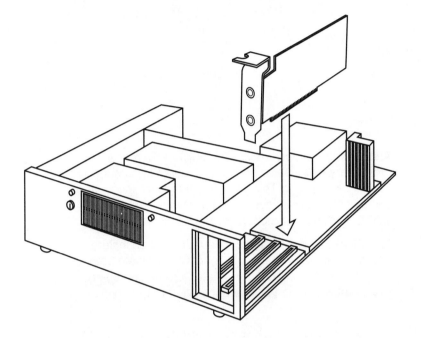

Figure 11.3
Installing the NIC.

7. Secure the network adapter in place by using the same screw you removed from the expansion slot cover.

8. Replace the cover on the case, and secure it in place with the screws you previously removed.

9. Plug one end of the Simply LANtastic cable into one of the jacks (it doesn't matter which one) on the Simply LANtastic network adapter (see fig. 11.4).

Figure 11.4

Connecting the Simply LANtastic cable to the Simply LANtastic network adapter.

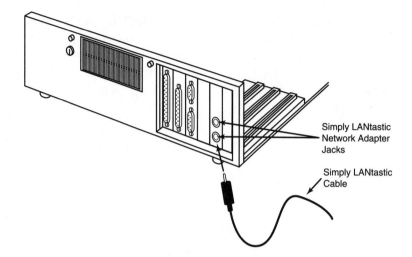

Simply LANtastic Network Adapter Jacks

Simply LANtastic Cable

Although the Simply LANtastic cabling scheme is proprietary because of the network cable and connectors used, it is similar to Thin Ethernet in most respects and can even be directly connected to Thin Ethernet cabling with the appropriate connector from Artisoft.

The Simply LANtastic network adapters each include an internal terminator. If a cable is not plugged into both jacks on the Simply LANtastic adapter, the cable segment that is plugged in is terminated at the adapter.

10. Return the computer back to its original position, and replace any cables or equipment you moved out of the way.

Your Simply LANtastic network adapter now is installed and ready for use. To install the Simply LANtastic network adapter in the second computer, repeat the preceding steps.

Configuring Simply LANtastic Using NRSETUP

In most situations, the default configuration of your Simply LANtastic network adapter is fine and you won't have to change any settings. The default configuration of the Simply LANtastic network adapter uses an *input/output* (I/O) Base address of 300h and an IRQ value of 15.

If you put your Simply LANtastic adapter in an 8-bit expansion slot, then you need to run the NRSETUP program to change the IRQ value used by the network adapter. You must change the IRQ value because the default IRQ value of 15 is not available if your network adapter is plugged into an 8-bit expansion slot.

Another adapter card in your computer, such as a CD-ROM drive adapter card, might possibly use the same I/O Base address as your Simply LANtastic network adapter. If an I/O Base conflict between the two adapters exists, either you'll be unable to load your network software or the network will operate incorrectly. To resolve the I/O Base conflict, you need to run NRSETUP and change the I/O Base address to a value different from the default 300h.

To run the NRSETUP utility, place the accompanying disk in drive A (or B) and type the following command at the DOS prompt:

     A:NRSETUP (or **B:NRSETUP**)

The NodeRunner Setup Utility program starts and displays the Main Options menu (see fig. 11.5). With the Automatic NodeRunner Configuration option selected from the Main Options menu, press Enter and the IRQ and I/O Bass address values are automatically configured for your computer.

In the event you are unable to run NRSETUP, you might have an I/O Base conflict that is preventing NRSETUP from executing properly. To temporarily move the I/O Base address from the default 300h to the second I/O Base option of 320h, type the following command at the DOS prompt with the accompanying disk in your floppy drive A (or B):

     A:NRMOVE (or **B:NRMOVE**)

continues

Try to run NRSETUP again. If NRSETUP still doesn't run, you can run NRMOVE again and specify two additional temporary I/O Base addresses of 340h and 360h. To change the temporary I/O Base address to 340h, type the following at the DOS prompt:

> **A:NRMOVE 340** (or **B:NRMOVE 340**)

To change the temporary I/O Base address to 360h, type the following at the DOS prompt:

> **A:NRMOVE 360** (or **B:NRMOVE 360**)

Remember that the I/O Base address determined using the NRMOVE utility is only temporary. You still need to run NRSETUP to make the change permanent.

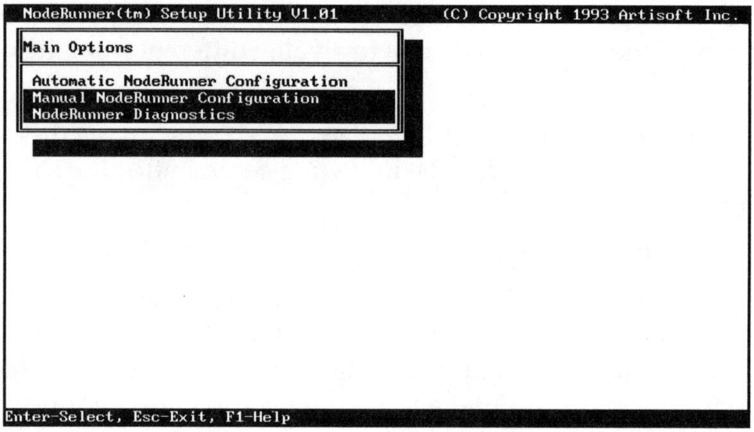

Figure 11.5

The NodeRunner Setup Utility Main Options menu.

```
NodeRunner(tm) Setup Utility V1.01          (C) Copyright 1993 Artisoft Inc.
 ┌Main Options────────────────────────────────┐
 │ Automatic NodeRunner Configuration          │
 │ Manual NodeRunner Configuration             │
 │ NodeRunner Diagnostics                      │
 └─────────────────────────────────────────────┘




Enter-Select, Esc-Exit, F1-Help
```

If you prefer to specify the IRQ or I/O Base address values used by your Simply LANtastic adapter manually, perform the following steps:

1. Use your arrow keys to select the Manual NodeRunner Configuration option from the Main Options menu and press Enter.

The NodeRunner Adapter Information/Statistics and the NodeRunner Adapter Configuration windows appear (see fig. 11.6).

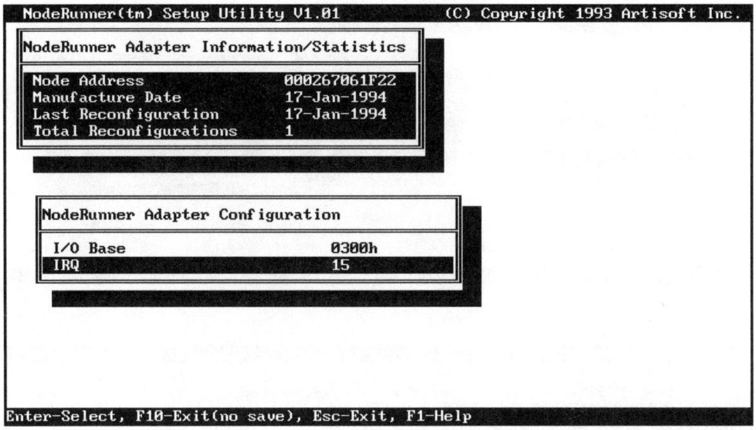

```
NodeRunner(tm) Setup Utility V1.01        (C) Copyright 1993 Artisoft Inc.

  NodeRunner Adapter Information/Statistics

    Node Address              000267061F22
    Manufacture Date          17-Jan-1994
    Last Reconfiguration      17-Jan-1994
    Total Reconfigurations    1


  NodeRunner Adapter Configuration

    I/O Base                  0300h
    IRQ                       15




Enter-Select, F10-Exit(no save), Esc-Exit, F1-Help
```

Figure 11.6

The NodeRunner Adapter Information/ Statistics and the NodeRunner Adapter Configuration windows.

2. To change the I/O Base address, select the I/O Base line in the NodeRunner Adapter Configuration window and press Enter. The I/O Base Options selection window appears (see fig. 11.7).

   Using your arrow keys, select the desired I/O Base address and press Enter.

3. To change the IRQ value, use your arrow keys to select the IRQ line in the NodeRunner Adapter Configuration window and press Enter. The IRQs window appears, listing the IRQ values from which you can select (see fig. 11.8).

   Using your arrow keys, select the desired IRQ value and press Enter.

4. When you are finished, press Esc and your changes are written to the memory on the Simply LANtastic adapter. If you don't want to save your changes, press F10 to exit.

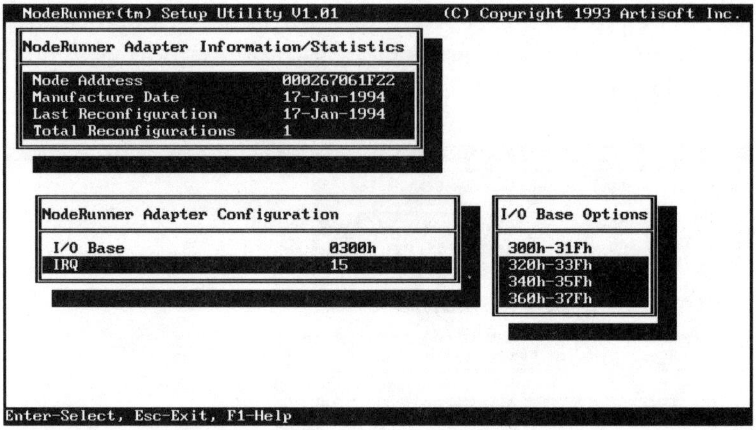

Figure 11.7

Selecting an I/O Base
address.

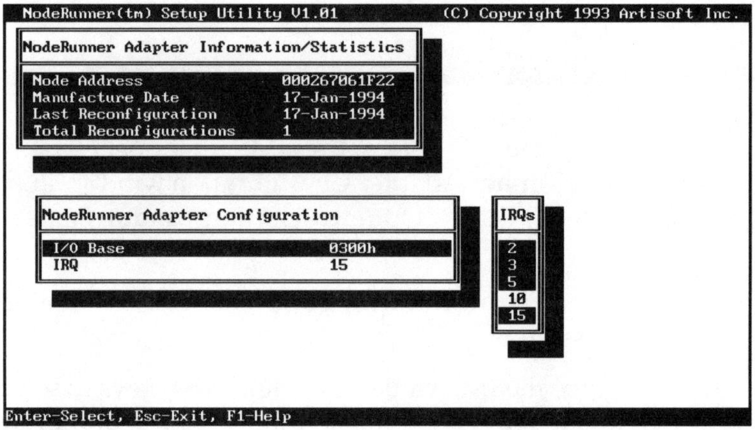

```
NodeRunner(tm) Setup Utility V1.01          (C) Copyright 1993 Artisoft Inc.
┌─NodeRunner Adapter Information/Statistics─┐
│ Node Address              000267061F22    │
│ Manufacture Date          17-Jan-1994     │
│ Last Reconfiguration      17-Jan-1994     │
│ Total Reconfigurations    1               │
└───────────────────────────────────────────┘

        ┌─NodeRunner Adapter Configuration─┐   ┌─I/O Base Options─┐
        │ I/O Base              0300h       │   │ 300h-31Fh        │
        │ IRQ                   15          │   │ 320h-33Fh        │
        └───────────────────────────────────┘   │ 340h-35Fh        │
                                                 │ 360h-37Fh        │
                                                 └──────────────────┘

Enter-Select, Esc-Exit, F1-Help
```

Figure 11.7
Selecting an I/O Base address.

Figure 11.8

Selecting an IRQ
value.

```
NodeRunner(tm) Setup Utility V1.01          (C) Copyright 1993 Artisoft Inc.
┌─NodeRunner Adapter Information/Statistics─┐
│ Node Address              000267061F22    │
│ Manufacture Date          17-Jan-1994     │
│ Last Reconfiguration      17-Jan-1994     │
│ Total Reconfigurations    1               │
└───────────────────────────────────────────┘

        ┌─NodeRunner Adapter Configuration─┐   ┌─IRQs─┐
        │ I/O Base              0300h       │   │ 2    │
        │ IRQ                   15          │   │ 3    │
        └───────────────────────────────────┘   │ 5    │
                                                 │ 10   │
                                                 │ 15   │
                                                 └──────┘

Enter-Select, Esc-Exit, F1-Help
```

Figure 11.8
Selecting an IRQ value.

Your Simply LANtastic network adapter is now configured for
your system and ready for use.

Checking Network Adapter Communication

After your Simply LANtastic network adapters are installed in
each computer and the Simply LANtastic cable connected between them, you can run a diagnostic routine in NRSETUP to

check the communication between the Simply LANtastic network adapters even before installing your Simply LANtastic software.

To run the diagnostic routine and check the network communication of the Simply LANtastic adapters, perform the following steps on each computer:

1. Put the accompanying disk in drive A (or B), and start the NRSETUP program by typing the following command at the DOS prompt:

   A:NRSETUP (or **B:NRSETUP**)

   The NodeRunner Setup Utility Main Options menu appears (see fig. 11.9).

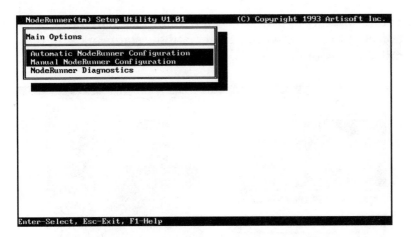

Figure 11.9

Selecting NodeRunner Diagnostics from the NRSETUP Main Options menu.

2. Use your arrow keys to select the NodeRunner Diagnostics option and press Enter.

3. When you are prompted to enter a unique station name, enter any name you desire (as long as the name hasn't already been specified on another node) and press Enter (see fig. 11.10).

Three windows appear, each containing different information about your network adapter and the status of communications on your network (see fig. 11.11).

The NodeRunner Statistics window shows the communication statistics for the adapter in your computer. The station
name shown is the name you entered when you were
prompted for a unique station name.

The Diagnostic Results window shows the results of the tests
performed on the Simply LANtastic adapter installed in
your computer.

The last window shows additional stations on your network running the same routine and the number of packets of information sent by the station. In the example shown, because the station ZAK appears, you know that nodes KSOFFICE and ZAK are communicating with each other.

4. When you are finished, press Esc once to return to the Main Options menu, and then press Esc again to return to the DOS prompt.

Installing the Simply LANtastic NOS

Included on the accompanying disk is a two-node version of Simply LANtastic. Simply LANtastic supports full network functionality in both DOS and Windows operating environments.

When you install the Simply LANtastic NOS on your computer, the installation program detects if you have Microsoft Windows installed on your computer. If Windows is installed, the Simply LANtastic Windows installation program begins. If you don't have Windows installed on your computer, the Simply LANtastic DOS installation program begins.

The Simply LANtastic Windows installation program installs all the Simply LANtastic DOS software in addition to the Simply LANtastic Windows software. Thus you can switch between DOS and Windows without any interruption in network activities.

You need to install Simply LANtastic on each computer in your network. To install Simply LANtastic on your computer, place the accompanying disk in drive A (or B) and type the following commands at the DOS prompt:

```
A: (or B:)
INSTALL
```

The Simply LANtastic installation program searches for Microsoft Windows in your path and, if found, runs the Simply LANtastic Windows installation program. If Windows is not found on your system, the installation program notifies you that Windows was not found and prompts you to press Enter to run the Simply LANtastic DOS installation program (see fig. 11.12).

```
A:\>install

Searching for Microsoft Windows(tm)
    Press [Esc] to abort this install program.
    Press [Space] to skip searching for Windows.

Microsoft Windows was not found.
    Press [Enter] and this program will run under MS-DOS.
    Press [Esc] and this program will exit...
```

If you encounter problems running the Simply LANtastic Windows installation program, you can run the Simply LANtastic DOS installation program and have it install the Simply LANtastic Windows programs by including the /DOS and /WIN switches on the INSTALL command line as follows:

INSTALL /DOS/WIN

DOS Installation

Once the Simply LANtastic DOS installation program starts, you can proceed by performing the following steps:

1. At the Simply LANtastic introduction screen, press any key (see fig. 11.13). The next screen provides some additional introductory information. Press any key to proceed with the installation.

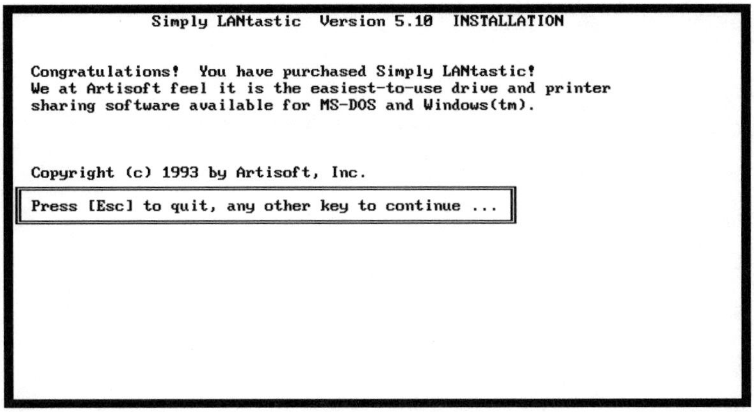

```
        Simply LANtastic  Version 5.10  INSTALLATION

Congratulations!  You have purchased Simply LANtastic!
We at Artisoft feel it is the easiest-to-use drive and printer
sharing software available for MS-DOS and Windows(tm).


Copyright (c) 1993 by Artisoft, Inc.
 ┌──────────────────────────────────────────────────┐
 │ Press [Esc] to quit, any other key to continue ... │
 └──────────────────────────────────────────────────┘
```

Figure 11.13

The Simply LANtastic
installation
introduction screen.

2. The next screen lists the available physical drives on your
    system from which you can select the drive on which you
    want Simply LANtastic to be installed (see fig. 11.14) .

    Accept the default Drive C selection, and press Enter to
    continue.

```
        Simply LANtastic  Version 5.10  INSTALLATION




Please select the drive where you want Simply LANtastic
to be installed on your computer.  Any available drive
can be used, but we suggest Drive C:




                    ┌────────────┐
                    │  Drive B:  │
                    │  Drive C:  │
                    └────────────┘
```

Figure 11.14

Selecting the drive for
installation.

3. You are then asked to specify the directory on the selected
    drive in which you want Simply LANtastic to be installed
    (see fig. 11.15).

    Accept the default \LANTASTI directory, and press Enter to
    continue.

```
              Simply LANtastic  Version 5.10  INSTALLATION


    Please select the directory on Drive C where
    you want Simply LANtastic to be installed.  Most people
    accept the default directory by pressing ENTER.



                  ─Enter directory────────────────
            \LANTASTI
```

4. The next screen prompts you to specify a name for the
   computer at which you are sitting (see fig. 11.16). The name
   you specify must be unique, which means that another node
   in the network cannot have the same name. The name can
   contain up to 15 alphanumeric characters with no spaces.

```
              Simply LANtastic  Version 5.10  INSTALLATION

    Each computer in the Simply LANtastic sharing group requires a
    name.  No two names in the group should be the same.  Usually,
    people use some variation of their own name for their computer.
    Or computers could be named by location (e.g. UPSTAIRS) or function
    (e.g. GAMES).  Please name your computer now with a word
    containing up to fifteen letters with no spaces.


                  ─Enter computer name────────────
            KSOFFICE
```

Enter the name for your computer, and press Enter to continue. In the example shown, KSOFFICE is the name specified.

5. You are next asked whether you want to share your computer's drives or printers (see fig. 11.17). If you select the SHARE my computer's drives or printers option, the Simply LANtastic installation program configures your computer as a nondedicated server; that is, your computer will be allowed to share its resources with other nodes. If you select the DO NOT share my computer's drives and printers option, the installation program configures your computer as a workstation; your computer will be allowed to access shared resources on other nodes but will not be able to share its own resources with others.

    Accept the default SHARE my computer's drives or printers option, and press Enter to continue.

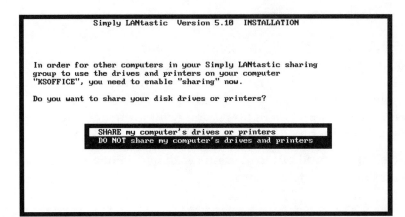

Figure 11.17

Specifying whether to share the computer's resources.

6. The next screen enables you to specify the maximum number of computers that may establish connections to you and the maximum number of computers to which you may be connected (see fig. 11.18). The KEEP maximum connected computers at 10 option allows up to 10 connections to exist between your computer and other network nodes. The INCREASE maximum connected computers to 30 option allows up to 30 connections to exist between your computer and other network nodes.

Accept the default KEEP maximum connected computers at 10 option, and press Enter to continue.

```
             Simply LANtastic   Version 5.10   INSTALLATION

If your computer  "KSOFFICE"  will NOT be connected to more
than 10 other computers, press ENTER now to "KEEP" the
maximum number of computers at 10.

But if your computer  "KSOFFICE"  WILL be connected to more
than 10 other computers, arrow down to  "INCREASE"  in the box
below, then press ENTER to allow all of those other computers to
use yours at the same time.  (This will result in a small increase
in the amount of memory Simply LANtastic uses on your computer.)



            KEEP      maximum connected computers at 10
            INCREASE  maximum connected computers to 30
```

7. The Simply LANtastic installation summary screen appears, displaying the selections you have specified so far (see fig. 11.19). You can select the OK to continue with installation option to continue, or you can select the Go back and re-enter the information option if you want to change any of the information you have specified so far.

Select the default OK to continue with installation option, and press Enter to continue.

```
             Simply LANtastic   Version 5.10   INSTALLATION

So far, you have specified the following installation
information for Simply LANtastic for DOS:

Installation Drive:        C:
Installation Directory:    \LANTASTI
Computer Name:             KSOFFICE
Share Drives & Printers:   YES - Allow  10  Connections




            OK to continue with installation
            Go back and re-enter the information
```

8. The next screen enables you to change the colors used in the Simply LANtastic NET program (see fig. 11.20).

   Accept the default DO NOT change colors, keep the "CLASSIC" set option, and press Enter to continue.

```
                Simply LANtastic   Version 5.10   INSTALLATION



  The DOS-based "Connections" program (NET.EXE) that comes
  with Simply LANtastic can be configured to run with several color
  combinations.   The traditional Artisoft colors (blue and red)
  will be used if you do not want to select another set of colors.

  Do you want to change colors for the Simply LANtastic NET program?


         DO NOT change colors, keep the "CLASSIC" set
         SELECT new colors for the Simply LANtastic NET program
```

Figure 11.20

Specifying the colors used in the Simply LANtastic NET program.

9. Next you are required to select the type of network adapter that is installed in your computer (see fig. 11.21). The first two selections—Simply LANtastic Internal Network Adapter and LANtastic NodeRunner 2000 Series Ethernet Adapter—actually install the same network adapter driver because the two adapters are similar. If you are not using an Artisoft adapter, select the NDIS Support for Network Adapters option, which enables you to use any other network adapter supplied with an NDIS driver.

   Select the Simply LANtastic Internal Network Adapter option, and press Enter to continue.

   If you do not have a network adapter installed in your computer and are planning to use the supplied stub driver to practice using Simply LANtastic, select the Simply LANtastic Internal Network Adapter option. You will change the network driver installed later.

Figure 11.21

Specifying the
network adapter
installed.

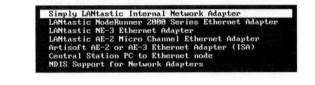

```
          Simply LANtastic   Version 5.10   INSTALLATION

Please select one of the following adapters to run with your
Simply LANtastic software.  If you do not know the name of
the adapter that is installed in your computer, check the
instructions that came with your adapter.  If the name of
your adapter does not appear on the list below, select
"NDIS Support for Network Adapters".


           Simply LANtastic Internal Network Adapter
           LANtastic NodeRunner 2000 Series Ethernet Adapter
           LANtastic NE-3 Ethernet Adapter
           LANtastic AE-2 Micro Channel Ethernet Adapter
           Artisoft AE-2 or AE-3 Ethernet Adapter (ISA)
           Central Station PC to Ethernet node
           NDIS Support for Network Adapters
```

10. The next screen enables you to specify if you want to set up
    network drive or printer connections that are automatically
    established when Simply LANtastic is started on your
    computer (see fig. 11.22).

    Select the SET UP permanent drive or printer connections
    option, and press Enter to continue.

Figure 11.22

Specifying the option
to set up permanent
drive or printer
connections.

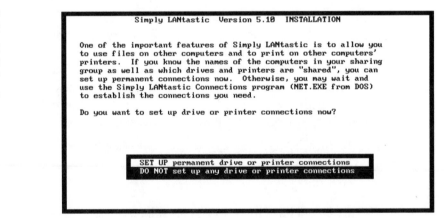

```
          Simply LANtastic   Version 5.10   INSTALLATION

One of the important features of Simply LANtastic is to allow you
to use files on other computers and to print on other computers'
printers.  If you know the names of the computers in your sharing
group as well as which drives and printers are "shared", you can
set up permanent connections now.  Otherwise, you may wait and
use the Simply LANtastic Connections program (NET.EXE from DOS)
to establish the connections you need.

Do you want to set up drive or printer connections now?




           SET UP permanent drive or printer connections
           DO NOT set up any drive or printer connections
```

11. After you choose to set up permanent drive or printer
    connections, the next screen asks for the name of the com-
    puter that has a drive you want to use (see fig. 11.23). If you

don't want to set up a permanent drive connection but want
to proceed to set up a printer connection, leave the Enter
computer name field blank and press Enter.

If you want to set up a permanent connection to a drive on
the computer named ZAK, type **ZAK** in the Enter computer
name field and press Enter.

```
            Simply LANtastic  Version 5.10  INSTALLATION
OTHER COMPUTER with a DRIVE you want to USE...
_____

Please type the name of the other computer that has
the drive you want to connect to and use.

Or just press ENTER to continue, skipping  drive setup.

If you skip permanent drive setup, you will have an extra
step to perform every time you turn on your computer.

>>> You can do this before the other computer is set up.<<<

         ═Enter computer name═══════════════════
│ ZAK                                            │
```

Figure 11.23

Specifying the name
of the computer with
the drive you want to
use.

The information for permanent drive and printer
connections you specify during installation appears
as commands in the STARTNET.BAT file created by
the Simply LANtastic installation program. The
STARTNET.BAT file contains the commands necessary
to start Simply LANtastic on your computer and establish
any drive or printer connections.

You can change the STARTNET.BAT file later to add,
delete, or modify any drive or printer connections.

12. The next screen asks you to specify the name of the shared-
     drive resource you want to use (see fig. 11.24). The Simply
     LANtastic installation program automatically creates shared
     resource names for the drives present on each computer and
     assigns the names C-DRIVE for your C hard disk, A-DRIVE

for your A floppy drive, and so on. If you know the name of a shared drive and directory resource on another computer, you can specify that name now.

For this installation, accept the default C-DRIVE drive resource name and press Enter.

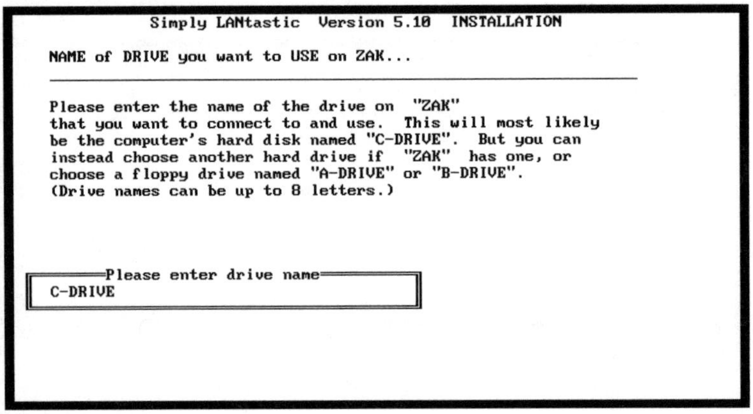

Figure 11.24

Specifying the name
of the shared-drive
resource to use.

```
                    Simply LANtastic   Version 5.10   INSTALLATION

          NAME of DRIVE you want to USE on ZAK...
          ─────────────────────────────────────────────────────────

          Please enter the name of the drive on  "ZAK"
          that you want to connect to and use.  This will most likely
          be the computer's hard disk named "C-DRIVE".  But you can
          instead choose another hard drive if  "ZAK"  has one, or
          choose a floppy drive named "A-DRIVE" or "B-DRIVE".
          (Drive names can be up to 8 letters.)




                     ═Please enter drive name═
                     C-DRIVE
```

13. Now you are asked for the drive letter on your computer to use to access the shared-drive resource on the other computer (see fig. 11.25). You can specify any drive letter you want, although it's advisable not to use a drive letter that corresponds to a physical drive that already exists in your computer.

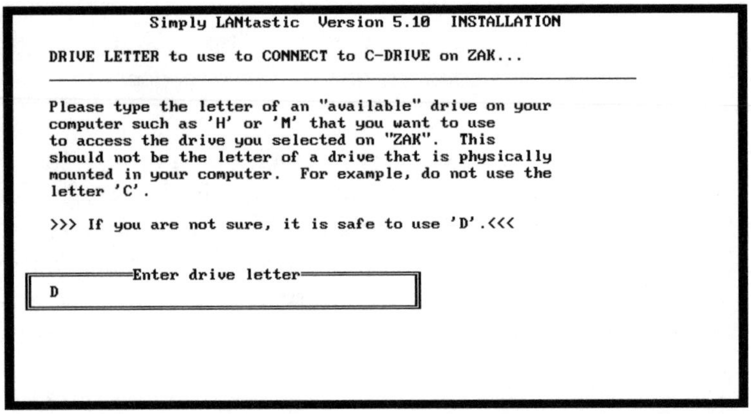

Figure 11.25

Specifying the drive
letter to redirect to a
shared-drive resource
on another computer.

```
                    Simply LANtastic   Version 5.10   INSTALLATION

          DRIVE LETTER to use to CONNECT to C-DRIVE on ZAK...
          ─────────────────────────────────────────────────────────

          Please type the letter of an "available" drive on your
          computer such as 'H' or 'M' that you want to use
          to access the drive you selected on "ZAK".  This
          should not be the letter of a drive that is physically
          mounted in your computer.  For example, do not use the
          letter 'C'.

          >>> If you are not sure, it is safe to use 'D'.<<<


                     ═Enter drive letter═
                     D
```

For this installation, accept the default drive letter D and press Enter.

14. The next screen asks for the name of another computer with a shared-drive resource you want to use. You can specify the name of another computer, or you can specify the name of the computer you specified in the previous connection if you want to use another drive on that computer. You also can leave the Enter computer name field blank if you don't want to specify another drive connection.

    Leave the Enter computer name field blank, and press Enter to continue.

You are given the option to identify a maximum of two network drive connections during installation. You can change your STARTNET.BAT file later to add connections, if desired.

15. Next you are asked for the name of the computer with the shared-printer resource you want to use (see fig. 11.26).

    If ZAK has a shared-printer resource you want to use, type **ZAK** in the Enter computer name field and press Enter.

```
              Simply LANtastic  Version 5.10   INSTALLATION

OTHER COMPUTER that has PRINTER ATTACHED...
_____

If you want to use the printer that may already be
attached to LPT1 on your computer, press ENTER now.

Otherwise type the name of the other computer that has the
printer you want to connect to and use.




         ══════Enter computer name══════
        ┌                              ┐
        │ ZAK                          │
        └                              ┘
```

Figure 11.26

Specifying the name of the computer with the shared-printer resource to use.

16. Next choose the name of the shared-printer resource on the other computer to which you want to establish a connection (see fig. 11.27).

    Accept the default @PRINTER name and press Enter.

Figure 11.27

Specifying the name of the shared-printer resource to use.

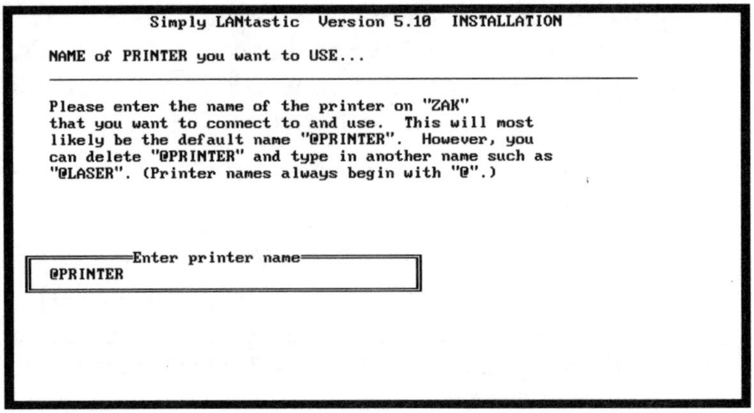

```
        Simply LANtastic  Version 5.10   INSTALLATION

    NAME of PRINTER you want to USE...
    ─────────────────────────────────────────────────────

    Please enter the name of the printer on "ZAK"
    that you want to connect to and use.  This will most
    likely be the default name "@PRINTER".  However, you
    can delete "@PRINTER" and type in another name such as
    "@LASER". (Printer names always begin with "@".)



    ┌──────────Enter printer name─────────────────────────┐
    │ @PRINTER                                             │
    └──────────────────────────────────────────────────────┘
```

The Simply LANtastic installation program automatically creates a shared-printer resource with the name @PRINTER, which is defined as the LPT1 device.

Shared-printer resources in Simply LANtastic always begin with the at character (@).

17. The next screen asks for the device name (printer port) on your computer to which you want to redirect the shared-printer resource on the specified server (see fig. 11.28).

    Accept the default LPT1 selection and press Enter.

The Simply LANtastic installation program enables you to specify a single network printer connection. You can change your STARTNET.BAT file later to specify additional connections, if desired.

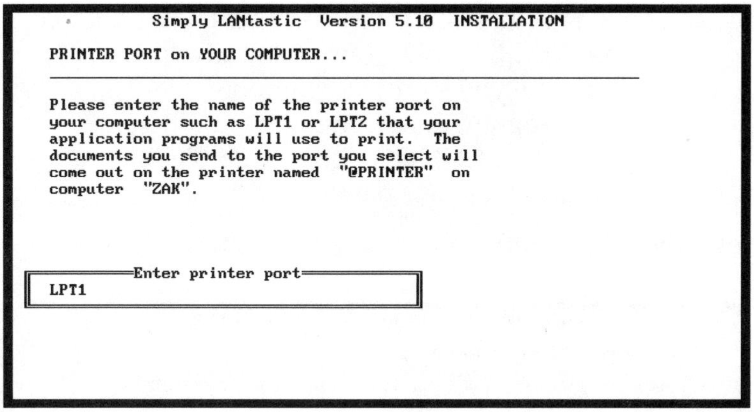

```
           Simply LANtastic  Version 5.10  INSTALLATION

PRINTER PORT on YOUR COMPUTER...
_____

Please enter the name of the printer port on
your computer such as LPT1 or LPT2 that your
application programs will use to print.  The
documents you send to the port you select will
come out on the printer named  "@PRINTER"  on
computer  "ZAK".


          ┌─────Enter printer port─────┐
          │ LPT1                        │
          └─────────────────────────────┘
```

Figure 11.28

Specifying the printer port to connect to the shared-printer resource on the server.

18. The Simply LANtastic installation summary information screen is displayed, which shows the parameters you have specified for installation (see fig. 11.29). At this point, you either can select OK to continue with installation option if the information listed is correct, or select Go back and re-enter the information option to make changes.

Select the OK to continue with installation option, and press Enter to continue.

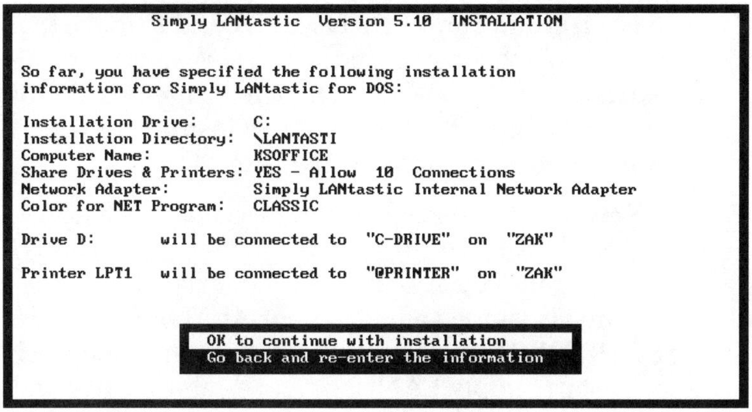

```
           Simply LANtastic  Version 5.10  INSTALLATION

So far, you have specified the following installation
information for Simply LANtastic for DOS:

Installation Drive:      C:
Installation Directory:  \LANTASTI
Computer Name:           KSOFFICE
Share Drives & Printers: YES - Allow  10  Connections
Network Adapter:         Simply LANtastic Internal Network Adapter
Color for NET Program:   CLASSIC

Drive D:      will be connected to  "C-DRIVE"  on  "ZAK"

Printer LPT1  will be connected to  "@PRINTER"  on  "ZAK"


          ┌──────────────────────────────────────────┐
          │   OK to continue with installation        │
          │   Go back and re-enter the information     │
          └──────────────────────────────────────────┘
```

Figure 11.29

The Simply LANtastic installation final information summary screen.

19. The next screen notifies you that a statement will be added to your AUTOEXEC.BAT file to automatically run Simply LANtastic each time you start your computer (see fig. 11.30). The installation program makes changes to both your AUTOEXEC.BAT and CONFIG.SYS startup files and saves the original files under a new name.

Press any key to continue with the installation.

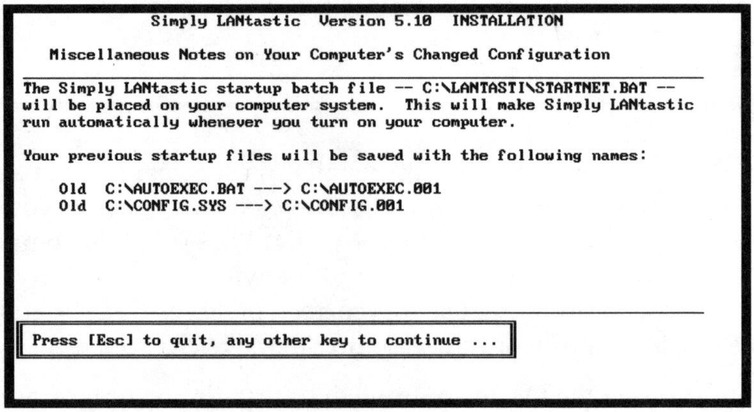

Figure 11.30

Screen displaying notes regarding changes made to the computer's configuration.

```
            Simply LANtastic  Version 5.10   INSTALLATION

    Miscellaneous Notes on Your Computer's Changed Configuration

  The Simply LANtastic startup batch file -- C:\LANTASTI\STARTNET.BAT --
  will be placed on your computer system.  This will make Simply LANtastic
  run automatically whenever you turn on your computer.

  Your previous startup files will be saved with the following names:

     Old   C:\AUTOEXEC.BAT ---> C:\AUTOEXEC.001
     Old   C:\CONFIG.SYS ---> C:\CONFIG.001




  Press [Esc] to quit, any other key to continue ...
```

The Simply LANtastic installation program proceeds to install Simply LANtastic on your computer's hard disk and to make the appropriate changes to your system startup files. When the installation is finished, the Installation Complete screen appears, notifying you that the installation was successful and instructing you to reboot your computer to start Simply LANtastic.

The Simply LANtastic installation program has created a batch file called STARTNET.BAT, which is located in your \LANTASTI directory (or the directory you specified during installation). The installation program also added a line to your AUTOEXEC.BAT file to call the STARTNET.BAT file, which contains the commands that automatically start Simply LANtastic and establish drive and printer connections. As a result, when your computer is turned on, Simply LANtastic is started and the drive and printer connections specified are established.

Windows Installation

After the Simply LANtastic Windows installation program starts, you can proceed by performing the following steps:

1. The Artisoft Install Message dialog box appears, congratulating you on your selection of Simply LANtastic (see fig. 11.31). Select OK or press Enter, and another dialog box with additional information appears. Select OK or press Enter again to proceed with the installation.

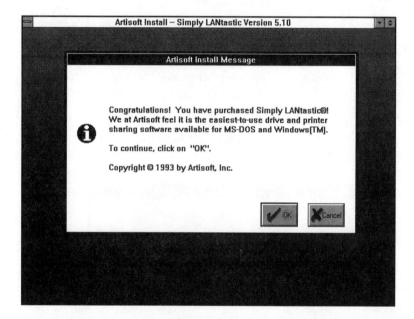

Figure 11.31

The Artisoft Install Message dialog box.

2. The Enter target drive dialog box appears (see fig. 11.32), listing the available physical drives on your system and allowing you to select the drive on which you want Simply LANtastic to be installed.

    Accept the default Drive C: selection, and select OK or press Enter to continue.

Figure 11.32

Selecting the drive for
installation.

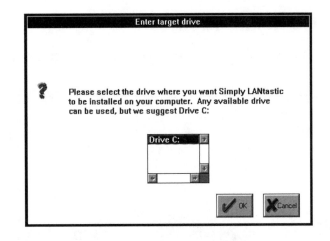

3. The Enter directory dialog box appears, asking you to
    specify the directory where you want to install Simply
    LANtastic (see fig. 11.33).

    Accept the default \LANTASTI directory, and select OK or
    press Enter to continue.

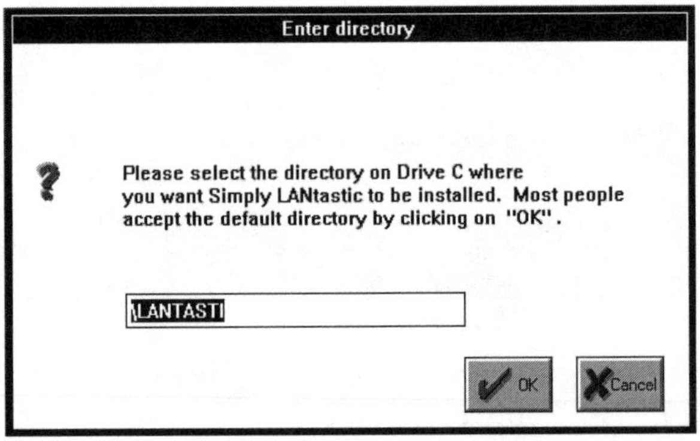

Figure 11.33

Specifying the
installation directory
for Simply LANtastic.

```
┌──────────────────────────────────────────────────────┐
│                    Enter directory                     │
├──────────────────────────────────────────────────────┤
│                                                        │
│   ?   Please select the directory on Drive C where     │
│       you want Simply LANtastic to be installed. Most people │
│       accept the default directory by clicking on "OK". │
│                                                        │
│       ┌──────────────────────────────┐                │
│       │\LANTASTI                     │                │
│       └──────────────────────────────┘                │
│                          ┌─────┐  ┌────────┐           │
│                          │✔ OK │  │✗ Cancel│           │
│                          └─────┘  └────────┘           │
└──────────────────────────────────────────────────────┘
```

4. The Enter computer name dialog box appears, asking you to
    specify a name for the computer at which you are sitting (see
    fig. 11.34). The name you specify must be unique, which
    means that another node in the network cannot have the
    same name. The name can contain up to 15 alphanumeric
    characters with no spaces.

Enter the name for your computer, and select OK or press
Enter to continue. In this example, KSOFFICE is the name
specified.

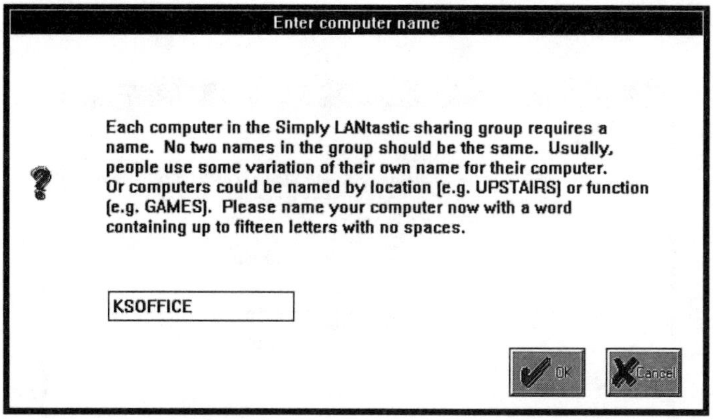

Figure 11.34

Entering the network
name for the node.

5. The Share drives and printers? dialog box appears, asking
    whether you want to share your computer's drives or print-
    ers (see fig. 11.35). If you select the SHARE my computer's
    drives or printers option, the Simply LANtastic installation
    program configures your computer as a nondedicated
    server; that is, your computer will be allowed to share its
    resources with other nodes. If you select the DO NOT share
    my computer's drives and printers option, the installation
    program configures your computer as a workstation; your
    computer will be allowed to access shared resources on
    other nodes but will not be able to share its own resources
    with others.

    Accept the default SHARE my computer's drives or printers
    option, and select OK or press Enter to continue.

6. The More than 10 computers connected to yours? dialog box
    appears (see fig. 11.36). This dialog box enables you to
    specify the maximum number of computers that may estab-
    lish connections to you and the maximum number of com-
    puters that you may be connected to. The KEEP maximum

connected computers at 10 option allows up to 10 connections to exist between your computer and other network
nodes. The INCREASE maximum connected computers to
30 option allows up to 30 connections to exist between your
computer and other network nodes.

Figure 11.35

Specifying whether to
share the computer's
resources.

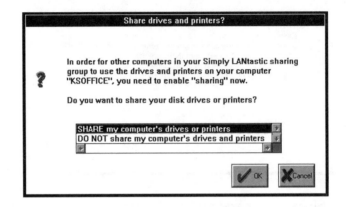

Accept the default KEEP maximum connected computers at
10 option, and select OK or press Enter to continue.

Figure 11.36

Specifying the
maximum number of
network connections
for your computer.

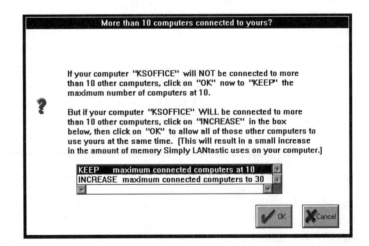

7. The Simply LANtastic Information Check dialog box appears, displaying a summary of the selections you have made so far (see fig. 11.37). You can select the OK to continue with installation option to continue, or you can select the Go back and re-enter the information option if you want to change any of the information you have specified so far.

   Select the default OK to continue with installation option, and select OK or press Enter to continue.

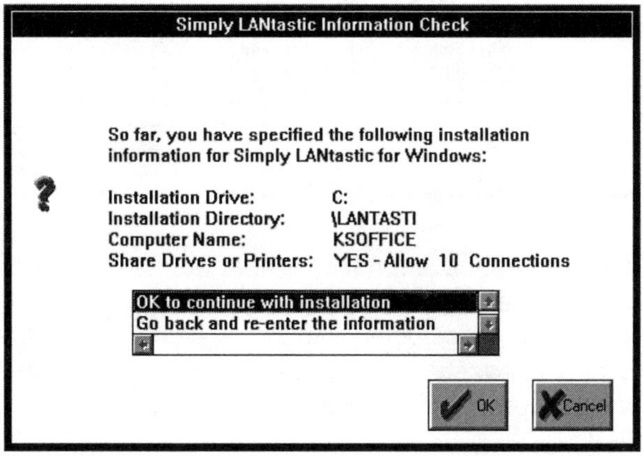

Figure 11.37

The Simply LANtastic Information Check dialog box showing the options specified so far.

8. The Select network adapter dialog box appears, requiring you to select the type of network adapter that is installed in your computer (see fig. 11.38). The first two selections— Simply LANtastic Internal Network Adapter and LANtastic NodeRunner 2000 Series Ethernet Adapter—actually install the same network adapter driver because the two adapters are similar. If you are not using an Artisoft adapter, select the NDIS Support for Network Adapters option. This option enables you to use any other network adapter supplied with an NDIS driver.

   Select the Simply LANtastic Internal Network Adapter option, and select OK or press Enter to continue.

Figure 11.38

Specifying the
network adapter.

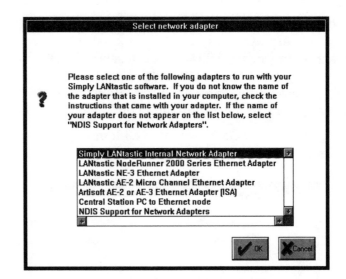

> If you do not have a network adapter installed in your
> computer and are planning to use the supplied stub
> driver to practice using Simply LANtastic, select the
> Simply LANtastic Internal Network Adapter option. You
> will change the network driver installed later.

9. The Set up drive or printer connections? dialog box appears
    (see fig. 11.39). This dialog box enables you to specify if you
    want to set up network drive or printer connections that are
    automatically established when Simply LANtastic is started.

    Select the SET UP permanent drive or printer connections
    option, and select OK or press Enter to continue.

10. The Enter computer name dialog box appears, asking for the
    name of the computer that has a drive you want to use (see
    fig. 11.40). If you don't want to set up a permanent drive
    connection but want to proceed to set up a printer connec-
    tion, leave the field blank and select OK or press Enter.

    If you want to set up a permanent connection to a drive on
    the computer named ZAK, type **ZAK** and select OK or press
    Enter.

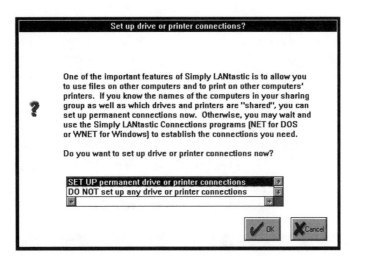

Figure 11.39

Specifying the option to set up permanent drive or printer connections.

Set up drive or printer connections?

One of the important features of Simply LANtastic is to allow you to use files on other computers and to print on other computers' printers. If you know the names of the computers in your sharing group as well as which drives and printers are "shared", you can set up permanent connections now. Otherwise, you may wait and use the Simply LANtastic Connections programs (NET for DOS or WNET for Windows) to establish the connections you need.

Do you want to set up drive or printer connections now?

SET UP permanent drive or printer connections
DO NOT set up any drive or printer connections

✓ OK   ✗ Cancel

Figure 11.40

Specifying the name of the computer with the drive you want to use.

Enter computer name

OTHER COMPUTER with a DRIVE you want to USE...

Please type the name of the other computer that has the drive you want to connect to and use.

Or just click on "OK" to continue, skipping drive setup.

>>> You can do this before the other computer is set up.<<<

ZAK

✓ OK   ✗ Cancel

The information you specify during installation for permanent drive and printer connections appear as commands in the STARTNET.BAT file created by the Simply LANtastic installation program. The STARTNET.BAT file contains the commands necessary to start Simply LANtastic on your computer and establish any drive or printer connections.

You can change the STARTNET.BAT file later to add, delete, or modify any drive or printer connections.

11. The Please enter drive name dialog box appears, asking you to enter the name of the shared-drive resource you want to use (see fig. 11.41). The Simply LANtastic installation program automatically creates shared resource names for the drives present on each computer and assigns the names C-DRIVE for your C hard disk, A-DRIVE for your A floppy drive, and so on. If you know the name of a shared-drive and shared-directory resource on the other computer that you want to use, you can specify that name now.

For this installation, accept the default C-DRIVE drive resource name and select OK or press Enter.

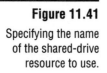

Please enter drive name

NAME of DRIVE you want to USE on ZAK...

_____

Please enter the name of the drive on "ZAK"
that you want to connect to and use. This will most likely
be the computer's hard disk named "C-DRIVE". But you can
instead choose another hard drive if "ZAK" has one, or
choose a floppy drive named "A-DRIVE" or "B-DRIVE".
(Drive names can be up to 8 letters.)

C-DRIVE

✔ OK   ✗ Cancel

12. The Enter drive letter dialog box appears, asking you for the drive letter on your computer to use to access the shared-drive resource on the other computer (see fig. 11.42). You can specify any drive letter you want, although it's advisable not to use a drive letter that corresponds to a physical drive that already exists in your computer.

For this installation, accept the default drive letter D and select OK or press Enter.

Figure 11.42

Specifying the drive
letter to redirect to a
shared-drive resource
on another computer.

13. The Enter computer name dialog box appears, asking for the
    name of another computer with a shared-drive resource you
    want to use. You can specify the name of another computer;
    or you can specify the name of the computer you specified in
    the previous connection if you want to use another drive on
    that computer. You also can leave the field blank if you don't
    want to specify another drive connection.

    Leave the field blank and select OK or press Enter to con-
    tinue.

    > You can specify a maximum of two network drive
    > connections during installation. You can change your
    > STARTNET.BAT file later to specify additional connec-
    > tions, if desired.

14. The Enter computer name dialog box appears, asking
    you for the name of the computer with the shared-printer
    resource you want to use (see fig. 11.43).

    If ZAK has a shared-printer resource you want to use, type
    ZAK in the field and select OK or press Enter.

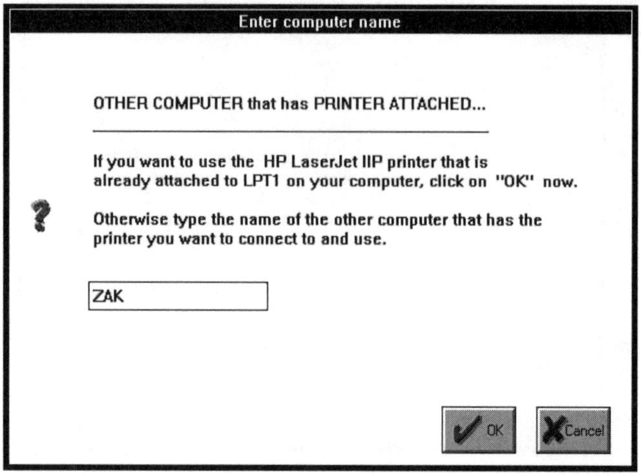

Figure 11.43

Specifying the name
of the computer with
the shared-printer
resource to use.

```
                    Enter computer name

        OTHER COMPUTER that has PRINTER ATTACHED...

        If you want to use the  HP LaserJet IIP printer that is
        already attached to LPT1 on your computer, click on  "OK"  now.

  ?     Otherwise type the name of the other computer that has the
        printer you want to connect to and use.

        ┌─────────────────────────────┐
        │ ZAK                         │
        └─────────────────────────────┘

                                        ✔ OK    ✗ Cancel
```

15. The Enter printer name dialog box appears, asking you to
    specify the name of the shared-printer resource on the other
    computer to which you want to establish a connection (see
    fig. 11.44).

    Accept the default @PRINTER name, and select OK or press
    Enter.

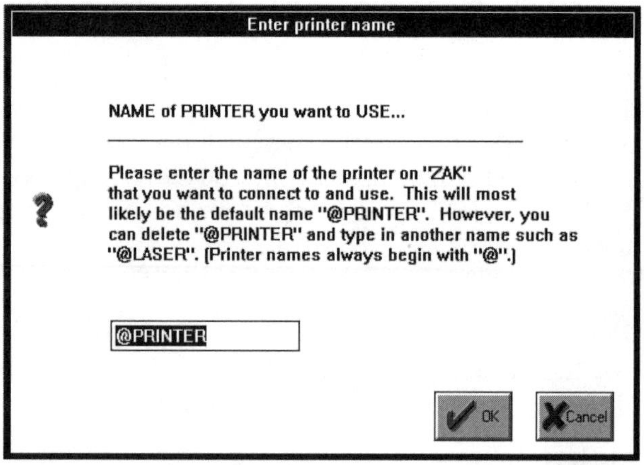

Figure 11.44

Specifying the name
of the shared-printer
resource to use.

```
                      Enter printer name

        NAME of PRINTER you want to USE...

        Please enter the name of the printer on "ZAK"
        that you want to connect to and use. This will most
  ?     likely be the default name "@PRINTER". However, you
        can delete "@PRINTER" and type in another name such as
        "@LASER". [Printer names always begin with "@".]

        ┌─────────────────────────────┐
        │ @PRINTER                    │
        └─────────────────────────────┘

                                        ✔ OK    ✗ Cancel
```

The Simply LANtastic installation program automatically creates a shared-printer resource with the name @PRINTER, which is defined as the LPT1 device.

Shared-printer resources in Simply LANtastic always begin with the at character (@).

16. The Enter printer port dialog box appears (see fig. 11.45), asking for the device name (printer port) on your computer you want to redirect to point to the shared-printer resource on the specified server.

    Accept the default LPT1 selection, and select OK or press Enter.

```
+=========================================================+
|                    Enter printer port                   |
+=========================================================+
|                                                         |
|       PRINTER PORT on YOUR COMPUTER...                   |
|       _____         |
|                                                         |
|       Please enter the name of the printer port on      |
|   ?   your computer such as LPT1 or LPT2 that your      |
|   •   application programs will use to print. The       |
|       documents you send to the port you select will    |
|       come out on the printer named "@PRINTER" on       |
|       computer "ZAK".                                    |
|                                                         |
|                                                         |
|                                                         |
|        +-------------------------------------+          |
|        | LPT1                                |          |
|        +-------------------------------------+          |
|                                                         |
|                            +------+   +--------+        |
|                            | ✔ OK |   | ✘ Cancel|       |
|                            +------+   +--------+        |
+=========================================================+
```

Figure 11.45

Indicating the printer port to connect to the shared-printer resource on the server.

The Simply LANtastic installation program enables you to designate a single network printer connection. You can change your STARTNET.BAT file later to specify additional connections, if desired.

17. The Simply LANtastic Information Check dialog box appears, showing a summary of the installation information you have specified (see fig. 11.46). Select the OK to continue

with installation option if the information shown is correct. Otherwise, select the Go back and re-enter the information option to make changes.

Select the OK to continue with installation option, and select OK or press Enter to continue.

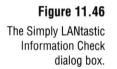

Figure 11.46

The Simply LANtastic Information Check dialog box.

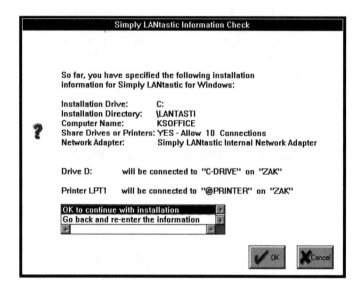

18. The Artisoft Install Message dialog box appears, notifying you that a statement will be added to your AUTOEXEC.BAT file to automatically run Simply LANtastic each time you start your computer (see fig. 11.47). The installation program makes changes to both your AUTOEXEC.BAT and CONFIG.SYS startup files and saves the original files as a new name. In addition, changes also are made to your Windows configuration files.

    Select OK or press Enter to continue with the installation.

The Simply LANtastic installation program proceeds to install Simply LANtastic on your computer's hard disk and to make the appropriate changes to your system startup files and your Windows configuration files. When installation is finished, the Artisoft

Install Message dialog box appears, notifying you that the installation is complete and instructing you to shut down Windows and reboot your computer to start Simply LANtastic.

```
┌──────────────────────────────────────────────────────────┐
│                  Artisoft Install Message                  │
├──────────────────────────────────────────────────────────┤
│                                                            │
│   Miscellaneous Notes on Your Computer's Changed Configuration │
│                                                            │
│   The Simply LANtastic startup batch file – C:\LANTASTI\STARTNET.BAT – │
│   will be placed on your computer system.  This will make Simply LANtastic │
│   run automatically whenever you turn on your computer.    │
│                                                            │
│   Your previous startup files will be saved with the following names: │
│                                                            │
│      Old  C:\AUTOEXEC.BAT —> C:\AUTOEXEC.001               │
│      Old  C:\CONFIG.SYS —> C:\CONFIG.001                   │
│      Old  C:\LANTASTI\STARTNET.BAT —> C:\LANTASTI\STARTNET.001 │
│      Old  C:\WINDOWS\SYSTEM.INI —> C:\WINDOWS\SYSTEM.001   │
│      Old  C:\WINDOWS\WIN.INI —> C:\WINDOWS\WIN.001         │
│      Old  C:\WINDOWS\PROGMAN.INI —> C:\WINDOWS\PROGMAN.001 │
│                                                            │
│   Please click on  "OK"  to continue...                    │
│                                                            │
│                                  [✓ OK]  [✗ Cancel]        │
└──────────────────────────────────────────────────────────┘
```

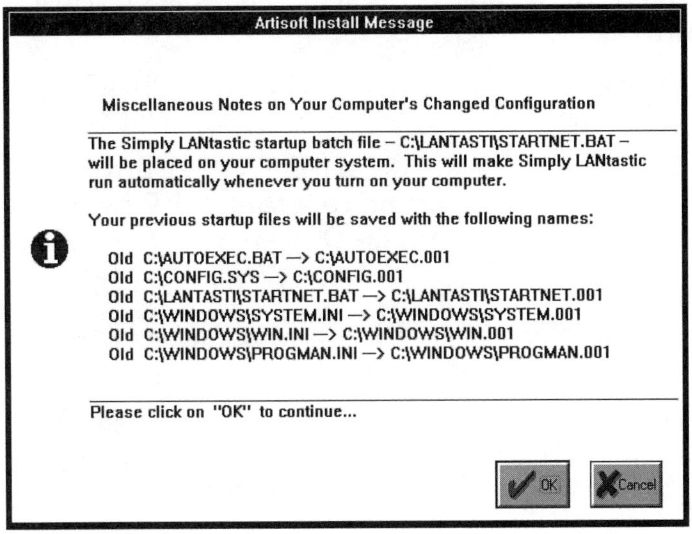

Figure 11.47

Notes regarding changes made to the computer's configuration.

The Simply LANtastic installation program has created a batch file called STARTNET.BAT, which is located in your \LANTASTI directory (or the directory you specified during installation). The installation program also adds a line to your AUTOEXEC.BAT file to call the STARTNET.BAT file, which contains the commands that automatically start Simply LANtastic and establish drive and printer connections. As a result, when your computer is turned on, Simply LANtastic is started and the drive and printer connections specified are established.

Stub Driver Installation

The stub driver included on the accompanying disk enables you to start Simply LANtastic on a computer that has no network adapter installed and is not connected to another computer. With the stub driver installed, you can practice using all the features of

Simply LANtastic. The only exception is that you are not able to communicate with any other computers.

After installing Simply LANtastic on your computer as described in the preceding section, perform the following steps to install the stub driver:

1. Place the accompanying disk in the A (or B) drive on your computer.

2. Copy the file STUB.EXE from the A (or B) drive to the \LANTASTI directory on your hard disk C by issuing the following command at the DOS prompt:

   COPY A:STUB.EXE C:\LANTASTI*.*

   If the accompanying disk is in your B drive, substitute B for A in the preceding command.

3. Using the DOS editor or another editor, change the STARTNET.BAT file in the \LANTASTI directory to replace the network adapter driver NR with STUB.

If you are using the DOS editor, perform the following steps to change the STARTNET.BAT file:

1. Start editing the STARTNET.BAT file by typing the following command at the DOS prompt:

   EDIT C:\LANTASTI\STARTNET.BAT

2. Locate the line in STARTNET.BAT that loads the network adapter driver NR (see fig. 11.48). Depending on your configuration, the command appears as NR or LOADHIGH NR.

3. Using your arrow keys, position the cursor at the first character in the line that loads NR. Then type **REM** to remark the command so it won't be loaded the next time STARTNET.BAT is run (see fig. 11.49).

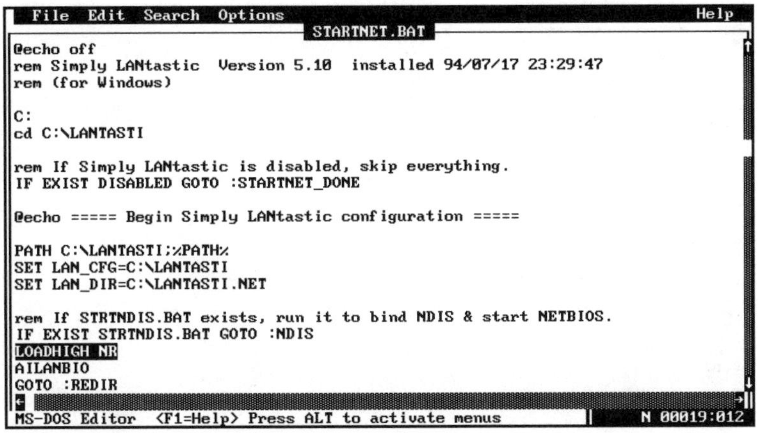

```
  File  Edit  Search  Options                                   Help
─────────────────────────────── STARTNET.BAT ──────────────────────────
@echo off
rem Simply LANtastic  Version 5.10  installed 94/07/17 23:29:47
rem (for Windows)

C:
cd C:\LANTASTI

rem If Simply LANtastic is disabled, skip everything.
IF EXIST DISABLED GOTO :STARTNET_DONE

@echo ===== Begin Simply LANtastic configuration =====

PATH C:\LANTASTI;%PATH%
SET LAN_CFG=C:\LANTASTI
SET LAN_DIR=C:\LANTASTI.NET

rem If STRTNDIS.BAT exists, run it to bind NDIS & start NETBIOS.
IF EXIST STRTNDIS.BAT GOTO :NDIS
LOADHIGH NR
AILANBIO
GOTO :REDIR

MS-DOS Editor   <F1=Help> Press ALT to activate menus        N 00019:012
```

Figure 11.48

Locating the network
adapter driver NR in
STARTNET.BAT.

Figure 11.48

Locating the network
adapter driver NR in
STARTNET.BAT.

```
  File  Edit  Search  Options                                   Help
─────────────────────────────── STARTNET.BAT ──────────────────────────
@echo off
rem Simply LANtastic  Version 5.10  installed 94/07/17 23:29:47
rem (for Windows)

C:
cd C:\LANTASTI

rem If Simply LANtastic is disabled, skip everything.
IF EXIST DISABLED GOTO :STARTNET_DONE

@echo ===== Begin Simply LANtastic configuration =====

PATH C:\LANTASTI;%PATH%
SET LAN_CFG=C:\LANTASTI
SET LAN_DIR=C:\LANTASTI.NET

rem If STRTNDIS.BAT exists, run it to bind NDIS & start NETBIOS.
IF EXIST STRTNDIS.BAT GOTO :NDIS
REM LOADHIGH NR
AILANBIO
GOTO :REDIR

MS-DOS Editor   <F1=Help> Press ALT to activate menus        N 00019:016
```

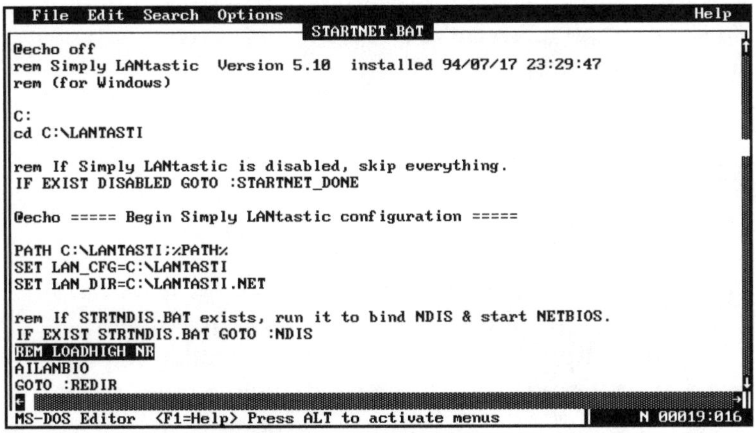

Figure 11.49

Remarking the NR
driver in the
STARTNET.BAT file.

4. Using your arrow keys, position the cursor at the first char-
    acter of the following line and press Enter to insert a blank
    line. Move the cursor to the first character in the blank line
    and type **STUB** (see fig. 11.50).

5. Save the changes made to the STARTNET.BAT file by
    selecting **S**ave from the **F**ile menu (press Alt+F+S). Then exit
    the DOS editor by selecting E**x**it from the **F**ile menu (press
    Alt+F+X).

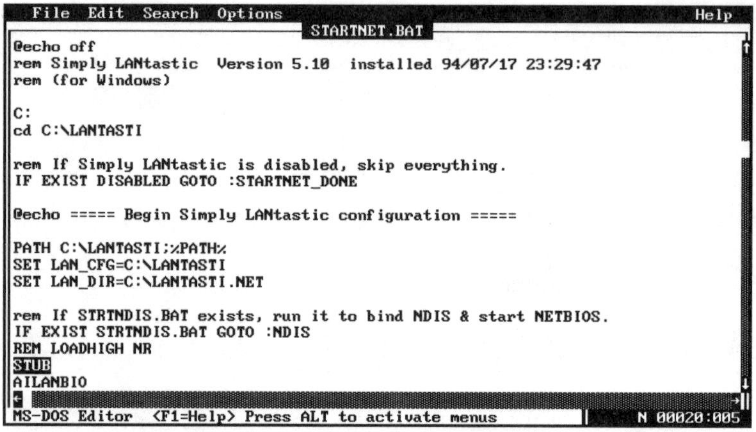

Figure 11.50

Including the STUB
command in
STARTNET.BAT.

```
   File  Edit  Search  Options                                        Help
                            STARTNET.BAT
@echo off
rem Simply LANtastic   Version 5.10   installed 94/07/17 23:29:47
rem (for Windows)

C:
cd C:\LANTASTI

rem If Simply LANtastic is disabled, skip everything.
IF EXIST DISABLED GOTO :STARTNET_DONE

@echo ===== Begin Simply LANtastic configuration =====

PATH C:\LANTASTI;%PATH%
SET LAN_CFG=C:\LANTASTI
SET LAN_DIR=C:\LANTASTI.NET

rem If STRTNDIS.BAT exists, run it to bind NDIS & start NETBIOS.
IF EXIST STRTNDIS.BAT GOTO :NDIS
REM LOADHIGH NR
STUB
AILANBIO
MS-DOS Editor   <F1=Help> Press ALT to activate menus        N 00020:005
```

The stub driver is now installed in place of the network adapter
driver. To start Simply LANtastic using the stub driver, you need
to reboot your computer.

Summary

This chapter illustrated in detail how to install the Simply
LANtastic network adapters and the Simply LANtastic NOS on
your computer. Both the Simply LANtastic DOS installation
program and the Simply LANtastic Windows installation program were demonstrated. This chapter also included instructions
for changing the STARTNET.BAT file to include the stub driver,
which enables you to run Simply LANtastic on a single computer
not physically connected to any other computer.

In This Chapter. . .

This chapter discusses how to establish network connections to shared-drive and shared-printer resources using the Simply LANtastic DOS and Windows utilities. You also learn to set up shared-drive and shared-printer resources using the Simply LANtastic DOS and Windows utilities. Specifically, this chapter discusses the following topics:

- Connecting to shared drives and printers in DOS using the DOS Simply LANtastic Connections program.

- Connecting to shared drives and printers in DOS using Simply LANtastic NET commands from a DOS command line.

- Connecting to shared drives and printers in Windows using the Windows Simply LANtastic Connections program.

- Setting up shared-drive and shared-printer resources in DOS using the DOS Simply LANtastic Connections program.

- Setting up shared-drive and shared-printer resources in Windows using the Windows Simply LANtastic Connections program.

Users, Printers, and Shared Drives

Now that your Simply LANtastic network is installed and running, you can begin using your new network.

When you installed Simply LANtastic, you may have specified some permanent connections to shared resources on another computer that are available as you turn on your computer. Remember, however, that to use another computer's shared resources, that other computer has to be turned on.

The Simply LANtastic installation program automatically creates shared resources for the drives and printer on each computer. The installation program creates a shared-resource name using the drive letter followed by a hyphen and the word DRIVE. For example, Simply LANtastic creates C-DRIVE—the shared-resource name for each computer's hard disk drive. Similarly, the A and B floppy drives are assigned the shared-resource names A-DRIVE and B-DRIVE, and the printer is assigned the shared-resource name @PRINTER.

The installation program creates shared resources that allow everyone Full Access rights to those resources. Simply LANtastic does not incorporate user accounts and passwords but rather enables you to specify which computers can have access to a particular shared resource and the type of access the computer can have (Full Access, Read-Only Access, or No Access).

This chapter discusses how to establish network connections to other computers' shared resources using the Simply LANtastic DOS and Windows utilities. You also learn to specify additional resources to share on your computer and to change the parameters (such as access rights) of your existing shared resources.

Establishing Network Connections

Before using a shared resource on another computer, you must establish a connection to the shared resource you want to use. To do this, you must specify a drive letter (such as K) if you are connecting to a shared-drive resource, or a device name (such as LPT1) if you are connecting to a shared-printer resource. Using the appropriate Simply LANtastic program or NET command, specify the computer with the shared-resource you want to use and then the name of the shared resource on that computer you want to access.

Simply LANtastic provides three methods for establishing network drive and printer connections: the DOS Simply LANtastic Connections program, a Simply LANtastic NET command issued at the DOS command line, and the Windows Simply LANtastic Connections program. In Microsoft Windows, you also can establish network drive connections using Windows File Manager, or you can establish network printer connections using the Windows Control Panel.

Connecting to Shared Drives and Printers in DOS

You can establish network connections to shared-drive or shared-printer resources in DOS either by using the DOS Simply LANtastic Connections program or by issuing a Simply LANtastic NET command at the DOS prompt. The following two sections discuss how to establish network connections using these two methods.

Using the DOS Simply LANtastic Connections Program

The Simply LANtastic Connections program in DOS can establish Network drive and printer connections. Start the Simply LANtastic Connections program by typing **NET** at the DOS prompt; the main menu appears (see fig. 12.1). The first two selections, Connect to Other Computers' Drives and Connect to Other Computers' Printers, establish network connections to shared-drive and shared-printer resources on other computers.

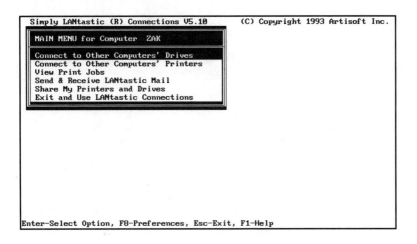

Figure 12.1

The DOS Simply LANtastic Connections program main menu.

To connect to a shared-drive resource, perform the following steps:

1. Select the Connect to Other Computers' Drives option from the main menu and press Enter.

2. The Drive Connections to Other Computers window appears. Using your arrow keys, select an available drive letter on your computer to use for the connection and press Enter.

3. The Connect To Computer window appears, listing the computers (servers) available (see fig. 12.2). Select the computer with the shared resource you want to use and press Enter.

Figure 12.2

Selecting a computer to which to establish a connection.

```
Simply LANtastic (R) Connections V5.10      (C) Copyright 1993 Artisoft Inc.
┌─ Drive Connections to Other Computers ──────┐  ┌─ Connect To Computer: ─┐
│  My A:    « Floppy Drive »                  │  │ \\ZAK                   │
│  My B:    « Floppy Drive »                  │  │ (KSOFFICE)              │
│  My C:    « Hard Drive »                    │  │                         │
│  My D:       « Available »                  │  │                         │
│  My E:       « Available »                  │  │                         │
│  My F:       « Available »                  │  │                         │
│  My G:       « Available »                  │  │                         │
│  My H:       « Available »                  │  │                         │
│  My I:       « Available »                  │  │                         │
│  My J:       « Available »                  │  │                         │
│  My K:       « Available »                  │  │                         │
│  My L:       « Available »                  │  │                         │
│  My M:       « Available »                  │  │                         │
│  My N:       « Available »                  │  │                         │
│  My O:       « Available »                  │  │                         │
│  My P:       « Available »                  │  │                         │
│  My Q:       « Available »                  │  │                         │
│  My R:       « Available »                  │  │                         │
└─────────────────────────────────────────────┘  └─────────────────────────┘
Enter-Select, Ins-Type Computer, Esc-Exit, F1-Help
```

Computers to which you have already established some kind of a connection appear with a double backslash (\\) in front of their names. Computers to which you haven't established a connection appear in parentheses in the Connect To Computer window.

4. The Select a Drive to Connect to window appears, showing a list of the available shared-drive resources on the selected computer (see fig. 12.3). Using your arrow keys, select the shared-drive resource you want to connect to and press Enter.

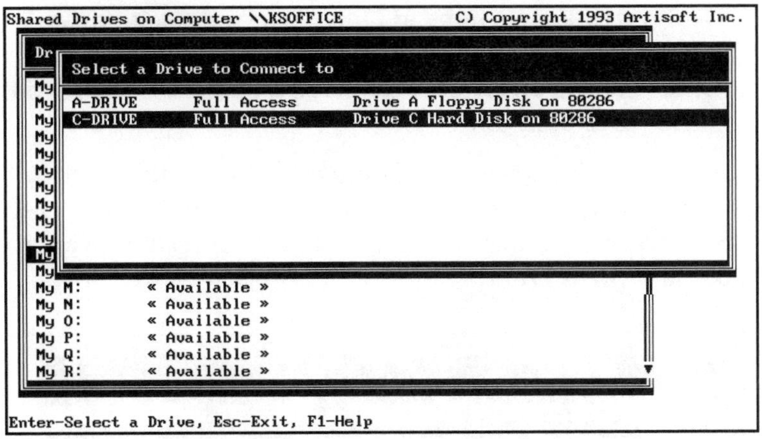

```
Shared Drives on Computer \\KSOFFICE          C) Copyright 1993 Artisoft Inc.
 Dr
My ┌─ Select a Drive to Connect to ─────────────────────────────────┐
My │                                                                 │
My │  A-DRIVE      Full Access      Drive A Floppy Disk on 80286      │
My │  C-DRIVE      Full Access      Drive C Hard Disk on 80286        │
My │                                                                 │
My │                                                                 │
My │                                                                 │
My │                                                                 │
My │                                                                 │
My │                                                                 │
My └─────────────────────────────────────────────────────────────────┘
My M:        « Available »
My N:        « Available »
My O:        « Available »
My P:        « Available »
My Q:        « Available »
My R:        « Available »

Enter-Select a Drive, Esc-Exit, F1-Help
```

Figure 12.3

Selecting a shared
drive resource.

5. The SUCCESS! window appears, indicating that the connection has been established. Press Enter or Esc to continue.

6. The Drive Connections to Other Computers window now shows the redirected drive and the shared-drive resource it points to (see fig. 12.4). Press Esc to return to the main menu.

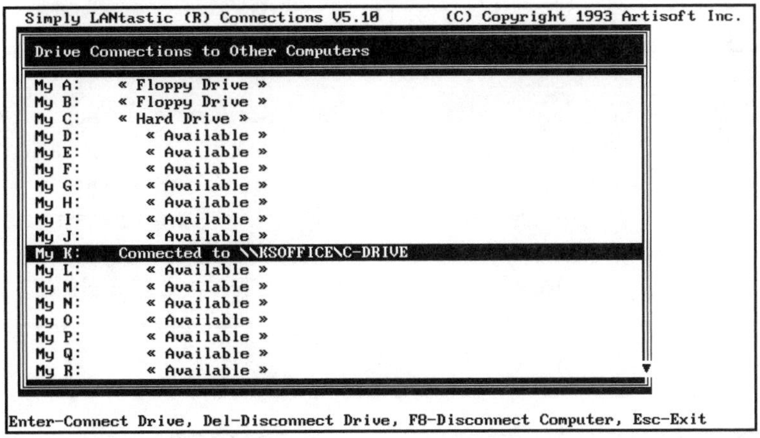

```
Simply LANtastic (R) Connections V5.10       (C) Copyright 1993 Artisoft Inc.
 ┌─ Drive Connections to Other Computers ──────────────────────────────┐
 │  My A:     « Floppy Drive »                                          │
 │  My B:     « Floppy Drive »                                          │
 │  My C:     « Hard Drive »                                            │
 │  My D:        « Available »                                          │
 │  My E:        « Available »                                          │
 │  My F:        « Available »                                          │
 │  My G:        « Available »                                          │
 │  My H:        « Available »                                          │
 │  My I:        « Available »                                          │
 │  My J:        « Available »                                          │
 │  My K:     Connected to \\KSOFFICE\C-DRIVE                           │
 │  My L:        « Available »                                          │
 │  My M:        « Available »                                          │
 │  My N:        « Available »                                          │
 │  My O:        « Available »                                          │
 │  My P:        « Available »                                          │
 │  My Q:        « Available »                                          │
 │  My R:        « Available »                                          │
 └─────────────────────────────────────────────────────────────────────┘
Enter-Connect Drive, Del-Disconnect Drive, F8-Disconnect Computer, Esc-Exit
```

Figure 12.4

The Drive Connections
to Other Computers
window showing the
redirected drive and
the shared resource it
points to.

To connect to a shared-printer resource, perform the following steps:

1. Select the Connect to Other Computers' Printers option from the main menu and press Enter.

2. The Printer Connections to Other Computers window appears. Using your arrow keys, select an available device name (such as LPT2) on your computer to use for the connection and press Enter.

3. Figure 12.5 illustrates the Connect To Computer window that appears with a list of the available computers (servers). Select the computer with the shared resource you want to use and press Enter.

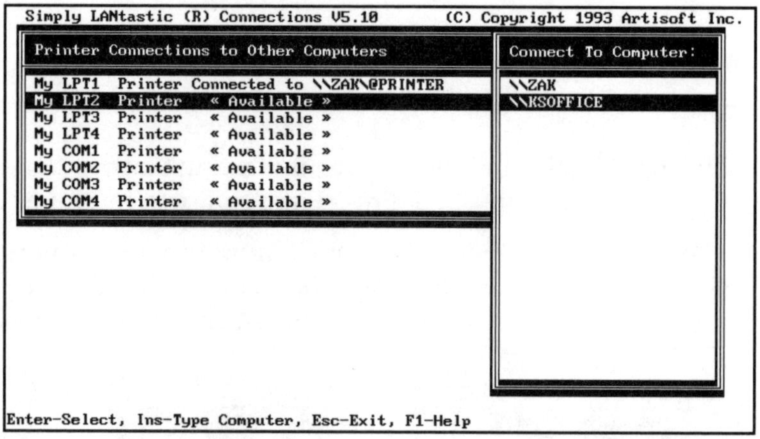

Figure 12.5

Selecting a computer to which to establish a connection.

```
Simply LANtastic (R) Connections V5.10          (C) Copyright 1993 Artisoft Inc.
┌───────────────────────────────────────────────────┐  ┌─────────────────────┐
│ Printer Connections to Other Computers              │  │ Connect To Computer:│
│ ┌─────────────────────────────────────────────────┐│  │┌───────────────────┐│
│ │My LPT1  Printer  Connected to \\ZAK\@PRINTER     ││  ││\\ZAK              ││
│ │My LPT2  Printer     « Available »                ││  ││\\KSOFFICE         ││
│ │My LPT3  Printer     « Available »                ││  ││                   ││
│ │My LPT4  Printer     « Available »                ││  ││                   ││
│ │My COM1  Printer     « Available »                ││  ││                   ││
│ │My COM2  Printer     « Available »                ││  ││                   ││
│ │My COM3  Printer     « Available »                ││  ││                   ││
│ │My COM4  Printer     « Available »                ││  ││                   ││
│ │                                                   ││  ││                   ││
│ │                                                   ││  │└───────────────────┘│
│ │                                                   ││  └─────────────────────┘
│ └─────────────────────────────────────────────────┘│
│Enter-Select, Ins-Type Computer, Esc-Exit, F1-Help   │
└─────────────────────────────────────────────────────┘
```

4. If there is only one shared-printer resource on the server you are attempting to connect to, the connection is automatically established and displayed in the Printer Connections to Other Computers window (see fig. 12.6). If more than one shared-printer resource is available, the Select a Printer to Connect to window appears, from which you can choose a shared-printer resource. Press Esc to return to the main menu.

Using Simply LANtastic NET Commands

You can establish network connections to shared resources on other computers by typing NET commands at the DOS prompt or by including them in a DOS batch file. You use the NET USE command to establish drive and printer connections to shared resources.

```
 Simply LANtastic (R) Connections V5.10        (C) Copyright 1993 Artisoft Inc.
┌──────────────────────────────────────────────────────────────────────────┐
│ Printer Connections to Other Computers                                     │
│┌──────────────────────────────────────────────────────────────────────────┐
││ My LPT1  Printer Connected to \\ZAK\@PRINTER                              │
││ My LPT2  Printer Connected to \\KSOFFICE\@PRINTER                         │
││ My LPT3  Printer    « Available »                                         │
││ My LPT4  Printer    « Available »                                         │
││ My COM1  Printer    « Available »                                         │
││ My COM2  Printer    « Available »                                         │
││ My COM3  Printer    « Available »                                         │
││ My COM4  Printer    « Available »                                         │
│└──────────────────────────────────────────────────────────────────────────┘
│                                                                            │
│                                                                            │
│                                                                            │
│                                                                            │
│                                                                            │
│                                                                            │
│                                                                            │
│                                                                            │
│ Enter-Connect Printer, Del-Disconnect Printer, Esc-Exit, F1-Help           │
└──────────────────────────────────────────────────────────────────────────┘
```

Figure 12.6

The Printer Connections to Other Computers window showing the redirected device and the shared-printer resource it points to.

The syntax for the NET USE command is as follows:

```
NET USE drive/device \\server-name\resource-name
```

The variable *drive/device* is the drive letter or device name on your computer that will be redirected to point to the shared resource; *server-name* is the name of the computer with the shared resource you want to use; and *resource-name* is the name of the shared drive or printer resource you are connecting to.

Use the /DEFERRED switch with the NET USE command to establish the connection when the drive or device is actually being used. A NET USE command issued with the /DEFERRED switch does not report an error or fail an attempted connection unless the computer with the shared resource is not turned on at the time an action is attempted using the redirected drive or device.

The /DEFERRED switch is placed immediately after the USE in the NET USE command. The syntax is as follows:

```
NET USE/DEFERRED drive/device \\server-
name\resource-name
```

Consider the following examples of NET commands. To establish a connection using your K drive to the shared-drive resource C-DRIVE on server KSOFFICE, type the following command at the DOS prompt:

```
NET USE K: \\KSOFFICE\C-DRIVE
```

To establish a connection using your LPT2 device to the shared-printer resource @PRINTER on server KSOFFICE, type the following command at the DOS prompt:

```
NET USE LPT2: \\KSOFFICE\@PRINTER
```

Connecting to Shared Drives and Printers in Windows

You can establish network drive and printer connections in Windows using the Windows Simply LANtastic Connections program. Windows also provides basic features to enable you to establish network drive and printer connections; you can use Windows File Manager to establish network drive connections and Windows Control Panel to establish network printer connections.

Using the Windows Simply LANtastic Connections Program

The Windows Simply LANtastic Connections program can be used to establish network drive and printer connections. When you install Simply LANtastic, the Simply LANtastic program group is created, which contains the Simply LANtastic Connections program and the Simply LANtastic SETUP program (see fig. 12.7).

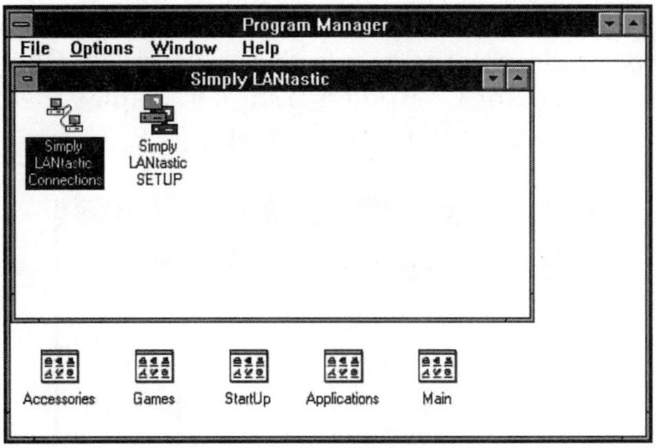

Figure 12.7
The Simply LANtastic
program group.

To start the Simply LANtastic Connections program, double-click
on the Simply LANtastic Connections icon or, with the icon
selected, choose **O**pen from the Program Manager **F**ile menu. The
Simply LANtastic Connections program main menu appears (see
fig. 12.8).

Figure 12.8
The Windows
Simply LANtastic
Connections program
main menu.

To establish a network drive connection using the Windows
Simply LANtastic Connections program, perform the following
steps:

1. Select the **D**rives button, or choose the Connect to **D**rives
   option from the **N**et menu. The Drive Connections dialog
   box appears, showing the shared resources available for
   connection and the drives on your computer that can be
   used for connecting to the shared resources.

2. If the computer (server) that has the resource you want to connect to does not appear in the Available for Connection section, select the Computers button to display the Computer Connections dialog box (see fig. 12.9).

Figure 12.9

The Computer
Connections
dialog box.

```
┌─────────────────────────────────────────────────────────────┐
│ ─                  Computer Connections                       │
├─────────────────────────────────────────────────────────────┤
│ Available for Connection:        Already Connected:           │
│ ┌─────────────────────┐          ┌─────────────────────┐     │
│ │ KSOFFICE            │          │ ZAK                 │     │
│ │                     │          │                     │     │
│ │                     │          │                     │     │
│ └─────────────────────┘          └─────────────────────┘     │
│                                                               │
│ Computer:  ┌──────────────────┐         ┌──────────┐         │
│            └──────────────────┘         │ Connect  │         │
│                      ┌──────────┐       ┌──────────┐         │
│                      │  Close   │       │Disconnect│         │
│                      └──────────┘       └──────────┘         │
└─────────────────────────────────────────────────────────────┘
```

3. Select the computer you want to connect to by clicking on the name listed in the Available for Connection section, and then select the Connect button to establish the connection. The selected computer appears in the Already Connected section.

4. Select the Close button, and you return to the Drive Connections dialog box with the selected computer and its resources listed in the Available for Connection section.

5. Establish the desired connection by selecting the shared-drive resource in the Available for Connection section and dragging and dropping it on the drive letter in the My Connections section you want to use to access the shared-drive resource. The connection is established and appears in the My Connections section (see fig. 12.10).

6. Select the Close button to return to the main menu.

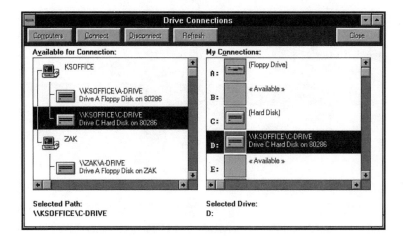

Figure 12.10

The D drive redirected to the C-DRIVE shared resource on server KSOFFICE.

Perform the following steps to establish a network printer connection using the Windows Simply LANtastic Connections program:

1. Select the **P**rinters button, or choose the Connect to **P**rinters option from the **N**et menu. The Printer Connections dialog box appears, showing the shared-printer resources available for connection and the devices on your computer that can be used for connecting to the shared resources.

2. Establish the connection you want by selecting the desired shared-printer resource in the A**v**ailable for Connection section and dragging and dropping it on the device name in the My C**o**nnections section you want to use to access the selected shared-printer resource. The connection is established and appears in the My C**o**nnections section (see fig. 12.11).

If the computer (server) that has the resource you want to connect to does not appear in the A**v**ailable for Connection section, select the Co**m**puters button to display the Computer Connections dialog box and connect to the computer as you did when establishing drive connections.

Figure 12.11

The LPT2 device
redirected to the
@PRINTER shared
resource on server
KSOFFICE.

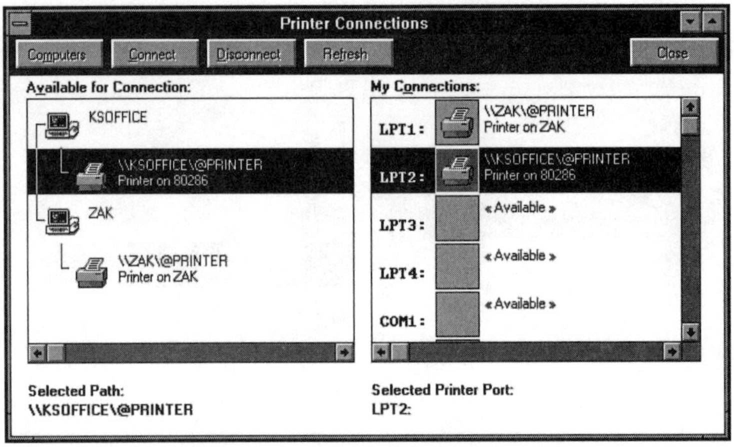

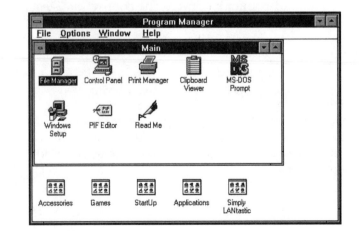

3. Select the Close button to return to the main menu.

Establishing Drive Connections Using Windows File Manager

You can use the Windows File Manager program to establish
network drive connections to shared-drive resources. File Manager is located in the Main program group (see fig. 12.12). The
Windows File Manager interface isn't as intuitive as the Simply
LANtastic interface and requires that you know the name of the
computer and the shared resource you want to connect to.

Figure 12.12

The Windows File
Manager program in
the Main program
group.

To establish a network drive connection using the Windows File Manager program, perform the following steps:

1. Start File Manager by double-clicking on the File Manager icon or, with the File Manager icon selected, choosing **O**pen from the Program Manager **F**ile menu.

2. Select **N**etwork Connections from the Windows File Manager **D**isk menu.

3. The Network Connections dialog box appears (see fig. 12.13). Type the path of the shared resource you want to connect to in the **N**etwork Path field, and type the drive letter you want to redirect to point to the specified shared resource in the D**r**ive field.

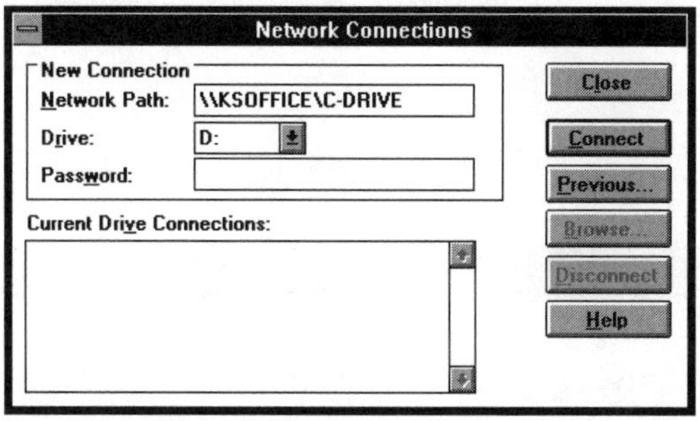

Figure 12.13

Specifying the Network Path and Drive in the Network Connections dialog box.

4. Select the **C**onnect button, and the network drive connection appears in the Current Dri**v**e Connections list.

5. Select C**l**ose to return to File Manager. The new network drive (D, in this example) now appears with the other drive icons (see fig. 12.14).

Establishing Printer Connections Using Windows Control Panel

You can establish network printer connections using Windows Control Panel. Control Panel is located in the Main program group next to File Manager. The Windows Control Panel interface isn't as intuitive as the Simply LANtastic interface and, like

Windows File Manager, requires that you know the name of the computer and the shared resource you want to connect to.

Figure 12.14

File Manager with the new D network drive.

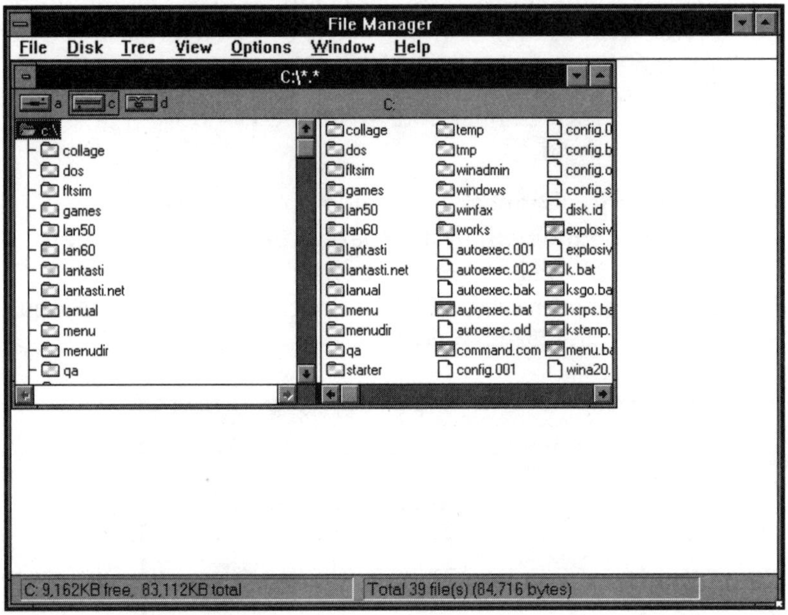

To establish a network printer connection using Control Panel, perform the following steps:

1. Start Control Panel by double-clicking on the Control Panel icon or, with the Control Panel icon selected, choosing **O**pen from the Program Manager **F**ile menu. Select the Printers routine by double-clicking on the Printers icon.

2. The Printers dialog box appears (see fig. 12.15). Select the **C**onnect button.

3. The Connect dialog box appears (see fig. 12.16). Select the device in the **P**orts section you want to redirect to point to the shared-printer resource, and then select the **N**etwork button.

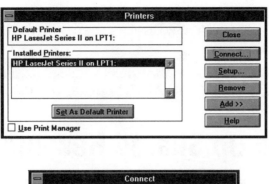

Figure 12.15

The Printers
Dialog box.

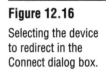

Figure 12.16

Selecting the device
to redirect in the
Connect dialog box.

4. The Printers - Network Connections dialog box appears.
   Type the network path of the shared-printer resource you
   want to connect to in the Network Path field (see fig. 12.17).

Figure 12.17

Specifying the
Network Path in the
Printer - Network
Connections
dialog box.

5. Select the Connect button, and the connection is established
   and appears in the Current Printer Connections list.

6. Select the Close button to return to the Connect dialog box, which now displays the new network printer connection.

7. Select OK to return to the Printers dialog box, and then select Close to exit the Control Panel Printers routine.

Setting Up Shared Resources

The Simply LANtastic installation program automatically creates shared-drive and shared-printer resources. Many situations arise, however, that require the creation of additional shared resources or the modification of existing shared resources.

Consider these examples that could occur after installing Simply LANtastic: you might add a drive or printer that you want to share with others in the network; you might choose to share specific directories; or perhaps a shared resource created by the Simply LANtastic installation program has been deleted, and you need to re-create the shared-resource name.

Simply LANtastic allows three levels of access to shared-drive resources: Full Access, Read-Only Access (shared printer resources don't have Read-Only Access), or No Access. In addition, Simply LANtastic enables you through the use of access lists to specify which computers can have which type of access to a shared resource.

You can create and configure shared resources using the DOS Simply LANtastic Connections program or the Windows Simply LANtastic Connections program.

Understanding Access Lists

Simply LANtastic *access lists* allow or restrict access to shared resources. Simply LANtastic does not require or support the use of individual user accounts and passwords; instead, Simply LANtastic enables you to specify access restrictions for individual

computers or for groups of computers with similar names. Assuming that each computer is always used by the same person,
specifying access restrictions by individual computers or groups
of computers provides adequate security features. Simply
LANtastic does not have security features to allow or deny access
[...] specific individuals—only to computers.

[...]es access lists to allow specific computers or
[...] Full Access, Read-Only Access, or No Access
[...]resource. In addition, Simply LANtastic uses
[...]pecific computers or groups of computers
[...]rinter resource.

[...]t to specify the access that other computers
[...]E resource. Because the C-DRIVE resource
[...]ter's entire hard disk drive, you don't want
[...]ss to your drive except the computer with
[...]en defining the access list for your C-DRIVE
[...]pecify Full Access for KATIE and No Access
[...]resented with the wild card character (*).
[...]ook like the following:

[...]ll Access

[...] Access

[...]stic evaluates the access rights of a
[...]ed on the first match found in the

[...]rder of the access list shown in the
[...]mple was switched so the wild card
[...]as first and KATIE second. When KATIE
[...] the C-DRIVE resource, No Access would
[...]ause the wild card (*) would be seen as a
match for KATIE first.

Consider another example of using access lists to restrict access.
Suppose you want to specify the access rights for INFO—a shared
resource on your computer. You want to allow Full Access to the

THANK YOU

CASHIER SIGNATURE

DATE

PARKING RECEIPT

$

Washington, D.C. 20007
Suite 100
2201 Wisconsin Avenue, N.W.
Diplomat Parking Corporation

computer named DANA, Read-Only Access to all computers whose names start with SALES, and No Access to all other computers. When defining INFO's access list, you would specify Full Access for DANA, Read-Only Access for SALES*, and No Access for everyone else (*). The access list would look like the following:

DANA	Full Access
SALES*	Read-Only Access
*	No Access

Setting Up Shared Resources in DOS

Using the DOS Simply LANtastic Connections program, you can set up the shared-drive and shared-printer resources in DOS. Shared-drive resources can point to entire drives or to directories contained on a drive.

To set up shared resources using the DOS Simply LANtastic Connections program, start the Simply LANtastic Connections program by typing **NET** at the DOS prompt and pressing Enter. The Simply LANtastic Connections program main menu appears (see fig. 12.18).

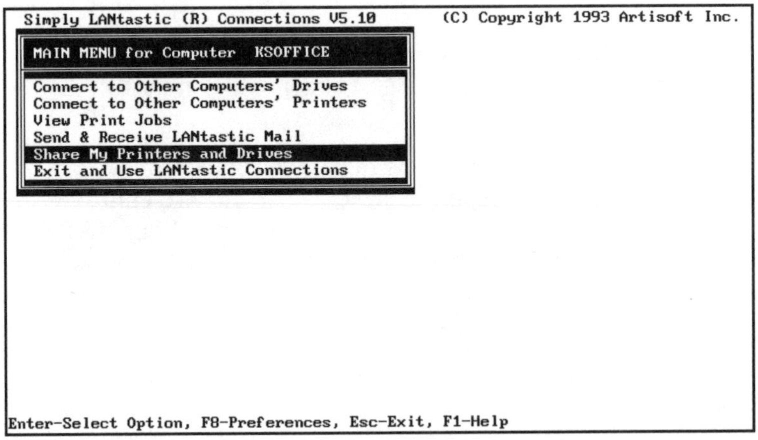

Figure 12.18

The DOS Simply LANtastic Connections program main menu.

```
Simply LANtastic (R) Connections V5.10     (C) Copyright 1993 Artisoft Inc.
┌──────────────────────────────────────┐
│ MAIN MENU for Computer   KSOFFICE      │
├──────────────────────────────────────┤
│ Connect to Other Computers' Drives     │
│ Connect to Other Computers' Printers    │
│ View Print Jobs                         │
│ Send & Receive LANtastic Mail           │
│ Share My Printers and Drives            │
│ Exit and Use LANtastic Connections      │
└──────────────────────────────────────┘




Enter-Select Option, F8-Preferences, Esc-Exit, F1-Help
```

The following two sections describe how to set up shared-drive and shared-printer resources using the DOS Simply LANtastic Connections program.

Shared-Drive and Shared-Directory Resources

To create a shared drive or directory using the DOS Simply LANtastic Connections program, perform the following steps:

1. Select the Share My Printers and Drives option from the main menu and press Enter. A list of shared-drive and -printer resources appears.

2. Press Ins to create a shared-drive-directory resource.

3. Type the name of the shared-drive-directory resource you want to create in the Type Printer or Drive Name window and press Enter. In this example, type MISCDATA.

4. When prompted, type the actual drive-directory that the shared resource points to. In this example, type C:\DATA.

5. The newly created resource appears on the list of shared-drive and shared-printer resources (see fig. 12.19). With the new shared-drive resource selected, press Enter.

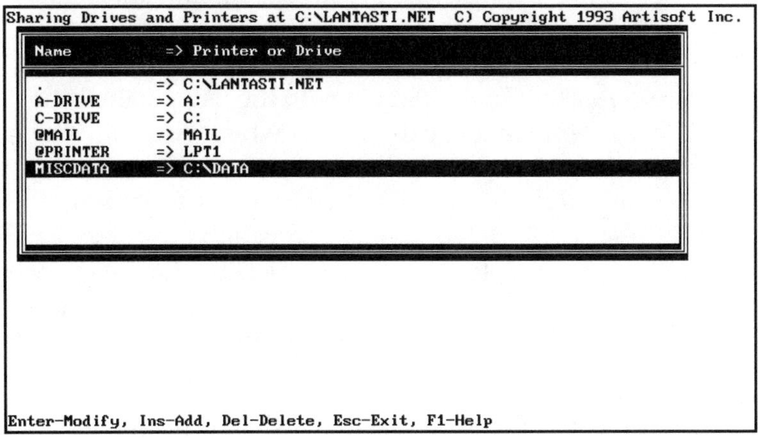

```
Sharing Drives and Printers at C:\LANTASTI.NET  C) Copyright 1993 Artisoft Inc.

  Name            => Printer or Drive

    .             => C:\LANTASTI.NET
  A-DRIVE         => A:
  C-DRIVE         => C:
  @MAIL           => MAIL
  @PRINTER        => LPT1
  MISCDATA        => C:\DATA




Enter-Modify, Ins-Add, Del-Delete, Esc-Exit, F1-Help
```

Figure 12.19

The list of shared-drive and shared-printer resources showing the newly added shared resource.

6. The Detailed Information screen appears, enabling you to specify or change the Description of the shared resource, the DOS Path, the Disk Drive Type, and the ACCESS LIST (see fig. 12.20). Use the arrow keys to move between fields. The following list describes each of these fields:

   - The optional Description field is shown to a user when connecting to shared resources using the Simply LANtastic Connections program. To add or change a description, press Enter, type the description when prompted, and press Enter when finished.

   - The DOS Path field shows the actual drive or directory on the local computer that is accessed when the shared resource is used. To change the DOS path, press Enter, change the DOS path when prompted, and press Enter when finished.

   - The Disk Drive Type field can be either DOS for a regular DOS drive on your computer or CD-ROM if the drive you are sharing is a CD-ROM drive. To change the disk drive type, press Enter to switch between DOS and CD-ROM.

   - The ACCESS LIST field is a list of computers or groups of computers (the wild card characters * and ? are allowed) and the access rights associated with each. Access rights can be Full Access, Read-Only Access, or No Access. To add an entry to the list, position the cursor on the entry in front of which you want the new entry to be located, press Ins, type the name of the computer when prompted, and press Enter when finished. To delete an entry, position the cursor on the entry to be deleted and press Del. To change the access rights for an entry, press F for Full Access, N for No Access, or R for Read-Only Access.

7. After changing the Detailed Information screen for your resource, press Esc to return to the shared resources list, and then press Esc again to return to the main menu.

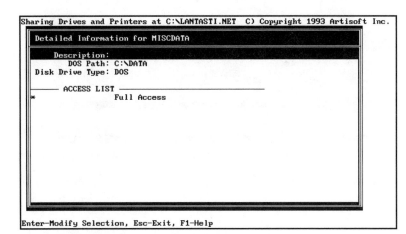

```
Sharing Drives and Printers at C:\LANTASTI.NET  C) Copyright 1993 Artisoft Inc.

  Detailed Information for MISCDATA

     Description:
       DOS Path: C:\DATA
  Disk Drive Type: DOS

   ───── ACCESS LIST ─────────────────────────────
  *                     Full Access






Enter-Modify Selection, Esc-Exit, F1-Help
```

Figure 12.20

The Detailed Information screen for the newly added MISCDATA resource.

Shared-Printer Resources

To create a shared-printer resource using the DOS Simply LANtastic Connections program, perform the following steps:

1. Select the Share My Printers and Drives option from the main menu and press Enter. A list of shared-drive and shared-printer resources appears.

2. Press Ins to create a shared-printer resource.

3. Type the name of the shared-printer resource you want to create in the Type Printer or Drive Name window and press Enter. In this example, type @LASER.

> In Simply LANtastic, shared-printer resource names must begin with the at character (@).

4. When prompted, select the actual device in the Printer Port window that the shared resource points to. In this example, choose LPT2.

5. The newly created resource appears on the list of shared-drive and shared-printer resources (see fig. 12.21). With the new shared-printer resource selected, press Enter.

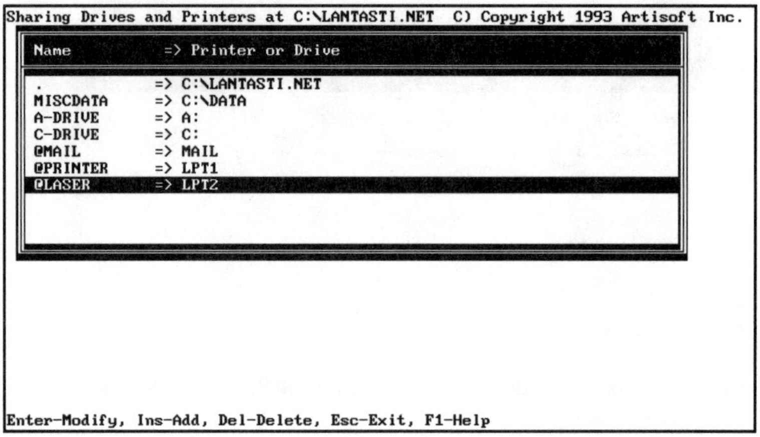

Figure 12.21

The list of shared-
drive and shared-
printer resources
showing the newly
added shared
resource.

```
Sharing Drives and Printers at C:\LANTASTI.NET   C) Copyright 1993 Artisoft Inc.

    Name              => Printer or Drive

       .              => C:\LANTASTI.NET
    MISCDATA          => C:\DATA
    A-DRIVE           => A:
    C-DRIVE           => C:
    @MAIL             => MAIL
    @PRINTER          => LPT1
    @LASER            => LPT2




Enter-Modify, Ins-Add, Del-Delete, Esc-Exit, F1-Help
```

6. The Detailed Information screen appears, enabling you to
    specify or change several parameters of the shared-printer
    resource (see fig. 12.22). Use the arrow keys to move be-
    tween fields. The following list describes these parameter
    fields:

    • The optional Description field is shown to a user when
      connecting to shared resources using the Simply
      LANtastic Connections program. To add or change a
      description, press Enter, type the description when
      prompted, and press Enter when finished.

    • The Printer Port field shows the actual port (device
      name) on the local computer that is accessed when the
      shared resource is used. To change the printer port
      press Enter, select the appropriate port when prompted,
      and press Enter when finished.

    • The Form Feeds field can be either enabled or disabled.
      If it is enabled, a form feed is sent to the printer at the
      end of each print job. Press Enter to switch the field
      between enabled and disabled.

    • The Lines Per Page field represents the number of lines
      that are printed on a page before a form feed is sent.
      Most application programs automatically handle the

lines per page, so changing the value in this field is usually not necessary. To change the Lines Per Page field, press Enter, type the number of lines per page when prompted, and press Enter when finished. Specifying 0 disables the Lines Per Page option.

- The Tab Width field represents the number of spaces sent to the printer if a tab character is received from an application. A Tab Width value of 0 causes the tab character to be sent to the printer. A Tab Width value is necessary only if your application sends tab characters and your printer does not support them. To change the Tab Width value press Enter, type a value for the tab width when prompted, and press Enter when finished.

- The Chars/Second field represents the minimum speed, in characters per second, at which print jobs are sent to the printer. Specifying a value other than the default of 0 (9600, for example) is sometimes necessary when running applications such as Microsoft Windows to force printing to occur at a reasonable rate. To change the Chars/Second field, press Enter, type the minimum characters per second (up to 32,767) when prompted, and press Enter when finished.

- The Setup Delay field represents the number of seconds to wait between the time the setup string is sent to the printer and the time the print job is sent to the printer. If you are using setup strings to initialize your printer, the setup delay is useful for printers that need a few seconds to reset before accepting data. To specify a Setup Delay value press Enter, type the number of seconds when prompted, and press Enter when finished.

- The Cleanup Delay field represents the number of seconds to wait after sending a cleanup file to the printer before allowing any other data to be sent. To specify a Cleanup Delay value press Enter, type the number of seconds when prompted, and press Enter when finished.

- The Edit Setup String field enables you to specify a setup string (or a setup file name) and a cleanup file name to be sent to the printer. A setup string or file name is sent before a print job, and a cleanup file name is sent after a print job. To specify setup or cleanup parameters press Enter, choose the appropriate action, and follow the prompts to enter the required information.

- The Access List field is a list of computers or groups of computers (the wild card characters * and ? are allowed) and the access rights associated with each. Access rights for printer resources can be Full Access or No Access. To add an entry to the list position the cursor on the entry in front of which you want the new entry to be located, press Ins, type the name of the computer when prompted, and press Enter when finished. To delete an entry position the cursor on the entry to be deleted and press Del. To change the access rights for an entry press F for Full Access or N for No Access.

Figure 12.22

The Detailed Information screen for the newly added @LASER printer resource.

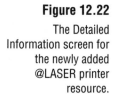

```
Sharing Drives and Printers at C:\LANTASTI.NET  C) Copyright 1993 Artisoft Inc.
┌──────────────────────────────────────────────────────────────────────────┐
│ Detailed Information for @LASER                                            │
│      Description:                                                          │
│     Printer Port: LPT2                                                     │
│       Form Feeds: DISABLED                                                 │
│   Lines Per Page: DISABLED                                                 │
│        Tab Width: 0                                                        │
│    Chars/Second: 0                                                         │
│      Setup Delay: 0                                                        │
│    Cleanup Delay: 0                                                        │
│   Edit Setup String                                                        │
│   ┌─── ACCESS LIST ───────────────────────────────────                    │
│   *              Full Access                                               │
│                                                                            │
└──────────────────────────────────────────────────────────────────────────┘
Enter-Modify Selection, Esc-Exit, F1-Help
```

7. After changing the Detailed Information screen for your shared-printer resource, press Esc to return to the shared resources list, and then press Esc again to return to the main menu.

Setting Up Shared Resources in Windows

Shared-drive and shared-printer resources are set up in Windows using the Windows Simply LANtastic Connections program. Shared-drive resources can point to entire drives or to directories contained on a drive.

To set up shared resources, start the Connections program by double-clicking on the Simply LANtastic Connections icon located in the Simply LANtastic program group or, with the icon selected, by choosing **O**pen from the Program Manager **F**ile menu. The Simply LANtastic main menu appears.

The following two sections describe how to set up shared-drive and shared-printer resources using the Windows Simply LANtastic Connections program.

Shared-Drive or Shared-Directory Resources

To create a shared drive or directory using the Windows Simply LANtastic Connections program, perform the following steps:

1. Select the **S**hare button, or choose the **S**hare Drives and Printers option from the **N**et menu. The Shared Drives and Printers dialog box appears, showing a list of the shared-drive and shared-printer resources (see fig. 12.23).

2. Select the **A**dd button, or choose **A**dd from the **E**dit menu.

3. The Add Drive or Printer dialog box appears (see fig. 12.24). Specify the name of the shared-drive resource in the Shared **N**ame field, an optional description in the **D**escription field, and the actual drive or directory pointed to by the shared resource in the **P**ath field.

Figure 12.23

The Shared Drives
and Printers
dialog box.

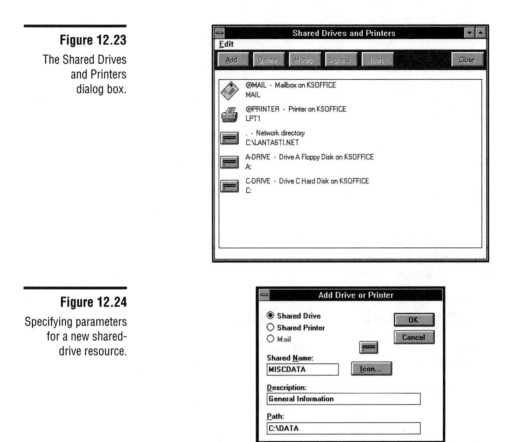

Figure 12.24

Specifying parameters
for a new shared-
drive resource.

4. Select OK to create the new shared resource and return to the Shared Drives and Printers dialog box, which now shows the newly added drive resource (see fig. 12.25).

To modify the parameters of a shared-drive resource, select the **M**odify button or choose **M**odify from the **E**dit menu. The Drive Parameters dialog box appears (see fig. 12.26). In this dialog box, you can change the description, path, and drive type of the shared resource in the **D**escription, **P**ath, and Dri**v**e Type fields, respectively. If the shared resource is for a CD-ROM drive, select the CD-ROM Dri**v**e Type option.

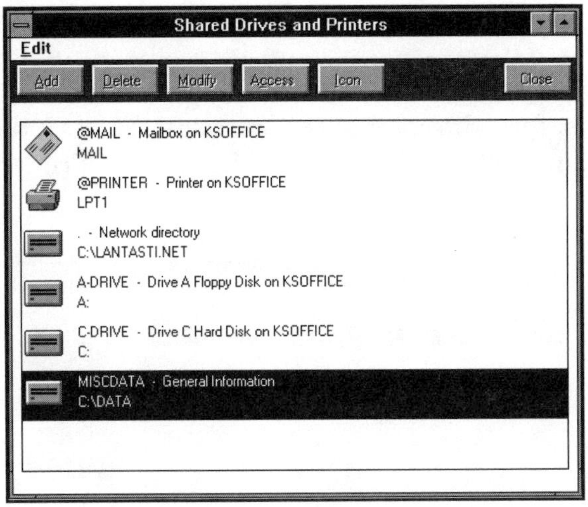

Figure 12.25

The Shared Drives and Printers dialog box showing the newly added shared resource.

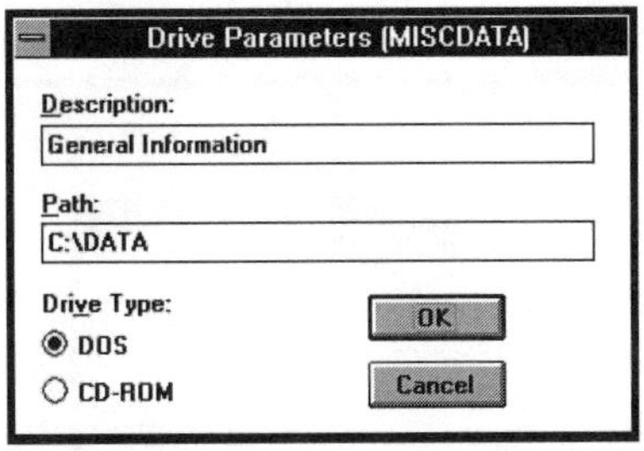

Figure 12.26

The Drive Parameters dialog box.

To specify an access list for the shared resource, select the Access button or choose Access from the Edit menu. The Access List dialog box appears (see fig. 12.27). To add entries to the list, select the Add button. The Access Entry dialog box then appears (see fig. 12.28). In this dialog box, you can add the name of a computer or group of computers (the * and ? wild card characters are allowed) in the Computer Name field, and you can specify No Access, Full Access, or Read-Only Access.

From the Access List dialog box, you also can delete, edit, or switch items in the access list, and copy the access list to the clipboard. To delete an entry from the access list, select the Delete button. To change the name or access rights or both of an entry in the access list, select the Edit button. To switch the access rights for an entry in the list between Full Access, Read-Only Access, or

No Access, select the Acce_ss_ button. You are also able to copy an individual item (_C_opy) or the entire access list (Copy _L_ist) to the Access Clipboard, which enables you to paste the item or list into the access list for a different shared resource. Select OK to accept the changes and return to the Shared Drives and Printers dialog box.

Figure 12.27

The Access List
dialog box.

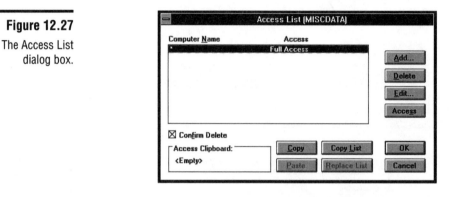

Figure 12.28

Adding a new entry to
the access list.

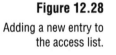

Shared-Printer Resources

To create a shared-printer resource using the Windows Simply LANtastic Connections program, perform the following steps:

1. Select the _S_hare button, or choose the _S_hare Drives and Printers option from the _N_et menu. The Shared Drives and Printers dialog box appears, listing the shared drive and printer resources.

2. Select the _A_dd button, or choose _A_dd from the _E_dit menu.

3. The Add Drive or Printer dialog box appears (see fig. 12.29).
   When you select the Shared Printer option, the fields in the
   dialog box change to reflect information required for a
   shared-printer resource.

Figure 12.29

The Add Drive or
Printer dialog box for
a shared-printer
resource.

4. Specify the name of the shared-printer resource in the
   Shared **N**ame field and an optional description in the
   Description field. To specify the port (device name), select
   the **P**ort button to open the Select Printer Port dialog box
   (see fig. 12.30).

Figure 12.30

Specifying a new
shared-printer
resource.

Shared-printer resource names must begin with the at
character (@) in Simply LANtastic.

5. Select OK to create the new shared resource and return to
   the Shared Drives and Printers dialog box, which now
   shows the newly added printer resource (see fig. 12.31).

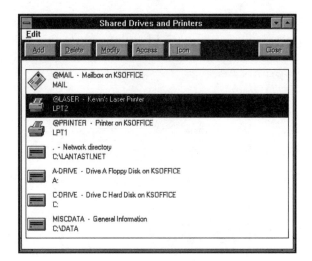

To change or specify the detailed parameters for a shared-printer resource, select the **M**odify button or choose **M**odify from the **E**dit menu. The Printer Parameters dialog box appears, enabling you to change the description, the port, and several other detailed printer parameters (see fig. 12.32). The following list describes these parameters:

- The Send **F**orm Feed option, if selected, sends a form feed to the printer at the end of each print job.

- The **T**ab Width field represents the number of spaces sent to the printer if a tab character is received from an application. A **T**ab Width value of 0 causes the tab character to be sent to the printer. **T**ab Width values are necessary only if applications send tab characters and your printer does not support them. To change the **T**ab Width value, type a new value in the field or use the increase and decrease icons to the right of the field.

- The **P**aper Width field represents the number of characters that can be printed across the page. This field is not necessary unless you are printing ASCII text on a wide carriage printer, and you want the text to fill the width of the page instead of the normal 80-column width. To change the **P**aper Width value, type a new value in the field or use the increase and decrease icons to the right of the field.

- The **L**ines per Page field represents the number of lines that are printed on a page before a form feed is sent. Most application programs automatically handle the lines per page, so changing the value in this field usually is not necessary. To change the **L**ines per Page value, type a new value in the field or use the increase and decrease icons to the right of the field. Specifying 0 disables the **L**ines per Page option.

- The **C**haracters per Second field represents the minimum speed, in characters per second, at which print jobs are sent to the printer. Specifying a value other than the default of 0 (9600, for example) is sometimes necessary when running applications such as Microsoft Windows to force printing to occur at a reasonable rate. To change the **C**haracters per Second value, type a new value in the field or use the increase and decrease icons to the right of the field.

- The **S**etup button opens the Printer Setup dialog box, in which you can specify special setup strings or files and cleanup files to be sent to the printer between print jobs (see fig. 12.33). The **S**etup Delay field represents the number of seconds to wait between the time the setup string or file is sent to the printer and the time the print job is sent to the printer. If you are using setup strings to initialize your printer, the setup delay is useful for printers that need a few seconds to reset before accepting data. The **C**leanup Delay field represents the number of seconds to wait after sending a cleanup file to the printer before allowing any other data to be sent. The **P**rinter Setup options enable you to specify a setup string or a setup file name and a cleanup file name to be sent to the printer. A setup string or file name is sent before a print job, and a cleanup file name is sent after a print job.

To specify an access list for the shared resource, select the Access
button or choose Access from the Edit menu. The Access List
dialog box appears. This dialog box enables you to specify access
lists and rights for a shared-printer resource just as you did for a
shared-drive resource. The only difference is that for shared-
printer resources, the access rights can be either No Access or Full
Access; Read-Only Access does not apply when dealing with
printer resources.

Summary

This chapter discussed how you can access and use shared resources in Simply LANtastic. You learned how to establish shared resources in DOS by using the DOS Simply LANtastic Connections program and Simply LANtastic NET commands. You learned how to establish shared resources in Windows by using the Windows Simply LANtastic Connections program and Windows File Manager and Control Panel. This chapter also described in detail how to set up shared-drive and shared-printer resources using the DOS and Windows Simply LANtastic Connections programs.

In This Chapter. . .

Managing a Simply LANtastic network is a relatively easy task. There are, however, issues that you need to consider to optimize your network and simplify its use. In this chapter, you learn about the issues that you face when managing a Simply LANtastic network.

Specifically, this chapter discusses the following topics:

- Managing shared resources, and organizational tips for making management easier.

- Changing a node in your network from a server to a workstation and disabling Simply LANtastic on a network node.

- Configuration issues when sharing a CD-ROM drive with other nodes in the network.

- Features of Simply LANtastic to manage print jobs in the queue.

- Making network use easier by setting up connections using batch files.

- Understanding the commands and purpose of the network startup batch file STARTNET.BAT.

- Issues of using Microsoft Windows with Simply LANtastic.

- Considerations for adding network stations to your Simply LANtastic network.

Managing a Network

Simply LANtastic makes networking your computers as easy as possible while providing the features you want a network to include. Managing a Simply LANtastic network also is a relatively simple task, and there are many things you can do to make using your Simply LANtastic network even easier.

You might discover that you want to change the organization or configuration of your network. Perhaps you have a common location on your network where you store all your data files and you want to move it to a different computer or directory. Or maybe you just installed a CD-ROM drive that you want to share on the network. Or you want to change the network connections established when your computer starts. Or perhaps you want to set up batch files to automatically establish the required network drive and printer connections to run a particular application. This chapter discusses the methods of performing these tasks and more.

Shared Resource Management

When you install Simply LANtastic on each computer in your network, the network automatically creates shared resources for the drives and printer. For example, if the computer on which you install Simply LANtastic has an A floppy drive, a C hard drive, and a printer, the Simply LANtastic installation program creates shared resources with the names A-DRIVE, C-DRIVE, and @PRINTER. Each drive resource is configured to provide any computer in the network full access to the entire drive. In many situations you might not want to allow others to access your entire drive. You might prefer to set up a shared-drive resource that points to a directory on the hard drive for others to access rather than the entire hard drive.

To prevent others from accessing your C-DRIVE shared resource, you can either delete the resource using the DOS or Windows Simply LANtastic Connections program, or change the access list for the C-DRIVE shared resource from Full Access for all users to No Access for all users. Chapter 12, "Users, Printers, and Shared Drives," describes changing the access list for a shared resource.

You might decide that although you do not want others to have access to everything on your hard disk, you do want to share specific directories. You can specify a different resource name for each directory to share or organize your hard disk so you can share everything you want using only a few or one shared-drive resource. Chapter 9, "Managing Users and Resources," discusses methods you can use to organize the directories on your hard disk so you can create a single shared-drive resource to share with others instead of creating several shared-drive resources. If you have three application programs on your hard drive that you want to share with others but you don't want to share your entire C drive, for example, you normally have to create three separate shared resources, each of which point to the directory in which the application is stored (see fig. 13.1). By creating a directory (APPS in this example) beneath which you can move the other application directories, you create a single shared resource that others can use to access all the applications, and you still prevent access to the rest of your C: drive.

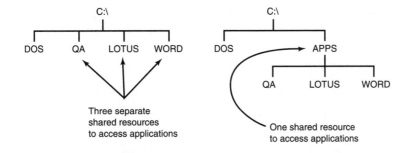

Figure 13.1
Organizing a directory structure so a single shared resource can access multiple applications.

Changing a Node from a Server to a Workstation

You might decide you no longer want to allow a node in your network to share its resources with other nodes. For example, you might have a node in your network that contains sensitive data. The node needs to access and use the shared resources on other computers, but you want to make sure that another computer cannot access this one. Configuring the node as a workstation rather than a server prevents other computers from accessing any resources on the node.

You also might want to change the configuration of a node from a server to a workstation if the computer you use isn't very powerful and the application you are trying to run requires more memory (RAM) to operate than your computer currently has available. Because the server program uses approximately 28 KB of RAM, if you configure the node as a workstation rather than a server, you have 28 KB additional memory for your application program to use.

To change a node configured as a server to a workstation, change the Simply LANtastic STARTNET.BAT file using the DOS editor or another editor to avoid loading the server program into memory when Simply LANtastic is started. To change the STARTNET.BAT file using the DOS editor, perform the following steps:

1. Start the DOS editor with the STARTNET.BAT file loaded by typing the following command at the DOS prompt:

    `EDIT C:\LANTASTI\STARTNET.BAT`

2. Using your arrow keys, locate the command in the STARTNET.BAT file that loads the server program (see fig. 13.2). The command usually is either SERVER C:\LANTASTI.NET or LOADHIGH SERVER C:\LANTASTI.NET.

Figure 13.2

The STARTNET.BAT file loading the Simply LANtastic SERVER program.

```
  File  Edit  Search  Options                              Help
                          STARTNET.BAT
:NDIS
@echo Binding NDIS & starting NETBIOS from STRTNDIS.BAT
rem Build STRTNDIS.BAT by hand or by using utilities
rem which may become available from Artisoft later.
call STRTNDIS.BAT

:REDIR
LOADHIGH REDIR ZAK
IF EXIST NOSHARE GOTO :NOSHARE
LOADHIGH SERVER C:\LANTASTI.NET
NET CONNECT \\ZAK
GOTO :CONTINUE

:NOSHARE
@echo Simply LANtastic sharing was installed but turned off.

:CONTINUE

rem If CONNECT.BAT exists, run it to set up connections.
IF EXIST CONNECT.BAT GOTO :CONNECT

MS-DOS Editor  <F1=Help> Press ALT to activate menus       N 00034:033
```

3. Using your arrow keys, position the cursor at the first character of the line and type REM (see fig. 13.3).

When you execute a batch file, DOS ignores any commands preceded by REM (which stands for REMark).

```
 File  Edit  Search  Options                              Help
                          STARTNET.BAT
:NDIS
@echo Binding NDIS & starting NETBIOS from STRTNDIS.BAT
rem Build STRTNDIS.BAT by hand or by using utilities
rem which may become available from Artisoft later.
call STRTNDIS.BAT

:REDIR
LOADHIGH REDIR ZAK
IF EXIST NOSHARE GOTO :NOSHARE
REM LOADHIGH SERVER C:\LANTASTI.NET
NET CONNECT \\ZAK
GOTO :CONTINUE

:NOSHARE
@echo Simply LANtastic sharing was installed but turned off.

:CONTINUE

rem If CONNECT.BAT exists, run it to set up connections.
IF EXIST CONNECT.BAT GOTO :CONNECT

MS-DOS Editor   <F1=Help> Press ALT to activate menus      CN 00034:037
```

Figure 13.3

Remarking the
SERVER command in
STARTNET.BAT.

4. Save the changes to the STARTNET.BAT file by selecting
    Save from the **F**ile menu (press Alt+F+S). Exit the DOS
    editor by selecting E**x**it from the **F**ile menu (press Alt+F+X).

The next time you start your computer, the server program is
excluded from loading and your computer is configured as a
workstation.

> To prevent error messages from appearing when you
> start your network, REMark any NET USE or NET
> CONNECT commands that specify the name of the
> computer that has been changed from a server to a
> workstation. For example, if the name of your computer
> is ZAK, you type REM in front of the NET CONNECT
> \\ZAK command and the NET USE LPT1:
> \\ZAK\@PRINTER commands.

Disabling Simply LANtastic

Occasionally you need to disable the network software from
running on a particular node. Some software, especially games,
does not operate properly with network software. Other software

requires the maximum amount of memory possible to run, some of which the network software is using.

You can use three different methods to disable Simply LANtastic network software: use Simply LANtastic commands to remove the network software from memory; remove the statement from your AUTOEXEC.BAT that starts the network: or use the DOS or Windows Simply LANtastic installation program to disable the network.

Removing Simply LANtastic Software Components

Use the same commands you use to start Simply LANtastic in your STARTNET.BAT file to remove Simply LANtastic from memory. For example, the following general commands in the STARTNET.BAT file load the Simply LANtastic software:

NR

AILANBIO

REDIR

SERVER

To remove each software component that comprises your Simply LANtastic software, at the DOS prompt type the command in the opposite order it was loaded in the STARTNET.BAT file and include the /REMOVE switch. For example, to remove every software component of Simply LANtastic type the following commands at the DOS prompt:

```
SERVER/REMOVE

REDIR/REMOVE

AILANBIO/REMOVE

NR/REMOVE
```

Removing STARTNET.BAT from the AUTOEXEC.BAT File

The second method of disabling the Simply LANtastic software on your computer is to change your AUTOEXEC.BAT file so the Simply LANtastic network startup batch file, STARTNET.BAT, does not execute. To change your AUTOEXEC.BAT file using the DOS editor, perform the following steps:

1. Start the DOS editor with the AUTOEXEC.BAT file loaded by typing the following command at the DOS prompt:

   `EDIT C:\AUTOEXEC.BAT`

2. Using your arrow keys, locate the command that calls the STARTNET.BAT file in the AUTOEXEC.BAT file. The command usually is CALL C:\LANTASTI\STARTNET.

3. Using your arrow keys, position the cursor at the first character of the line and type `REM`.

4. Save the changes to the AUTOEXEC.BAT file by selecting <u>S</u>ave from the <u>F</u>ile menu (press Alt+F+S). Exit the DOS editor by selecting E<u>x</u>it from the <u>F</u>ile menu (press Alt+F+X).

Running the Simply LANtastic Installation Program

The third method of disabling Simply LANtastic is to use the DOS or Windows Simply LANtastic installation program. To use the DOS Simply LANtastic installation program, perform the following steps:

1. Start the Simply LANtastic installation program by typing `INSTALL` at the DOS prompt.

If you have Windows installed on your computer and want to run the DOS Simply LANtastic installation program, type `INSTALL/DOS` at the DOS prompt.

2. Select the DISABLE option from the Simply LANtastic
   Installation program main menu (see fig. 13.4).

Figure 13.4

The DOS Simply
LANtastic Installation
program main menu.

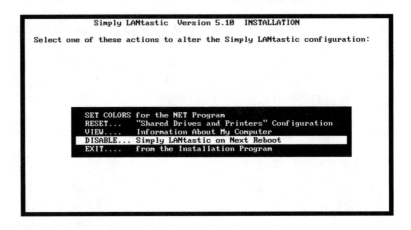

3. Select EXIT to quit the installation program.

When the computer is rebooted, Simply LANtastic does not start.
To later re-enable Simply LANtastic, run the installation program
again and select the ENABLE option.

To disable Simply LANtastic using the Windows Simply
LANtastic installation program, perform the following steps:

1. Double-click on the Simply LANtastic SETUP icon in the
   Simply LANtastic program group or, with the Simply
   LANtastic SETUP icon selected, choose **O**pen from the
   Program Manager **F**ile menu.

2. Select the DISABLE option from the Artisoft Install Setup
   Menu (see fig. 13.5).

3. Choose EXIT to quit the installation program.

When the computer is rebooted, Simply LANtastic does not start.
To later re-enable Simply LANtastic, run the installation program
again and select the ENABLE option.

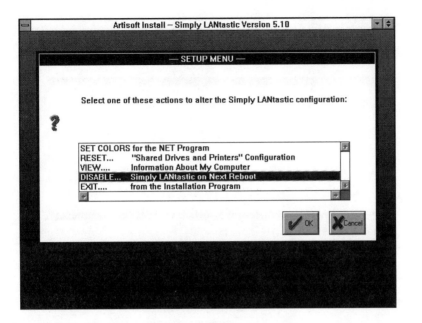

Figure 13.5

The Windows Simply LANtastic installation program Setup Menu.

Sharing CD-ROM Drives

Simply LANtastic enables you to set up a CD-ROM drive to share with others on the network. The only difference in setting up a shared resource for a CD-ROM drive as opposed to a standard drive is that you specify CD-ROM as the drive type when specifying the drive parameters in the DOS or Windows Simply LANtastic Connections program.

To specify that a shared resource is a CD-ROM drive in the DOS Simply LANtastic Connections program, specify CD-ROM in the Disk Drive Type field of the Detailed Information screen for the shared resource (see fig. 13.6).

To specify that a shared resource is a CD-ROM drive in the Windows Simply LANtastic Connections program, choose CD-ROM as the Drive Type in the Drive Parameters dialog box for the shared resource (see fig. 13.7).

Figure 13.6

Specifying CD-ROM as the Disk Drive Type in the DOS Simply LANtastic Connections program.

```
Sharing Drives and Printers at C:\LANTASTI.NET  C) Copyright 1993 Artisoft Inc.

 ┌─ Detailed Information for CDROM ──────────────────────────────────────────┐
 │       Description: CD-ROM Drive                                            │
 │          DOS Path: E:                                                      │
 │   Disk Drive Type: CD-ROM                                                  │
 │   ┌─ ACCESS LIST ──────────────────────────────────────────────┐          │
 │ * │              Full Access                                    │          │
 │                                                                            │
 │                                                                            │
 │                                                                            │
 │                                                                            │
 │                                                                            │
 │                                                                            │
 │                                                                            │
 └────────────────────────────────────────────────────────────────────────┘

 Enter-Modify Selection, Esc-Exit, F1-Help
```

Figure 13.7

Specifying CD-ROM as the Drive Type in the Windows Simply LANtastic Connections program.

```
┌──────────── Drive Parameters (CDROM) ────────────┐
│ Description:                                      │
│ [CD-ROM Drive                                  ]  │
│                                                   │
│ Path:                                             │
│ [E:                                            ]  │
│                                                   │
│ Drive Type:                                       │
│  ○ DOS              [   OK   ]                     │
│  ● CD-ROM           [ Cancel ]                     │
└───────────────────────────────────────────────────┘
```

For your CD-ROM and network to operate together correctly, move the DOS MSCDEX driver in the AUTOEXEC.BAT file to the STARTNET.BAT file (in the \LANTASTI directory). It must be located here after the Simply LANtastic REDIR program but before the SERVER program. Use the DOS editor to make the appropriate changes to the AUTOEXEC.BAT and STARTNET.BAT files.

Managing Print Jobs

When an application program sends information to the printer, Simply LANtastic intercepts the print job, routes it to a temporary holding location called the *print queue,* and then spools the print job to the appropriate printer. You can view the print jobs in the queue. You also can remove a print job from the queue if, for example, a print job accidentally is sent to the wrong printer.

Both the DOS and Windows Simply LANtastic Connections programs enable you to manage print jobs in the queues of various servers.

Managing Print Jobs in DOS

To manage print jobs in DOS, perform the following steps:

1. Start the DOS Simply LANtastic Connections program by typing **NET** at the DOS prompt, and press Enter.

2. Using your arrow keys, select View Print Jobs from the Simply LANtastic Connections Main Menu, and press Enter (see fig. 13.8).

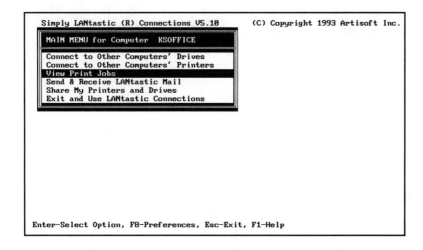

```
 Simply LANtastic (R) Connections V5.10      (C) Copyright 1993 Artisoft Inc.
 ┌─────────────────────────────────────────┐
 │ MAIN MENU for Computer   KSOFFICE         │
 ├─────────────────────────────────────────┤
 │ Connect to Other Computers' Drives        │
 │ Connect to Other Computers' Printers      │
 │ View Print Jobs                           │
 │ Send & Receive LANtastic Mail             │
 │ Share My Printers and Drives              │
 │ Exit and Use LANtastic Connections        │
 └─────────────────────────────────────────┘




 Enter-Select Option, F8-Preferences, Esc-Exit, F1-Help
```

Figure 13.8

Selecting View Print Jobs from the DOS Simply LANtastic Connections program Main Menu.

3. From the Viewing Print Jobs at window, select the computer that contains the print jobs you want to manage, and press Enter (see fig. 13.9).

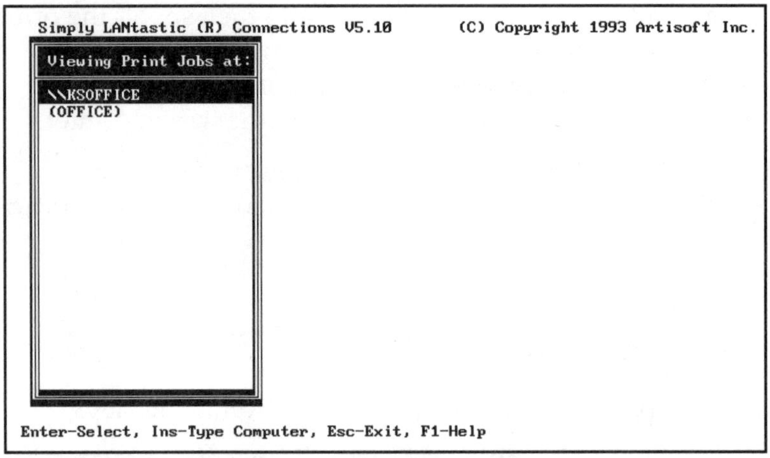

Figure 13.9

Selecting the
computer with the
print jobs to manage.

```
Simply LANtastic (R) Connections V5.10      (C) Copyright 1993 Artisoft Inc.
┌─────────────────────────┐
│ Viewing Print Jobs at:  │
├─────────────────────────┤
│ \\KSOFFICE              │
│ (OFFICE)                │
│                         │
│                         │
│                         │
│                         │
│                         │
│                         │
│                         │
│                         │
│                         │
│                         │
└─────────────────────────┘
 Enter-Select, Ins-Type Computer, Esc-Exit, F1-Help
```

4. The Viewing Print Jobs screen appears displaying the print
   jobs currently in the queue as well as the status of each job
   (see fig. 13.10).

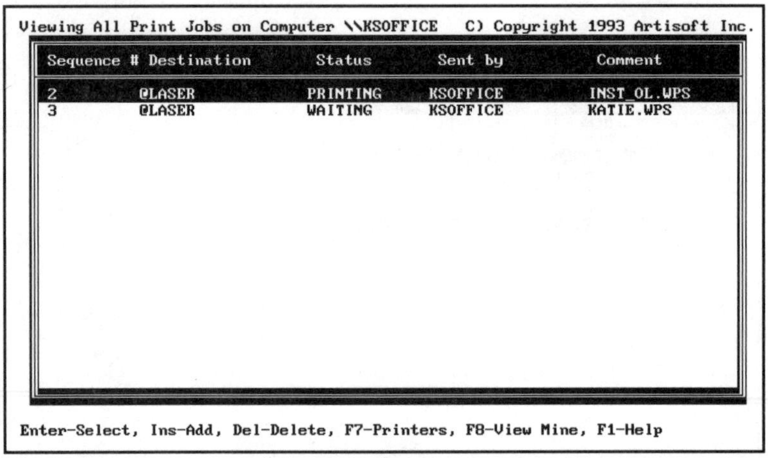

Figure 13.10

The Viewing Print
Jobs screen.

```
Viewing All Print Jobs on Computer \\KSOFFICE    C) Copyright 1993 Artisoft Inc.
┌─────────────────────────────────────────────────────────────────────┐
│ Sequence # Destination       Status      Sent by        Comment      │
├─────────────────────────────────────────────────────────────────────┤
│ 2          @LASER            PRINTING    KSOFFICE        INST_OL.WPS  │
│ 3          @LASER            WAITING     KSOFFICE        KATIE.WPS    │
│                                                                       │
│                                                                       │
│                                                                       │
│                                                                       │
│                                                                       │
│                                                                       │
│                                                                       │
│                                                                       │
│                                                                       │
│                                                                       │
└─────────────────────────────────────────────────────────────────────┘
 Enter-Select, Ins-Add, Del-Delete, F7-Printers, F8-View Mine, F1-Help
```

To control a specific print job in the queue, with the print job
selected, press Enter. The Job Control window appears that
enables you to perform several functions including deleting
the print job, viewing the contents of the print job, temporarily holding the print job so it doesn't print, and several
other functions (see fig. 13.11).

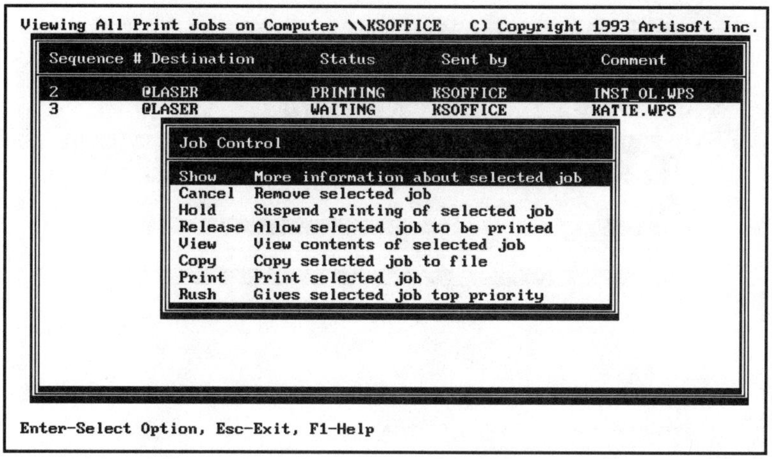

Figure 13.11

The Job Control window.

You can add a print job to the queue manually by pressing the Ins key from the Viewing All Print Jobs screen. You either can use an editor to type the information to be printed, or specify the name of a file to be added to the queue.

Pressing Del from the Viewing All Print Jobs screen deletes the selected entry from the queue.

Pressing the F7-Printers key from the Viewing All Print Jobs screen displays a window showing the printer devices and the status of each device (see fig. 13.12). To control a specific printer, with the printer device highlighted, press Enter. The Printer Control window appears enabling you to control the functions of the selected printer including halting, pausing, and restarting printing (see fig. 13.13).

Pressing the F8 key from the Viewing All Print Jobs screen toggles the display between viewing all the print jobs in the queue and viewing only the print job sent from your computer.

5. When you finish, press Esc to return to the main menu, and press Esc again to exit the Simply LANtastic Connections program.

Figure 13.12

The status of the
printer devices.

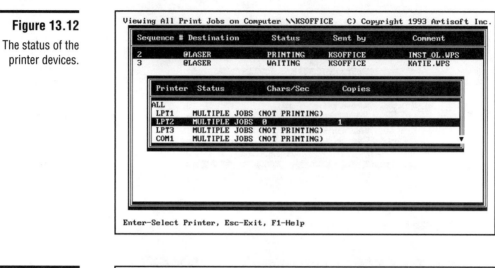

Figure 13.13

The Printer Control
window.

Managing Print Jobs in Windows

To manage print jobs in Windows, perform the following steps:

1. Start the Simply LANtastic Connections program by double-clicking on the Simply LANtastic Connections icon in the Simply LANtastic program group, or, with the icon selected, choose **O**pen from the Program Manager **F**ile menu.

2. Select the Jobs button, or choose View Print Jobs from the Net menu (see fig. 13.14).

Figure 13.14

Choosing Jobs from the Simply LANtastic Connections main menu.

3. Choose from the Current Connections list in the Select Computer dialog box the computer that contains the print jobs you want to manage, and then select OK (see fig. 13.15). If the computer you want to access does not appear in the Current Connections list, establish a connection to it by selecting the Connections button.

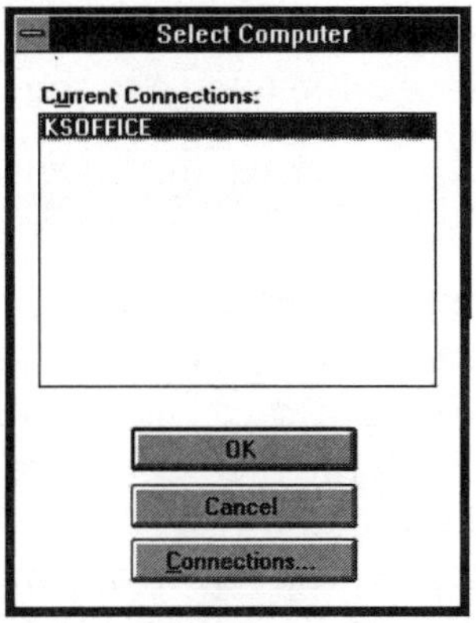

Figure 13.15

Selecting the computer with the print jobs to manage.

4. The All Print Jobs dialog box appears displaying the print jobs currently in the queue as well as the status of each job (see fig. 13.16).

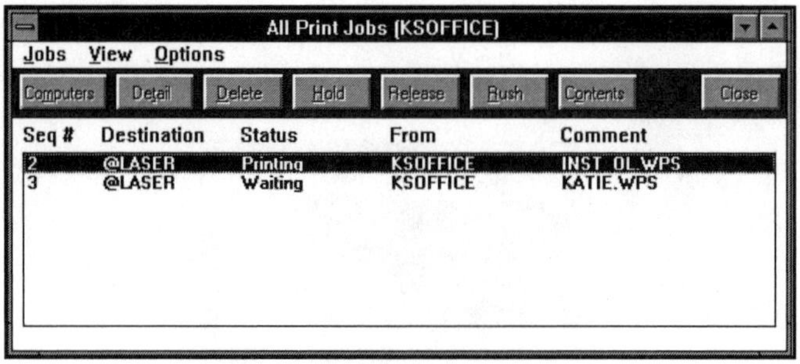

Figure 13.16

The All Print Jobs
dialog box.

To control a specific print job in the queue, with the print job selected, select the button associated with the action you want to perform, or choose the action from the Jobs menu. You can perform several functions including deleting a print job, viewing the contents of the print job, temporarily holding the print job so it doesn't print, and several other functions.

You can add a print job to the queue manually by selecting the Send Job option from the Jobs menu. You can either use an editor to type the information you want to print, or specify the name of a file to add to the queue.

Selecting the Del key deletes the selected entry from the queue.

Selecting the Control Printers option from the Jobs menu displays the Printers dialog box showing the printer devices and the status of each device (see fig. 13.17). To control a specific printer, with the printer device chosen, select the button corresponding to the desired action. The functions you can perform with the selected printer include halting, stopping, pausing, sending a single job, starting and restarting printing.

Selecting the My Jobs option from the View menu in the All Print Jobs dialog box displays only the print job sent from your computer rather than all the print jobs sent from every computer.

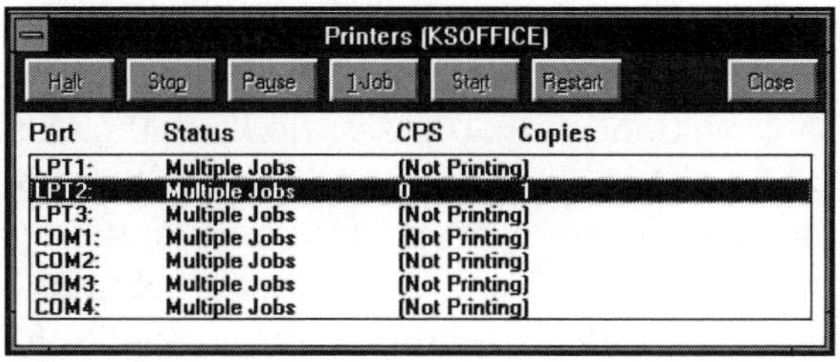

Figure 13.17
The Printers dialog
box.

5. When you finish, select the Close button or choose E_x_it from
    the Jobs menu.

Changing Permanent Connections

The permanent connections you specified when you installed
Simply LANtastic appear as NET USE commands in the Simply
LANtastic startup batch file STARTNET.BAT. If, during installa-
tion, you specify that you want a permanent connection to the
C-DRIVE resource on computer KATIE using your D drive, and a
permanent connection to the @PRINTER resource on computer
ZAK using your LPT1 device, the following two command lines
appear in your STARTNET.BAT file:

```
NET USE D: \\KATIE\C-DRIVE
NET USE LPT1: \\ZAK\@PRINTER
```

Using an editor such as DOS Edit, you can delete, change, or add
lines to the STARTNET.BAT file to establish connections when
your computer is started.

An easier way to change connections when you turn on your
computer is with the Simply LANtastic SETNET utility. SETNET
is a batch file that runs the DOS Simply LANtastic Connections
program to establish the network connections you want to save. It
then saves the network configuration as a series of NET USE
commands in a batch file called CONNECT.BAT. When you turn
on your computer and execute the STARTNET.BAT file to start
your network, if the CONNECT.BAT file exists, the commands
contained in it also are run.

To define permanent connections using SETNET.BAT, type **SETNET** at the DOS prompt and press Enter. Establish the network drive and printer connections you want by choosing the Connect to Other Computer's Drive or Connect to Other Computer's Printer options in the DOS Simply LANtastic Connections program as described in Chapter 12, "Users, Printers, and Shared Drives." When you finish, exit the program as you normally do, and the CONNECT.BAT file is created. The network connections specified in CONNECT.BAT are established automatically when you start your computer.

Setting Up Connections Using Batch Files

DOS batch files are extremely valuable when you use them to establish network connections. When your network starts, the DOS batch file STARTNET.BAT contains the commands necessary to load the Simply LANtastic network software into the memory on your computer and set up any drive or printer connections specified during installation. If you change the network connections using the SETNET routing described in the preceding section, the network commands in the DOS batch file CONNECT.BAT establish the desired network connections.

Batch files can establish specific network connections for a variety of different purposes. You can set up batch files to connect to different computers or shared resources. You can change batch files you use to start a specific program to include network commands to connect to a printer or a shared-drive resource.

Suppose you have a dot-matrix printer connected to the computer named ZAK, for example, and a laser printer connected to the computer named KATIE. When you start Simply LANtastic on your computer, you have configured your STARTNET.BAT file so the LPT1 device on your computer points to the laser printer on KATIE, and the LPT2 device on your computer points to the dot-matrix printer on ZAK. Normally the default printer connections configuration works fine. Perhaps, however, you have one application program that has to print to the dot-matrix printer using your LPT1 device instead of LPT2. In this situation, you can create a batch file that contains the network commands to connect to the dot-matrix printer on ZAK as LPT1. Using the DOS editor you can create a batch file named DOTPRINT.BAT that contains the following network commands:

NET UNUSE LPT1:

NET USE LPT1: \\ZAK\@PRINTER

The NET UNUSE command disconnects the previous network connection using LPT1, which in this example is the connection to the laser printer on KATIE. The second network command redirects the LPT1 device on your computer to point to the @PRINTER resource on ZAK, which is a dot-matrix printer. Because these two commands are in the DOS batch file name DOTPRINT.BAT, typing **DOTPRINT** at the DOS prompt executes the network commands contained in the batch file.

For the next example, suppose you do not establish any network connections when you first start Simply LANtastic. You decide instead to create for each application you run a DOS batch file that establishes the desired network connections, runs the application program, and then disconnects the network connections when finished.

Suppose the word processor you use is Microsoft Word, which is located on your hard disk drive C in the WORD5 directory. Start Word by typing **WORD**. With Word you want to use the laser printer that is connected to the computer named DANA. Access the printer using the shared printer resource name @LASER. When you print from Word to your LPT1 device, you want to route the print job to the laser printer. In addition, you store all your word processing files on a computer named KEVIN in a directory you access using the DATA shared resource name. When you save or read a file from the K drive, you want the data to be read from or saved to the DATA shared resource on KEVIN. Based on this information, you can create a batch file named WP.BAT that contains the following commands:

    NET USE LPT1: \\DANA\@LASER

    NET USE K: \\KEVIN\DATA

    C:

    CD\WORD5

    WORD

    CD\

    NET UNUSE LPT1:

    NET UNUSE K:

The first line redirects the LPT1 device on your computer to point to the @LASER shared-printer resource on DANA. The next line redirects your K drive to point to the DATA resource on server KEVIN. The C: statement makes your current default drive the C drive and the CD\WORD5 command makes your current default directory the WORD5 directory. WORD starts the Microsoft Word program, from which you proceed to work. At this point, Word sends anything you print to the LPT1 device, which Simply LANtastic then redirects to the network laser printer. When you access K, the data is read from and written to the shared resource DATA on KEVIN. When you finish using Word and exit the program, the remainder of the commands in the batch file are automatically executed by your computer. The CD\ command changes your default directory to the root directory. The NET UNUSE LPT1: command disconnects the connection between your LPT1 device and the @LASER shared printer resource on DANA. The NET UNUSE K: command disconnects the connection between your K drive and the DATA shared resource on KEVIN.

Understanding the Network Startup Batch File

The DOS batch file STARTNET.BAT in the LANTASTI directory contains the commands necessary to start the Simply LANtastic *network operating system* (NOS) on your computer. Additionally,

STARTNET.BAT might contain commands that establish certain default network drive and printer connections.

To better understand what happens when your network starts, it's beneficial to know the purpose of the various commands in the Simply LANtastic STARTNET.BAT file.

The following is a typical STARTNET.BAT file created by the Simply LANtastic installation program:

```
@echo off
rem Simply LANtastic  Version 5.10  installed 94/07/17
23:29:47
rem (for Windows)

C:
cd C:\LANTASTI

rem If Simply LANtastic is disabled, skip everything.
IF EXIST DISABLED GOTO :STARTNET_DONE

@echo ===== Begin Simply LANtastic configuration =====

PATH C:\LANTASTI;%PATH%
SET LAN_CFG=C:\LANTASTI
SET LAN_DIR=C:\LANTASTI.NET

rem If STRTNDIS.BAT exists, run it to bind NDIS & start
NETBIOS.
IF EXIST STRTNDIS.BAT GOTO :NDIS
LOADHIGH NR
AILANBIO
GOTO :REDIR

:NDIS
@echo Binding NDIS & starting NETBIOS from STRTNDIS.BAT
rem Build STRTNDIS.BAT by hand or by using utilities
rem which may become available from Artisoft later.
call STRTNDIS.BAT

:REDIR
REDIR KSOFFICE
IF EXIST NOSHARE GOTO :NOSHARE
SERVER C:\LANTASTI.NET
NET CONNECT \\KSOFFICE
GOTO :CONTINUE
```

```
:NOSHARE
@echo Simply LANtastic sharing was installed but turned off.

:CONTINUE

rem If CONNECT.BAT exists, run it to set up connections.
IF EXIST CONNECT.BAT GOTO :CONNECT

rem Otherwise set up connections specified during install.
NET CONNECT/wait \\ZAK
NET USE D: \\ZAK\C-DRIVE
NET USE LPT1: \\ZAK\@PRINTER
NET LPT TIMEOUT 10
GOTO :CONNECT_DONE

:CONNECT
@echo Setting up Simply LANtastic connections from CONNECT.BAT
rem Build CONNECT.BAT like this: "NET SHOW/BATCH >
C:\LANTASTI\CONNECT.BAT"
rem   (or run the batch file SETNET.BAT)
call CONNECT.BAT

:CONNECT_DONE
NET POSTBOX

@echo ===== End Simply LANtastic configuration =====
:STARTNET_DONE
```

Lines in the STARTNET.BAT file that begin with REM are remarks used for information purposes only; they do not perform any task.

Lines in the STARTNET.BAT file that begin with @ECHO display the contents of the line when the line is encountered in the batch file; otherwise the line performs no other task.

Following is a description of the commands in the STARTNET.BAT file:

- C:
  cd C:\LANTASTI

These two commands change the current default drive to the C drive and the current default directory to \LANTASTI.

- IF EXIST DISABLED GOTO :STARTNET_DONE

  This command looks for a file with the name DISABLED in the current directory. If the file exists, execution of the batch file jumps to the :STARTNET_DONE section, skipping everything else in between. When you run the Simply LANtastic installation program after you install Simply LANtastic, one of your options is to disable Simply LANtastic. If you choose to disable Simply LANtastic, a file with the name DISABLED is created, and when STARTNET.BAT runs, all the commands in the middle that load the Simply LANtastic NOS are skipped.

- PATH C:\LANTASTI;%PATH%

  This command adds the C:\LANTASTI directory to your DOS path statement so that DOS can execute and understand NET commands independent of your current default drive or directory. Without C:\LANTASTI in your path, if you type **NET** or issue a NET command, such as NET USE K: \\KEVIN\DATA, a `Bad command or filename` error message appears.

- SET LAN_CFG=C:\LANTASTI
  SET LAN_DIR=C:\LANTASTI.NET

  These two commands set environment variables. Simply LANtastic uses *environment variables* to locate the network control directory and the Simply LANtastic configuration files.

- IF EXIST STRTNDIS.BAT GOTO :NDIS

  This command looks for the STRTNDIS.BAT file in the current directory. If the file exists, the command jumps to the :NDIS section. If you use a network adapter that has an NDIS driver, you have a STRTNDIS.BAT file that loads the required NDIS drivers. Therefore, skip the equivalent section, in the STARTNET.BAT file, that contains the commands between this statement and the :NDIS section.

- LOADHIGH NR

  This command loads into memory the Simply LANtastic
  network adapter driver NR. The LOADHIGH prefix causes
  NR to be loaded into upper memory (the region between
  640 KB and 1024 KB).

- AILANBIO

  This command loads the Simply LANtastic NETBIOS into
  memory.

- GOTO :REDIR

  This command causes execution of the batch file to jump to
  the :REDIR section. This command is required to jump over
  the following :NDIS section.

- :NDIS

  This is the label that marks the start of the NDIS section.
  Any GOTO :NDIS statement in the batch file jumps to this
  location.

- call STRTNDIS.BAT

  This command executes the commands in the
  STRTNDIS.BAT file and then returns to this
  STARTNET.BAT file at the line following the preceding
  command. Note that this section is jumped over unless the
  STRTNDIS.BAT file exists when tested for in a preceding
  statement.

- :REDIR

  This is the label that marks the start of the REDIR section.
  Any GOTO :REDIR statement in the batch file jumps to this
  location.

- REDIR KSOFFICE

  This command loads the Simply LANtastic redirector program that enables this computer to be a Simply LANtastic
  workstation with the name KSOFFICE.

- IF EXIST NOSHARE GOTO :NOSHARE

  This command looks for a file with the name NOSHARE. If it finds such a file, the command jumps to the :NOSHARE section, thereby skipping the following command that allows the computer to share its resources with others.

- SERVER C:\LANTASTI.NET

  This command loads the Simply LANtastic server program that enables the computer to share its resources with others. The C:\LANTASTI.NET statement following SERVER specifies the location of the Simply LANtastic control directory that, among other things, stores information about the shared resources on this server.

- NET CONNECT \\KSOFFICE

  This command establishes a connection (or logs in) to the computer. Any computer connected with the NET CONNECT or NET LOGIN command automatically appears in the list of available computers in the DOS and Windows Simply LANtastic Connections programs.

- GOTO :CONTINUE

  This command jumps to the :CONTINUE section, thereby skipping the following :NOSHARE section.

- :NOSHARE

  This label marks the start of the NOSHARE section. The only purpose of this section is to display on-screen the following line:

  ```
  Simply LANtastic sharing was installed but turned off.
  ```

- :CONTINUE

  This label marks the start of the CONTINUE section, which is where the network connections are established. Any GOTO :CONTINUE statement in the batch file jumps to this location.

- IF EXIST CONNECT.BAT GOTO :CONNECT

  This command checks to see if the file CONNECT.BAT exists, and if it does, jumps to the :CONNECT section. If CONNECT.BAT does not exist, execution continues.

- NET CONNECT/wait \\ZAK
  NET USE D: \\ZAK\C-DRIVE
  NET USE LPT1: \\ZAK\@PRINTER

  These commands are installed when you specify the permanent connections to establish when you install Simply LANtastic.

  The first command, NET CONNECT, establishes a connection to the computer named ZAK. The /wait switch causes execution of the batch file to wait until the connection to ZAK is established. When turning on the computers in your network, the /wait switch pauses until the computer to which you are connecting can start the network software. Your computer then connects to ZAK.

  The second command, NET USE D:, redirects your D drive to point to the C-DRIVE shared resource on computer ZAK.

  The third command, NET USE LPT1:, redirects your LPT1 device to point to the @PRINTER shared printer resource on computer ZAK.

- NET LPT TIMEOUT 10

  This command specifies that if more than ten seconds have elapsed since the Simply LANtastic spooler received the last information from a print job, the print job will close and be released for printing.

- GOTO :CONNECT_DONE

  This command jumps to the :CONNECT_DONE section, thereby skipping the following :CONNECT section, which executes only if the CONNECT.BAT file exists.

- :CONNECT

  This label marks the beginning of the CONNECT section, which executes if the CONNECT.BAT file is found when checked for in a preceding statement. Any GOTO :CONNECT statement in the batch file jumps to this location.

- CALL CONNECT.BAT

  This command executes the commands in the CONNECT.BAT batch file, and then returns to the statement in the STARTNET.BAT file following this statement.

- :CONNECT_DONE

  This label marks the beginning of the CONNECT_DONE section.

- NET POSTBOX

  This command checks for any mail for this computer from other computers on the network.

- :STARTNET_DONE

  This label marks the beginning of the STARTNET_DONE section, which is the end of the STARTNET.BAT file. Any GOTO :STARTNET_DONE statement in the batch file jumps to this location.

Saving and Restoring Connections Established in Windows

Each time you start Microsoft Windows, the Simply LANtastic Connections program also starts. When the Simply LANtastic Connections program starts, it restores the network connections saved during a previous Windows session. This feature provides the same basic functionality in Windows that the SETNET utility provides in DOS.

The Options menu in the Simply LANtastic Connections program has four selections that you can select or deselect by clicking on them (see fig. 13.18). If selected, a check mark appears next to the selected items. The four selections are described below:

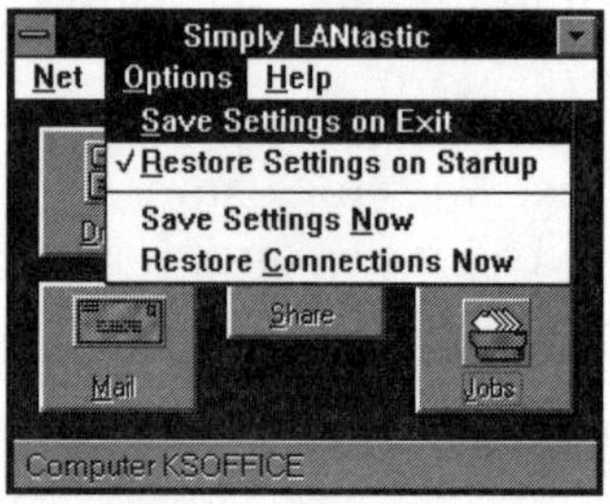

Figure 13.18

The Simply LANtastic
Connections program
Options menu.

- **Save Settings on Exit.** This option saves your current settings including your drive and printer connections when you exit Windows.

- **Restore Settings on Startup.** This option restores your saved settings including your drive and printer connections when you start Windows.

- **Save Settings Now.** This option saves your current settings including your drive and printer connections.

- **Restore Connections Now.** This setting restores your drive and printer connections.

Considerations for Running Microsoft Windows

Simply LANtastic and Microsoft Windows work great together. You need to be aware of a few issues, however, to ensure trouble-free operation of Microsoft Windows.

If you use a shared-printer resource on another computer in Windows, perform the following steps to set up and configure the printer:

1. Double-click on the Control Panel icon in the Main program group.

2. Double-click on the Printers icon in the Control Panel.

3. The Printers dialog box appears displaying the installed printers (see fig. 13.19). If the type of printer you want to access on the other computer does not appear in the Installed Printers list, you can add the printer at this time by selecting the Add button.

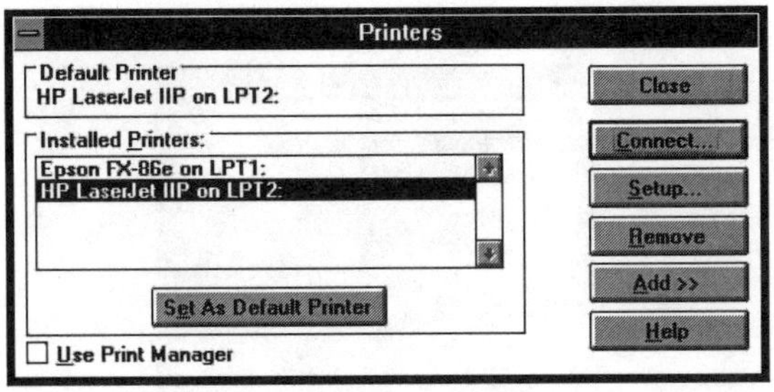

Figure 13.19

The Printers dialog box with the list of installed printers.

4. Make sure the Use Print Manager box is not selected. Simply LANtastic has its own print spooler, so the Windows Print Manager is not necessary.

5. Select the Connect button. The Connect dialog box appears (see fig. 13.20). Make sure the Fast Printing Direct to Port box is not selected. Also, change the Device Not Selected value to 900 and the Transmission Retry value to 950.

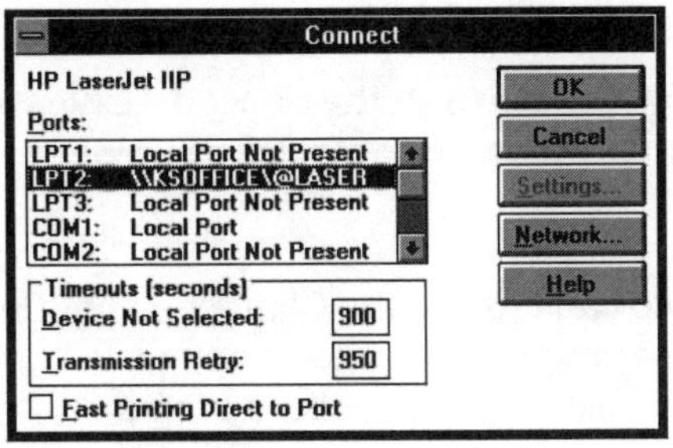

Figure 13.20

The Connect dialog box.

6. Click on OK when you finish to return to the Printers dialog box. Choose Close to exit.

When you run Microsoft Windows, printers connected to the computer often print extremely slowly. To increase the printing speed on a printer connected to a computer running Windows, perform the following steps:

1. From the Windows Simply LANtastic Connections program select the <u>S</u>hare button or choose <u>S</u>hare Drive and Printers from the <u>N</u>et menu (see fig. 13.21).

Figure 13.21

Selecting the Share button in the Simply LANtastic Connections program.

2. The Shared Drives and Printers dialog box appears displaying a list of shared-drive and -printer resources (see fig. 13.22). Select the shared-printer resource you want to change, and select the <u>M</u>odify button or choose the <u>M</u>odify option from the <u>E</u>dit menu.

3. The Printer Parameters dialog box for the specified shared-printer resource appears. Change the <u>C</u>haracters per Second field to 9600 (see fig. 13.23).

4. Click on OK to return to the Shared Drives and Printers dialog box and then choose Close to exit.

You also can change the Characters per Second value for a specific shared-printer resource using the DOS Simply LANtastic Connections program.

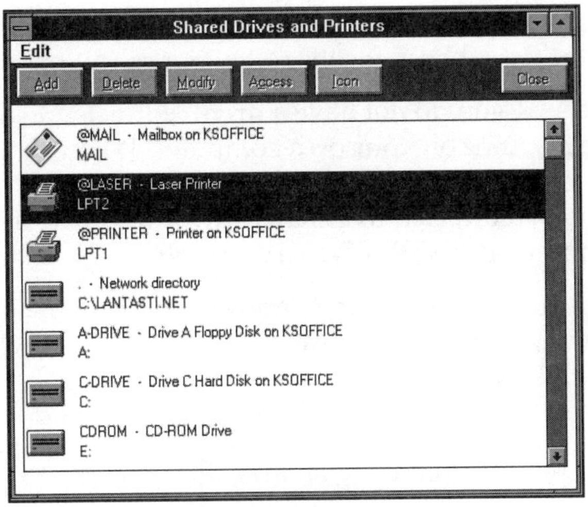

Shared Drives and Printers

Edit

| Add | Delete | Modify | Access | Icon | Close |

@MAIL · Mailbox on KSOFFICE
MAIL

@LASER · Laser Printer
LPT2

@PRINTER · Printer on KSOFFICE
LPT1

. · Network directory
C:\LANTASTI.NET

A-DRIVE · Drive A Floppy Disk on KSOFFICE
A:

C-DRIVE · Drive C Hard Disk on KSOFFICE
C:

CDROM · CD-ROM Drive
E:

Figure 13.22

The Shared Drive and Printers dialog box displaying a list of shared resources.

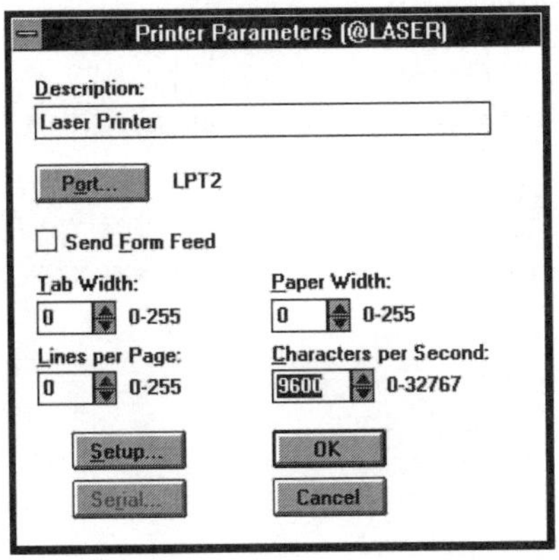

Printer Parameters (@LASER)

Description:

Laser Printer

Port...   LPT2

☐ Send Form Feed

Tab Width: Paper Width:
0 0-255   0 0-255

Lines per Page: Characters per Second:
0 0-255   9600 0-32767

Setup...   OK

Serial...   Cancel

Figure 13.23

Changing the Characters per Second field in the Printer Parameters dialog box to 9600.

When you install Simply LANtastic, several changes occur in your Windows WIN.INI and SYSTEM.INI configuration files. These changes are made automatically; normally you don't have to be concerned about them.

If you install Microsoft Windows on a computer that already has Simply LANtastic, re-install Simply LANtastic to make the appropriate changes to Windows.

If you encounter problems when running Simply LANtastic and Windows together, check for the following conditions:

- Make sure you do not have a drive redirected to a shared-drive resource on your own computer. When running Microsoft Windows, you should not have your D drive, for example, redirected to a shared-drive resource on your own computer, such as the C-DRIVE resource.

- Using the DOS editor or Windows Notepad, make sure the following command appears in the [BOOT] section of your WIN.INI file:

```
network.drv=c:\lantasti\lantnet.drv
```

- Make sure the following commands appear in the [386Enh] section:

```
UniqueDOSPSP=TRUE
NetAsynchFallback=TRUE
NetAsynchTimeout=5.0
network=*vnetbios;c:\lantasti\lantasti.386
InDOSPolling=TRUE
PSPIncrement=5
```

- Make sure there is a [LANtastic] section with the following command:

```
Network_IRQ=15
```

  If the IRQ that your network adapter uses is different than the factory default setting of 15, replace the 15 with the IRQ used by your adapter.

Adding Stations

Adding computers to your Simply LANtastic network is a relatively easy task. As described in Chapter 11, "Installing Simply LANtastic," proceed to install the network adapter and Simply LANtastic software on the computer you are adding. Then connect the cable between the new computer and a computer at the end of a network cable segment (a jack is available at each end of the adapters if you're using Simply LANtastic adapters).

After you install the network adapter and Simply LANtastic, configure Simply LANtastic and set up any batch files used for network connections or for running application programs. You can establish a connection to another computer, and copy the desired batch files from the other computer to your computer.

If by adding stations to your Simply LANtastic network your network exceeds 10 nodes, you need to change the STARTNET.BAT file on each computer. Using the DOS editor, include in each computer's STARTNET.BAT file the @MAXIMUM setting after the AILANBIO, REDIR, and SERVER commands (see fig. 13.24). Including the @MAXIMUM setting allows as many as 30 network connections between each node.

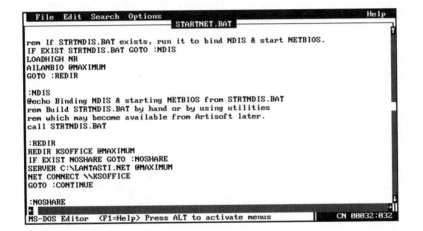

Figure 13.24

The AILANBIO, REDIR, and SERVER commands with the @MAXIMUM setting.

Summary

This chapter discussed the many areas relating to the management of your Simply LANtastic network. Management configuration topics discussed include managing shared resources, changing a node from a server to a workstation, and disabling Simply LANtastic on your computer. You also learned how to share a CD-ROM drive in your Simply LANtastic network, and how to manage print jobs in the queue. Establishing network connections to the shared resources on other computers using batch files also was covered in detail, including a discussion of the commands in the STARTNET.BAT file. You learned how to add, save, and re-establish network connections in Windows, and you became familiar with issues to consider when running Microsoft Windows. Finally, you learned the necessary requirements to add new stations to your Simply LANtastic network.

In This Chapter. . .

This chapter contains several example sessions that demonstrate how you can use Simply LANtastic with your application software to increase your productivity and to increase the flexibility of your computer. Specifically, the following example sessions are demonstrated:

- A session in which you send and receive Simply LANtastic mail in both the DOS and Windows environments.

- A Works for Windows session using a shared-drive and shared-printer resource for storing data and printing.

- A Word for DOS session that accesses the program, data, and printer from a different computer.

- A Q&A database session in which multiple users are accessing the same database. The program and data are located on different computers and accessed over the network.

- A session using the Windows File Manager program to change the directory organization of a drive on a different computer.

Running DOS and Windows Sessions

By now you have acquired a significant amount of general network knowledge and specific Simply LANtastic experience. Although you are familiar with the features and capability of your Simply LANtastic network, you may be wondering exactly how to use your network with your application programs to perform your daily tasks.

This chapter demonstrates how you can use your Simply LANtastic network with your application software to perform a variety of routine tasks. Several example sessions are included that show how to incorporate your Simply LANtastic network into your daily routines.

Most of the example sessions demonstrated in this chapter establish network connections using one of the manual methods described in previous chapters. You would probably want to set up batch files to automate your network connections if you were running a selected application with the same network connections on a consistent basis.

Using Simply LANtastic Mail

Your Simply LANtastic network has electronic mail built in that enables you to exchange messages with others in your network. You can send and receive mail in both the DOS and Windows environments. In addition to sending messages to other users, you also can send files.

You send and receive mail in Simply LANtastic using the DOS or Windows Simply LANtastic Connections program. Mail that has been sent using Simply LANtastic in Windows can be read using the Simply LANtastic Connections program in Windows or in DOS; and conversely, mail that has been sent using Simply LANtastic in DOS can be read using the Simply LANtastic Connections program in DOS or in Windows.

To use Simply LANtastic's mail feature, you should choose a server in your network that will act as the post office to store Simply LANtastic mail. Although any computer that has the @MAIL resource defined can act as a Simply LANtastic post office, it's a good idea to select a single computer for the post office. By doing so, each person has to look in only a single location when checking for mail. When you install Simply LANtastic on your computer, the @MAIL resource is automatically created. As soon as you decide which computer in your Simply LANtastic network to use as the post-office computer, it is a good idea to delete the @MAIL resource from the other computers so they are not inadvertently used as post offices.

Simply LANtastic Mail in DOS

In this example session, you send Simply LANtastic mail in DOS. Suppose you have been working on a proposal for a prospective client named Mr. Thomas. You have just finished the proposal and want your partner to review it before you send it out. You decide to send a Simply LANtastic mail message as well as a copy of the proposal for your partner to review. The following steps accomplish your objectives:

1. Start the Simply LANtastic Connections program by typing
    NET at the DOS prompt. Select the Send and Receive Simply
    LANtastic Mail option from the Simply LANtastic Connec-
    tions program main menu.

    You can go directly to the mail section of the Simply
    LANtastic Connections program by typing **NET MAIL** at
    the DOS prompt.

2. Select the computer used as the post office from the Mail
    services at window.

3. The Viewing My Mail screen appears, showing your incom-
    ing and outgoing mail (see fig. 14.1).

```
Viewing My Mail on Computer \\KSOFFICE        C) Copyright 1993 Artisoft Inc.
┌─────────────────────────────────────────────────────────────────────────┐
│ INcoming Mail          From              Comment                          │
│                                                                           │
│                                                                           │
│                                                                           │
│                                                                           │
└─────────────────────────────────────────────────────────────────────────┘
┌─────────────────────────────────────────────────────────────────────────┐
│ OUTgoing Mail          To                Comment                          │
│                                                                           │
│                                                                           │
│                                                                           │
└─────────────────────────────────────────────────────────────────────────┘
Enter-Select, Ins-Send Del-Delete Tab-Next Window, F8-View All, F1-Help
```

Figure 14.1

The Viewing My Mail
screen.

4. You want to send a message to your partner (the OFFICE
    computer in this example), so press Ins to send a message.

5. The Send Mail Options menu appears offering three selec-
    tions: Use LANtastic Editor, Use Another Editor, or Send
    Existing DOS File.

    First you'll send the message, and then you'll send a copy of
    the file; you therefore choose the Use LANtastic Editor
    option and press Enter.

6. Type the message you want to send using the Simply
   LANtastic Editor (see fig. 14.2), and press F2-Send when you
   are finished.

Figure 14.2

Composing a message
using the Simply
LANtastic Editor.

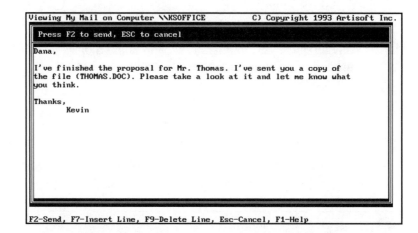

Figure 14.2

Composing a message
using the Simply
LANtastic Editor.

7. You are next asked to type the name of the user to receive
   the mail. The name you specify should be the name of the
   person's computer that is to receive the mail. In this example, you would type **OFFICE** and press Enter to continue
   (see fig. 14.3).

You also can use the wild card character * to enter
recipients for your mail, or you can press F10 to choose
from a list of computers that are currently connected to
the post-office computer.

Figure 14.3

Specifying the name
of the user to receive
the mail.

8. You are then asked to type a comment, which appears on the
   Viewing My Mail screen. Type a comment and press Enter.

9. The Viewing My Mail screen appears, showing the message you created in the OUTgoing Mail section (see fig. 14.4).

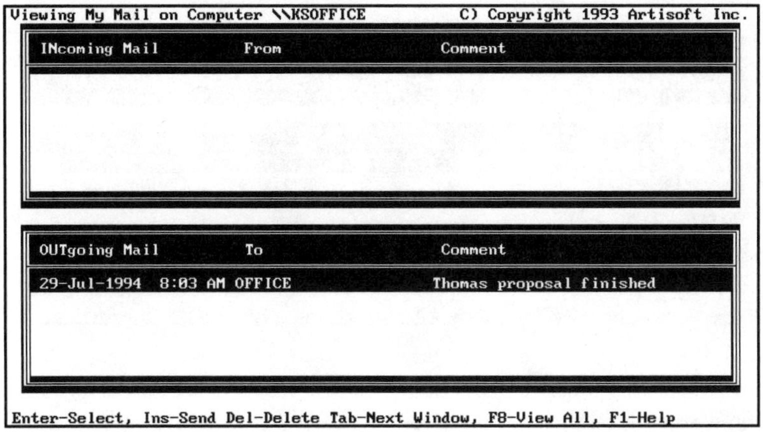

```
Viewing My Mail on Computer \\KSOFFICE          C) Copyright 1993 Artisoft Inc.
┌──────────────────────────────────────────────────────────────────────────┐
│ INcoming Mail        From              Comment                             │
│                                                                            │
│                                                                            │
│                                                                            │
│                                                                            │
│                                                                            │
│ OUTgoing Mail        To                Comment                             │
│ 29-Jul-1994  8:03 AM OFFICE            Thomas proposal finished            │
│                                                                            │
│                                                                            │
│                                                                            │
└──────────────────────────────────────────────────────────────────────────┘
Enter-Select, Ins-Send Del-Delete Tab-Next Window, F8-View All, F1-Help
```

Figure 14.4

Your message in the OUTgoing Mail section of the Viewing My Mail screen.

10. Now that you have sent your message, you need to send a copy of the file for your partner to review. Press Ins to create a new mail item to send.

11. When the Send Mail Options menu appears this time, you select the Send Existing DOS File option and press Enter.

12. You are next asked to type the pathname of the file to mail. In this example, you type c:\WORD\THOMAS.DOC and press Enter (see fig. 14.5).

```
┌──────────────────────────────────────────────────┐
│ Type pathname of file to mail.                     │
│ C:\WORD\THOMAS.DOC                                 │
└──────────────────────────────────────────────────┘
```

Figure 14.5

Specifying the pathname of the file to mail.

13. When prompted, type the name of the user to receive the mail (OFFICE, in this example) and press Enter.

14. When prompted, type a comment and press Enter.

15. The mail is sent and appears in the OUTgoing Mail section of the Viewing My Mail screen (see fig. 14.6).

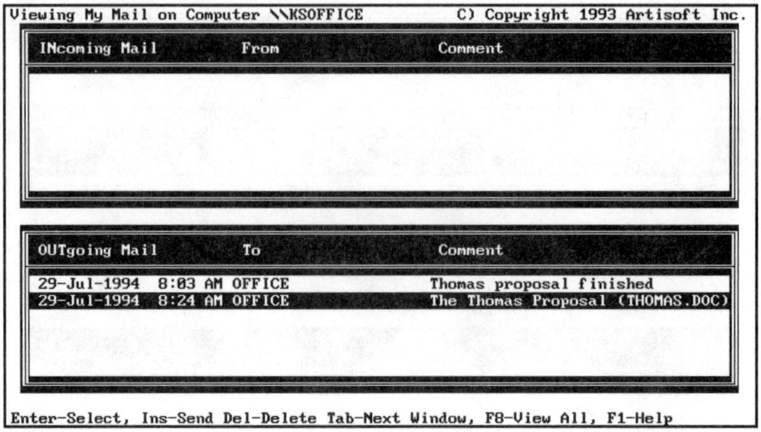

Figure 14.6

The OUTgoing Mail
section of the Viewing
My Mail screen
showing both the mail
items sent to OFFICE.

```
Viewing My Mail on Computer \\KSOFFICE            C) Copyright 1993 Artisoft Inc.
┌──────────────────────────────────────────────────────────────────────────┐
│  INcoming Mail          From              Comment                          │
│                                                                            │
│                                                                            │
│                                                                            │
│                                                                            │
│                                                                            │
└──────────────────────────────────────────────────────────────────────────┘

┌──────────────────────────────────────────────────────────────────────────┐
│  OUTgoing Mail          To                Comment                          │
│  29-Jul-1994  8:03 AM OFFICE              Thomas proposal finished          │
│  29-Jul-1994  8:24 AM OFFICE              The Thomas Proposal (THOMAS.DOC)  │
│                                                                            │
│                                                                            │
│                                                                            │
└──────────────────────────────────────────────────────────────────────────┘
Enter-Select,  Ins-Send Del-Delete Tab-Next Window, F8-View All, F1-Help
```

The mail you sent your partner consists of two separate mail
items: a message indicating that you have finished the Thomas
proposal; and a mail item containing the Thomas proposal, which
is a copy of the THOMAS.DOC file on your computer. When your
partner receives the mail you sent, he reads the first mail item (the
message). Because the second mail item is a document file and is
in a Simply LANtastic mail format, your partner uses an option in
Simply LANtastic Mail to copy the mail item to a file so he can
review and change the file's contents using his word processing
program.

Simply LANtastic Mail in Windows

In this example session, you receive mail from your partner using
Simply LANtastic Mail in Windows. You receive two separate
mail items. The first item is a message responding to your request
for your partner to review the Thomas proposal. The second mail
item is a revised copy of the proposal, which you will save to a file
so you can view and edit the changes with your word processor.

The following steps accomplish the described objectives:

1. From the Simply LANtastic program group, double-click on
    the Simply LANtastic Connections icon. The Simply
    LANtastic Connections program starts and displays the
    main menu.

2. Select the Mail button, or choose Send and Receive Mail from the Net menu.

3. Choose the computer used as the post office from the Current Connections list in the Select Computer dialog box. If the post-office computer is not listed, choose the Connections button to establish a connection to the post-office computer. In this example, KSOFFICE is the post-office computer used to store mail items.

4. The My Mail dialog box appears (see fig. 14.7), showing your incoming and outgoing mail. Note that the mail you sent to your partner (OFFICE) using Simply LANtastic Mail in DOS also appears in the Outgoing Mail list in the Windows Simply LANtastic Mail.

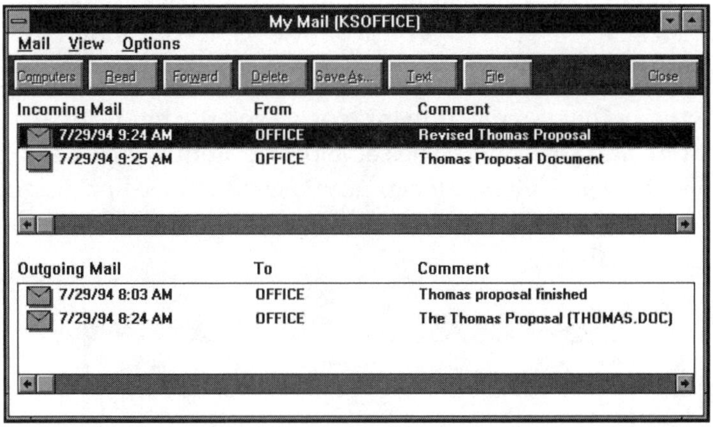

Figure 14.7

Viewing incoming and outgoing mail in the My Mail dialog box.

5. The Incoming Mail list contains two mail items sent from OFFICE. Select the first item by clicking on it, and then select the Read button to view the mail. The Read Mail Message dialog box appears, displaying the message sent to you (see fig. 14.8).

6. When you have finished reading your message, you select Exit from the File menu and return to the My Mail dialog box.

After reading the message sent to you, you realize the next mail item from OFFICE is the revised document. You therefore want to save the second mail item as a file, which you can then edit in your word processor.

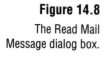

Figure 14.8

The Read Mail
Message dialog box.

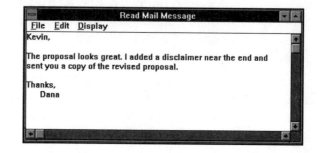

7. Select the second mail item in the list by clicking on it, and then select the Save As button. The Save As dialog box appears.

8. Specify the name you want to save the file name as (see fig. 14.9), and select OK. The second mail item is saved as THOMAS2.DOC. You can now use your word processor to view the changes and make any additional modifications as you see fit.

Figure 14.9

Saving the mail item
as a file.

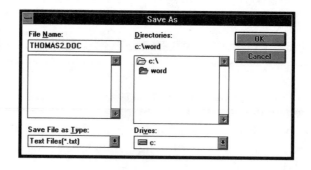

You are now able to open the revised document in your word processor and make any last-minute changes to it. When you have finished, you can save the document and print it. The finished proposal is ready to be sent to your client.

Running a Works for Windows Session

Microsoft Works for Windows is an application that provides word processing, spreadsheet, and database features in a single integrated program. In this example session, you use Simply LANtastic to establish two network connections to ease your task of working with a spreadsheet in your Works for Windows program.

You have decided to store all your data files used for various programs in the DATA directory on the computer named OFFICE. OFFICE also has a laser printer physically connected to it that you use for all your printing. You have decided to purchase a new computer to add to your network. Last week you priced the different configurations available and created a spreadsheet in Works for Windows. Now you want to use the spreadsheet you created to do some "what if" analysis on the different configurations with which you could order your new PC. When you have decided which configuration you want to go with, you'll print a copy of the spreadsheet.

In this example session, you access the following resources, files, and program:

Program:	Microsoft Works for Windows Spreadsheet. Works is installed on your computer.
Data Files:	PCPRICE.WKS located on server OFFICE in the C:\DATA directory.
Shared Drive Resource Name:	C-DRIVE
Redirected Drive Letter:	K
Shared Printer Resource Name:	@PRINTER. Points to laser printer on server OFFICE.
Redirected Printer Device:	LPT1

Before starting the Works for Windows program, you want to establish the network drive and printer connections you'll be using. Your data file is located on the server OFFICE, so you redirect your K drive to point to the C-DRIVE resource on server OFFICE. You'll also be printing to the laser printer on server OFFICE, so you need to redirect your LPT1 device to point to the @PRINTER resource on server OFFICE. Because you are working in Windows, you choose to use the Simply LANtastic Connections program to establish the desired connections.

To establish the network connections necessary to accomplish your objectives for this example session, you perform the following steps:

1. Start the Windows Simply LANtastic Connections program by double-clicking on the Simply LANtastic Connections icon from the Simply LANtastic program group; or with the Simply LANtastic Connections icon selected, choose Open from the Program Manager File menu.

   The Simply LANtastic Connections program menu appears (see fig. 14.10).

Figure 14.10

The Simply LANtastic Connections program main menu.

2. To establish the desired network drive connection, select Drives. The Drive Connections dialog box appears.

3. Redirect the K drive on your computer to point to the C-DRIVE shared drive resource on server OFFICE by selecting the C-DRIVE shared drive resource in the Available for

Connection section and dragging and dropping it on the K drive slot in the My Connections section. The connection is established and appears in the My Connections section (see fig. 14.11).

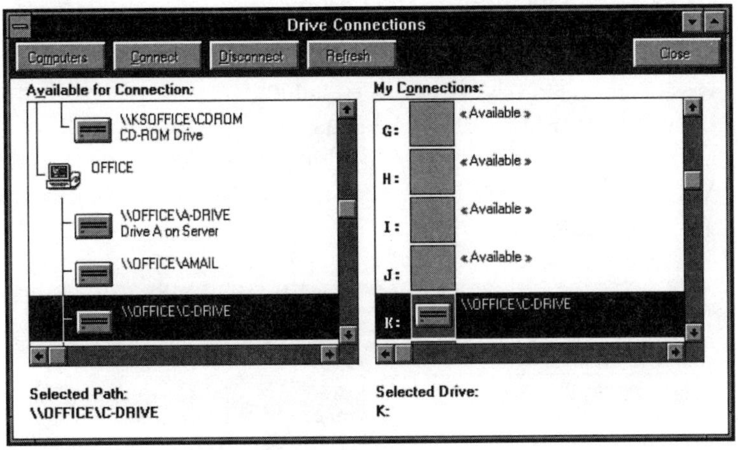

Figure 14.11

Redirecting the K drive to point to the C-DRIVE resource on server OFFICE.

4. Select Close to return to the Simply LANtastic Connections program menu.

5. To establish the network printer connection, select Printers. The Printer Connections dialog box appears.

6. Redirect the LPT1 device on your computer to point to the @PRINTER shared printer resource on server OFFICE by selecting the @PRINTER shared printer resource in the Available for Connection section and dragging and dropping it on the LPT1 printer slot in the My Connections section. The connection is established and appears in the My Connections section (see fig. 14.12).

7. Select Close to return to the Simply LANtastic Connections program menu.

You have established the network connections you need to use and are now ready to start using your Works for Windows application program. Start your application by double-clicking on Microsoft Works icon. Then perform the following steps to open your PCPRICE file located on the server:

1. From the Microsoft Works Startup dialog box, select Open an Existing Document. The Open dialog box appears.

2. You have redirected your K drive to point to the C-DRIVE resource on server OFFICE, so select the K drive from the Drives list and specify DATA as the directory from the Directories list (see fig. 14.13). Note that the network path \\OFFICE\C-DRIVE appears next to the K drive, indicating a redirected drive.

Figure 14.12

Redirecting the LPT1 device to point to the @PRINTER shared resource on server OFFICE.

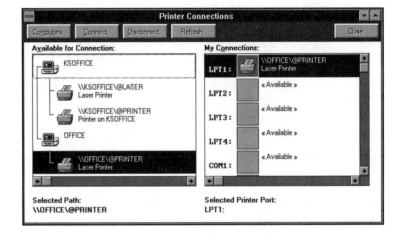

Figure 14.13

The Open dialog box accessing the redirected K drive.

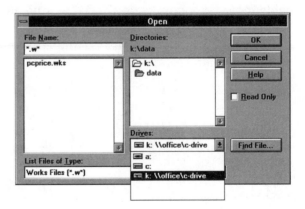

3. Open the file by selecting PCPRICE.WKS from the File
   Name list and selecting OK.

The Microsoft Works spreadsheet program starts and opens your
PCPRICE.WKS file for you to use (see fig. 14.14). You are now able
to work with your spreadsheet and make any changes necessary
to perform your analysis. When you save your changes to the K
drive, your changes overwrite your previous PCPRICE.WKS.
When you print your spreadsheet, because your LPT1 device is
redirected to the @PRINTER resource on server OFFICE, your
results are printed on the laser printer connected to OFFICE.

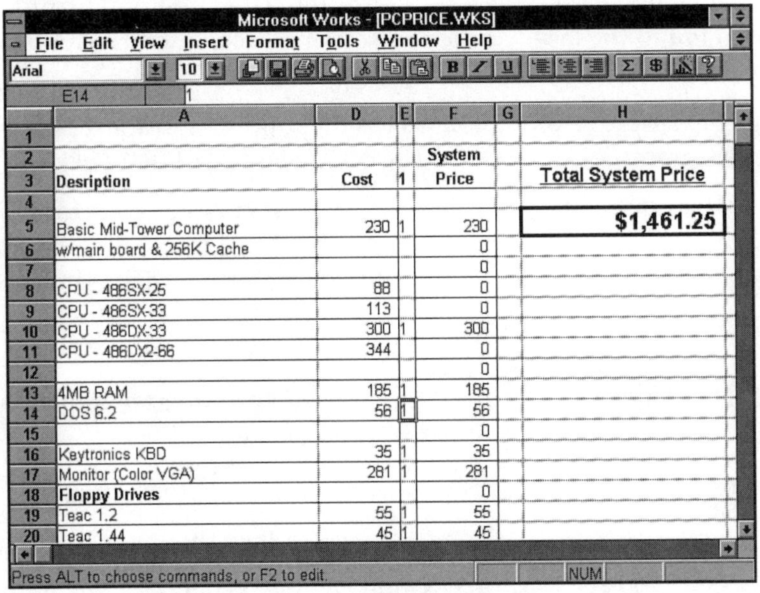

Figure 14.14

Microsoft Works for
Windows with the
PCPRICE.WKS
spreadsheet loaded.

Running a Word for DOS Session

Microsoft Word for DOS is a popular word processing program
used for anything from writing simple memos to developing
entire books. In this example session, you access the Microsoft
Word program from another computer to create a document.
When you are finished, save the document on the other computer
and then print your document on a laser printer connected to the
other computer.

You don't use Word very often, so you have decided not to install it on your hard disk drive but rather to access the Word program from another computer when you need it. Microsoft Word for DOS is installed in the C:\WORD directory on server OFFICE. OFFICE also has the accounting program on it; therefore, the access rights to the C-DRIVE resource have been set so no one is allowed to access the C-DRIVE resource except for key personnel. To access the Word for DOS program, another shared resource named MSWORD has been created on server OFFICE, which points to the C:\WORD directory. You will save your document to the C:\WORD\DOCS directory on server OFFICE, which is accessible using the MSWORD resource. Then you will print your document to the laser printer on server OFFICE, which can be accessed using the @PRINTER resource.

In this example session, you access the following resources, files, and program:

Program:	Microsoft Word for DOS. Word is installed on the computer named OFFICE in the C:\WORD directory.
Data Files:	Word document will be saved in the C:\WORD\DOCS directory on server OFFICE.
Shared Drive Resource Name:	MSWORD. Points to the C:\WORD directory on server OFFICE.
Redirected Drive Letter:	W
Shared Printer Resource Name:	@PRINTER. Points to laser printer on server OFFICE.
Redirected Printer Device:	LPT1

Before starting Microsoft Word, you need to establish the network drive and printer connections you'll be using. You access Word from the server OFFICE, so you need to redirect your W drive to point to the MSWORD resource on server OFFICE. You'll also be printing to the laser printer on server OFFICE, so you need to redirect your LPT1 device to point to the @PRINTER resource on server OFFICE. Because you are working in DOS, you choose to use the Simply LANtastic Connections program to establish the desired connections.

To establish the network connections necessary to accomplish your objectives for this example session, you perform the following steps:

1. Start the DOS Simply LANtastic Connections program by typing **NET** at the DOS prompt and pressing Enter. The Simply LANtastic Connections main menu appears (see fig. 14.15).

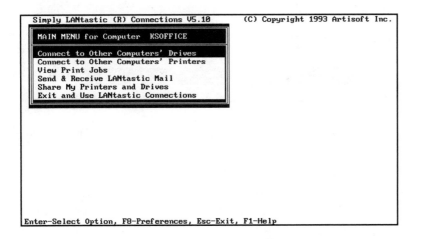

Figure 14.15

The DOS Simply LANtastic Connections program main menu.

2. To establish the desired network drive connection, select the Connect to Other Computers' Drives option from the main menu and press Enter.

3. The Drive Connections to Other Computers screen appears. Redirect your W drive to point to the MSWORD shared resource on server OFFICE by using your arrow keys to select the My W: selection and press Enter.

4. The Connect to Computer window appears, listing the available servers with which you can establish a connection. Select OFFICE and press Enter.

5. The Select a Drive to Connect to window appears, listing the available shared resources for server OFFICE. Choose the MSWORD resource and press Enter.

    You return to the Drive Connections to Other Computers screen, which now displays your network drive connection (see fig. 14.16).

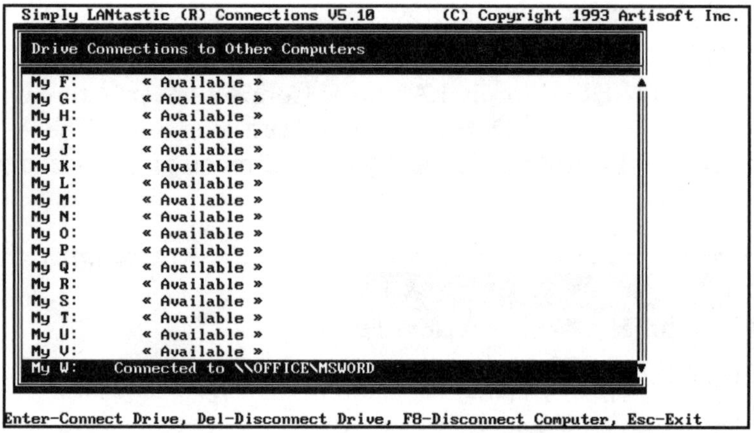

Figure 14.16

The Drive Connections
to Other Computers
screen showing the W
network connection.

```
Simply LANtastic (R) Connections V5.10      (C) Copyright 1993 Artisoft Inc.
┌─────────────────────────────────────────────────────────────────────────┐
│ Drive Connections to Other Computers                                      │
├─────────────────────────────────────────────────────────────────────────┤
│ My F:      « Available »                                               ▲  │
│ My G:      « Available »                                                  │
│ My H:      « Available »                                                  │
│ My I:      « Available »                                                  │
│ My J:      « Available »                                                  │
│ My K:      « Available »                                                  │
│ My L:      « Available »                                                  │
│ My M:      « Available »                                                  │
│ My N:      « Available »                                                  │
│ My O:      « Available »                                                  │
│ My P:      « Available »                                                  │
│ My Q:      « Available »                                                  │
│ My R:      « Available »                                                  │
│ My S:      « Available »                                                  │
│ My T:      « Available »                                                  │
│ My U:      « Available »                                                  │
│ My V:      « Available »                                                  │
│ My W:      Connected to \\OFFICE\MSWORD                                ▼  │
└─────────────────────────────────────────────────────────────────────────┘
Enter-Connect Drive, Del-Disconnect Drive, F8-Disconnect Computer, Esc-Exit
```

6. Press Esc to return to the Simply LANtastic Connections program menu.

7. To establish your network printer connection, select the Connect to Other Computers' Printers option and press Enter. The Printer Connections to Other Computers' screen appears.

8. Use your arrow keys to select the My LPT1 selection and press Enter.

9. The Connect to Computer window appears, listing the available servers with which you can establish a connection. Select OFFICE and press Enter.

10. The Select a Printer to Connect to window appears, listing the available shared printer resources for server OFFICE. Choose the @PRINTER resource and press Enter.

You return to the Printer Connections to Other Computers screen, which now displays your network printer connection (see fig. 14.17).

```
Simply LANtastic (R) Connections V5.10        (C) Copyright 1993 Artisoft Inc.
┌─Printer Connections to Other Computers──────────────────────────────┐
│  My LPT1  Printer Connected to \\OFFICE\@PRINTER                     │
│  My LPT2  Printer  « Available »                                     │
│  My LPT3  Printer  « Available »                                     │
│  My LPT4  Printer  « Available »                                     │
│  My COM1  Printer  « Available »                                     │
│  My COM2  Printer  « Available »                                     │
│  My COM3  Printer  « Available »                                     │
│  My COM4  Printer  « Available »                                     │
└─────────────────────────────────────────────────────────────────────┘



  ─

 Enter-Connect Printer, Del-Disconnect Printer, Esc-Exit, F1-Help
```

Figure 14.17

The Printer Connections to Other Computers screen showing the redirected LPT1 printer connection.

11. Press Esc to return to the Simply LANtastic Connections program menu. Press Esc again to return to the DOS prompt.

You have established your network connections and are now ready to run Microsoft Word from your redirected W drive. To start Microsoft Word for DOS, type the following commands at the DOS prompt:

W:
WORD

The first command (W:) changes your default drive to the redirected W drive, which points to the MSWORD shared resource on server OFFICE. The second command (WORD) is the command that actually starts Word.

Remember that the MSWORD shared resource points to the C:\WORD directory on server OFFICE. For this reason, you do not have to change to the WORD directory because you are already there. W:\ on your computer is the same as C:\WORD on server OFFICE.

If this concept is not clear, review the "Sharing and Accessing Network Resources" section in Chapter 2, "Network Nodes and Their Function."

Word is loaded from the W drive and executes on your computer (see fig. 14.18). You compose your document and are now ready to save your work. You want to save your document to the C:\WORD\DOCS directory on server OFFICE. Your W drive is redirected to the MSWORD resource on server OFFICE, which points to the C:\WORD directory. Therefore, to save your document to the C:\WORD\DOCS directory on the server, you specify W:\DOCS.

Figure 14.18

Microsoft Word for DOS.

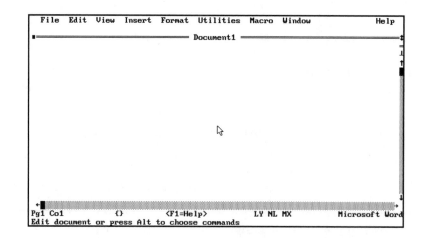

To save your document created in Word to the W:\DOCS directory, perform the following steps:

1. Select Save from the Word File menu (press Alt+F+S). The Save As window appears.

2. Choose the [-W-] option from the Directories list to specify that you want to save your document to the W drive. The list changes to show the directories on the W drive, which contains only the DOCS directory.

3. Select the DOCS directory from the Directories list (see fig. 14.19), and specify the name of the file you want to save your document as. Select OK, and your document is saved.

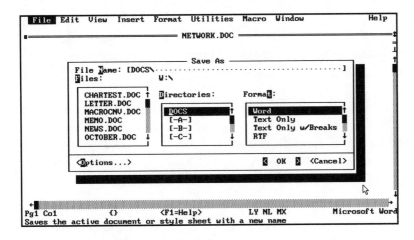

Figure 14.19

Saving a document in Word for DOS.

With your document saved, you decide to run the Word spell-checker routine to see if you misspelled any words in your document. When you try to run the spell checker, however, you receive an error message stating that the speller dictionary file cannot be found.

You know that the spell checker works fine when Word is run on the OFFICE computer. You therefore determine that Word must be configured to look for the speller dictionary file on the C drive instead of on the W drive, which is the drive you are using to access Word. By selecting View, then Preferences, and then Customize, you display the Customize window. This window shows C:\WORD\SPELL-AM.LEX in the Speller Name field (see fig. 14.20). You realize that C:\WORD on the server is the same as W:\ on your computer. You then replace C:\WORD with W:\ in the Speller Name field, and the spell checker works fine.

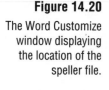

Figure 14.20

The Word Customize window displaying the location of the speller file.

```
 File   Edit  View  Insert  Format  Utilities  Macro  Window              Help
■─────────────────────────── NETWORK.DOC ──────────────────────────────$
                                 Customize
  ┌─Autosave──────────────────────┐      ┌─Line Draw─────────────────┐
  │ Frequency: [3···]  [ ] Confirm │      │ Character: [(|)·]↓        │
  ├─Settings──────────────────────┤      ├─Default Tab:──────────────┤
  │ [X] Background Pagination      │      │ [0.5"····]                │
  │ [X] Prompt for Summary Info    │      │                           │
  │ [X] Widow/Orphan Control       │      │ Speller Name:             │
  │ [ ] Use Word 5.0 Function Keys │      │ [C:\WORD\SPELL-A]↓        │
  │ [X] Use INS for Overtype Key   │      ┌────────────────────────┐  │
  │ [X] Show Keys on Menus         │      │▓  SPELL-AM.LEX       ↑ │  │
  │                                │      │                        │  │
  │ Decimal: [,·······]↓  [ ] Mute │      │                        │  │
  │ Date:    [MDY·····]↓           │      │                      ▓ │  │
  │ Time:    [12 hour·]↓           │      │  [-A-]               ↓ │  │
  │ Measure: [In······]↓           │      └────────────────────────┘  │
  │                                                                    │
  │ <Preferences...>                        ◄ OK ►    <Cancel>         │
  ◄■▓▓▓█────────────────────────────────────────────────────────────  
          {}            <F1=Help>          LY NL MX      Microsoft Word
  Sets display options for document window
```

Finally, with your document spell-checked, you save it one more time and are ready to print. Your LPT1 device is redirected to point to the @PRINTER resource on server OFFICE; therefore, when you select Print from the Word File menu, your document is printed on the laser printer connected to server OFFICE.

> **NOTE**
>
> Although the network sends anything printed to your LPT1 device to the specified network laser printer on server OFFICE, you must still ensure that your application program is configured to send to the appropriate device (in this example, LPT1) and the correct printer.
>
> If your application program is configured for the wrong type of printer, the printed document may contain many unwanted characters or may print pages of useless information.

Running a Multiuser Q&A DOS Session

Symantec Q&A is a popular database program with word processor. This program is especially well suited for managing information such as mailing lists and many other types of lists. Q&A is available in a single-user version and a multiuser network version that enables multiple users to run it from a network server. Both the single-user and network versions enable multiple users to access the same database concurrently. Q&A implements record-locking to prevent more than one user from changing the same record at the same time.

In this example session, you run the network version of Q&A from a server and access a database located on a different server. You create a DOS batch file that establishes the required network connections and then starts Q&A.

The network version of Q&A is installed in the C:\QA directory on server OFFICE. The shared resource QA has been created on server OFFICE to access the C:\QA directory. The database files for Q&A are stored in the C:\DATA\QA directory on server SERVER1. The shared resource DATA has been created on SERVER1 to point to the C:\DATA directory. To run Q&A in this exercise, you must redirect your drive Q to point to the QA resource on server OFFICE. You then redirect your K drive to point to the DATA resource to access the Q&A database files.

In this example session, you access the following resources, files, and program:

Program:	Symantec Q&A 4-node network version. Q&A installed on the computer named OFFICE in the C:\QA directory.
Data Files:	Q&A database files located in C:\DATA\QA directory on server SERVER1.
Shared Drive Resource Name:	QA. Points to the C:\QA directory on server OFFICE.

Redirected Drive Letter:	Q
Shared Drive Resource Name:	DATA. Points to the C:\DATA\QA directory on server SERVER1.
Redirected Drive Letter:	K

To establish the required network connections and to start Q&A, you create a DOS batch file named QANET.BAT using the DOS editor. Once you create QANET.BAT, you can copy it to each computer in your network for others to use when they want to run the network version of Q&A. When you type **QANET** at the DOS prompt, the commands in QANET.BAT are executed. The QANET.BAT file contains the following commands:

```
NET USE Q: \\OFFICE\QA
NET USE K: \\SERVER1\DATA
Q:
QA
C:
NET UNUSE Q:
NET UNUSE K:
```

The first command redirects your Q drive to point to the QA shared resource on server OFFICE. The next command redirects your K drive to point to the DATA shared resource on server SERVER1. The third line changes your current default drive to Q, which is where the Q&A program is located. QA is the command that actually starts the Q&A application program. After you run Q&A and then exit, execution of the batch file continues. The fifth line changes the current default drive back to C, which is a required step. If you left the default drive at Q and then issued a NET UNUSE Q command (as you do in the following line), you would receive an error message because you would be canceling your current default drive Q. The last two NET UNUSE commands cancel the Q and K drive redirections previously established.

Now that you have created your QANET.BAT batch file that every computer in your network can use to establish the required network connections, you can run Q&A by typing **QANET** at the DOS prompt.

The Q&A application starts and displays the Q&A main menu (see fig. 14.21). The statement There are 2 current users out of 4 permitted under your license indicates that a total of two people (including yourself) are currently accessing the network version of Q&A. This particular network version allows up to four simultaneous users.

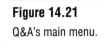

Figure 14.21
Q&A's main menu.

```
                    ┌──────────────────────────┐
                    │      Q&A MAIN MENU        │
                    ├──────────────────────────┤
                    │  F - File                │
                    │  R - Report              │
                    │  W - Write               │
                    │  A - Assistant           │
                    │  U - Utilities           │
                    │  X - Exit Q&A            │
                    └──────────────────────────┘


      There are 2 current users out of 4 permitted under your license.


 Q&A Version 4.0        Copyright (C) 1985-1992, Symantec    All Rights Reserved
 X-Exit to DOS          F1-Description of choices              ←┘ Continue
```

Before you actually start updating the information in your Q&A database, you want to specify the default location where Q&A looks for your database files. Select U - Utilities from the main menu and press Enter; then select S - Set global options and press Enter. The Set Global Options screen appears. You change the location of the Q&A Document files and the Q&A Database files to K:\QA; from now on, the default location Q&A looks to for files is the K:\QA directory (see fig. 14.22). Press F10 to continue, and then press Esc to return to the main menu.

When you change the location of the Q&A database files on the Set Global Options screen, the default location is changed for everyone accessing Q&A. Therefore, each person should access Q&A using the same drive letters, which is automatically taken care of if everyone uses the QANET batch file you created.

```
┌─────────────────────────────────────────────────────────────────────┐
│                        SET GLOBAL OPTIONS                             │
│                                                                       │
│   Type the Drive and, optionally, the Path where the following        │
│   kinds of files will be stored.  This will save you extra typing     │
│   because Q&A will always know where to look first for these files:   │
│                                                                       │
│        Q&A Document files : K:\QA\                                     │
│        Q&A Database files : K:\QA\                                     │
│        Q&A Temporary files: Q:\                                        │
│                                                                       │
│   You can make the program execute menu items as soon as you type the │
│   first letter of the selection.  (If you select this option, you may │
│   have to re-record macros that expect ENTER after the letter.)       │
│                                                                       │
│        Automatic Execution:   Yes  ►No◄                               │
│                                                                       │
│   Type your name and phone number for network identification purposes:│
│                                                                       │
│        Network ID........: KSOFFICE                                   │
│                                                                       │
│                                                                       │
│  Esc-Exit                                               F10-Continue  │
└─────────────────────────────────────────────────────────────────────┘
```

Now you're ready to start working with your Q&A database. The work you have done so far—which includes creating the QANET.BAT batch file and setting up the global options in Q&A—has to be done only once. From now on, you'll type QANET at the DOS prompt; Q&A will start, and you can begin working.

In this example session, you want to change some information for a particular customer in your database. From the Q&A main menu, you select F - File and press Enter. The File Menu appears, and you select S - Search/Update and press Enter. You are then prompted for the file name of the database you want to use in the K:\QA directory. You select the database from the list and press Enter. You next specify the search criteria and press F10 to continue, and the desired record appears (see fig. 14.23).

Notice the message near the bottom of the screen indicating that this record is being edited by OFFICE. Someone at the OFFICE computer is actually changing this particular record. Q&A therefore locks the record to prevent anyone else from making changes until the OFFICE computer finishes with the record. You are allowed to view the record but not to change it. After the person at the OFFICE computer finishes her changes, she presses F10 to continue. The record is then updated and released for others to make changes to it. If you are currently viewing the record when the changes are saved (when the person at the OFFICE computer presses F10), the changes automatically appear on your screen.

```
┌─────────────────────────────────────────────────────────────┐
│     ┌───────────────────────────────────────────────┐         │
│     │ NORTHWEST EXPERIMENTAL AIRCRAFT ASSOCIATION FLY-IN │      │
│     └───────────────────────────────────────────────┘         │
│                  P I L O T   R E G I S T R A T I O N            │
│  ▐DATE:▌ Aug 7, 1994     ▐N NUMBER:▌ 4330D                      │
│  ┌──────────────────────────────────────────────────────────┐ │
│  │     ▐PILOT NAME:▌ Wayne Walcott                            │ │
│  │   ▐COMPANY NAME:▌                                          │ │
│  │       ▐ADDRESS:▌ 1234 Fobes Rd.                            │ │
│  │          ▐CITY:▌ Snohomish      ▐STATE:▌ WA    ▐ZIP:▌ 98275 │ │
│  │         ▐PHONE:▌ 206-353-9623                              │ │
│  │   ▐EAA MEMBER#:▌ 1285344        ▐CHAPTER:▌ U/L 26          │ │
│  └──────────────────────────────────────────────────────────┘ │
│                      AIRCRAFT  INFORMATION                      │
│                                                                │
│   ▐OWNER:▌                              ▐PAID(Y/N)?:▌ Y        │
│   ▐TYPE:▌ Piper Archer                  ▐JUDGED(Y/N)?:▌ n      │
│                                                                │
│   ▐NOTES▌                                                      │
│                                                                │
│                                                                │
│ PILOTS.DTF      Retrieved form 1      of --      Total Forms: 464    Page 1  of 1 │
│ This record is being edited by OFFICE. You can view it only.   │
│ Esc-Exit   F1-Help     Alt+F6-Table     F7-Search     F8-Calc      F10-Continue │
└─────────────────────────────────────────────────────────────┘
```

Figure 14.23

Viewing a Q&A database record.

As soon as the record is released, you plan to change the zip code. The person at the OFFICE computer saves her changes, the record is released, and your screen is updated with the changes. As it turns out, the zip code field (which is what you were about to change) is now correct; the person at the OFFICE computer already made the change.

When you are finished with Q&A, press Esc to return to the Q&A main menu and then press X - Exit Q&A to exit. The execution of your QANET.NET batch file continues, which cancels your Q and K network drive redirections and returns you to the DOS prompt.

Running a Windows File Manager Session

The Windows File Manager program is primarily used for organizing the files on your hard disk. File Manager enables you to copy files, delete files, move files, change the names of files, create and delete directories, and do several other file-management functions.

Currently, the D drive on the computer with the network named OFFICE has an accounting program and several other applications that are shared with the network. Because the accounting program, which you don't want others to have access to, is on this D drive, you have had to set up separate shared resources for each of the other application directories (see fig. 14.24). In this example session, you use the Windows File Manager program to change the organization of the D drive on the OFFICE computer so you can access the four applications using a single shared resource instead of four separate shared resources.

Figure 14.24

The directory structure of D before and after organization.

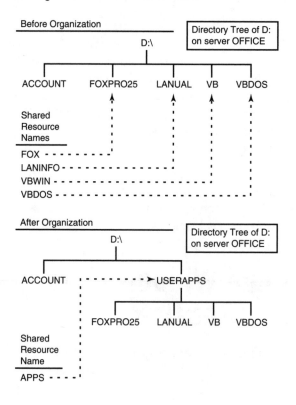

You want to organize the D drive on OFFICE from your computer because the OFFICE computer is constantly being used. Your computer has been given access to the D-DRIVE shared resource on OFFICE; you therefore have access to the entire drive. You have decided to redirect your O drive to point to the D-DRIVE resource on server OFFICE. Using File Manager, you create the USERAPPS directory (see fig. 14.24) and then move the four application program directories under it. By moving the four application directories under a single directory (USERAPPS, in this example), you can set up a single shared resource (APPS, in this example) that points to the USERAPPS directory. Anyone accessing the APPS resource has access to the USERAPPS directory as well as to the four application program directories under it.

In this example session, you access the following resources, files, and program:

Program:	Windows File Manager. File Manager is located on your computer.
Data File:	Will be organizing the directories on the D drive on server OFFICE. Directories FOXPRO25, LANUAL, VB, and VBDOS will be moved under a new USERAPPS directory.
Shared Drive Resource Name:	D-DRIVE. Points to the D:\ directory on server OFFICE.
Redirected Drive Letter:	O

You first need to establish your network drive connection so you can access the D drive on the OFFICE computer. To redirect your O drive to point to the D-DRIVE resource on server OFFICE, you perform the following steps:

1. Start the Windows Simply LANtastic Connections program by double-clicking on the Simply LANtastic Connections icon from the Simply LANtastic program group; or with the Simply LANtastic Connections icon selected, choose Open from the Program Manager File menu. The Simply LANtastic Connections program menu appears.

2. To establish the desired network drive connection, select Drives. The Drive Connections dialog box appears.

3. Redirect the O drive on your computer to point to the D-DRIVE shared drive resource on server OFFICE by selecting the D-DRIVE resource in the Available for Connection section and dragging and dropping it on the O drive slot in the My Connections section. The connection is established and appears in the My Connections section (see fig. 14.25).

Figure 14.25

Redirecting the O drive to point to the D-DRIVE resource on server OFFICE.

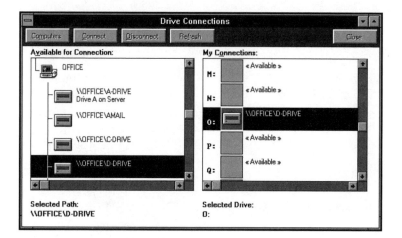

4. Select Close to return to the Simply LANtastic Connections program menu.

With your network connection established, you are ready to run the Windows File Manager program. To start File Manager, double-click on the File Manager icon located in the Main program group.

Select the O drive icon to view the contents of the O drive (see fig. 14.26). Notice how File Manager lists the network path name \\OFFICE\D-DRIVE next to the redirected drive letter O.

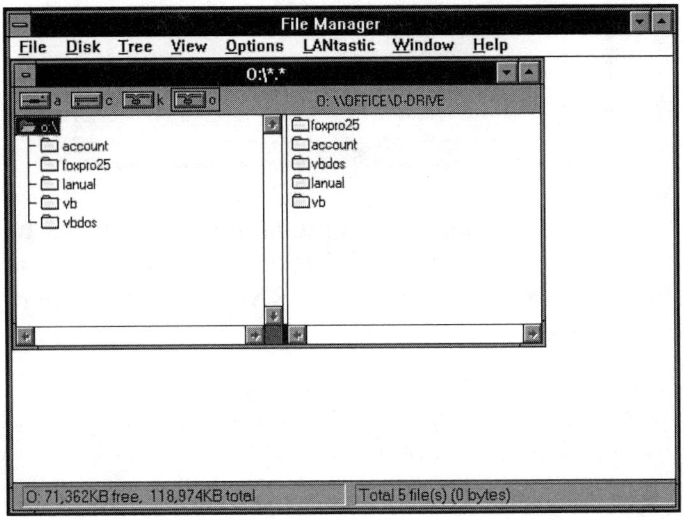

Figure 14.26

Viewing the directory structure of the O drive in File Manager.

You are now ready to start organizing the D drive on server OFFICE, which you are accessing using your redirected O drive.

First you need to create a directory named USERAPPS under the root directory (O:\, in this example). To create the USERAPPS directory, perform the following steps:

1. Select the root directory of the O drive by clicking on the O:\ in the directory tree list.

2. With the O:\ directory selected, choose Create Directory from the File Manager File menu.

3. The Create Directory dialog box appears. Type the name of the directory to create (USERAPPS) in the Name field, and select OK. The USERAPPS directory now appears on the list (see fig. 14.27).

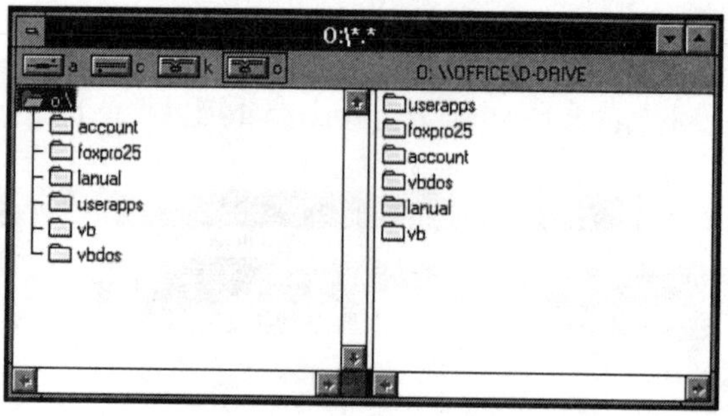

Figure 14.27

The list of directories
on drive O showing
the newly created
USERAPPS directory.

You are now ready to start moving the application program
directories under the USERAPPS directory. To move the four
application directories under the USERAPPS directory, perform
the following steps:

1. Move each of the four directories under the USERAPPS
    directory by selecting the directory to be moved and drag-
    ging and dropping it on the USERAPPS directory.

2. When you are asked to confirm the operation, select Yes. The
    specified directory is moved and appears under the
    USERAPPS directory.

3. When you have finished, the four directories you moved
    (FOXPRO25, LANUAL, VB, and VBDOS) appear as
    subdirectories to the USERAPPS directory (see fig. 14.28).

4. Exit File Manager by selecting Exit from the File Manager
    File menu.

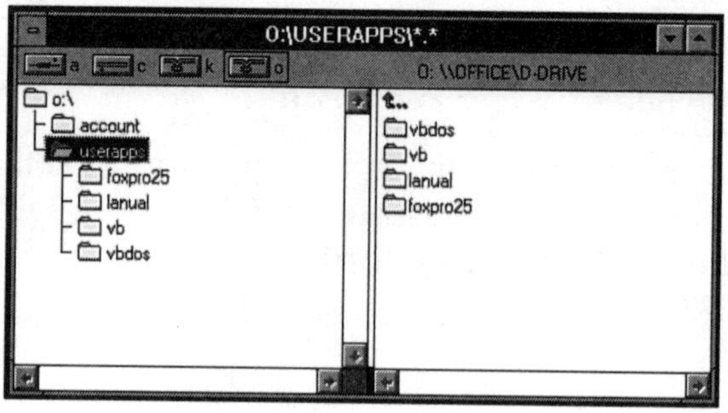

Figure 14.28

The newly organized
directory structure of
the network O drive.

You have finished reorganizing the D drive on server OFFICE and can now proceed to set up a shared resource named APPS, which will point to the D:\USERAPPS directory. To set up the APPS shared resource on the OFFICE computer, you must be sitting at the OFFICE computer. You need to delete the previous four shared resources (FOX, LANINFO, VBWIN, and VBDOS) and create the new shared resource (APPS), which will be used to access any of the four application programs.

To delete the old shared resources and create the new APPS shared resource, you perform the following steps:

1. Start the Windows Simply LANtastic Connections program by double-clicking on the Simply LANtastic Connections icon from the Simply LANtastic program group; or with the Simply LANtastic Connections icon selected, choose Open from the Program Manager File menu. The Simply LANtastic Connections program menu appears.

2. Select Share from the program menu, and the Shared Drives and Printers dialog box appears (see fig. 14.29).

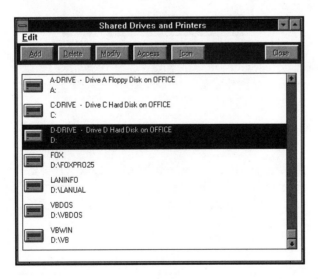

Figure 14.29

The Shared Drives and Printers dialog box on server OFFICE.

3. Delete the FOX shared resource by selecting the resource name on the list and then selecting the Delete button. When you are asked if you want to delete the resource, select Yes.

4. Repeat step 3 to delete the LANINFO, VBWIN, and VBDOS shared resources.

5. Add the APPS shared resource by selecting the Add button.

6. The Add Drive or Printer dialog box appears. Specify APPS as the shared resource name in the Shared Name field, and specify D:\USERAPPS as the directory in the Path field (see fig. 14.30).

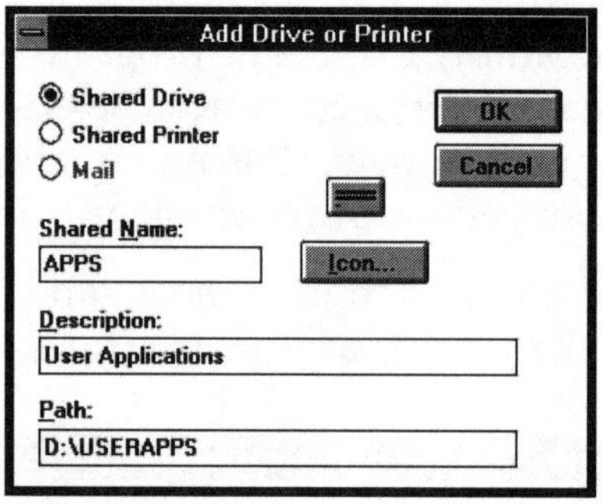

Figure 14.30

Specifying the new APPS shared resource on server office.

Add Drive or Printer
◉ Shared Drive
○ Shared Printer
○ Mail
Shared Name:
APPS
Description:
User Applications
Path:
D:\USERAPPS
OK
Cancel
Icon...

7. When you select OK, the Shared Drives and Printers dialog box appears, listing the newly added APPS shared resource (see fig. 14.31).

8. Select Close when you have finished specifying the shared resources on server OFFICE.

The new directory structure is ready to use. Anyone can now establish a connection to the APPS resource on server OFFICE to access any of the four application directories (FOXPRO25, LANUAL, VB, and VBDOS).

If the application you are using has a default drive and directory specified in the application for its support or configuration files, you may have to change the specified directory in the application.

As an example, if you previously redirected your F drive to point to the FOX resource, F:\ on your computer is actually D:\FOXPRO25 on server OFFICE. With the new organization, if you redirected your F drive to point to the APPS resource, F:\FOXPRO25 (not F:\) on your computer is the same as D:\FOXPRO25 on server OFFICE. In other words, if your FoxPro application previously looked for files in the F:\ directory, now you would need to specify F:\FOXPRO25 to find the same files.

If this concept is not clear, review the "Sharing and Accessing Network Resources" section in Chapter 2.

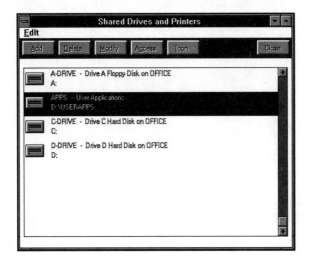

Figure 14.31

The Shared Drives and Printers dialog box showing the newly added APPS shared resource.

Summary

This chapter contained several example sessions to demonstrate how you can use your Simply LANtastic network to help with your daily activities. A session in which you sent and received Simply LANtastic mail (in both the DOS and Windows environments) illustrated how you can communicate with others in the network. A session using Works for Windows demonstrated the ability to access data from another computer and also print to the shared printer on another computer. A session using Microsoft Word for DOS explained how to actually run an application program from another computer in addition to accessing the data. A session using Symantec Q&A showed how you can use a multiuser network version of the Q&A database program to enable multiple users to access the same program and database concurrently. Finally, a session using Windows File Manager demonstrated how to organize the directories on a server's hard drive to make network access to various programs easier while maintaining required security.

You now have a good understanding of the many facets of networks and have the specific hands-on knowledge required to successfully install, configure, use, and manage a network.

Part Three: Appendix and Glossary

Appendix

Planning a Network

Glossary

In This Appendix. . .

This appendix guides you through the planning process required to successfully implement a network—a functioning network that meets current needs as well as a flexible network that meets future needs. You must make several decisions before installing a network, including what type of physical layout, *network operating system* (NOS), and network adapters to use.

In this appendix, you learn the following:

- The steps required to determine your network requirements.

- How to decide whether a server-based network or a peer-to-peer network is best for your situation.

- How to establish the layout of the computers in your network and identify the workstations and the servers.

- How to choose the network standard to use (such as Ethernet) and the layout of the network cable (topology) to connect the nodes.

- Considerations for choosing a NOS.

Planning a Network

A network provides many features to improve productivity, reduce costs, and allow for the exchange and sharing of important information. If your network meets these needs is determined in part prior to implementation by how well you plan your network.

Your current as well as future network requirements determine how extensive the planning process should be. Small networks with a few nodes located in the same physical area require minimal planning. Networks that consist of several nodes in different rooms or even on different floors, and that require additional nodes in the future, however, impose more extensive planning.

Whatever your network requirements, understanding and using the following planning guidelines can benefit your own network planning and implementation.

Determining Network Requirements

As obvious as it may sound, in order for your network to meet your requirements, the first thing you have to do is determine what you require of your network. The following list of questions helps identify your network requirements:

- What is the purpose of the network (file sharing, printer sharing, multiuser applications, and so on)?

- How many nodes will be connected?

- What are the performance requirements?

- Which nodes need to share resources with others? Which resources need to be shared (printers, files, and so forth)?

- How much will the network cost?

The following sections include a detailed discussion of each of the preceding questions. Answer the questions to define a good portion of your network requirements, and you are well on your way to having a detailed network implementation plan.

What Is the Purpose of the Network?

Determining the purpose of your network helps establish many factors, including which NOS you eventually choose.

You need to determine if more than one person needs to have access to such files as a document about company policies, or templates used to create other documents.

You also may want to store and access the data files used by several computers in one common location. Storing data files on one computer with a relatively large hard disk enables you to have smaller, less expensive disk drives on other nodes in the network.

Networks almost always are used for printer sharing and, even though other non-network devices are available for sharing printers among computers, sometimes printer-sharing requirements alone sufficiently justify a network.

The ability for more than one person to use a common application program to access the same data is one of the most powerful features of a network. You need to consider if your network will be used for multiuser applications, such as sharing a customer database or an accounting program.

How Many Nodes Need To Be Connected?

An important consideration when planning your network is determining how many computers you want to connect immediately and in the future. The maximum number of nodes that can be connected in a given network configuration depends on several factors, including the NOS, the physical topology (layout), and the type of network (Ethernet, ARCNET, Proprietary, and so on).

What Are the Performance Requirements?

The performance requirements of your network depend on a number of factors. Each NOS performs differently and some might be better suited to your performance requirements than others. The type of network adapter, network topology, as well as network protocols used affect performance.

If sharing network printers is your network's primary purpose, then even the lowest-performance network configuration probably is more than adequate. Printers rarely are able to accept data faster than the speed of the parallel port on the computer. Also, because even the slowest network adapters available are faster than a parallel port, network adapter speed typically isn't an issue in this situation.

If files and data are shared with other nodes on the network, performance is an issue. You therefore should consider a network that has the same 10-Mbps performance as Ethernet. The relatively low cost and high performance of Ethernet causes it to be the most popular network standard in use today.

If you have many nodes in your network that access a common server, you want to consider a dedicated server to provide the necessary bperformance. In situations in which only a few users heavily access a common database, a dedicated server can offer significant performance improvements.

Which Nodes Need To Share Resources with Others?

When determining your network requirements, you need to establish the nodes that share resources and those that don't. Nodes that share with other nodes such resources as disk drives, directories, and printers are configured as servers. The NOS you choose needs to support multiple servers if you need to share the resources on more than a single node. Additionally, if any of the nodes designated as sharing resources also are used as workstations, then you need to configure those servers as nondedicated servers.

If a node only needs to share a printer that is connected to it with other nodes in the network, you might be able to use a feature of the selected NOS to share a printer without configuring the node as a server.

How Much Will It Cost?

Cost is a major factor in determining which of the specified network requirements are a priority and which are not. The costs incurred to implement various network features aren't so much related to each function as they are to the technology available to perform the required function. As a result, it's very possible that the cost to implement what you might consider a trivial task is excessive, whereas the cost to implement what might seem a complicated task is relatively low.

Because of costs, you may choose to prioritize the requirements you have established and implement certain features at a later date. You still want to ensure that the chosen NOS and network hardware can be upgraded later to perform the deferred functions. Because cost typically decreases as technology develops, you may actually benefit by waiting to implement features that are not a high priority.

Server-Based or Peer-to-Peer?

Based on your network requirements, you can determine if you need a server-based network or a peer-to-peer network.

Recall that a peer-to-peer network primarily consists of non-dedicated servers that allow any node in the network to share its resources with any other node in the network. A server-based network primarily consists of a dedicated server that can share its resources with workstations (or clients). The workstations (clients) are able to access the shared resources on the server but are not able to access any resources on other workstations.

When deciding whether a server-based network or a peer-to-peer network is best for your situation, consider the following points:

- A peer-to-peer network gives you the capability to share resources with any computer in the network. In a server-based network you can share only the resources on a server, which typically is configured as a dedicated server.

- A server-based network usually provides better performance than a peer-to-peer network because it uses dedicated servers. With a peer-to-peer network, however, applications can be distributed over a number of different nondedicated servers, which can result in better performance.

- A peer-to-peer network can be more difficult to administer than a server-based network because of its flexible resource sharing capabilities.

- A server-based network usually is more expensive to implement because it requires a dedicated server. A peer-to-peer network doesn't require a dedicated server and usually works with your existing equipment.

Locating Existing and New Equipment

The next step in planning your network is to determine where to locate the computers.

After determining whether your network will be server-based or peer-to-peer, you'll know whether a dedicated server is required in addition to your other network nodes. You also may purchase additional computers to use as nodes on your network.

To assist in your planning, draw a sketch of the area where your computers will be located (see fig. A.1). On the sketch, show the location of the existing equipment (computers and printers) and any new equipment you will add when the network is installed. If you have a dedicated server, consider putting it in a secure area to prevent unauthorized access.

Figure A.1

A layout of the computers connected in the network.

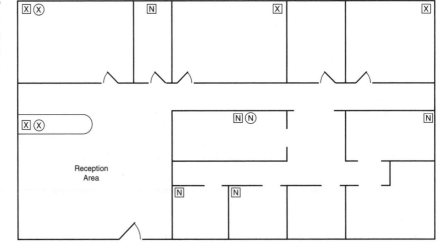

X̄ — Existing Computer

Ⓧ — Existing Printer

N̄ — New Computer

Ⓝ — New Printer

After you determine the location of the computers and the printers on your layout, it's time to establish which computers to configure as servers and which to configure as workstations.

Identifying Workstations

The workstations on your layout are the computers that can access the shared resources on the servers but cannot share their own resources with other nodes in the network.

In a dedicated server network, most of the nodes are configured as workstations (clients). In a peer-to-peer network, however, no nodes can be configured as workstations. Instead, they are configured as nondedicated servers.

> Printers, physically connected to a node configured as a workstation, that you want to share on the network, require a NOS with provisions to allow a printer on a workstation to be shared with the rest of the network.

Identifying Servers and Shared Printers

After identifying the workstations on your layout, you need to identify the nodes to be configured as servers and the printers to be shared with other nodes.

In a server-based network, you probably only need to identify a dedicated server and the shared network printers connected to that server.

In a peer-to-peer network, you probably need to identify nondedicated servers, which could be every computer in the network. In addition, you can identify one or more servers as dedicated servers. If you identify any servers as dedicated servers in your network, consider locating the dedicated server in a secure area to prevent the possibility of unauthorized use.

Figure A.2 is an example of the layout showing the locations of the nodes in the network as well as the type of use identified with each node (server or workstation). The example shown is a peer-to-peer network with a combination of workstations, nondedicated servers, and a dedicated server.

Figure A.2

Layout of a peer-to-peer network with a combination of workstations, non-dedicated servers, and a dedicated server.

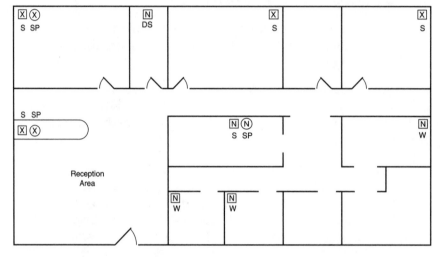

$\boxed{X}$ – Existing Computer

$\textcircled{X}$ – Existing Printer

$\boxed{N}$ – New Computer

$\textcircled{N}$ – New Printer

W – Workstation

DS – Dedicated Server

S – Non-Dedicated Server

SP – Shared Printer

L – Local Printer

Determining the Network Topology and Standard

After locating the computers in your network, the next step in the planning process is to determine the physical network topology and the standard used to connect the nodes. The network standard you choose usually determines the physical network topologies available to you as well as the type of network adapter to use.

Choosing a Network Standard

Several standards exist for connecting your computers to form a network including Ethernet, Token Ring, and ARCnet. Other proprietary methods that are not standards also exist. It's important at this point in the planning process to think about the NOS you want to use so you can be assured that it supports the standard or scheme to connect the computers in your network.

While choosing a standard, anticipate the effect that standard will have on any planned future expansion. Consider the ease of expansion with the chosen standard, as well as limitations that might exist.

The majority of new network installations use the Ethernet standard. As you learned previously, Ethernet supports the bus, star, and even a tree physical topology.

Layout of Network Cable and Devices

The next step in the planning process is to determine the physical layout of the cable used to connect the network nodes. The following three examples illustrate how the nodes in an Ethernet network are connected using a physical star, bus, and tree topology.

Figure A.3 illustrates how the example network described previously is connected using a physical star topology. The physical star topology in this example is known as *10Base-T* (UTP). A cable runs from each node in the network to a central location (concentrator) where it is connected. Diagnosing a network UTP cable problem is relatively simple because cable problems affect only the communications between the concentrator and the node with the bad cable; they don't affect the rest of the network.

Figure A.3

Connecting network
nodes using a
physical star
topology.

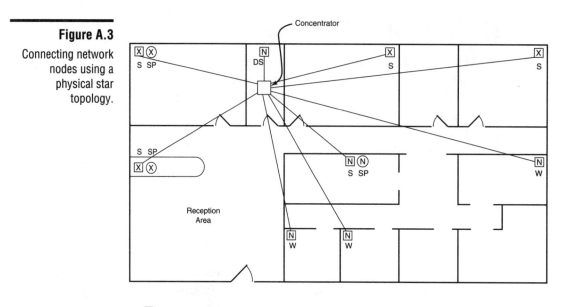

X – Existing Computer

Ⓧ – Existing Printer

N – New Computer

Ⓝ – New Printer

W – Workstation

DS – Dedicated Server

S – Non-Dedicated Server

SP – Shared Printer

L – Local Printer

Figure A.4 illustrates how the example network is connected using a physical bus topology. The physical bus topology used in this example is known as *Thin Ethernet* or *10BASE2 Ethernet*. The main cable runs next to every node where each node is connected to the cable. A network using Thin Ethernet can be less expensive than 10BASE-T, because Thin Ethernet doesn't require concentrators. As more nodes are connected, however, the price differential between UTP and Thin Ethernet becomes less significant because the coax cabling used for Thin Ethernet is more expensive than that used for UTP. Diagnosing a cable problem when using Thin Ethernet can be extremely difficult, especially in a network with many nodes, because a single break in the cable can disable the entire network.

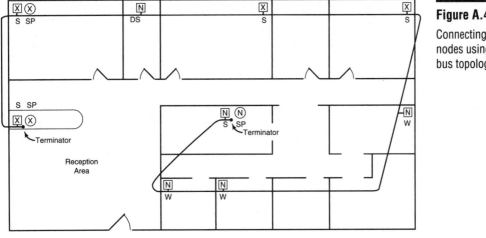

X — Existing Computer
X — Existing Printer
N — New Computer
N — New Printer
W — Workstation
DS — Dedicated Server
S — Non-Dedicated Server
SP — Shared Printer
L — Local Printer

Figure A.5 illustrates how the example network would be connected using a *physical tree topology,* which is a combination of a
physical star and bus topology. In this example, four nodes are
connected to a concentrator. The remaining nodes are connected
to the Thin Ethernet cable segment. The concentrator has a BNC
connector on the back allowing a Thin Ethernet cable segment
connection. The BNC connector allows the concentrator to bridge
the two network cable types.

Network Interface Cards

As soon as you determine the network standard and the physical
topology of the cabling, you establish the type of network adapter
cards required for your network. The network cable is connected

to the back of the card. The right type of connector must be used for the network to operate properly. For example, as discussed in Chapter 3, "Hardware Components," if you use Thin Ethernet, a BNC connector is used. If you use UTP Ethernet, an RJ-45 connector is used.

Figure A.5

Connecting network nodes using a physical tree topology.

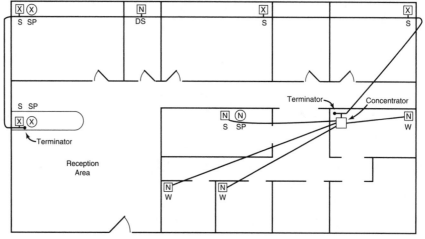

X — Existing Computer
Ⓧ — Existing Printer
N — New Computer
Ⓝ — New Printer
W — Workstation
DS — Dedicated Server
S — Non-Dedicated Server
SP — Shared Printer
L — Local Printer

Another consideration when choosing a *network interface card* (NIC) for each computer is to evaluate the interface between the NIC and the computer's expansion bus. Because the bottleneck in network communications usually is the interface between the network adapter and the computer's expansion bus into which the adapter is plugged, anything that increases the speed of data flow through the bottleneck improves network speed. For example, if your primary dedicated server serves the network needs of several computers, and the server uses an *Extended Industry Standard Architecture* (EISA) bus, you might want to purchase a network adapter card that supports the EISA bus rather than a standard *Industry Standard Architecture* (ISA) adapter. The EISA network adapter takes advantage of the higher throughput capability of the EISA bus, thereby improving network performance. The network adapters used in the rest of the nodes probably are the less expensive and lower quality ISA adapters.

Choosing the NOS

The decision of which NOS to use for your network is an important one, and should be considered carefully early in the network planning process. Determining whether a server-based or peer-to-peer network is best for your requirements helps narrow your choices for a NOS. Several NOSs, however, whether server-based or peer-to-peer, have strong support of features normally found in the opposite type of network. For example, a peer-to-peer network such as LANtastic has robust features that enable the use of a high-performance dedicated server, whereas Novell NetWare 2.2 enables the use of a non-dedicated server that usually is a feature of peer-to-peer networks only.

When evaluating the various NOSs to determine which is right for your situation, refer to the information in Chapter 5, "Peer-to-Peer Networks," to help determine the best peer-to-peer network for your situation or the information in Chapter 6, "Server-Based Networks," to help determine the best server-based network for your situation.

Summary

This appendix discussed the network planning process. You first learned how to determine the requirements for your network. Based on those specified network requirements, you identified whether a server-based network or a peer-to-peer network best suits your needs. Next, the specific layout of the computers in the network was determined as well as the physical topology and network cable layout. Finally, by considering your network requirements, the NOS to use was determined.

Complete Glossary
of Terms

10BASE2. The implementation of the IEEE 802.3 Ethernet standard that uses thin coax cable. Data travels at 10 Mbps, and the physical connection uses a bus topology. The maximum segment length is 607 feet (185 meters).

10BASE5. The implementation of the IEEE 802.3 Ethernet standard that uses thick coax cable. Data travels at 10 Mbps, and the physical connection uses a bus topology. The maximum segment length is 1,641 feet (500 meters).

10BASE-T. The implementation of the IEEE 802.3 Ethernet standard that uses UTP cable. Data travels at 10 Mbps, and the physical connection uses a star topology. The maximum segment length between a node and the hub or concentrator is 328 feet (100 meters).

Access control list (ACL). A list used by the NOS to provide specific access rights for a specific shared resource. Each shared resource typically has a separate ACL that contains a list of user or group accounts and each account's associated rights to the shared resource. See *network operating system (NOS)*.

Account. A record of information used to permit and keep track of the users accessing a server. Accounts are the records used to allow access to a network and include information such as account name, description, and other parameters used to specify the access rights to a server. An *individual account* is an account assigned to a single person, whereas a *group account* may be used by several individuals.

Address. A term used to identify a specific location in a computer's memory.

American National Standards Institute (ANSI). The primary group in the United States responsible for defining standards to benefit business and industry by providing common techniques for accomplishing similar tasks.

American Standard Code for Information Interchange (ASCII). The standard that represents 128 characters using a 7-bit binary representation. Extended ASCII uses an 8-bit representation for 256 characters. ASCII is the standard for transmitting characters between different computers and devices.

Application layer. The seventh layer of the OSI model. The application layer is responsible for providing user applications and network management functions, and for providing the operating system with services including file transfer. See *Open Systems Interconnection (OSI) model*.

ARCnet. A 2.5 Mbps network standard designed by Datapoint Corporation in the 1970s. ARCnet uses a token-passing bus topology with a physical star/tree topology.

Asynchronous Transfer Mode (ATM). A method of data transmission that transmits fixed-length packets over a cell-switched network provided by a telephone company. ATM can carry voice, video, and data at speeds up to 2.2 Gbps (1,000,000,000 bps). ATM is considered the solution for high-speed WAN communications. See *wide area network (WAN)*.

Attributes. Properties or parameters associated with an object that identify specific characteristics of the object. For example, a file may be assigned the read-only attribute, which allows the file to be read but not written to.

Auditing. A method used to keep track of specific activities that have occurred. Auditing usually creates an audit trail or an audit log, which is a list of the activities that have occurred.

Backbone. A main network communication medium to which servers are connected. In large networks, the servers typically are connected directly to the backbone, with the smaller sub-networks connected to the backbone through a bridge or router. This keeps network traffic on the backbone at a minimum.

Bandwidth. The amount of data that may be transmitted over a specific data channel. Bandwidth is measured in bits per second (bps). For example, Ethernet has a bandwidth of 10 Mbps.

Batch processing. A mode of computer operation in which the instructions in a computer program are executed one after another without user interaction. The process seen by the user is the following: the job is submitted, the computer processes the information without any user interaction, and the results are returned.

Binary. The most basic number system used by computers, consisting of the digits 0 and 1. Binary uses a series of on (1) and off (0) digits to represent numbers and characters (1001010, for example).

Bit. A single unit of information in the binary number system. A bit can have a value of 0 or 1.

Bridge. A device that connects two similar networks, such as Ethernet to Ethernet. A bridge looks at the address associated with each packet of information. Then, if the address is that of a node on the other network segment, the bridge passes the packet across the bridge. Bridges operate at the OSI's media access layer.

Brouter. A device that acts as a bridge and a router.

Bus topology. A network layout in which all the computers are connected to a single network cable segment.

Byte. A unit consisting of eight bits, commonly used to report the memory capacity of computers. A byte represents a single character.

Cabling. Media used to physically connect nodes in a network over which data is transferred as a series of electrical signals. Also referred to as *network cable*.

Carrier Sense Multiple Access with Collision Detection (CSMA/CD). The method of transmitting data in an Ethernet network by which each station listens for other network activity and transmits data when there is no other traffic. If two stations transmit at the same time, a collision is detected and each station waits a random amount of time before retransmitting.

Channel Service Unit/Digital Service Unit (CSU/DSU). A device, basically a sophisticated high-speed modem, used to connect a LAN to lines provided by the telephone company.

Client-server. A term used to refer to a server-based network. The client computer uses the shared resources of the server computer.

Coaxial cable. A type of cable consisting of a wire center conductor surrounded by insulation and wrapped in a thin, insulated metal shield. Coaxial cable is used as the transmission media in several networks such as 10BASE2 Ethernet.

Communications software. Software that provides features to enable two computers to communicate and exchange information, usually using a modem.

Compact Disk Read Only Memory (CD-ROM). A read-only technology that uses compact discs to store large quantities of information. A typical computer CD-ROM disc is capable of holding up to 650 MB of data.

Concentrator. A device used as a central connection point for cables from network nodes arranged in a physical star topology. Usually refers to the device used in an Ethernet 10BASE-T network.

Connectivity. The result of connecting computers so that they can communicate and share data in a network environment.

Data link layer. The second layer of the OSI model. The data link layer defines the protocol that detects and corrects errors, which may occur when transmitting data through the network cable. See *Open Systems Interconnection (OSI) model*.

Database server. A server used specifically to store database files that may be accessed and modified by other nodes in a network.

Dedicated server. A computer that shares its resources with other nodes on the network and cannot be used as a workstation.

Directory. A list of files stored on a disk drive or a specific location on a disk drive. Also refers to a specific, named location for storing files on a disk drive (for example, the DATA directory or the DOS directory).

Disk caching. The process of using part of the RAM in a computer as a temporary storage location for data read from and written to a hard disk. Disk caching speeds up the rate at which data is read from and written to a disk drive.

Disk drive. A device in a computer used for storing programs and files. Information stored on a disk drive is not lost when the power to the computer is turned off.

Disk duplexing. The process of concurrently writing data to two separate hard disks using separate channels, involving separate hard drive controllers in addition to separate disk drives.

Disk mirroring. The process of concurrently writing data to two separate hard disks when both hard disks are connected to the same hard disk controller.

Disk Operating System (DOS). A term referring to an operating system loaded from a disk when the computer boots. Commonly refers to the operating system used for PCs. DOS, MS-DOS (Microsoft DOS), and PC-DOS (Personal Computer DOS, which is IBM's version of DOS) are used to refer to the operating system of a PC. See *Operating system*.

Diskless workstation. A computer that uses only shared network drives and does not contain any physical disk drives of its own.

Domain. A term used to refer to a group of computers in a network that are administered as a related group or as a single entity.

Download. The process of transferring data from a host computer to a PC through a modem.

Downsizing. The process of adapting or moving applications from a larger computer system such as a mainframe or minicomputer to a smaller system such as a PC or LAN. See *local area network (LAN)*.

Downwardly compatible. Computer components or software that operate, without modification, with earlier components or software versions.

Dumb terminal. A device consisting of a monitor and keyboard that has no internal processing capability. Dumb terminals connect to host computers that perform the processing.

Enterprise network. A company-wide WAN. See *wide area network (WAN)*.

Ethernet. A network standard that uses CSMA/CD and a data transfer rate of 10 Mbps. Often referred to as IEEE 802.3, Ethernet runs over thick coax, thin coax, and unshielded twisted-pair cabling. See *Carrier Sense Multiple Access with Collision Detection (CSMA/CD)*.

EtherTalk. Apple Computer's implementation of Ethernet.

Extended Industry Standard Architecture (EISA). A 32-bit expansion bus specification developed by a group of PC-compatible computer manufacturers that is downwardly compatible with the standard PC 16-bit expansion bus.

Fiber Distributed Data Interface (FDDI). An ANSI standard that defines a 100 Mbps network using fiber-optic cable. FDDI uses a logical, counter rotating, token-passing ring topology. See *American National Standards Institute (ANSI)*.

Fiber-optic cable. A cable that consists of a strand or strands of glass fiber that carry data transmitted in the form of light. Fiber-optic cable can transmit data over relatively long distances and is not affected by electromagnetic radiation as is conventional cable.

File server. A computer whose primary purpose is to share files with other nodes on the network. Sometimes file server and server are used interchangeably.

File Transfer Protocol (FTP). The primary protocol used to transfer files in TCP/IP. See *Transmission Control Protocol/Internet Protocol (TCP/IP).*

Fractional T1. A standard 1.544 Mbps T1 line divided into 64 Kbps increments. A service offered by the telephone company.

Gateway. A device used to connect two dissimilar systems such as a PC network and a Macintosh network.

Group account. A network account that more than one person can use at a time. Network accounts allow network access only to those with valid accounts. Accounts also restrict or grant usage of shared resources to specific individuals or groups.

Groupware. Software developed specifically to help users in a network environment work together better.

Heterogeneous network. A network comprised of systems from a multitude of different manufacturers.

Host. The computer being accessed or used. When connecting to or accessing another computer using a modem, the other computer is the host.

Hub. A device used as a central connection point for the cables from network nodes arranged in a physical star topology.

Individual account. A network account assigned to and used by a single user. Network accounts allow network access only to those with valid accounts. Accounts also restrict or grant usage of shared resources to specific individuals or groups.

Industry Standard Architecture (ISA). The standard expansion bus interface used for PCs that consists of 8-bit or 16-bit expansion slots.

Infrared. A technology that uses electromagnetic waves for wireless LANs. See *local area network (LAN)*.

International Standards Organization (ISO). The group responsible for establishing standards for international and national data communications. The ISO developed the OSI network model. See *Open Systems Interconnection (OSI) model*.

Internet. A huge, global network consisting of over 5,000 networks with five to ten million users worldwide. The Internet also is referred to as the "Information Superhighway."

Internetwork. Several networks connected with bridges and routers, enabling nodes on different networks to communicate with each other.

Internetwork Packet Exchange (IPX). A protocol based on the Xerox Network System used by Novell that governs the exchange of network packets between networks.

LAN Manager. Microsoft's NOS based on the OS/2 operating system.

LAN Server. IBM's NOS based on the OS/2 operating system. See *network operating system (NOS)*.

LANtastic. Artisoft's peer-to-peer NOS. See *network operating system (NOS)*.

Leaf object. An object in the outermost extremities of the NetWare 4.*x* NDS hierarchical tree structure.

Local area network (LAN). A high-speed communications system that connects microcomputers or PCs that are in close proximity to each other (usually in the same building).

Log in. The process of establishing a logical connection to a server in a network to perform management activities or to access shared resources.

Logical drive. A drive on a workstation or client that is redirected to a drive resource on a server. A logical drive does not exist physically.

Mail. Messages and/or files sent to others across the network. Often referred to as e-mail (electronic mail).

Mainframe. A large, powerful computer able to process information from many users or other computers concurrently.

Map. The process of assigning a logical drive letter or device name to a shared resource. For example, "Map the K drive to the C-DRIVE resource."

Micro Channel Architecture (MCA). A proprietary 32-bit expansion bus architecture developed by IBM for use in its PS/2 computers. MCA is not downwardly compatible with ISA and therefore has not gained a significant market share as IBM had hoped. See *Industry Standard Architecture (ISA)*.

Microcomputer. A small computer that usually fits on a desktop and is used by an individual. As the power of microcomputers increases, the distinction between a microcomputer and a minicomputer becomes unclear. PCs are microcomputers.

Minicomputer. A multiuser computer typically used by a single company. Users access minicomputers by means of a terminal. All processing is performed on the minicomputer rather than at each station as in a LAN. Minicomputers are larger than microcomputers but smaller than mainframes. See *local area network (LAN)*.

Modem. A device that converts digital signals from a computer to analog signals for use over a telephone line. A modem is the interface used to connect your computer to a host computer using standard telephone lines.

Multiplex. The process of putting multiple signals on a single circuit.

Multistation Access Unit (MAU). A central connection point for the wiring from nodes on a Token Ring network.

Multitasking. The execution of more than one function or program at a time. Windows is a multitasking operating environment.

Multithreaded. The capability of a task in a multitasking operating system to have separate processes within the task that are executing concurrently.

Multiuser. Supporting more than one user at a time. A multiuser application enables more than one person to use the application at the same time.

NetWare. Novell's NOS.

NetWare Core Protocol (NCP). Novell's set of protocols used by a server to accept and respond to service requests.

NetWare Lite. Novell's former peer-to-peer NOS. NetWare Lite has been replaced by Personal NetWare.

Network. Two or more computers connected to enable the sharing of information and resources.

Network adapter driver. A software program that communicates directly with the network adapter in a computer and transfers information to the next layer of software in the network.

NetBEUI (NetBIOS Extended User Interface). Microsoft's version of NetBIOS.

Network Basic Input/Output System (NetBIOS). Developed by IBM, NetBIOS is a protocol that provides network access and data exchange. NetBIOS is the software that provides the interface between the network adapter in your computer and your operating system, such as DOS. See *Disk Operating System (DOS)*.

Network Driver Interface Specification (NDIS). A low-level network driver standard developed by Microsoft. Most network adapter manufacturers ship their network adapters with NDIS drivers that are supported by most NOSs. This ensures compatibility between the network adapter and the NOS. See *network operating system (NOS)*.

Network File System (NFS). A file-sharing protocol developed by Sun Microsystems for use on TCP/IP networks. See *Transmission Control Protocol/Internet Protocol (TCP/IP)*.

Network interface card (NIC). The hardware interface between the network and a computer. The NIC plugs into an expansion slot in the computer.

Network layer. The third layer of the OSI model that defines how data is routed from one network node to the next. See *Open Systems Interconnection (OSI) model*.

Network operating system (NOS). The software that enables computers in a network to communicate with each other. The NOS enables servers to share resources, and workstations to access and use shared resources.

Network transport. The process of transferring data between nodes in a network.

Node. A computer connected to a network.

Nondedicated server. A computer that can share its resources with other computers while being used as a workstation.

Object. An element that has properties associated with it that may contain values which define the object. For example, a user account object could consist of properties such as account name, address, access privileges, etc.

On-line service. A service connected to a computer by a modem and communications software that provides information such as news, weather, encyclopedias, and other services such as airline reservations, stock market quotes, and so on.

Open Datalink Interface (ODI). Novell's specification for a low-level network adapter driver. A NOS that supports ODI can use any network adapter if the manufacturer provides an ODI driver for the adapter. See *network operating system (NOS)*.

Open Systems Interconnection (OSI) model. A seven-layer model defined by ISO to specify how to accomplish communications between computers in a network. The names of the seven layers are physical, data link, network, transport, session, presentation, and application. See *International Standards Organization (ISO)*.

Operating system. The software that manages the internal functions of the computer and provides the interface between the computer hardware and the user or application program. The most popular operating system for PCs is DOS. See *Disk Operating System (DOS)*.

OS/2. IBM's single user, 32-bit, graphical, multitasking, multithreaded operating system.

Packet. A unit of information in a network consisting of data and control information that generally includes the intended destination of the packet. Transferring a file across the network might require the transfer of hundreds or even thousands of packets.

Packet burst. A network performance improvement technique that allows multiple packets of information to be sent over the network without waiting for verification from the receiving node that a packet was received.

Packet switching. A service available from most telephone companies that connects several LANs. Packet switching recognizes which LAN an information packet is destined for and then routes the packet accordingly. See *local area network (LAN)*.

Partition. A part of a hard disk which is treated as an entirely different hard disk. A single, physical hard disk may be partitioned into several logical hard disks, each of which is viewed by the operating system as a separate hard disk.

Peer-to-peer. A type of network in which every node is able to share its resources and use the shared resources of every other node in the network.

Peripheral Component Interconnect (PCI) local bus. An expansion bus standard developed by Intel that supports a 32-bit or 64-bit data path and runs at 33 MHz.

Personal NetWare. Novell's peer-to-peer NOS. See *network operating system (NOS)*.

Physical layer. The first layer of the OSI model that defines the interface with the physical media, including the network cable. See *Open Systems Interconnection (OSI) model*.

Presentation layer. The sixth layer of the OSI model responsible for the format of the data. See *Open Systems Interconnection (OSI) model*.

Print queue. A temporary storage location used to hold print jobs sent from an application program, through the network, until the printer is ready to print the job.

Protocol. A standard set of rules defining how network communications occur.

Real-time processing. A mode of computer operation that immediately processes data and presents output as the data is input. Compare with batch processing, in which the instructions in a computer program are executed without user interaction: data is submitted as a job, processed without user interaction, and presented as output.

Record. A group of items in a database, such as the name and address of a customer. Each customer's name and address is considered a separate record.

Record locking. A method used by network applications to prevent different users from accessing the same record concurrently. Record locking prevents multiple users from inadvertently overwriting each other's modifications.

Redirect. The process of causing a drive letter or device name to point to a shared resource on a server. If your K drive is to point to the C-DRIVE resource on the server, for example, redirect K to point to the C-DRIVE resource.

Redirector. A program in the NOS that redirects drives and devices on a workstation (or client) across the network to a shared resource on a server. See *network operating system (NOS)*.

Redundant Array of Inexpensive Disks (RAID). A set of specifications defining methods of preventing data loss due to drive failures. The RAID specifications include five levels. Level 1, the most basic, defines disk mirroring, by which the same data is written to two different drives, and duplexing.

Remote booting. The process of starting a PC by accessing the boot files and operating system from a server across the network.

Repeater. A device that amplifies and retransmits the network signal, allowing longer network cable segments.

Resource. An item or device on a computer that can be shared with a network such as a program, disk drive, printer, modem, CD-ROM drive, and so on.

Ring topology. A connection scheme by which network data is passed between computers that are connected in a ring.

Router. A device that connects networks using the same network layer (Level 3) protocol such as TCP/IP or IPX. Routers are able to connect networks using different logical topologies such as Ethernet and Token Ring.

RS232C. The hardware standard that defines how Data Terminal Equipment (DTE) and Data Communications Equipment (DCE) are connected. Now the overwhelming standard for connecting two devices using serial communications.

Sequential Packet Exchange (SPX). Novell's protocol for enabling two workstations to communicate across a network. Data is transferred in sequence, and checked that it arrives at its intended destination.

Server. A computer that shares its resources with other nodes in the network.

Session. A network communications connection between two nodes.

Session layer. The fifth layer of the OSI model; responsible for creating, maintaining, and terminating network sessions. See *Open Systems Interconnection (OSI) model.*

Simply LANtastic. Artisoft's entry-level peer-to-peer network designed for the small business and home office.

Stand-alone. A computer that is not connected to a network.

Star topology. A network connection scheme by which the computers are connected to a central connection point such as a concentrator.

Structured Query Language (SQL). A standard language that extracts information from a database. In some client-server applications, the client issues a SQL command to the SQL server, which processes the request and then returns the results to the client application.

Switched 56. A dial-up service provided by the telephone company for use with WANs that provides a 56 Kbps communication channel. See *wide area network (WAN)*.

Systems Application Architecture (SAA). IBM's specifications for network communications and application development.

Systems Network Architecture (SNA). IBM's protocols for specifying terminal-to-mainframe connections.

T1. A service provided by the telephone company for use with WANs that provides up to 24 channels of 64 Kbps speed for a total of 1.544 Mbps.

Telnet. The TCP/IP protocol used for terminal emulation. See *Transmission Control Protocol/Internet Protocol (TCP/IP)*.

Terminal. A station used to connect one or more computers to a host computer. There are various types of terminals. A dumb terminal has no processing capability; the processing is performed by the host computer. Some terminals (intelligent terminals) have processing capabilities such as features that enable the capturing and storage of data sent from the host computer. A PC can act as an intelligent terminal using terminal-emulation software.

Terminal-emulation software. Software that makes a PC appear to a host computer as a terminal.

Thicknet. The thick coax cable used in the 10BASE5 implementation of Ethernet.

Thinnet. The thin coax cable used in the 10BASE2 implementation of Ethernet.

Time sharing. The process used by host computers to allow several terminals to access the host at the same time.

Time-sharing service. A service whereby several terminals can access a host computer for the purpose of processing data.

Token Ring. A network topology whereby a token is passed between computers connected in a ring. When a computer is in possession of the token, it may transmit data across the network. When finished, the token is passed to the next computer and the process continues.

Topology. The scheme used to connect computers. Physical topology is the actual physical layout of the computers; logical topology is the path taken by the data.

Transceiver. A device for transmitting and receiving network data. The transceiver usually is integrated on the network adapter.

Transmission Control Protocol/Internet Protocol (TCP/IP). A very popular protocol, TCP/IP was developed by ARPA and is the primary protocol used to connect the thousands of computers on the Internet. The TCP/IP protocol is well suited for use when connecting diverse computers and large networks.

Transport layer. The fourth layer of the OSI model; responsible for maintaining the communications link and for responding appropriately if the link has failed or cannot be established. See *Open Systems Interconnection (OSI) model.*

Tree. A hierarchical structure of organizing directories in which the organization resembles a tree with a root and branches extending from it.

UNIX. A 32-bit, multitasking, multiuser operating system.

Unshielded twisted pair (UTP). The cable used in the 10BASE-T implementation of Ethernet.

Upload. The process of transferring data from a PC to a host computer via a modem.

User. Any person who performs tasks at a computer.

VESA local bus. An expansion bus specification developed by the Video Electronics Standards Association (VESA) that supports a 32-bit or 64-bit data path and runs at speeds up to 50 MHz.

Volume. The highest level in the NetWare directory structure; comparable to the root directory in DOS. A volume represents a physical amount of hard disk storage.

Wide area network (WAN). Two or more LANs connected using telephone company services or another method of communication such as fiber optics, infrared, microwave, or satellite. WANs are not geographically limited in size as are LANs, but they usually operate at a slower speed than LANs. See *local area network (LAN)*.

Wild card account. A network account that has a wild card character as part of its name. A wild card account enables users to log in using names that are similar to the wild card account name.

Windows NT Server. Microsoft's 32-bit multitasking NOS. See *network operating system (NOS)*.

Wireless LAN. A LAN that does not use cable as its communications medium. Most wireless LANs use a radio signal to communicate with other nodes. See *local area network (LAN)*.

Workstation. A computer that is able to access the shared resources on other computers but is not able to share its resources with others. Also referred to as a *client*. Workstation is also sometimes used to refer to a stand-alone computer.

X.25. A CCITT standard that defines the communications protocol for packet-switched networks providing communications channels up to 64Kbps.

Xerox Network System (XNS). Xerox's network communications protocol on which Novell's IPX and SPX network protocols are based. See *Internetwork Packet Exchange (IPX)* and *Sequential Packet Exchange (SPX)*.

INDEX

Symbols

A

M

X–Z

The Network Starter Kit
REGISTRATION CARD

NRP

Fill out this card to receive information about future networking books and other New Riders titles!

Name _____ **Title** _____

Company _____

Address _____

City/State/ZIP _____

I bought this book because: _____

_____

I purchased this book from:

☐ A bookstore (Name _____)

☐ A software or electronics store (Name _____)

☐ A mail order (Name of Catalog _____)

I purchase this many computer books each year:

☐ 1–5   ☐ 6 or more

I currently use these applications: _____

_____

_____

_____

I found these chapters to be the most informative: _____

_____

I found these chapters to be the least informative: _____

_____

Additional comments: _____

_____

☐ I would like to see my name in print! You may use my name and quote me in future New Riders products and promotions. My daytime phone number is: _____

New Riders Publishing 201 West 103rd Street • Indianapolis, Indiana 46290 USA

- Fold Here -

PLACE
STAMP
HERE

New Riders Publishing
201 West 103rd Street
Indianapolis, Indiana 46290
USA

WANT MORE INFORMATION?

CHECK OUT THESE RELATED TITLES:

	QTY	PRICE	TOTAL

Inside Novell NetWare, Special Edition. This #1 selling tutorial/reference is perfect for beginning system administrators. Each network management task is thoroughly explained and potential trouble spots are noted. The book also includes a disk with an extremely easy-to-use workstation menu program, an MHS capable E-Mail program, and workgroup management tools. ISBN: 1-56205-096-6.

____ $34.95 _____

NetWare 4: New Business Strategies. The ultimate guide to planning, installing, and managing a NetWare 4.0 network. This book explains how best to implement the new features of NetWare 4.0 and how to upgrade to NetWare 4.0 as easily and efficiently as possible. ISBN: 1-56205-159-8.

____ $27.95 _____

Downsizing to NetWare. Get the real story on downsizing with *Downsizing to NetWare*. This book identifies applications that are suitable for use on LANs and shows how to implement downsizing projects. This book lists the strengths and weaknesses of NetWare—making it perfect for managers and system administrators. ISBN: 1-56205-071-0.

____ $39.95 _____

LAN Operating Systems. Learn how to connect the most popular LAN operating systems. All major LAN operating systems are covered, including: NetWare 3.11, Appleshare 3.0, Banyan VINES 5.0, UNIX, LAN Manger 2.1, and popular peer-to-peer networks. The following client operating systems are covered as well: MS-DOS, Windows, OS/2, Macintosh System 7, and UNIX. This book clears up the confusion associated with managing large networks with diverse client workstations and multiple LAN operating systems. ISBN: 1-56205-054-0.

____ $39.95 _____

Name _____

Company _____

Address _____

City _____ State ____ ZIP _____

Phone _____ Fax _____

☐ Check Enclosed ☐ VISA ☐ MasterCard

Card #_____Exp. Date _____

Signature _____

Prices are subject to change. Call for availability and pricing information on latest editions.

Subtotal _____

Shipping _____

$4.00 for the first book and $1.75 for each additional book.

Total _____
Indiana residents add 5% sales tax.

New Riders Publishing 201 West 103rd Street • Indianapolis, Indiana 46290 USA

- Fold Here -

New Riders Publishing
201 West 103rd Street
Indianapolis, Indiana 46290
USA

GO AHEAD. PLUG YOURSELF INTO
MACMILLAN COMPUTER PUBLISHING.

Introducing the Macmillan Computer Publishing Forum on CompuServe®

Yes, it's true. Now, you can have CompuServe access to the same professional, friendly folks who have made computers easier for years. On the Macmillan Computer Publishing Forum, you'll find additional information on the topics covered by every Macmillan Computer Publishing imprint—including Que, Sams Publishing, New Riders Publishing, Alpha Books, Brady Books, Hayden Books, and Adobe Press. In addition, you'll be able to receive technical support and disk updates for the software produced by Que Software and Paramount Interactive, a division of the Paramount Technology Group. It's a great way to supplement the best information in the business.

WHAT CAN YOU DO ON THE MACMILLAN COMPUTER PUBLISHING FORUM?

Play an important role in the publishing process—and make our books better while you make your work easier:

- Leave messages and ask questions about Macmillan Computer Publishing books and software—you're guaranteed a response within 24 hours
- Download helpful tips and software to help you get the most out of your computer
- Contact authors of your favorite Macmillan Computer Publishing books through electronic mail
- Present your own book ideas
- Keep up to date on all the latest books available from each of Macmillan Computer Publishing's exciting imprints

JOIN NOW AND GET A FREE COMPUSERVE STARTER KIT!

To receive your free CompuServe Introductory Membership, call toll-free, **1-800-848-8199** and ask for representative **#597**. The Starter Kit Includes:

- Personal ID number and password
- $15 credit on the system
- Subscription to CompuServe Magazine

HERE'S HOW TO PLUG INTO MACMILLAN COMPUTER PUBLISHING:

Once on the CompuServe System, type any of these phrases to access the Macmillan Computer Publishing Forum:

GO MACMILLAN   **GO BRADY**
GO QUEBOOKS   **GO HAYDEN**
GO SAMS   **GO QUESOFT**
GO NEWRIDERS   **GO ALPHA**

Once you're on the CompuServe Information Service, be sure to take advantage of all of CompuServe's resources. CompuServe is home to more than 1,700 products and services—plus it has over 1.5 million members worldwide. You'll find valuable online reference materials, travel and investor services, electronic mail, weather updates, leisure-time games and hassle-free shopping (no jam-packed parking lots or crowded stores).

Seek out the hundreds of other forums that populate CompuServe. Covering diverse topics such as pet care, rock music, cooking, and political issues, you're sure to find others with the same concerns as you—and expand your knowledge at the same time.

Need cards and cables to build your network?

The disks at the back of this book contain Simply LANtastic software to network two IBM-compatible personal computers. Simply LANtastic software works with a wide variety of network interface cards that you may already own. If you do not have compatible hardware, mail or fax this coupon to Artisoft to order the hardware you need.

❏ Yes. Send me a Simply LANtastic hardware kit (part #8410), priced at $120.00 (plus tax and FedEx economy shipping). This kit will include all the hardware I need plus a 25-foot cable to connect two PCs in a Simply LANtastic network.

Name _____

Company _____

Address _____

City _____ State_____ ZIP_____

Phone _____ Fax _____

Payment Method:

❏ COD cashier's check   ❏ VISA   ❏ MasterCard   ❏ AmEx

Card # _____ Exp. Date _____

Signature _____

Prices are subject to change. Call 800-233-5564 for product availability and shipping information. Or fax inquiries to 602-670-7359, Attn: Sales Dept. Allow 4 to 6 weeks for delivery.

Artisoft, Inc.   2202 North Forbes Boulevard   Tuscon, AZ 85745
Headquarters: 602-670-7100
Fax: 602-670-7101

ARTISOFT, INC.

SOFTWARE LICENSE AND WARRANTY AGREEMENT

CAREFULLY READ ALL OF THE TERMS AND CONDITIONS OF THIS LICENSE AGREEMENT BEFORE USING THE SOFTWARE. BY OPENING THIS PACKAGE, YOU INDICATE YOUR COMPLETE AND UNCONDITIONAL ACCEPTANCE OF THESE TERMS AND CONDITIONS.

This document is a legal agreement between you and ARTISOFT, INC., concerning the use of the ARTISOFT® software. THIS AGREEMENT CONSTITUTES THE COMPLETE AGREEMENT BETWEEN YOU AND ARTISOFT.

AGREEMENT

1. LICENSE: ARTISOFT grants the licensee a non-exclusive license to use the Software in this package on one (1) server/workstation in a single network installation, which installation shall consist of no more than 500 servers/workstations. A network is defined as any continuously connected group of computers on one cabling scheme without hardware or software bridges. ARTISOFT retains title to an ownership of this copy and all backup copies and any proprietary rights related to the Software. You may make copies of the software for backup. You may not copy the User's or Reference Manual, make alterations or modifications to the software, or attempt to discover the source code of the software. The software may not be sublicensed, rented, or leased. Both the license and your right to use the software terminate automatically if you violate any part of this agreement. In the event of termination, you must immediately destroy all copies of the software or return them to ARTISOFT.

2. LIMITED SOFTWARE WARRANTY: If you discover physical defects in the media on which the software is distributed or in the User's or Reference Manual, ARTISOFT will replace the media or manuals for a period of ninety (90) days after purchase by the retail customer. You must return the disk or manuals to ARTISOFT or an authorized ARTISOFT dealer within the warranty period, accompanied by proof of purchase.

   THIS WARRANTY DOES NOT APPLY TO DEFECTS DUE DIRECTLY OR INDIRECTLY TO MISUSE, ABUSE, NEGLIGENCE, ACCIDENT, REPAIRS, OR ALTERATIONS MADE BY THE CUSTOMER OR ANOTHER PARTY OR IF THE ARTISOFT SERIAL NUMBER HAS BEEN REMOVED OR DEFACED.

   ARTISOFT DISCLAIMS ALL IMPLIED WARRANTIES, INCLUDING WITHOUT LIMITATION WARRANTIES OR MERCHANTABILITY, PERFORMANCE, AND FITNESS FOR A PARTICULAR PURPOSE. ARTISOFT WILL NOT BE LIABLE FOR ANY BUG, ERROR, OMISSION, DEFECT, DEFICIENCY, OR NONCONFORMITY IN ANY SOFTWARE. AS A RESULT, THE SOFTWARE IS SOLD "AS IS", AND THE PURCHASER ASSUMES THE ENTIRE RISK AS TO ITS QUALITY AND PERFORMANCE.

3. LIMITATIONS OF LIABILITY

ARTISOFT SHALL IN NO EVENT BE LIABLE FOR DIRECT, INDIRECT, SPECIAL INCIDENTAL, CONTINGENT, OR CONSEQUENTIAL DAMAGES RESULTING FROM ANY DEFECT IN THE SOFTWARE OR ITS DOCUMENTATION, INCLUD-ING DAMAGES FROM LOSS OF DATA, DOWNTIME, GOODWILL, DAMAGE TO OR REPLACEMENT OF EQUIPMENT OR PROPERTY, AND ANY COSTS OF RECOVERING, REPROGRAMMING, OR REPRODUCING ANY PROGRAM OR DATA USED IN CONJUNCTION WITH ARTISOFT PRODUCTS, EVEN IF ARTISOFT OR AN AUTHORIZED ARTISOFT DEALER HAS BEEN ADVISED OF THE POSSIBILITY OF SUCH DAMAGES. YOU AGREE THAT ARTISOFT'S LIABILITY ARISING OUT OF CONTRACT, NEGLIGENCE, STRICT LIABILITY IN TORT OR WARRANTY SHALL NOT EXCEED ANY AMOUNT PAID BY YOU FOR THIS PRODUCT. ANY WRITTEN OR ORAL INFORMATION OR ADVICE GIVEN BY ARTISOFT DEALERS, DISTRIBUTORS, AGENTS, OR EMPLOYEES WILL IN NO WAY INCREASE THE SCOPE OF THIS WARRANTY. NOR MAY YOU RELY ON ANY SUCH WRITTEN OR ORAL COMMUNICATION. Some states do not allow the exclusion or limitation of implied warranties or liability for incidental or consequential damages, so the above limitation may not apply to you. This warranty gives you specific legal rights, and you may also have other rights which vary from state to state.

4. GOVERNMENT RESTRICTED RIGHTS

The software and documentation are provided with RESTRICTED RIGHTS. Use, duplication, or disclosure by the Government is subject to restrictions as set forth in subparagraph (c)(1)(ii) of The Rights in Technical Data and Computer Software clause at DFARS 252.227-7013 or subparagraphs (c)(1) and (2) of the Commercial Computer Software - Restricted Rights at 48 CPR 52.277-19, as applicable. Manufac-turer is Artisoft, Inc. 2202 North Forbes Blvd., Tucson, AZ 85745.

The laws of the State of Arizona shall govern this agreement.

#8218   6/93

Installing the Simply LANtastic Companion Disk

The accompanying disks contain a two-node version of Simply LANtastic. With the appropriate cards and a cable, you can build a fully functional network for home or office.

Installing the Software

The installation process is fully detailed in Chapter 11, "Installing Simply LANtastic." Details as to all operations that are possible with Simply LANtastic are further explained in Chapters 11 through 14.

This book contains a special offer on networking cards and cable from Artisoft in the event you should need them as well.